Performance Notes by Adam Perlmutter

ISBN: 978-1-4234-7388-6

HAL•LEONARD®
CORPORATION
7777 W. BLUEMOUND RD. P.O. BOX 13819 MILWAUKEE, WI 53213

Visit Hal Leonard Online at
www.halleonard.com

Table of Contents

Introduction

Welcome to *Children's Piano Songs For Dummies!* In this book, you'll find everything you need to play some of the world's greatest children's songs — from traditional to folk to rock, from the television to the silver screen — many of which were actually first written for adults.

About This Book

For every song here, I include a little background or history. Sometimes I discuss the artist, the song, the movie, or some other interesting element of the song. This information is followed by a variety of tidbits that struck me as I made my way through the teaching of these songs, including some of the following:

- A run-down of the parts you need to know.
- A breakdown of some of the chord progressions important to playing the song effectively.
- Some of the critical information you need to navigate the sheet music.
- Some tips and shortcuts you can use to expedite the learning process.

In many cases, you may already know how to do a lot of this. If so, feel free to skip over those familiar bits.

How to Use This Book

The music in this book is in standard piano notation, a staff for the melody and lyrics above the traditional piano grand staff. I assume you know a little something about reading music, and that you know a little bit about playing piano, such as how to hold your fingers, basic chords, and how to look cool while doing it. If you need a refresher course on piano, please check out *Piano For Dummies* by Blake Neely (Wiley).

Glossary

As you might expect, I use quite a few musical terms in this book. Some of these may be unfamiliar to you, so here are a few right off the bat that can help your understanding of basic playing principles:

- **Arpeggio:** Playing the notes of a chord one at a time rather than all together.
- **Bridge:** Part of the song that is different from the verse and the chorus, providing variety and connecting the other parts of the song to each other.
- **Coda:** The section at the end of a song, which is sometimes labeled with the word "coda."
- **Chorus:** The part of the song that is the same each time through, usually the most familiar section.
- **Hook:** A familiar, accessible, or sing-along melody, lick, or other section of the song.
- **Verse:** The part of the song that tells the story; each verse has different lyrics, and each song generally has between two and four of these.

Icons Used in This Book

In the margins of this book are lots of little icons that will help make your life easier:

A reason to stop and review advice that can prevent personal injury to your fingers, your brain, or your ego.

These are optional parts, or alternate approaches that those who'd like to find their way through the song with a distinctive flair can take. Often these are slightly more challenging routes, but encouraged nonetheless, because there's nothing like a good challenge!

This is where you will find notes about specific musical concepts that are relevant but confusing to non-musical types — stuff that you wouldn't bring up, say, at a frat party or at your kid's soccer game.

You get lots of these tips, because the more playing suggestions I can offer, the better you'll play. And isn't that what it's all about?

Traditional

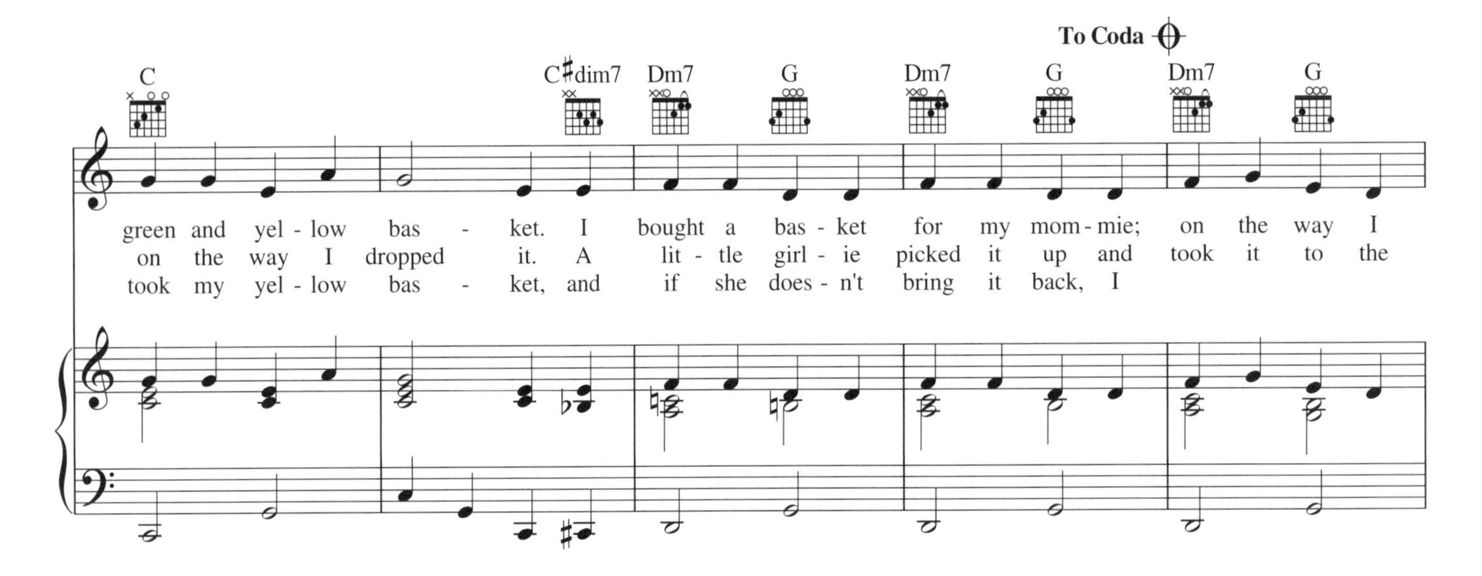

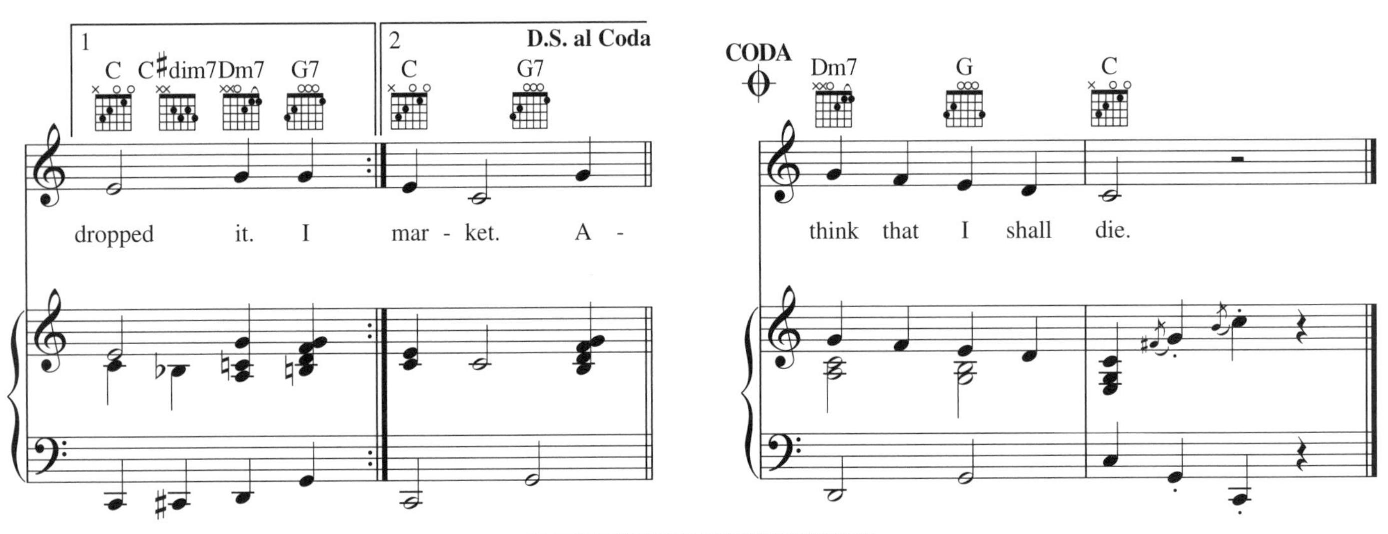

Alley Cat Song

Words by Jack Harlen
Music by Frank Bjorn

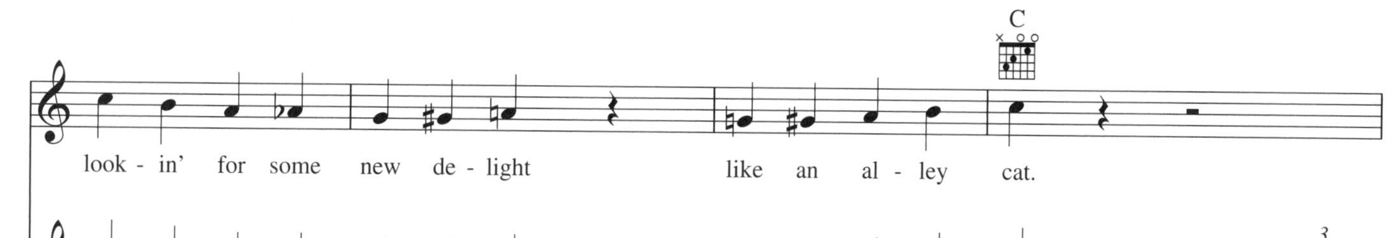

C
He just don't know wrong from right like an al - ley cat.
He's too bus - y mak - in' scenes like an al - ley cat.
He

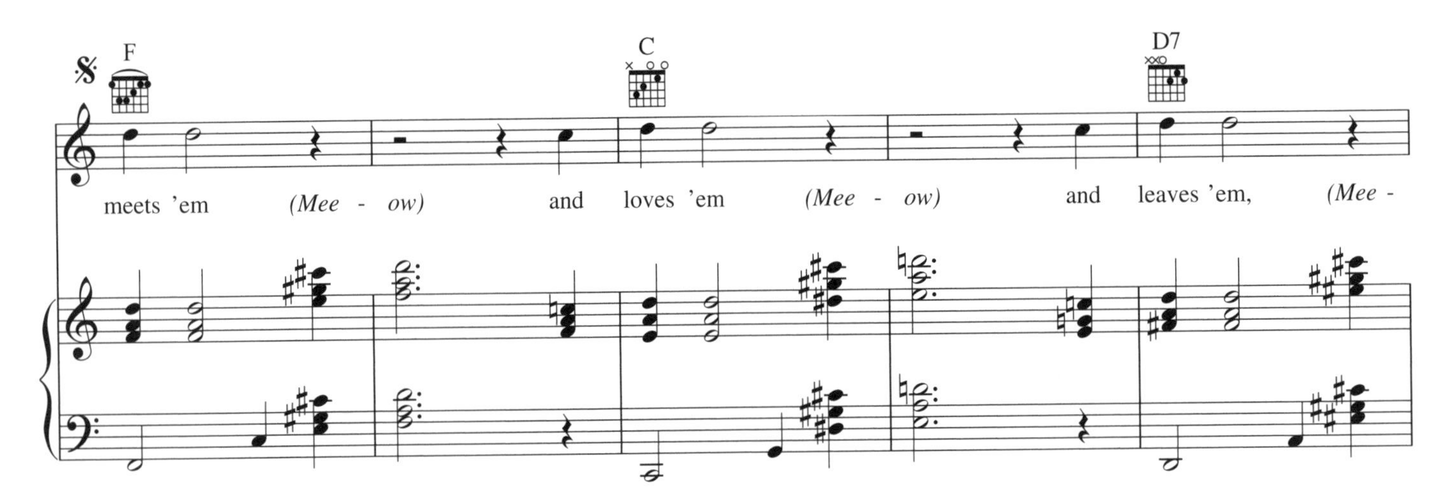
F
C
D7
meets 'em (Mee - ow) and loves 'em (Mee - ow) and leaves 'em, (Mee -

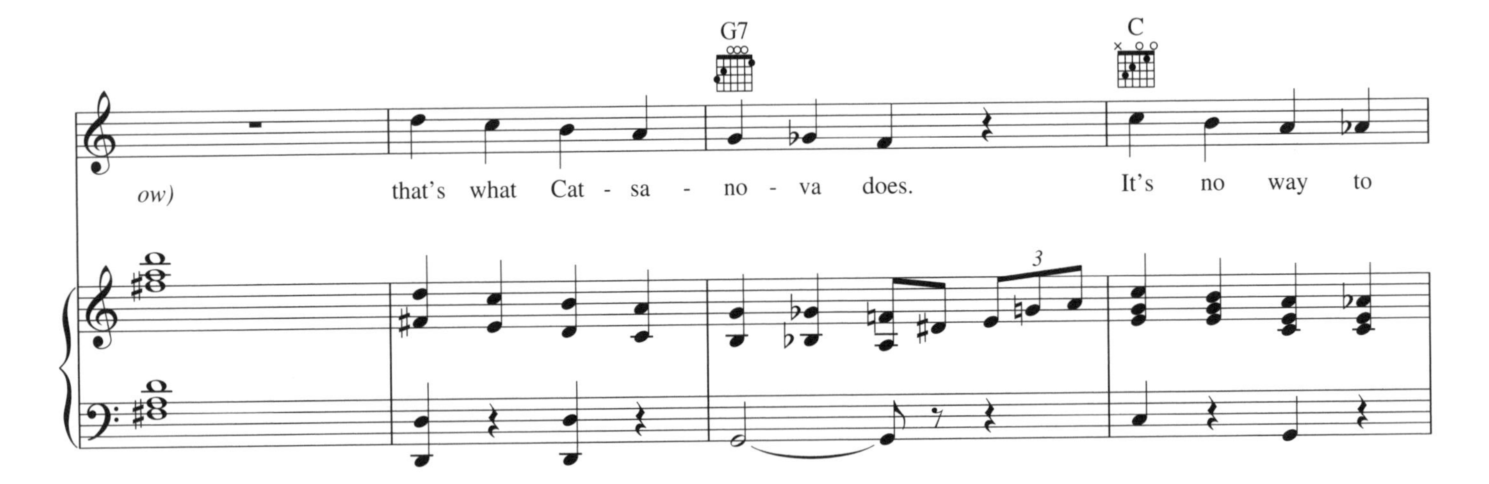
G7
C
ow) that's what Cat - sa - no - va does. It's no way to

G7
treat a pal, she should tell him, scat! Aren't you sor - ry

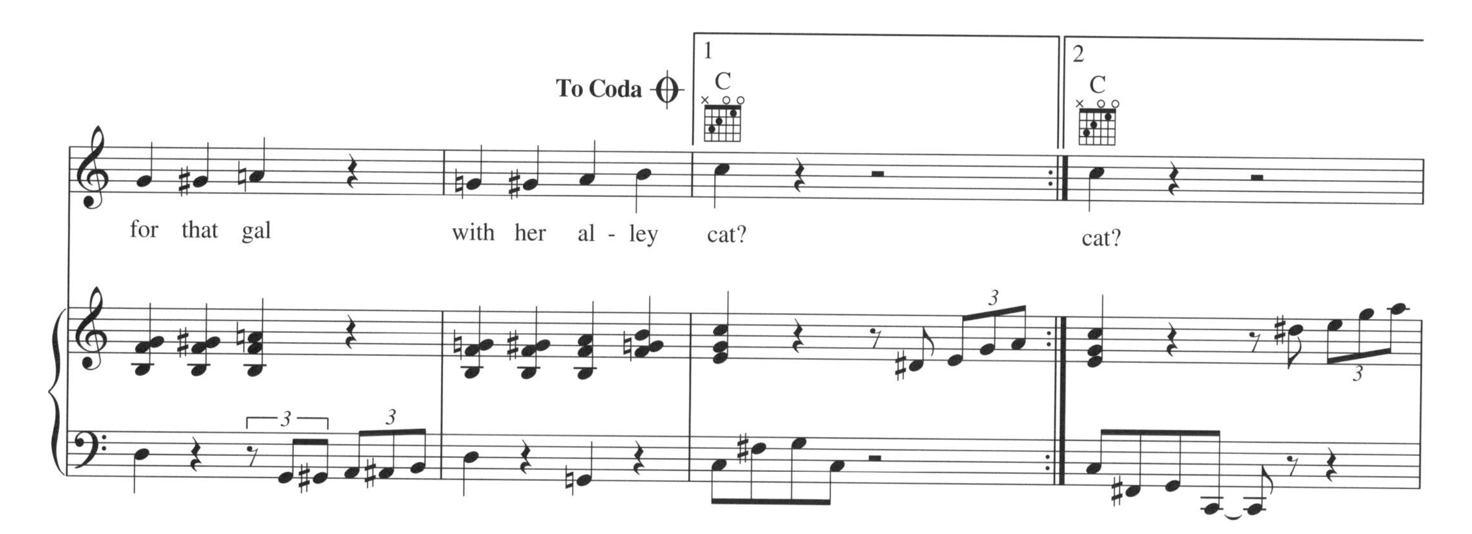
To Coda
1
C
2
C
for that gal with her al - ley cat?
cat?
3
3
3
3

G7

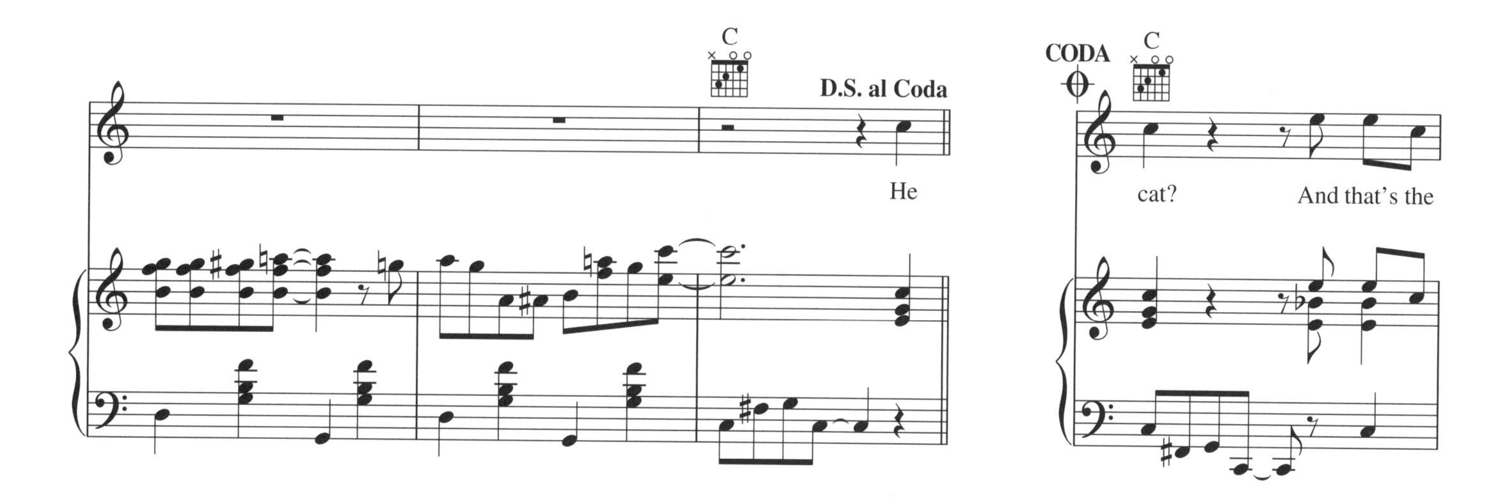
C
D.S. al Coda
He
CODA
C
cat? And that's the

F
F♯dim7
C/G
A7
D7
G7
C
sad, sad tale of a lone - some frail, and her al - ley cat.

The Addams Family Theme

Theme from the TV Show and Movie
Music and Lyrics by Vic Mizzy

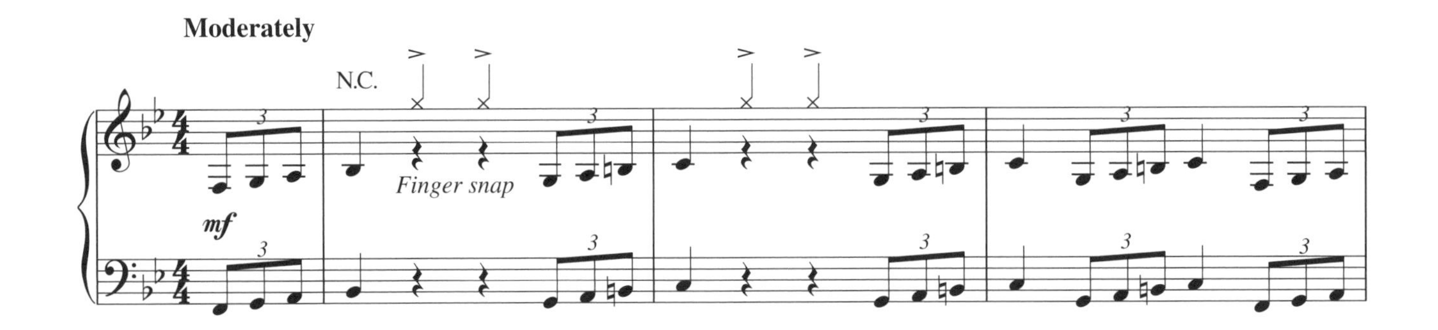

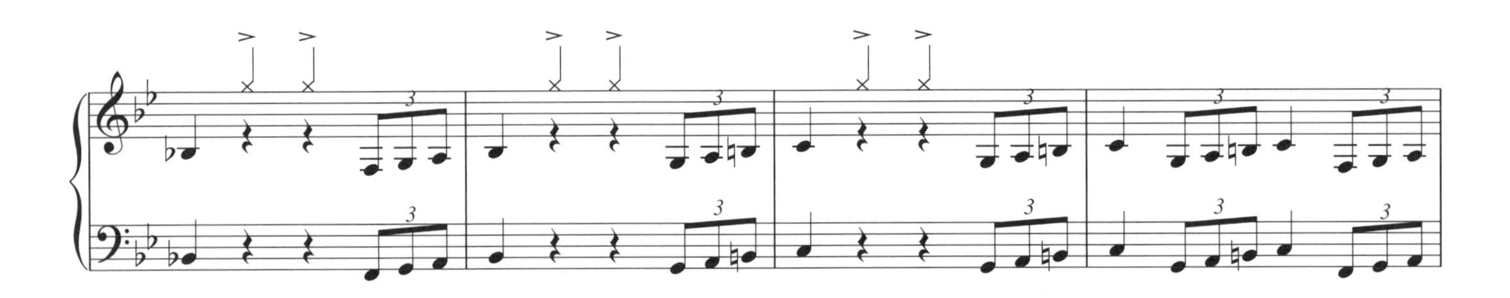

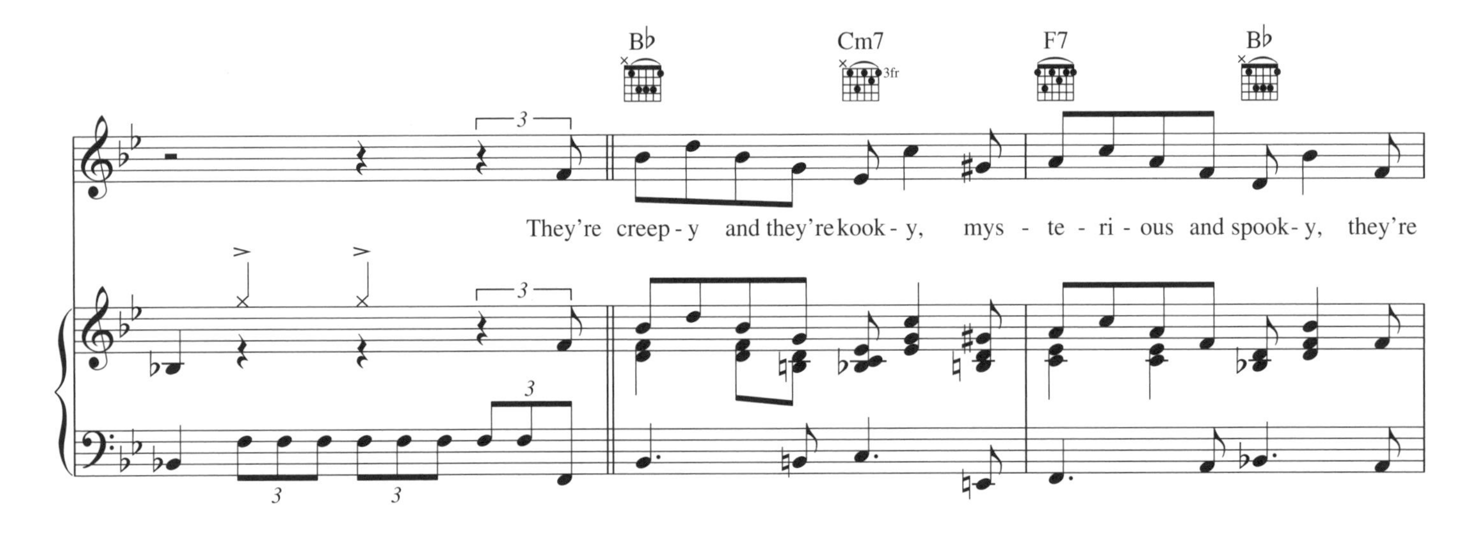

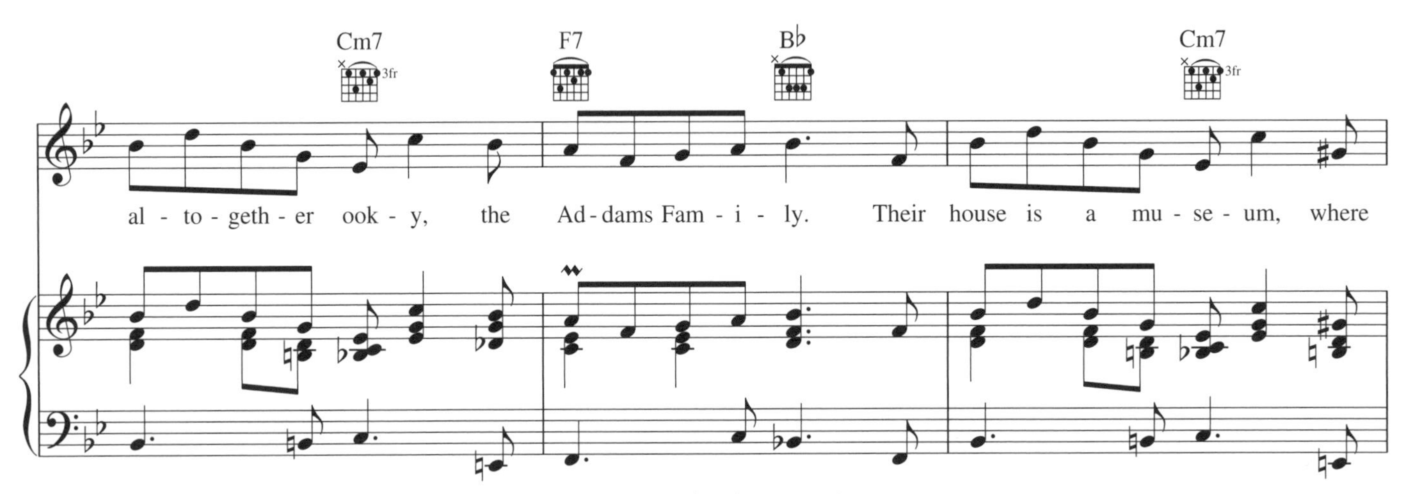

F7
B♭
Cm7
3fr
F7
B♭
N.C.
peo - ple come to see 'em, they real - ly are a scree - um, the Ad - dams Fam - i - ly.

(Spoken:) Neat.
Sweet.

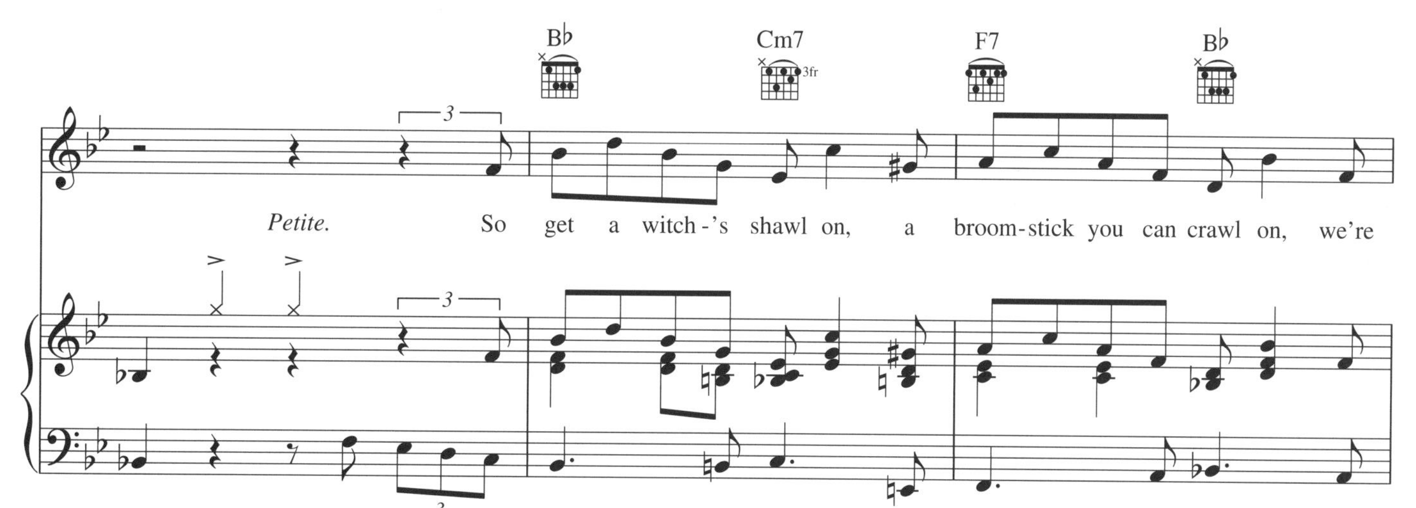
B♭
Cm7
3fr
F7
B♭
Petite.
So get a witch - 's shawl on, a broom - stick you can crawl on, we're

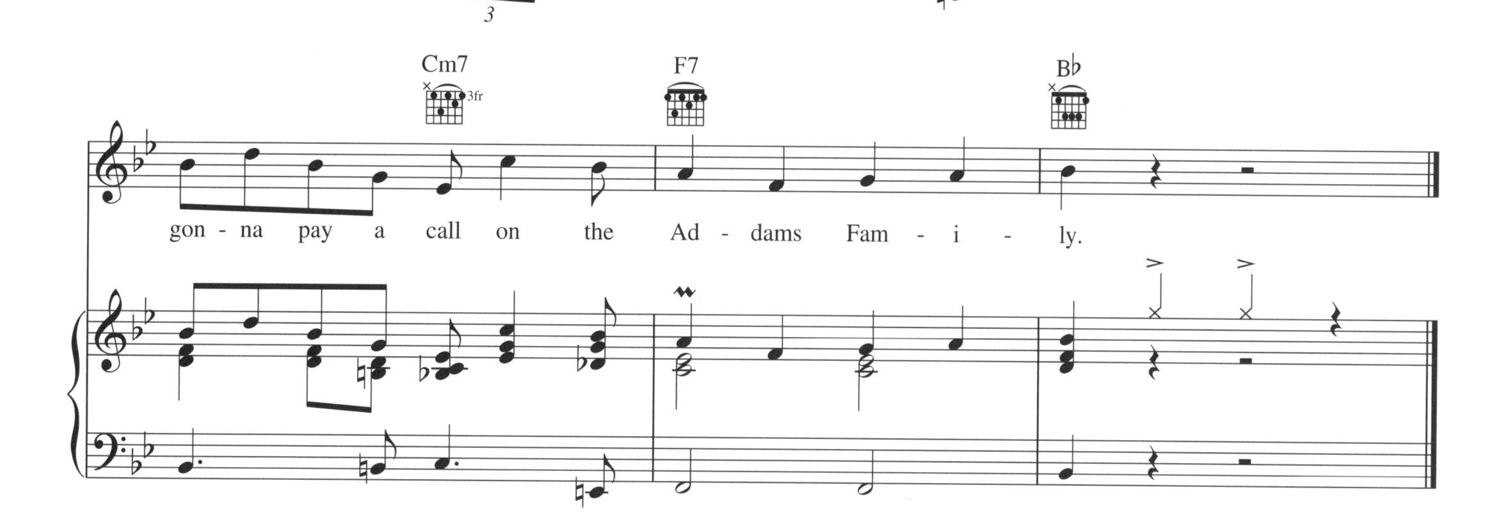
Cm7
3fr
F7
B♭
gon - na pay a call on the Ad - dams Fam - i - ly.

Alouette

Traditional

*Each chorus adds a new part of the body, in reverse order. For example, Chorus 3 is sung:

Et le nez, et le nez;
Et le bec, et le bec;
Et la têt', et le têt';
Alouett', Alouett'.
Oh, *etc.*

2. le bec (*beak*)
3. le nez (*nose*)
4. les yeux (*eyes*)
5. le cou (*neck*)
6. les ailes (*wings*)
7. le dos (*back*)
8. les pattes (*feet*)
9. la queue (*tail*)

Any Dream Will Do

from JOSEPH AND THE AMAZING TECHNICOLOR® DREAMCOAT
Music by Andrew Lloyd Webber
Lyrics by Tim Rice

C
G6
C
way
some - one was weep - ing,

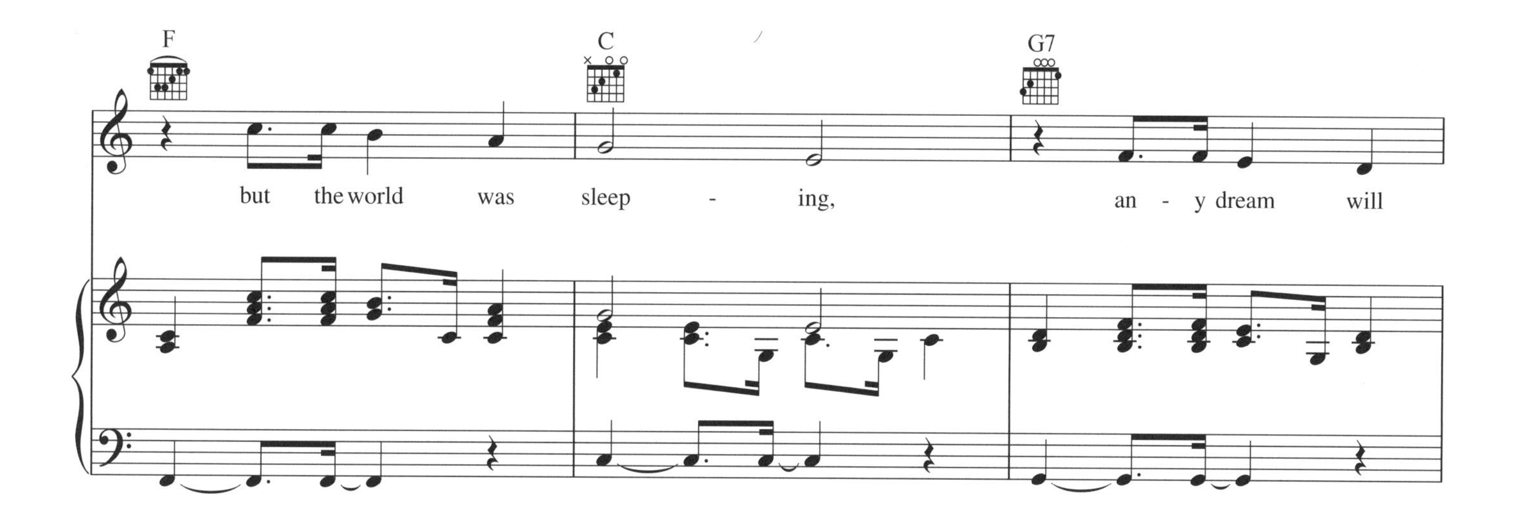
F
C
G7
but the world was sleep - ing,
an - y dream will

C
G6
G7
C
do.
I wore my coat
CHOIR:
I wore my

G6
C
F
with gold - en lin - ing, bright col - ours
coat,
ah,

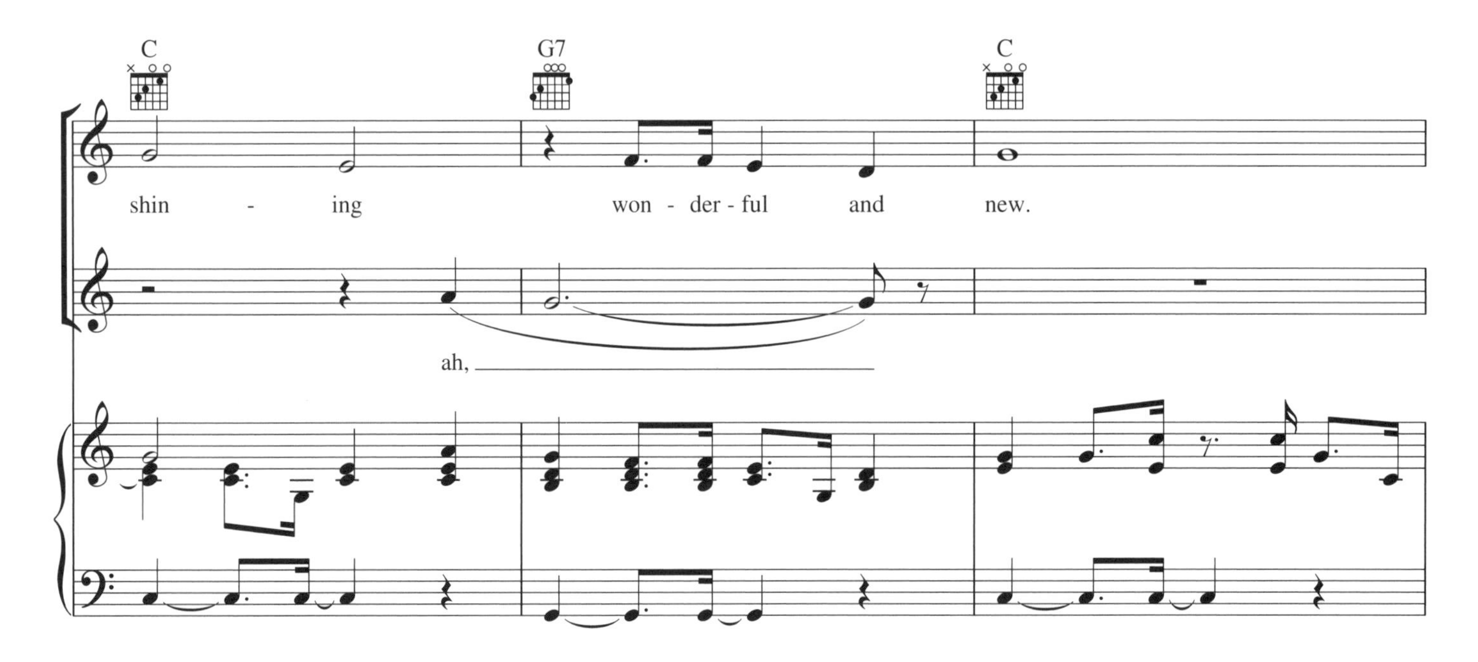
C
G7
C
shin - ing won - der - ful and new.
ah,

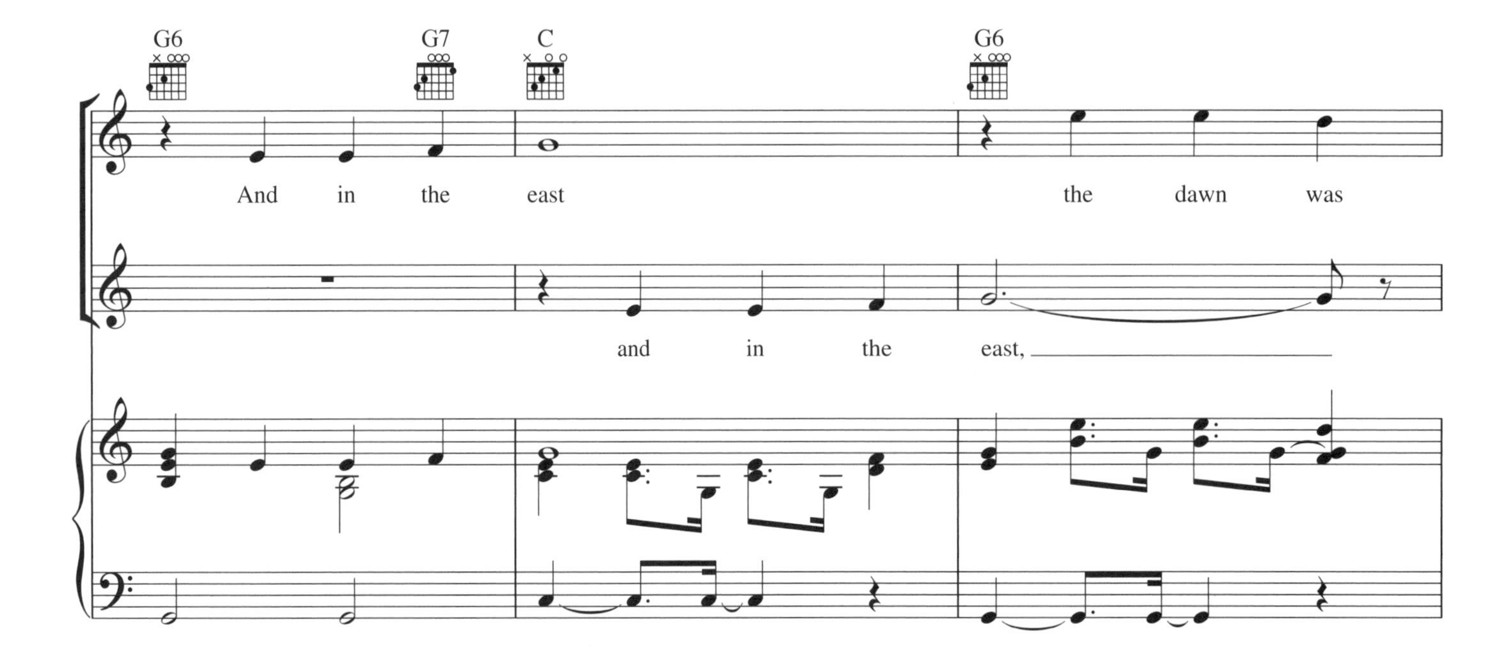
G6
G7
C
G6
And in the east the dawn was
and in the east,

C
F
C
break - ing,
and the world was
wak - ing,
ah,
ah,

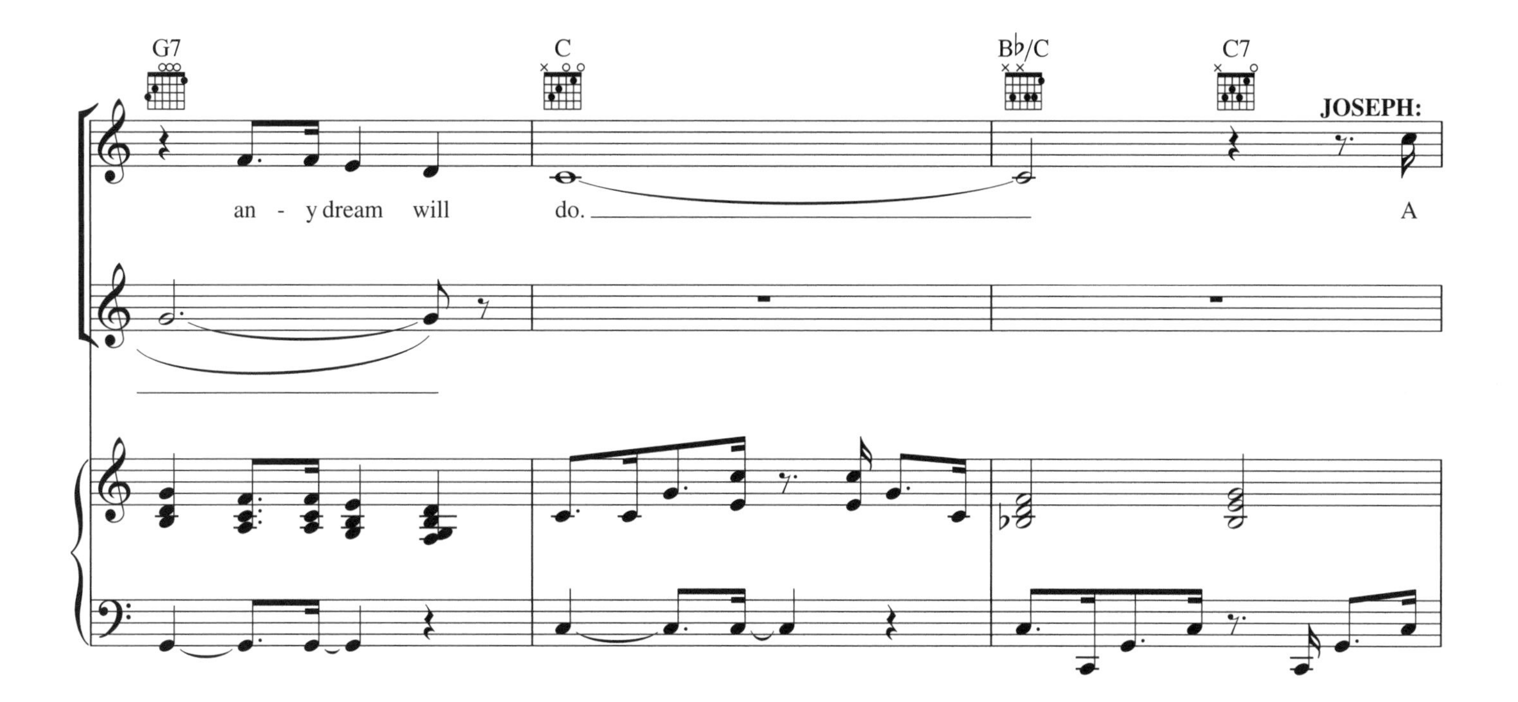
G7
C
B♭/C
C7
JOSEPH:
an - y dream will
do.
A

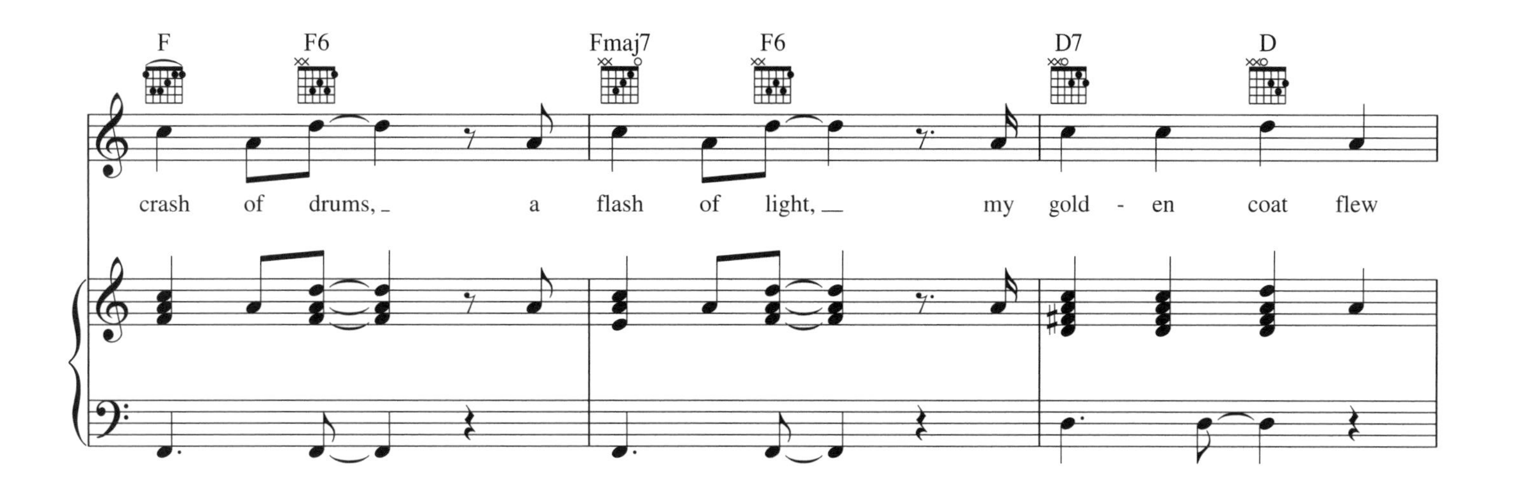
F
F6
Fmaj7
F6
D7
D
crash of drums,
a
flash of light,
my gold - en coat flew

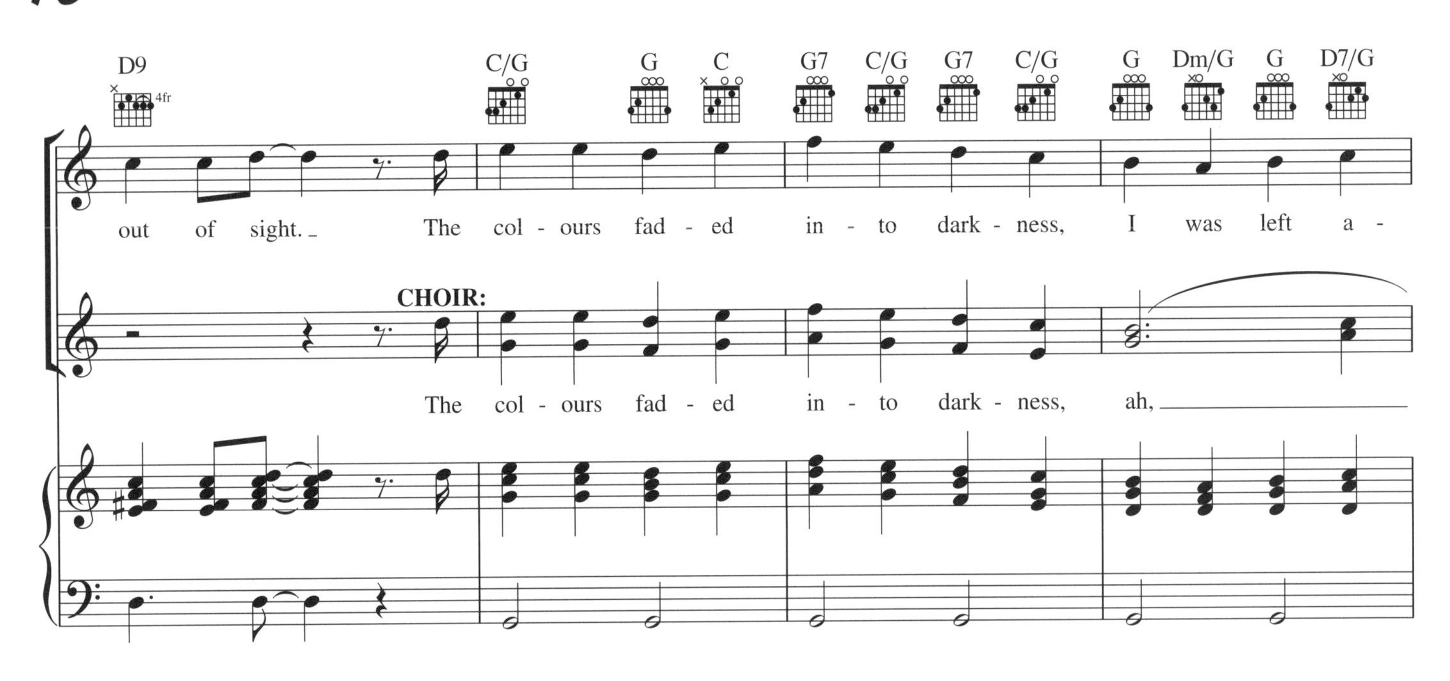
D9
C/G
G
C
G7
C/G
G7
C/G
G
Dm/G
G
D7/G
out of sight. The col - ours fad - ed in - to dark - ness, I was left a -
CHOIR:
The col - ours fad - ed in - to dark - ness, ah,

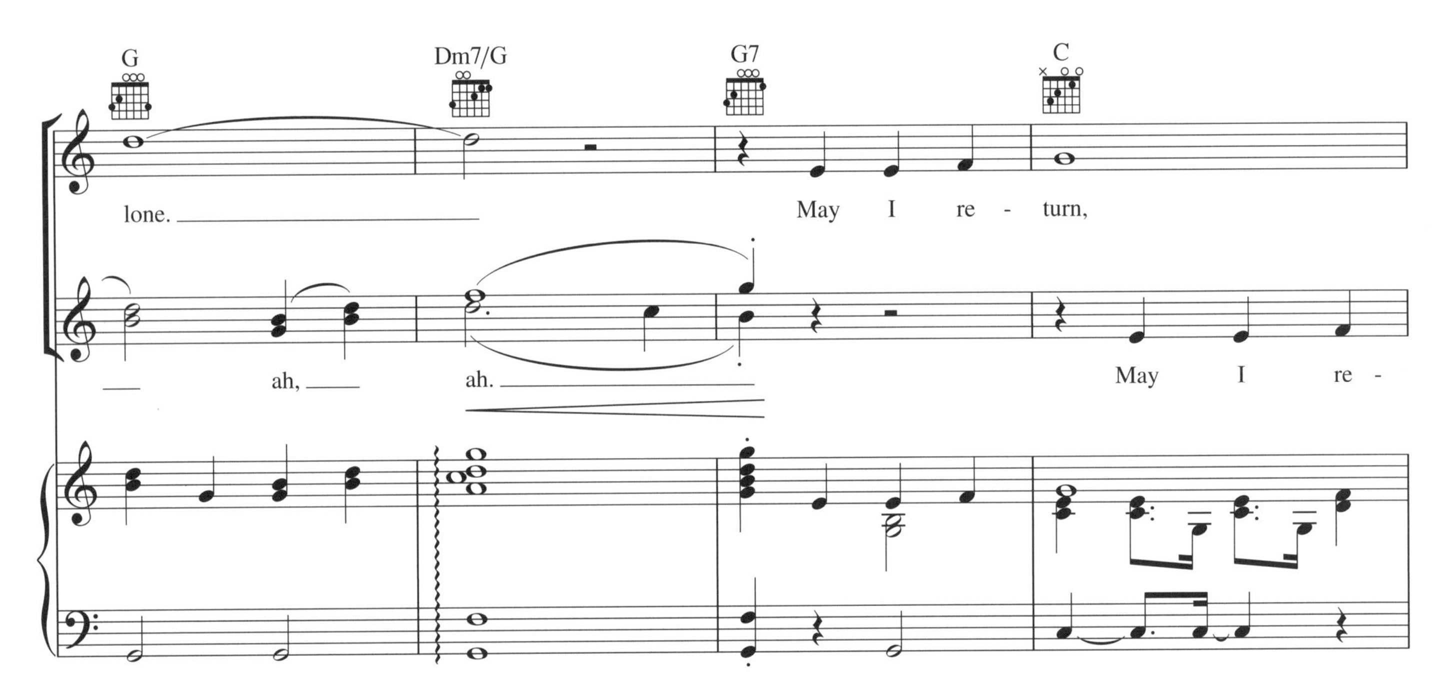
G
Dm7/G
G7
C
lone. May I re - turn,
ah, ah. May I re -

G6
C
F
to the be - gin - ning, the light is
turn, ah,

C
G7
C
dim - ming and the dream is too.
ah.
G6
G7
C
G6
The world and I, we are still
The world and I,

C
F
C
wait - ing, still hes - i - tat - ing,
ah,
ah.

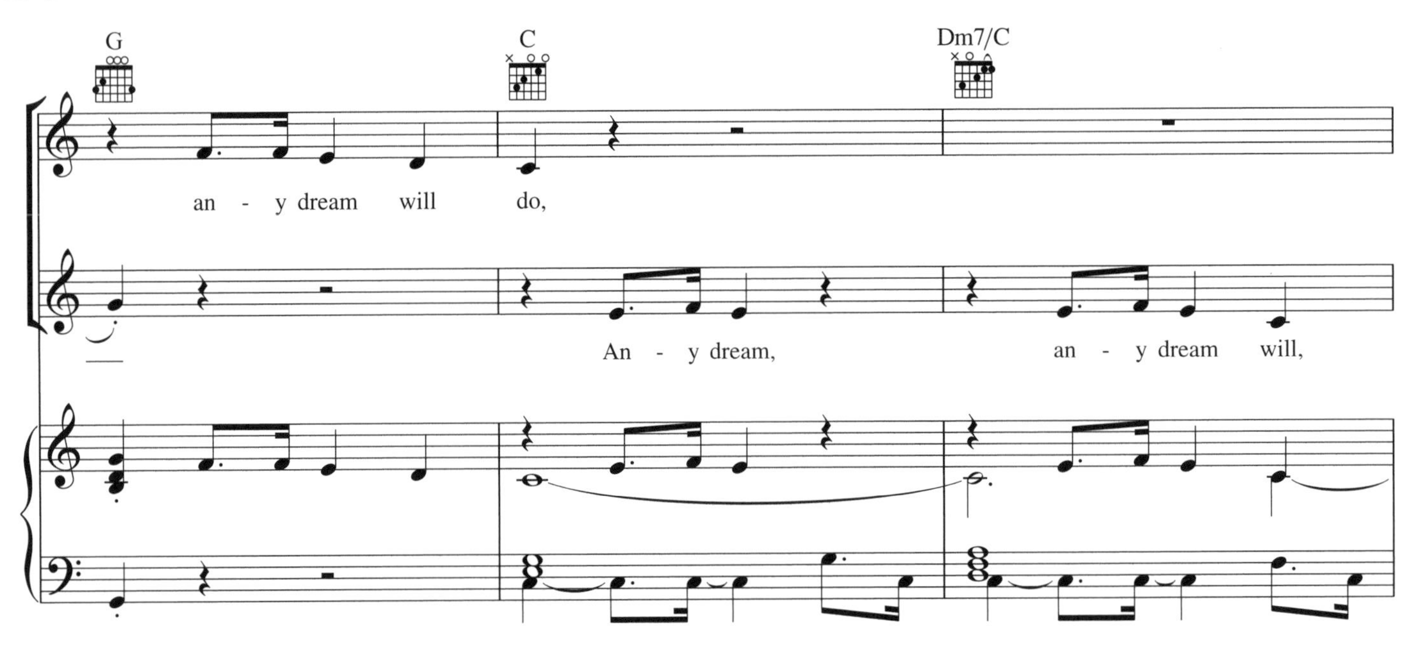
G
C
Dm7/C
an - y dream will do,
An - y dream,
an - y dream will,

C
Dm7/C
C
an - y dream will do,
an - y dream,
an - y dream will do, an - y dream,

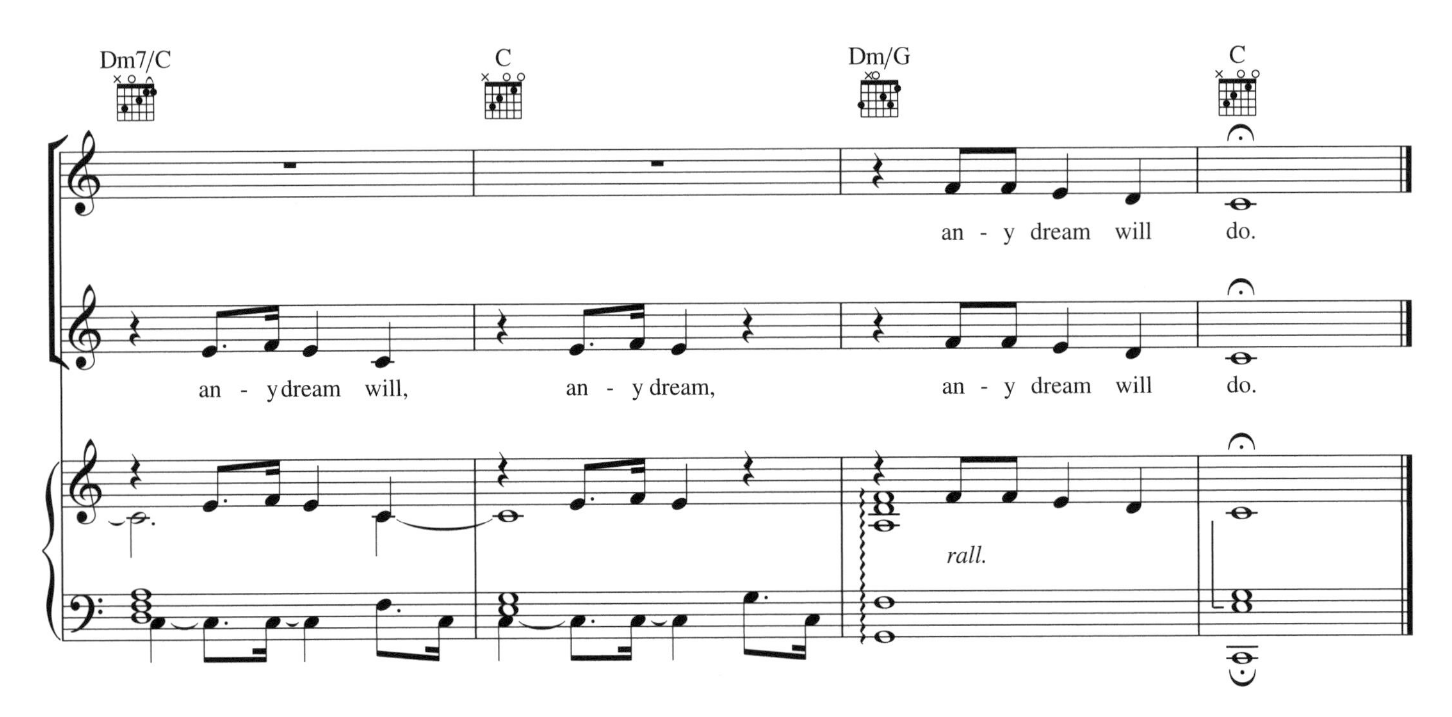
Dm7/C
C
Dm/G
C
an - y dream will do.
an - y dream will,
an - y dream,
an - y dream will do.
rall.

The Bible Tells Me So

Words and Music by Dale Evans

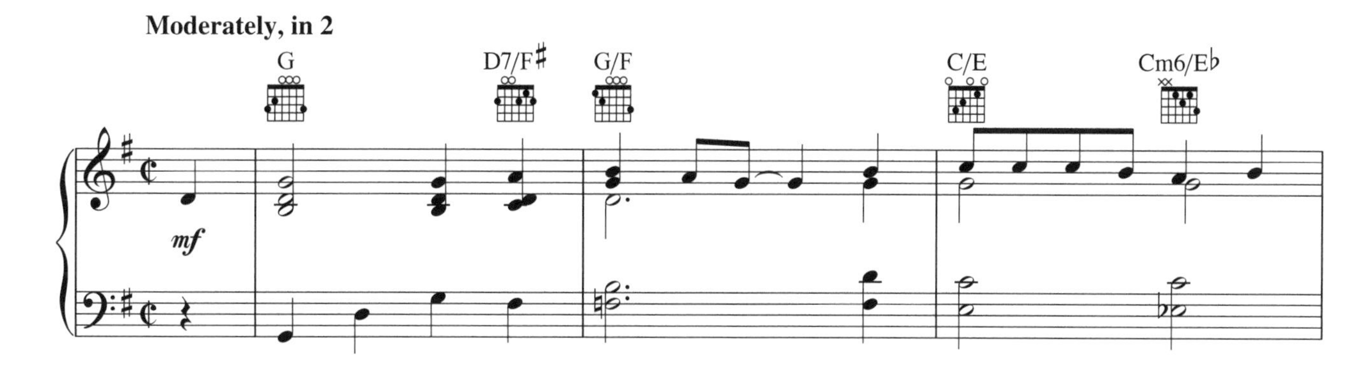

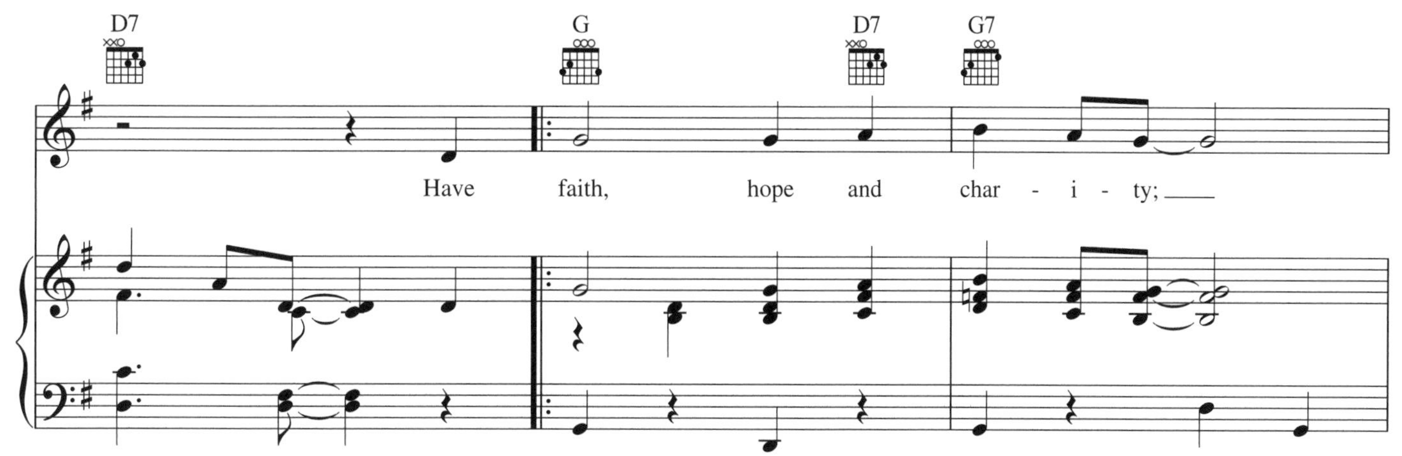

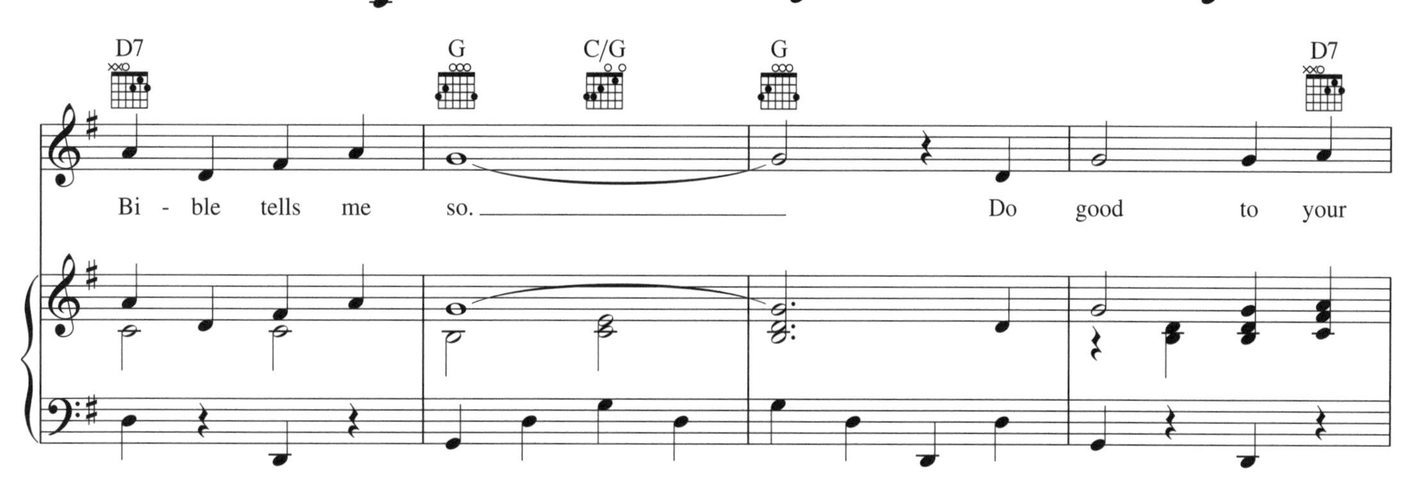

G7
C
G
en - e - mies
and the bless - ed Lord you'll
sure - ly please.

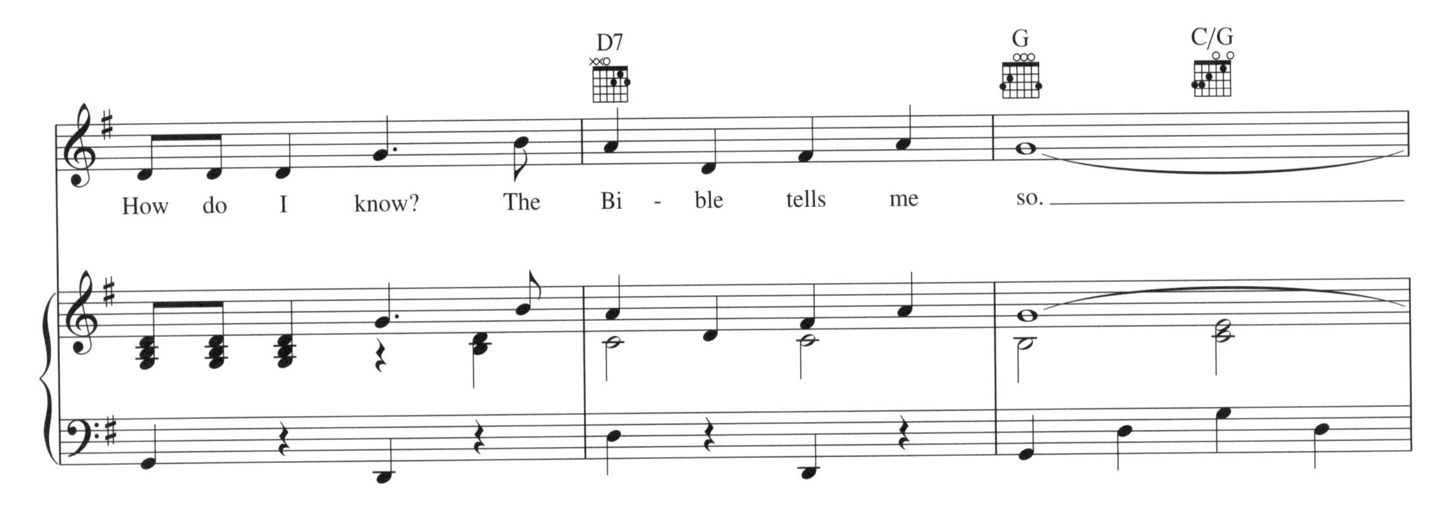
D7
G
C/G
How do I know? The
Bi - ble tells me
so.

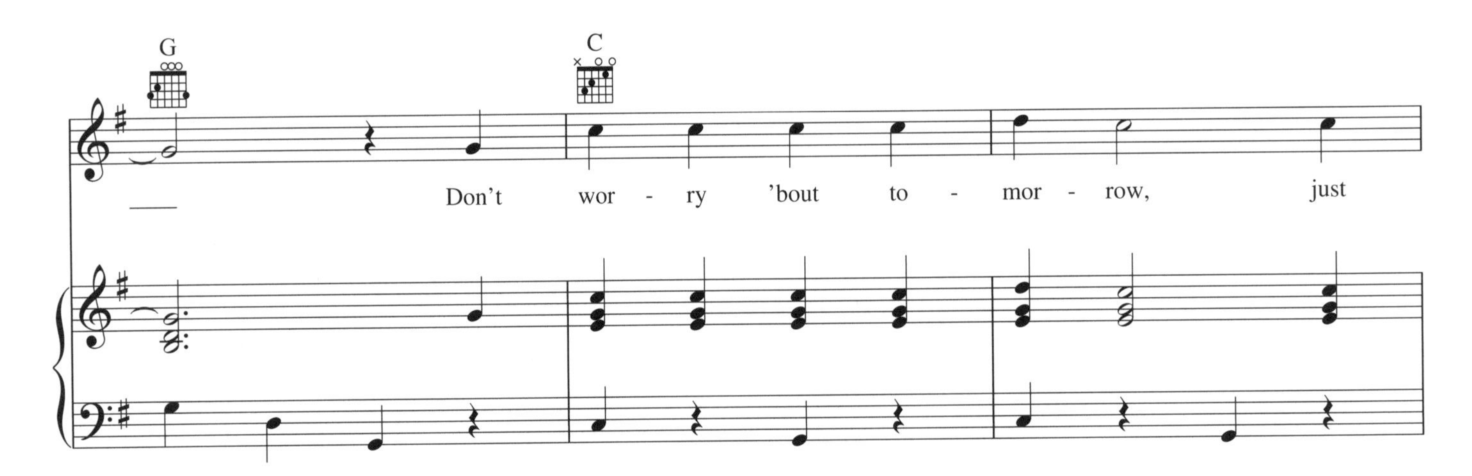
G
C
Don't
wor - ry 'bout to -
mor - row, just

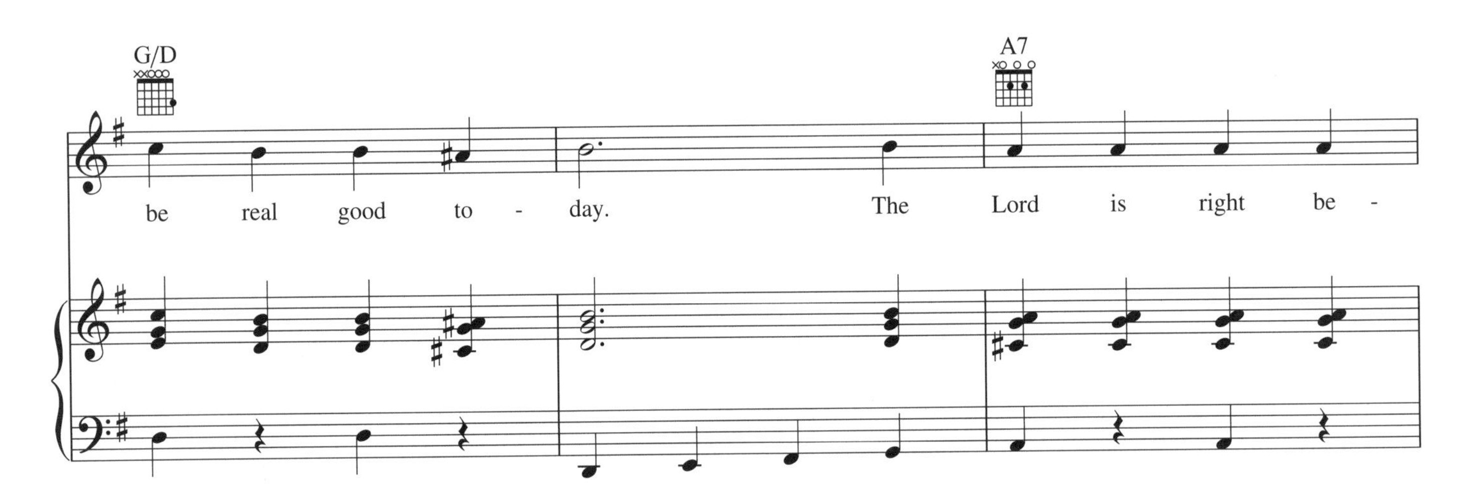
G/D
A7
be real good to -
day. The
Lord is right be -

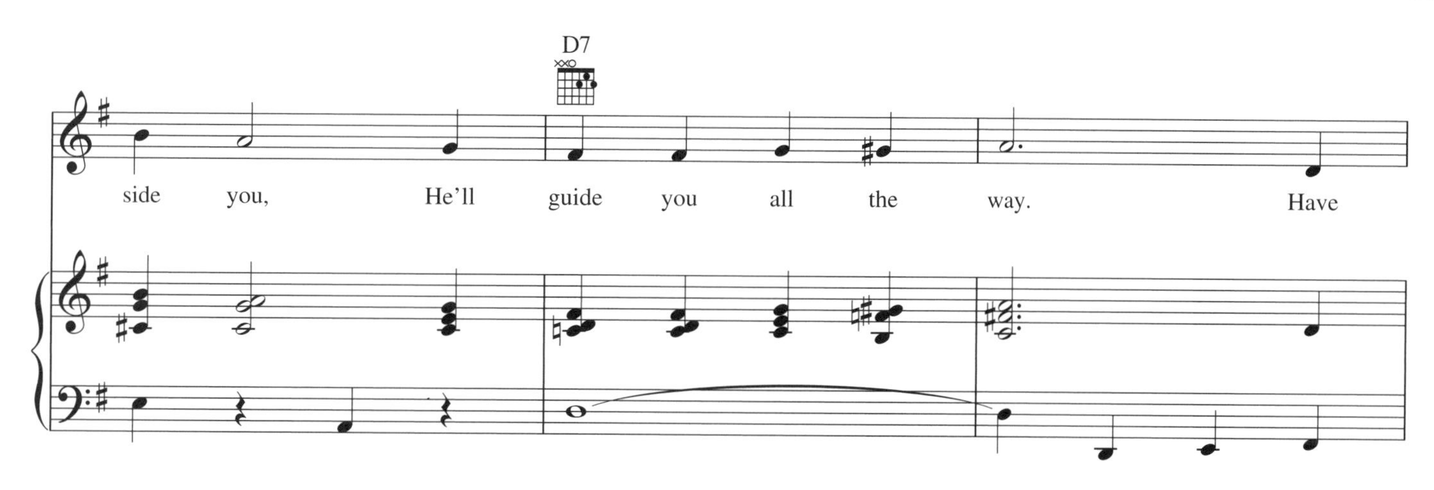
D7
side you, He'll guide you all the way. Have

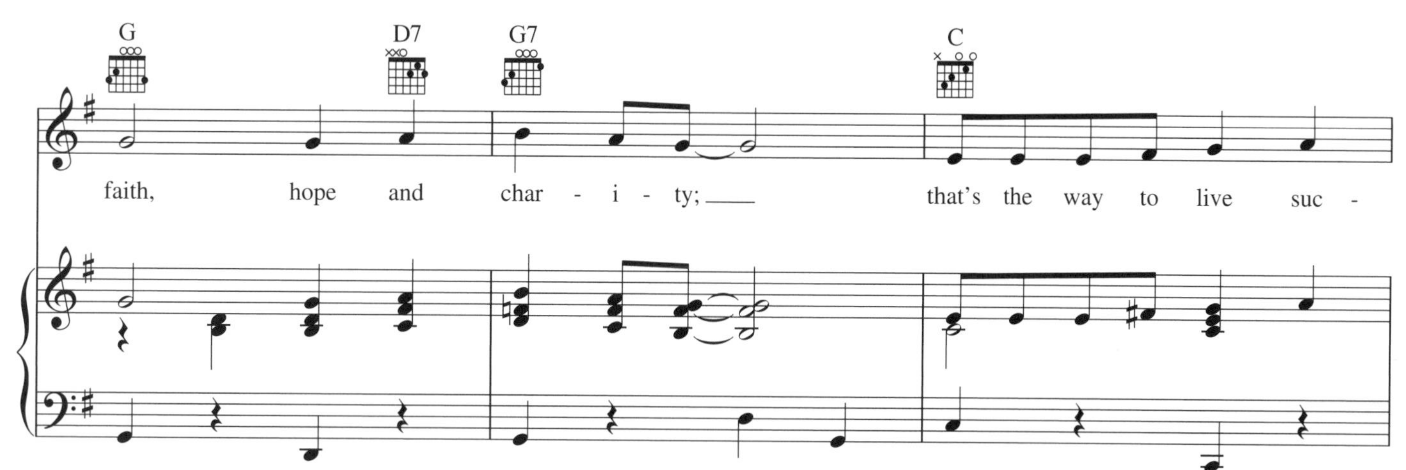
G D7 G7 C
faith, hope and char - i - ty; that's the way to live suc -

G D7
cess - ful - ly. How do I know? The Bi - ble tells me

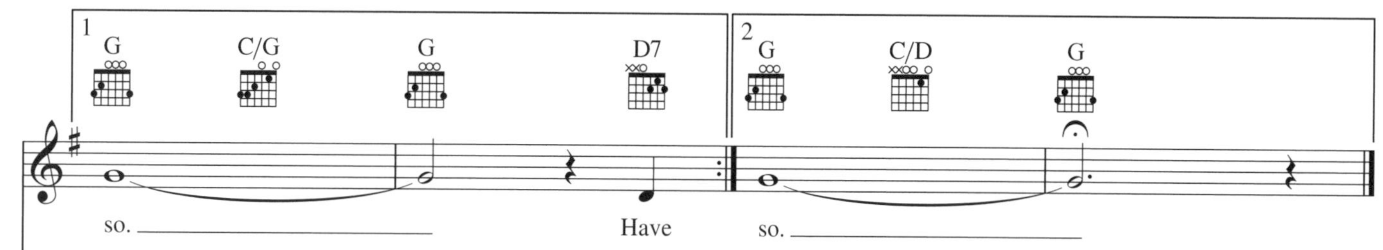
1 G C/G G D7
2 G C/D G
so. Have so.

rall.

Words and Music by Joe Raposo

B♭
A♭
G♭
F7
B♭maj7
B♭6
that. It's not eas-y be-in' green.
A7♯5
Fm6/A♭
It seems you blend in with so man-y oth-er or-di-nar-y things,
G7sus
G7♭9
Cm7
and peo-ple tend to pass you o-ver 'cause you're not stand-ing out like flash-y

Cm7/F
F9
B♭

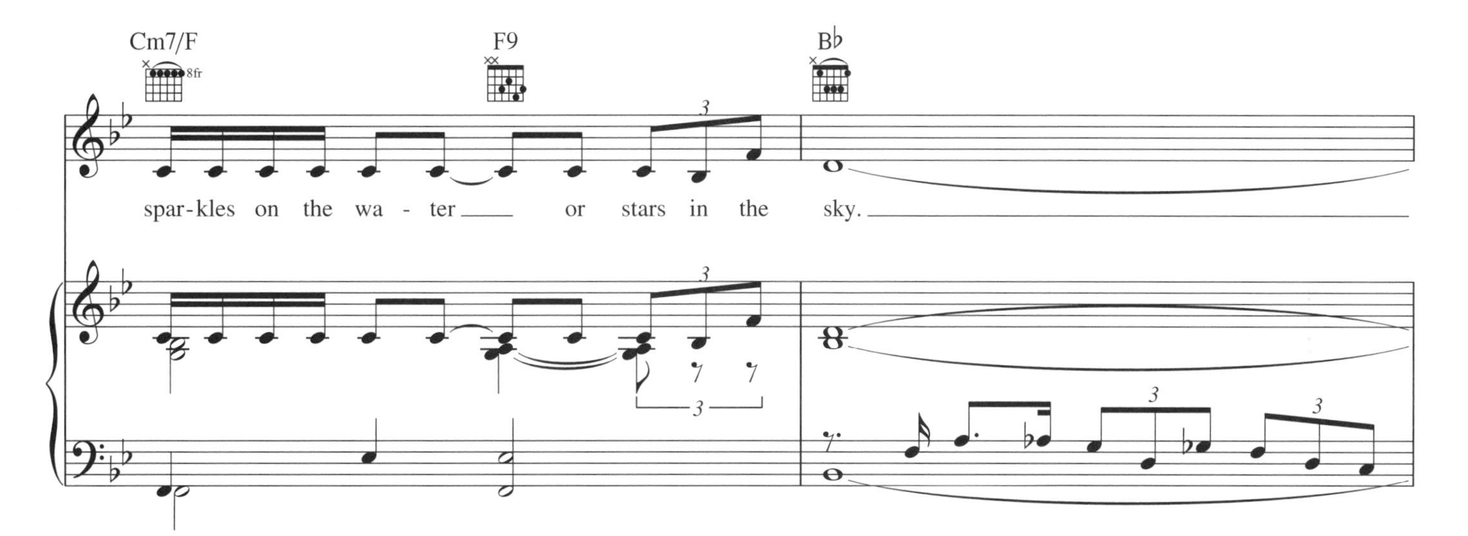
spar-kles on the wa-ter or stars in the sky.

Dm/A
A♭maj7
But green is the col - or of spring,
cresc.
mf
D♭maj7
B♭
and green can be cool and friend - ly - like,
Dm/A
Gm7
Gm(maj7)
3fr
and green can be big like an o - cean or im -
cresc.
Gm7/C
C9
Cm7
3fr
por - tant like a moun - tain or tall like a tree.
f
decresc.

Cm7/F
F7
B♭maj9
B♭6/9
When green is all there is to be,
mp
A7♯5
Fm6/A♭
Dm7/G
G7
it could make you won-der why, but why won-der, why won-der? I am
Cm7
Cm7/F
F9
green, and it-'ll do fine. It's beau-ti-ful, and I think it's
B♭
B♭(add2)
what I want to be.
decresc.
pp

Traditional

NOTE: Each time a letter of BINGO is deleted in the lyric, clap your hands in place of singing the letter.

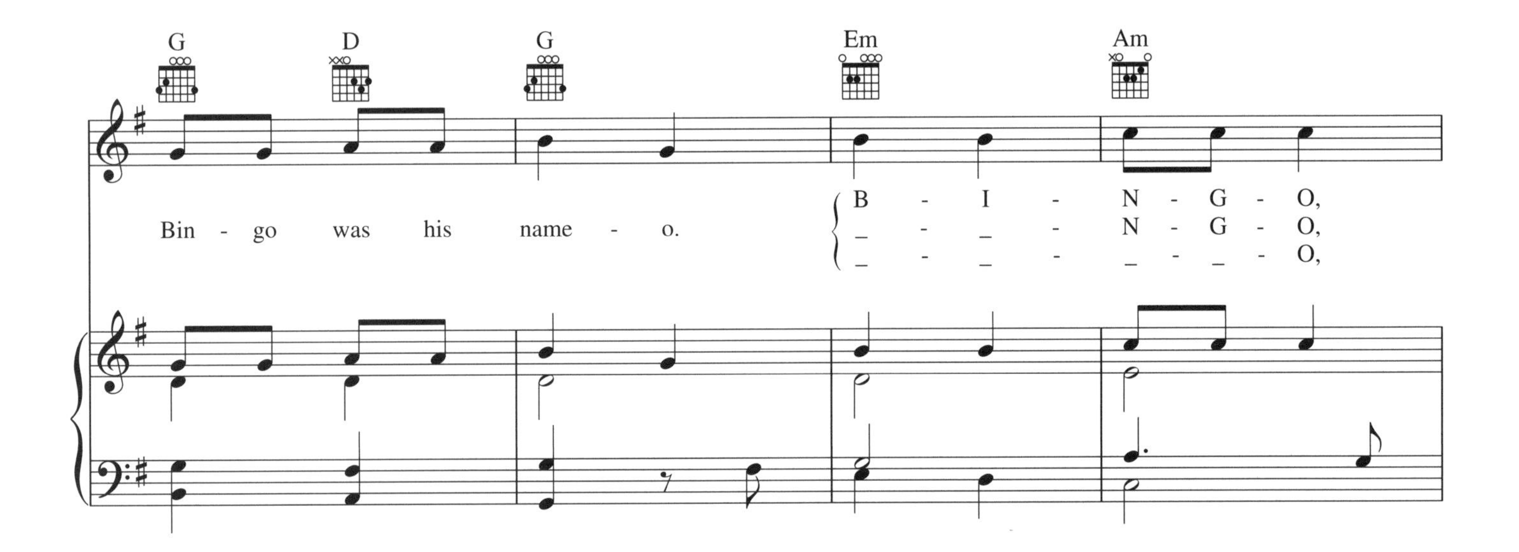

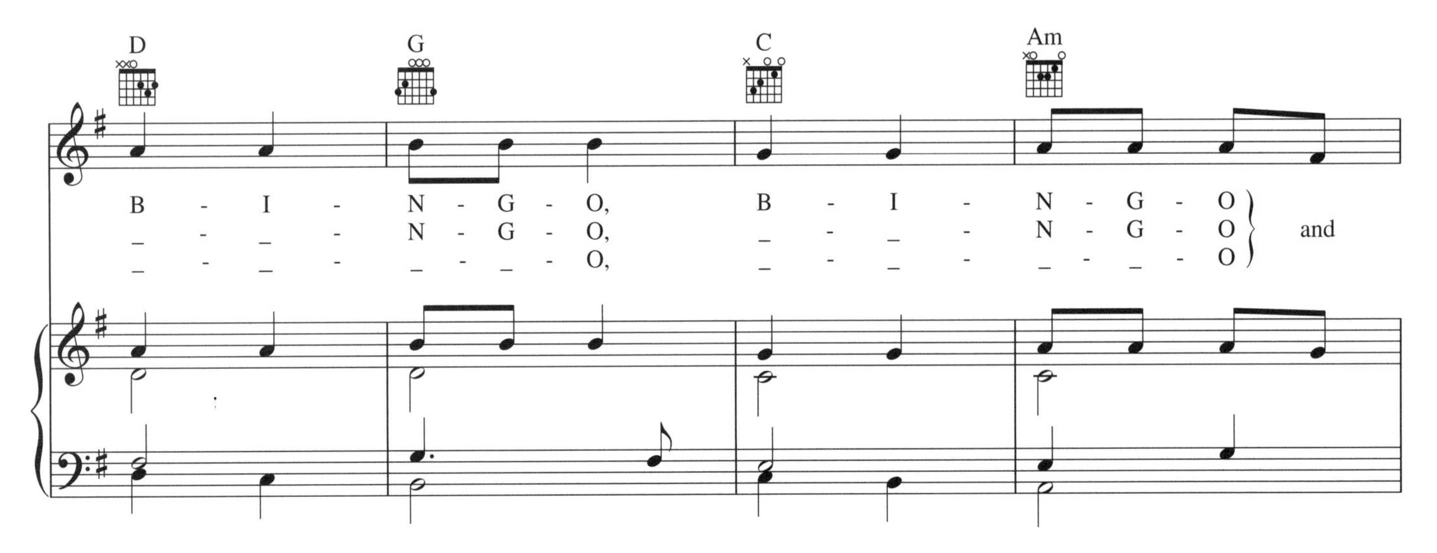

D7
C/G
G
C
D
Bin - go was his name - o. There was a farm - er had a dog and

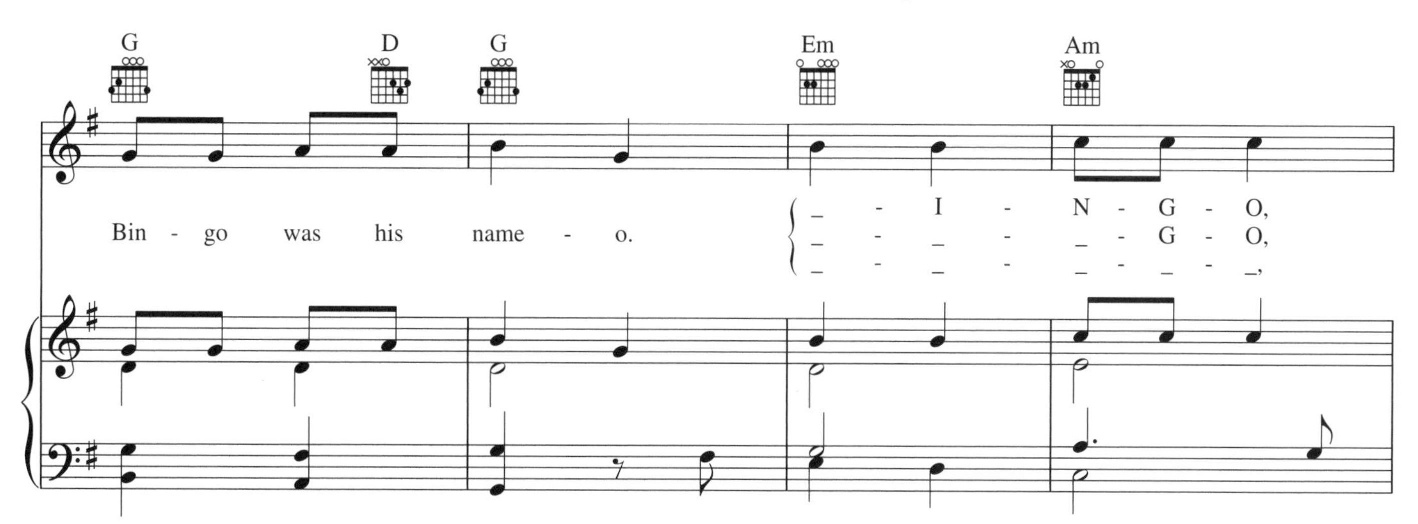
G
D
G
Em
Am
Bin - go was his name - o.
_ - I - N - G - O,
_ - _ - _ - G - O,
_ - _ - _ - _ - _,

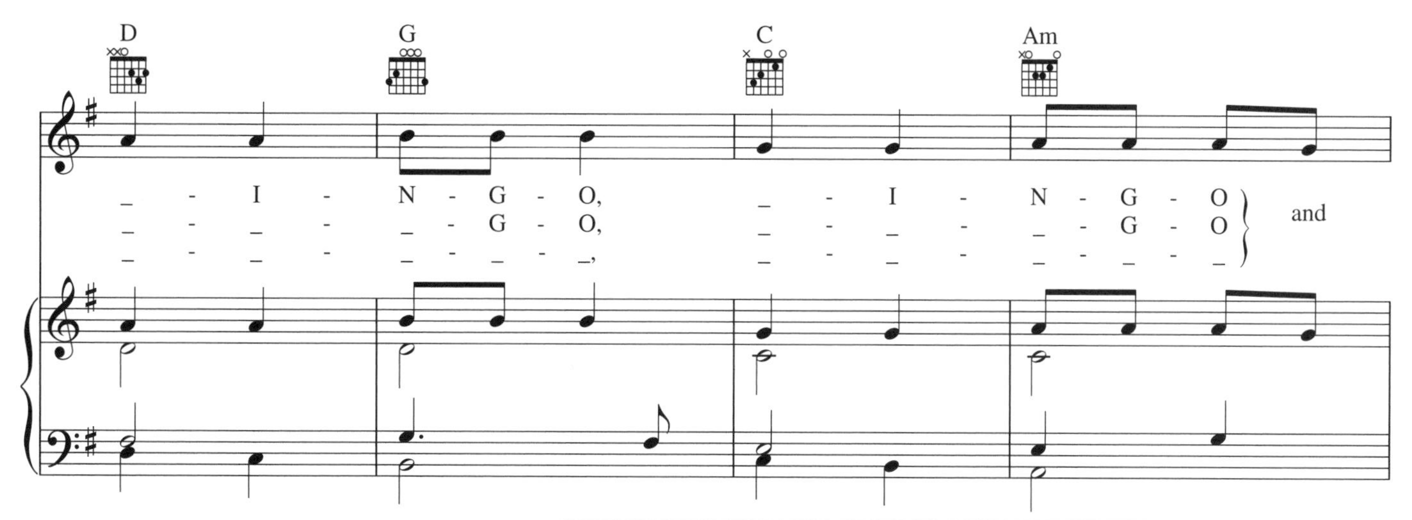
D
G
C
Am
_ - I - N - G - O, _ - I - N - G - O
_ - _ - _ - G - O, _ - _ - _ - G - O
_ - _ - _ - _ - _, _ - _ - _ - _ - _
and

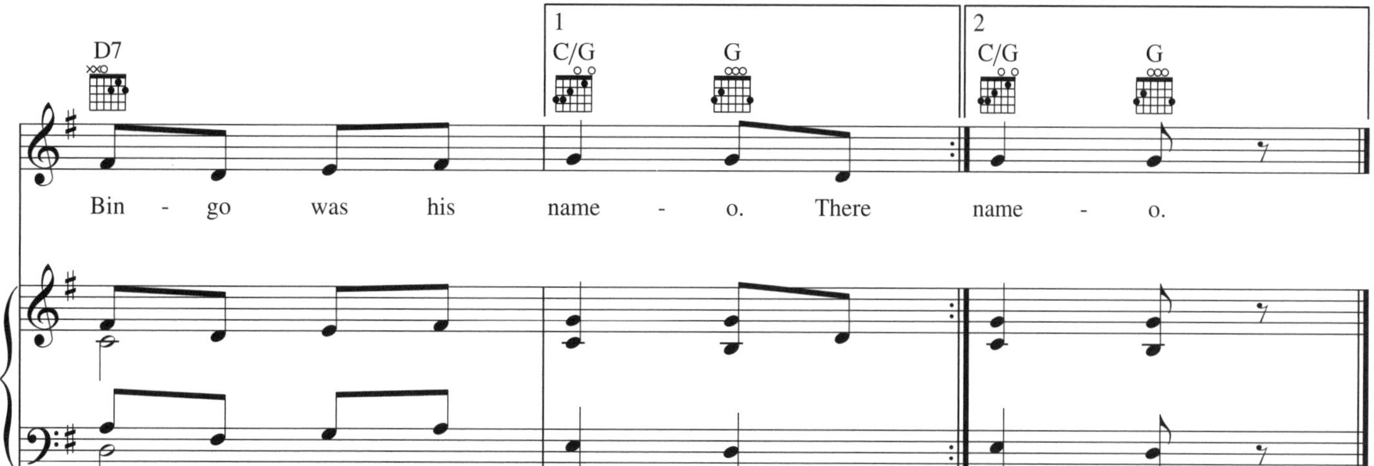
D7
1
C/G
G
2
C/G
G
Bin - go was his name - o. There name - o.

Theme from the Paramount Television Series THE BRADY BUNCH
Words and Music by Sherwood Schwartz and Frank Devol

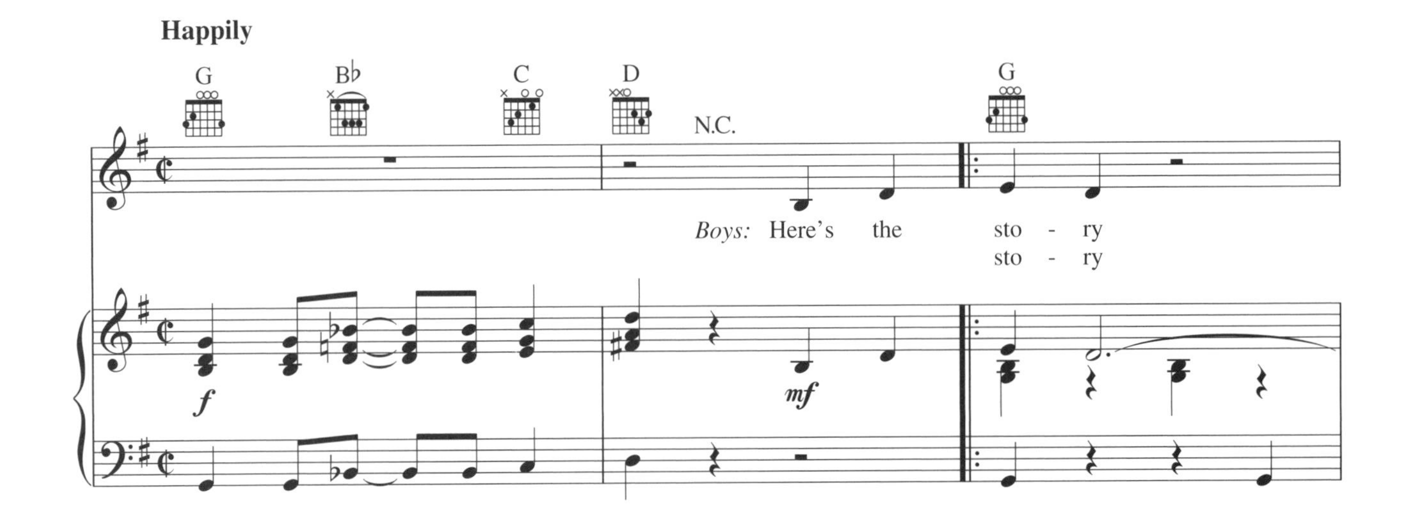

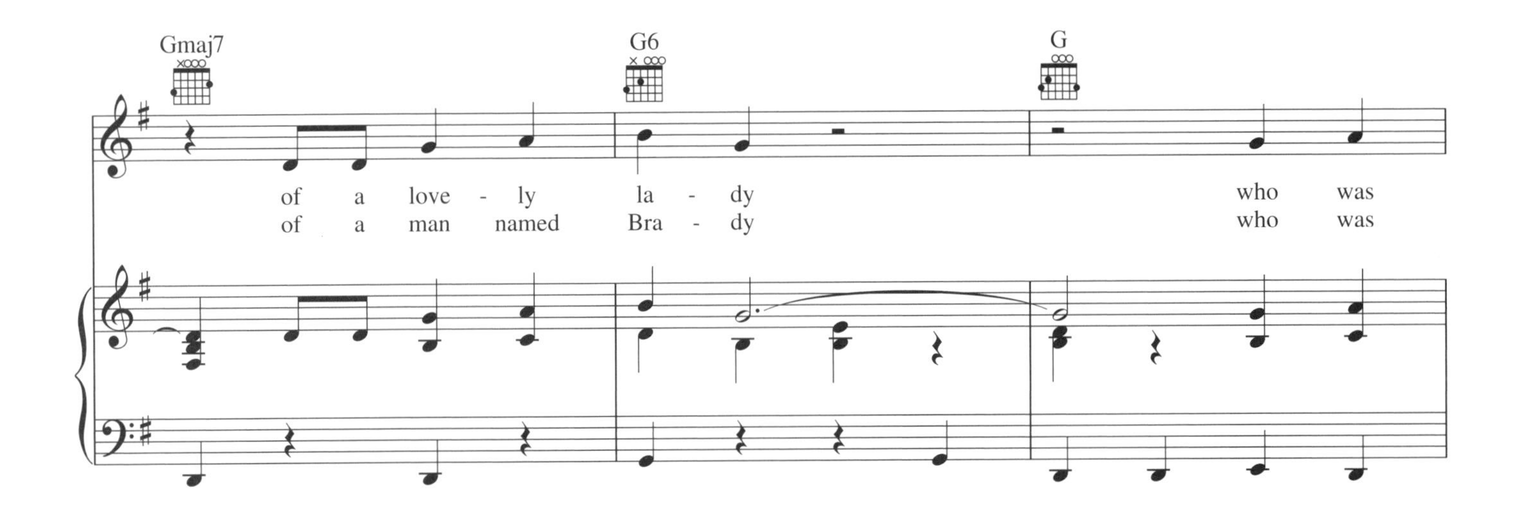

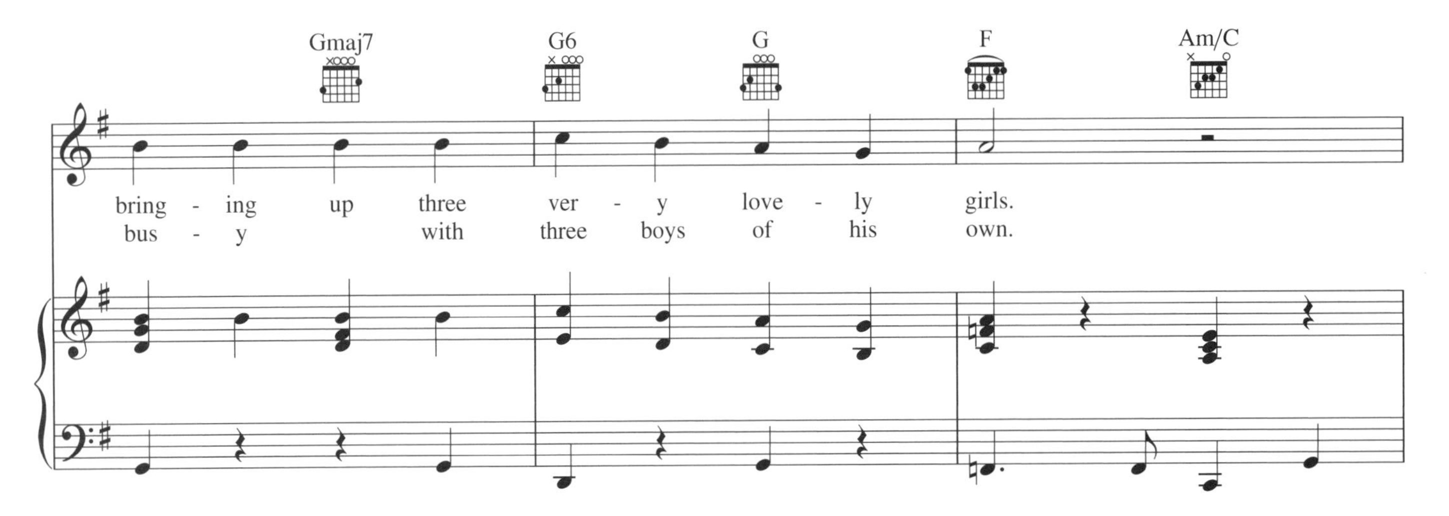

D7
Am7
D7
All of them had hair of gold
They were four men liv - ing all to -
Am7
D7
1
like their moth - er, the young - est
geth - er, yet they were
G
2
one in curls. Girls: It's the all a -
G G7 C/G G E♭7 A♭
4fr
lone. All: 'Til the one day when the
f
mf

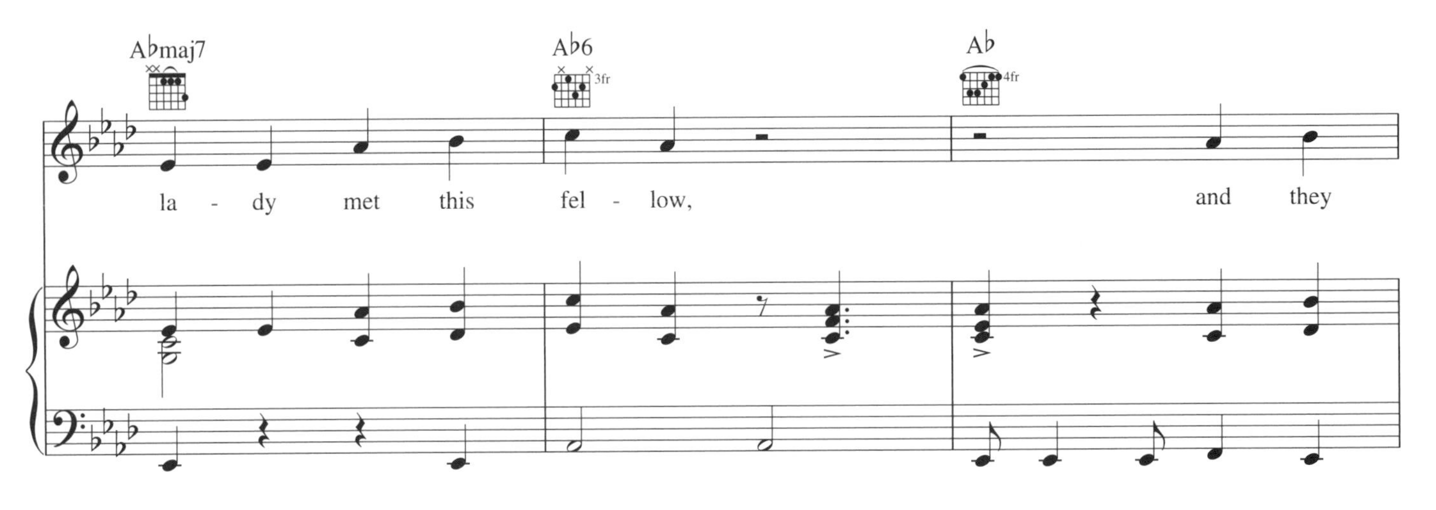
A♭maj7
A♭6
3fr
A♭
4fr
la - dy met this fel - low, and they

B♭m7
knew that it was much more than a hunch

E♭
3fr
B♭m7
E♭7
that this group must some - how form a

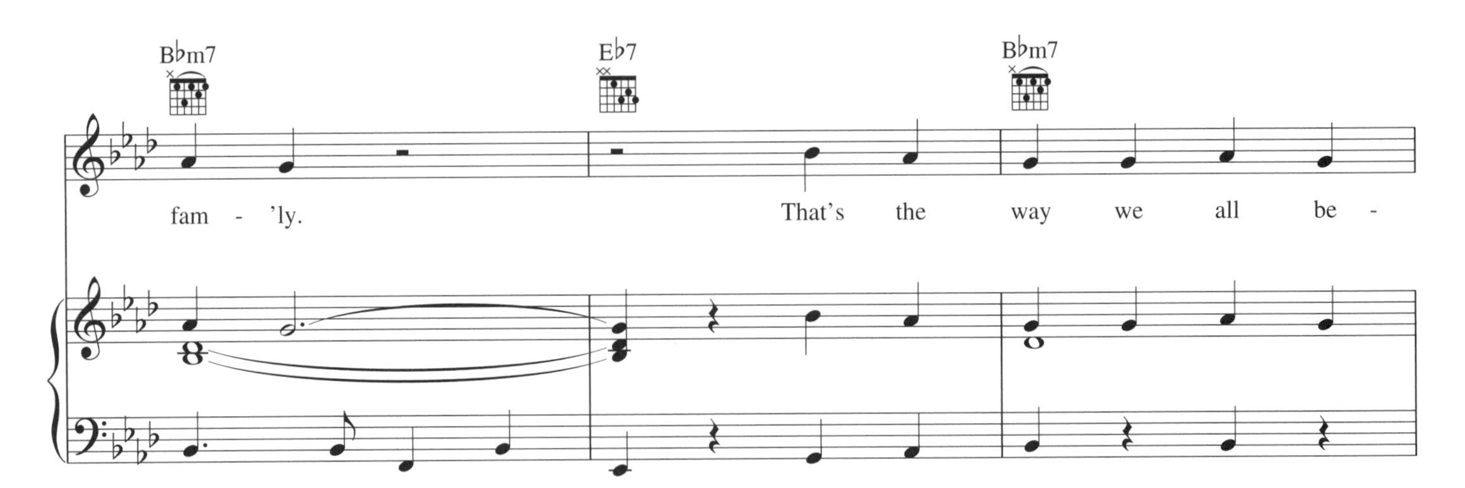
B♭m7
E♭7
B♭m7
fam - 'ly. That's the way we all be -

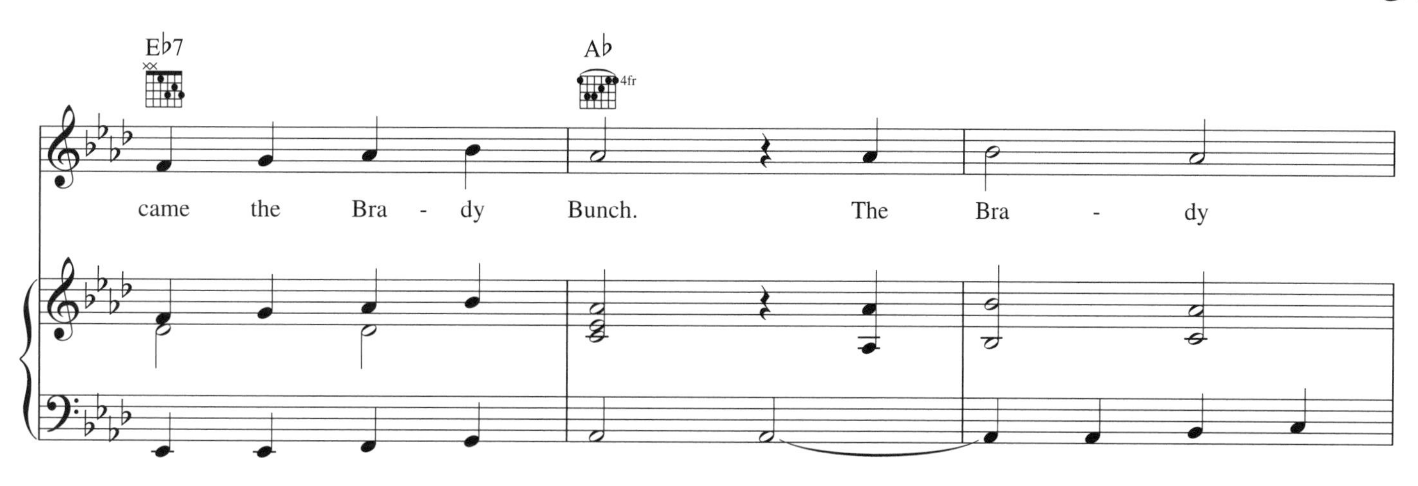
E♭7
A♭
4fr
came the Bra - dy Bunch. The Bra - dy

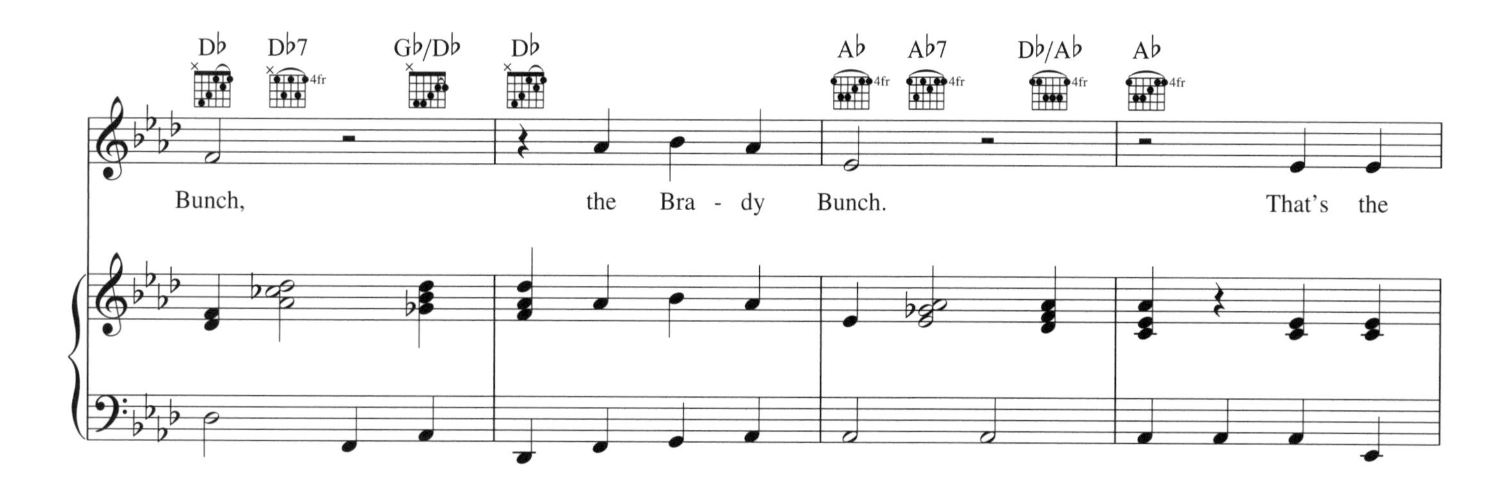
D♭
D♭7
G♭/D♭
D♭
A♭
A♭7
D♭/A♭
A♭
4fr
Bunch, the Bra - dy Bunch. That's the

B♭
E♭
3fr
E♭7
way we be - came the Bra - dy

A♭
D♭/A♭
A♭
N.C.
A♭
A♭7
D♭/A♭
A♭
4fr
Bunch.
f

"C" Is for Cookie

Words and Music by Joe Raposo

A♭
Fm7
E♭/B♭
B♭7
To Coda
good e - nough for me! Oh, cook - ie, cook - ie, cook - ie starts with
Oh, and the moon sometimes looks like a C,
1
2
3
D.S. al Coda
E♭
N.C.
C.
C. (Spoken:) Hey, you know what? but you can't eat that. So
CODA
C. Yeah! Cook - ie, cook - ie, cook - ie starts with
C. Oh boy! Cook - ie, cook - ie, cook - ie starts with C.

The Candy Man

from WILLY WONKA AND THE CHOCOLATE FACTORY
Words and Music by Leslie Bricusse and Anthony Newley

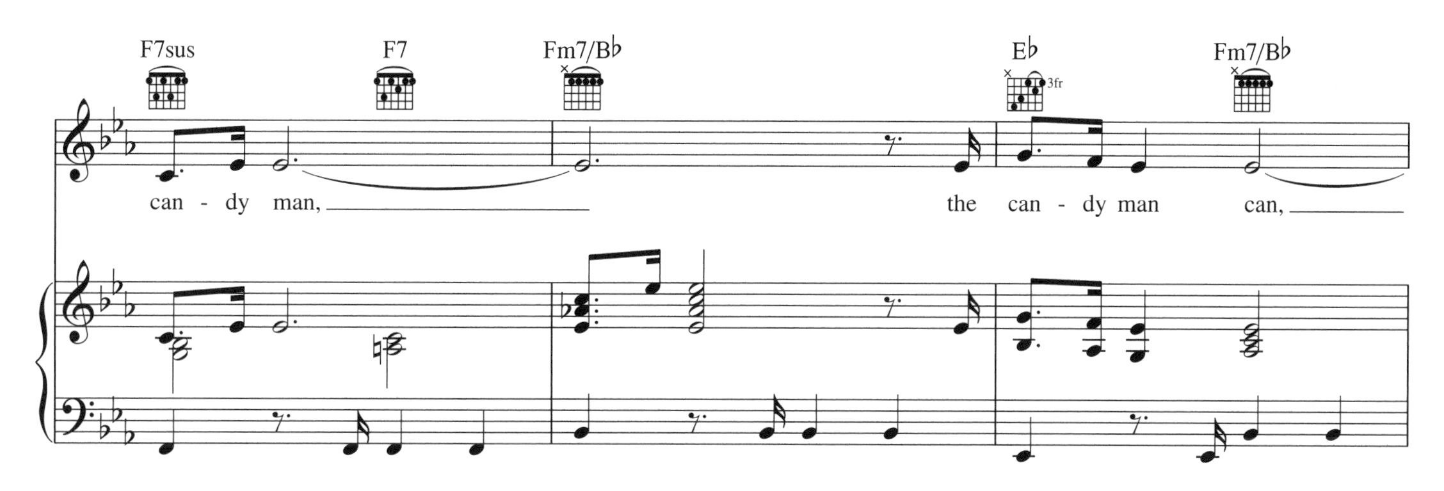
F7sus
F7
Fm7/B♭
E♭
3fr
Fm7/B♭
can - dy man,
the can - dy man can,

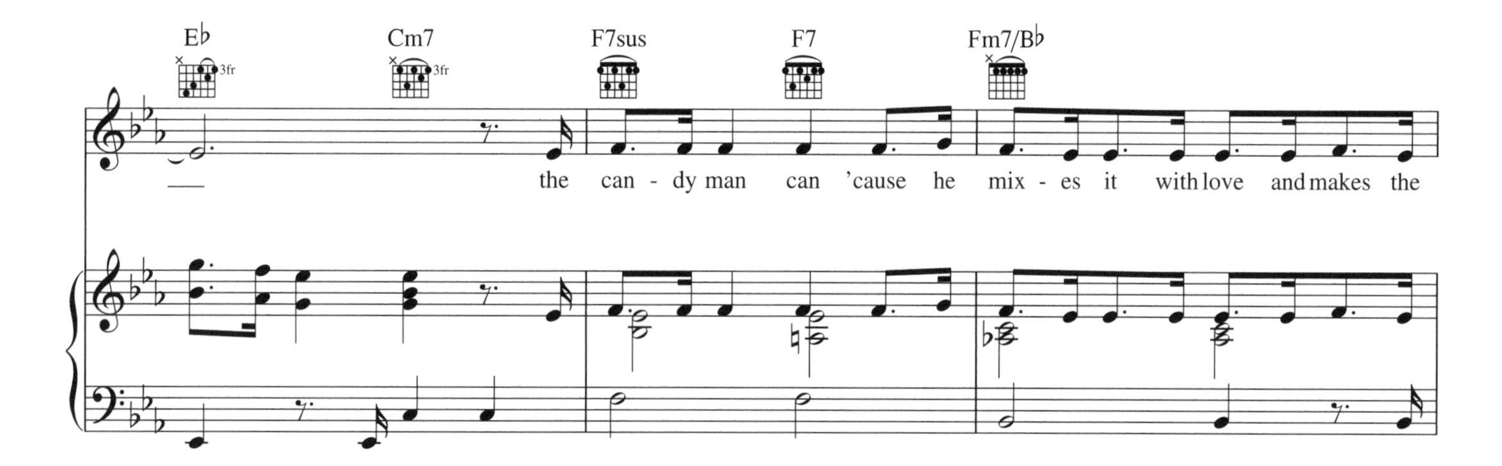
E♭
3fr
Cm7
3fr
F7sus
F7
Fm7/B♭
the can - dy man can 'cause he mix - es it with love and makes the

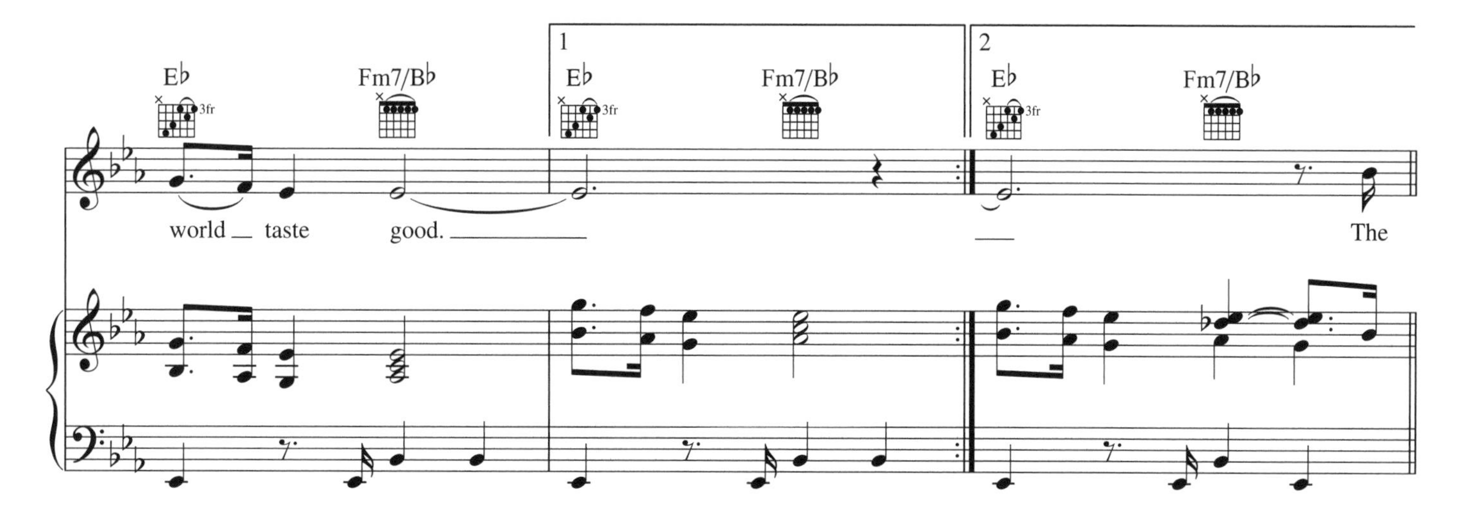
E♭
3fr
Fm7/B♭
1
E♭
3fr
Fm7/B♭
2
E♭
3fr
Fm7/B♭
world taste good.
The

A♭maj7
Adim7
E♭/B♭
6fr
can - dy man makes ev - 'ry-thing he bakes sat - is - fy - ing and de -

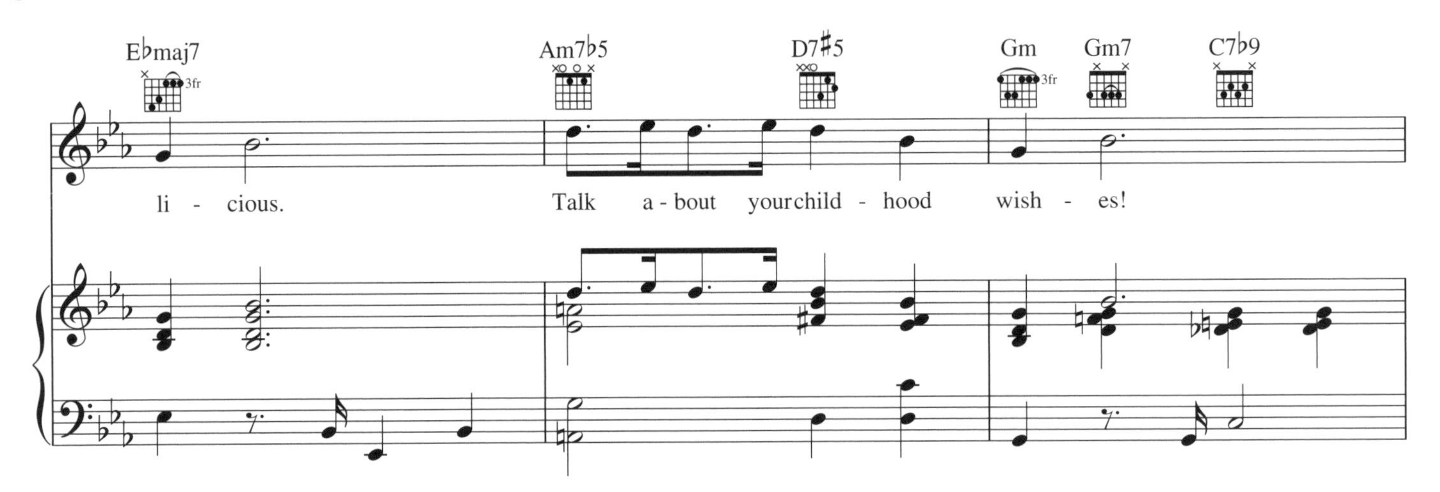
E♭maj7
Am7♭5
D7♯5
Gm
Gm7
C7♭9
li - cious. Talk a - bout your child - hood wish - es!

Fm7
B♭7
E♭
You can e - ven eat the dish - es! Who can take to - mor - row,

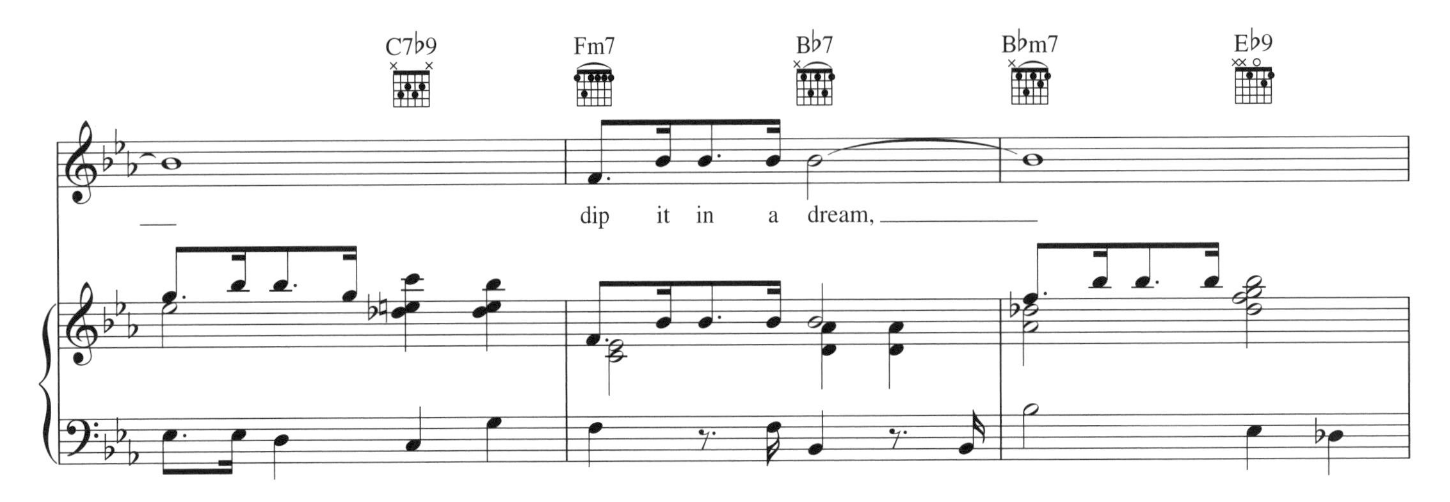
C7♭9
Fm7
B♭7
B♭m7
E♭9
dip it in a dream,

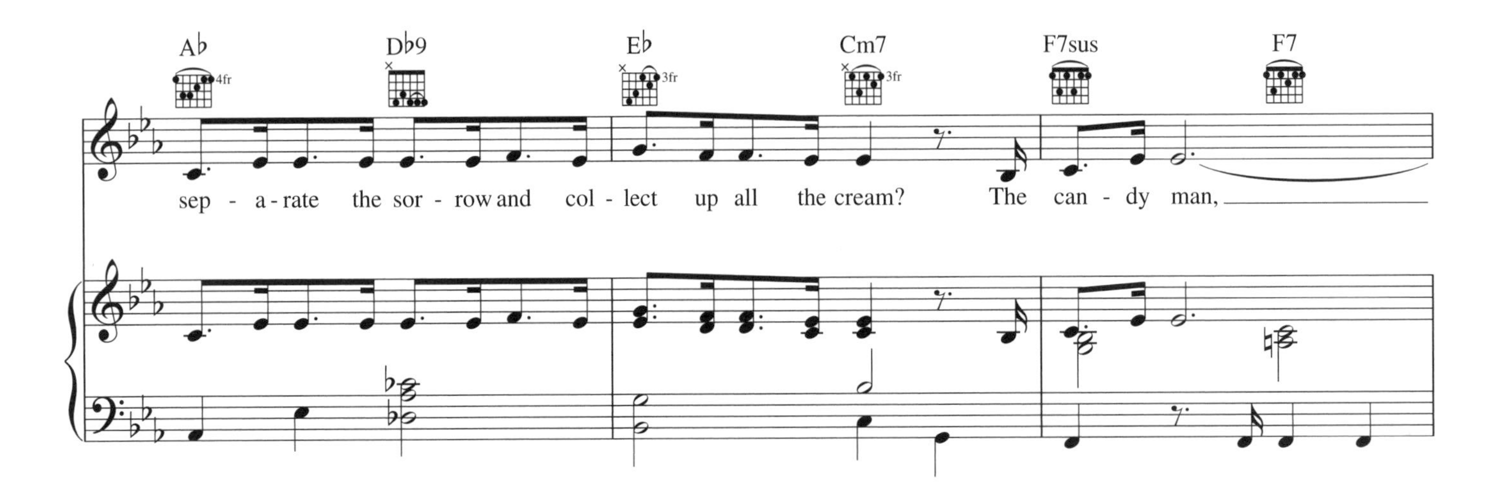
A♭
D♭9
E♭
Cm7
F7sus
F7
sep - a - rate the sor - row and col - lect up all the cream? The can - dy man,

Fm7/B♭
E♭
Fm7/B♭
E♭
Cm7
the can - dy man can, the
F7sus
F7
Fm7/B♭
E♭
Fm7/B♭
can - dy man can 'cause he mix - es it with love and makes the world taste good.
1
E♭
Fm7/B♭
The
2
E♭
Cm7
F7sus
F7
And the world tastes good 'cause the
Fm7/B♭
E♭
A♭
E♭
can - dy man thinks it should.

Casper the Friendly Ghost

F C G7 C
al - ways says "Hel - lo," and he's real - ly glad to meet cha. Wher -

F C D7 G7
ev - er he may go, he's kind to ev - 'ry liv - ing crea - ture.

C C#dim7
Grown - ups don't un - der - stand why chil - dren love him the most, but

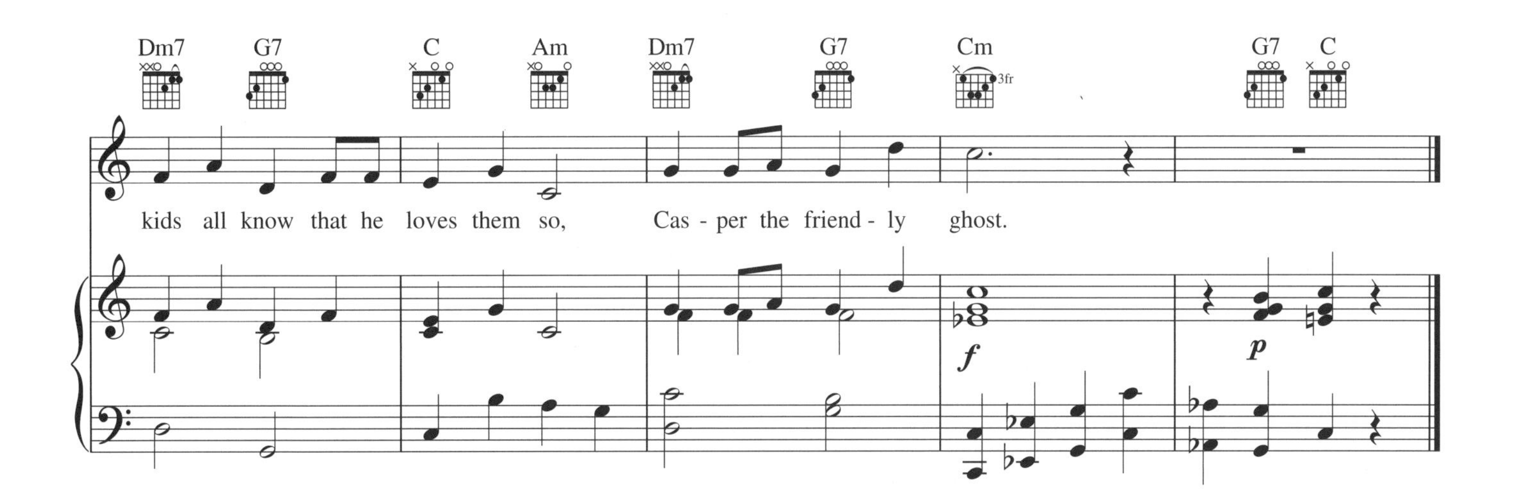
Dm7 G7 C Am Dm7 G7 Cm G7 C
3fr
kids all know that he loves them so, Cas - per the friend - ly ghost.
f
p

The Chicken Dance

By Terry Rendall and Werner Thomas
English Lyrics by Paul Parnes

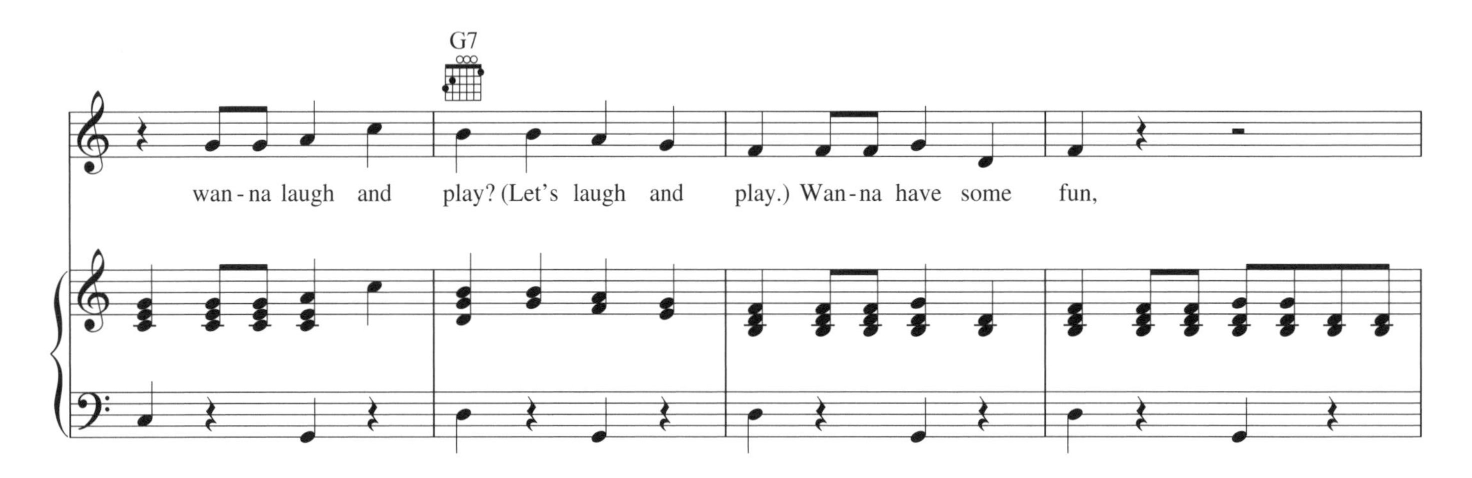

G7
Got a prob-lem? Here's a cure. (We got the cure.) Do the chick - en dance;
To Coda
C
Chorus
make you hap - py for sure.
1.,3. Reach out your arms and
swing your part - ner.
Make like a bird and

G7
try to fly.
Come on out there, you

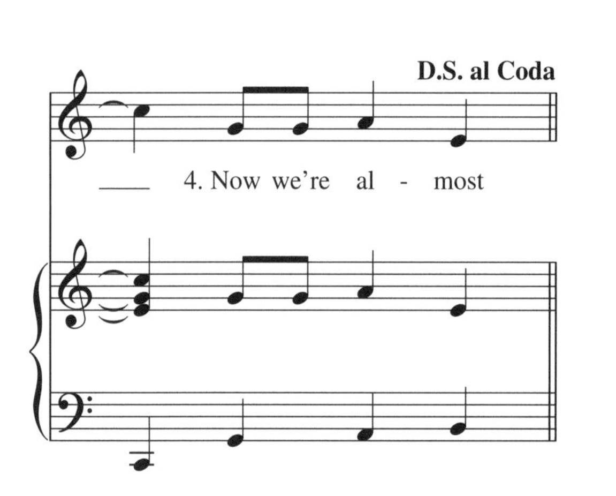

Additional Lyrics

2. Hey, you're in the swing.
   You're cluckin' like a bird. (Pluck, pluck, pluck, pluck.)
   You're flappin' your wings.
   Don't you feel absurd. (No, no, no, no.)
   It's a chicken dance,
   Like a rooster and a hen. (Ya, ya, ya, ya.)
   Flappy chicken dance;
   Let's do it again. *(To Chorus 2:)*

Chorus 2:
Relax and let the music move you.
Let all your inhibitions go.
Just watch your partner whirl around you.
We're havin' fun now; I told you so.

3. Now you're flappin' like a bird
   And you're wigglin' too. (I like that move.)
   You're without a care.
   It's a dance for you. (Just made for you.)
   Keep doin' what you do.
   Don't you cop out now. (Don't cop out now.)
   Gets better as you dance;
   Catch your breath somehow.
   Chorus

4. Now we're almost through,
   Really flyin' high. (Bye, bye, bye, bye.)
   All you chickens and birds,
   Time to say goodbye. (To say goodbye.)
   Goin' back to the nest,
   But the flyin' was fun. (Oh, it was fun.)
   Chicken dance was the best,
   But the dance is done.

Chim Chim Cher-ee

from Walt Disney's MARY POPPINS

Words and Music by Richard M. Sherman and Robert B. Sherman

Lightly, with gusto

Cm G7♭9 Am7♭5 G7/B Cm G7♭9 Am7♭5 G7/B

mf

Cm G+ Cm7 F

Chim chim-in-ey, chim chim-in-ey, chim chim cher-ee! A

Fm Cm D D7♭5 G7

sweep is as luck-y as luck-y can be.

Cm G+ Cm7 F Fm

Chim chim-in-ey, chim chim-in-ey, chim chim cher-oo! Good luck will rub

Cm/G
G7
G7♯5
Cm
Fm
Cm/G
off when I shakes 'ands with you, or blow me a kiss and

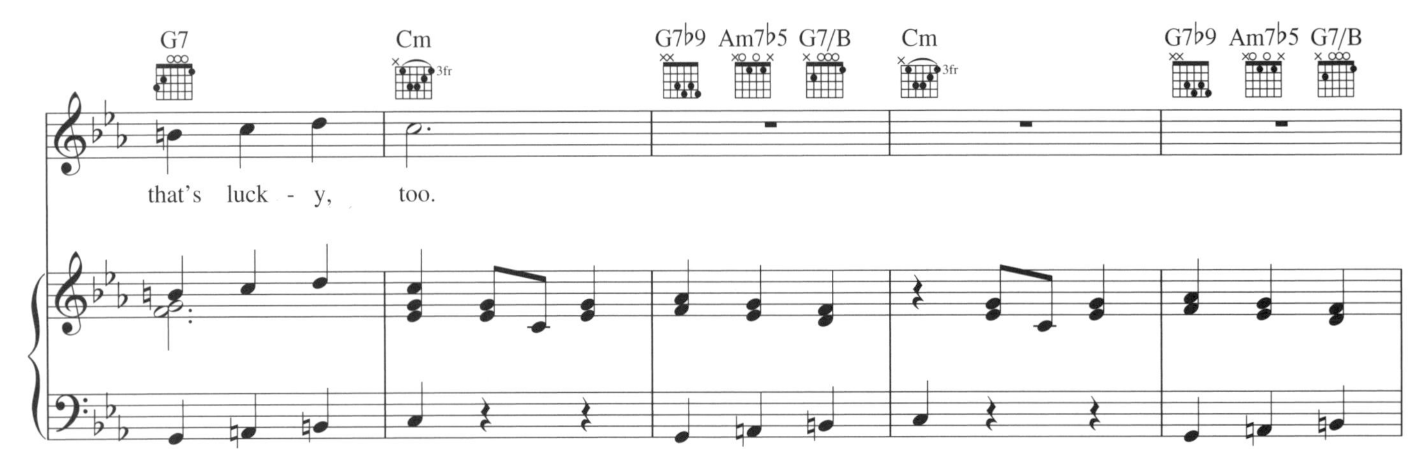
G7
Cm
G7♭9
Am7♭5
G7/B
Cm
G7♭9
Am7♭5
G7/B
that's luck - y, too.

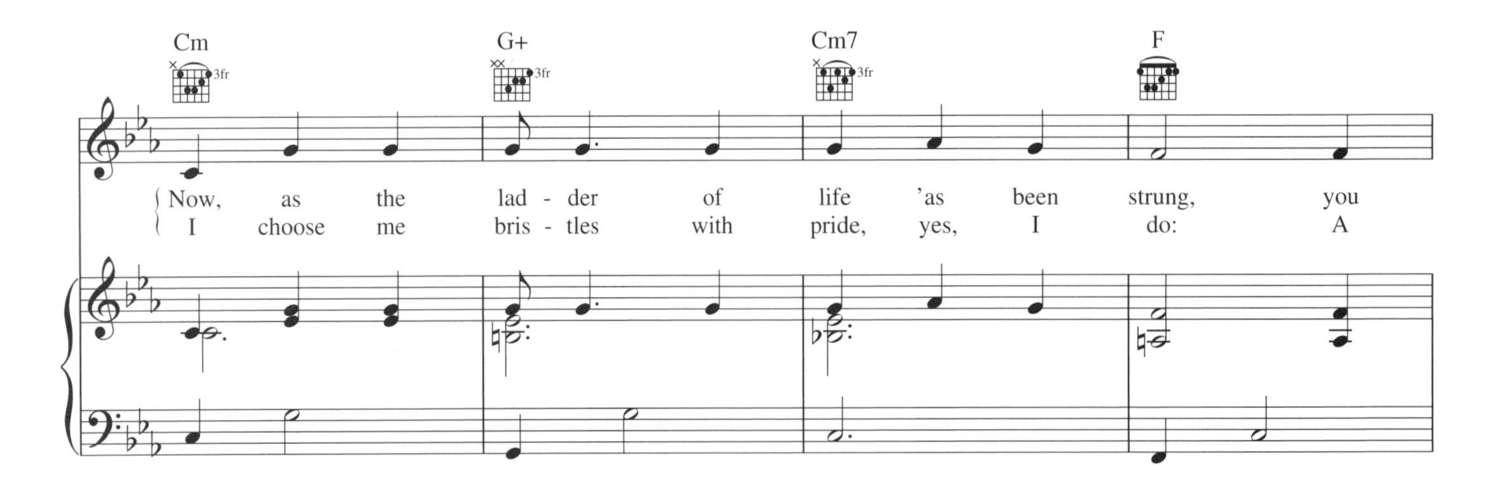
Cm
G+
Cm7
F
Now, as the lad - der of life 'as been strung, you
I choose me bris - tles with pride, yes, I do: A

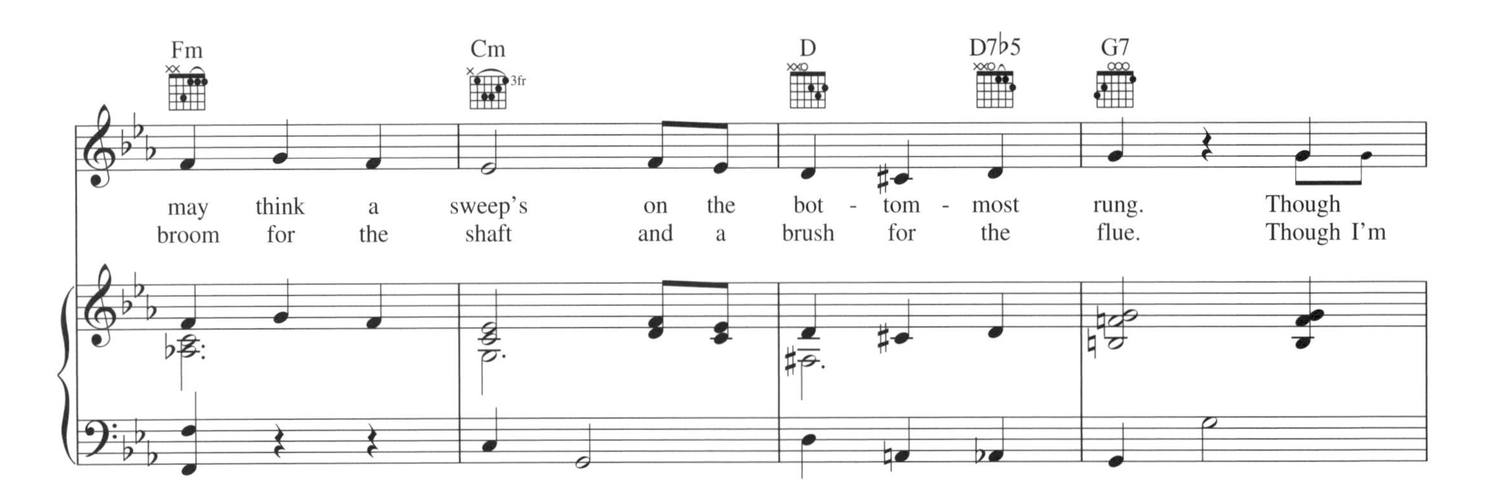
Fm
Cm
D
D7♭5
G7
may think a sweep's on the bot - tom - most rung. Though
broom for the shaft and a brush for the flue. Though I'm

Cm G+ Cm7 F
3fr
I spends me time in the ash - es and smoke, in
cov - ered with soot from me 'ead to me toes, a
Fm Cm/G G7 1 Cm 2 Cm
this 'ole wide world there's no 'ap - pi - er bloke.
sweep knows 'e's wel - come wher - ev - er 'e goes.
Freely
G+ Cm7 F
Up where the smoke is all bill - ered and curled, 'tween
Fm Cm/G D/A D7♭5 G7
pave - ment and stars, is the chim - ney sweep world. When there's

Cm
G+
Cm7
F
'ard - ly no day nor 'ard - ly no night, there's
Fm
Cm/G
G7
Cm
things 'alf in shad - ow and 'alf - way in light, on the
Fm
Cm/G
G7
Cm
roof - tops of Lon - don, coo, what a sight!

Tempo I
Cm
G+
Cm7
F
Chim chim - in - ey, chim chim - in - ey, chim chim cher - ee! When

Fm
Cm
D
D7♭5
G7
you're with a sweep you're in glad com - pa - ny.
Cm
G+
Cm
F
No - where is there a more 'ap - pi - er crew than
Fm
Cm/G
G7
Cm
them wot sings, "Chim chim cher - ee, chim cher - oo!"
Fm
Cm/G
G7
Cm
Chim chim - in - ey, chim chim, cher - ee, chim cher - oo!
rit.

Chopsticks

By Arthur de Lulli

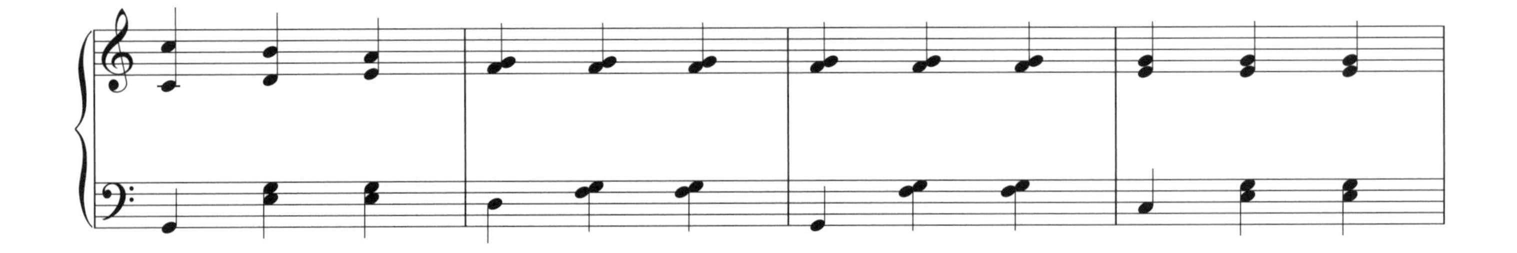

mp

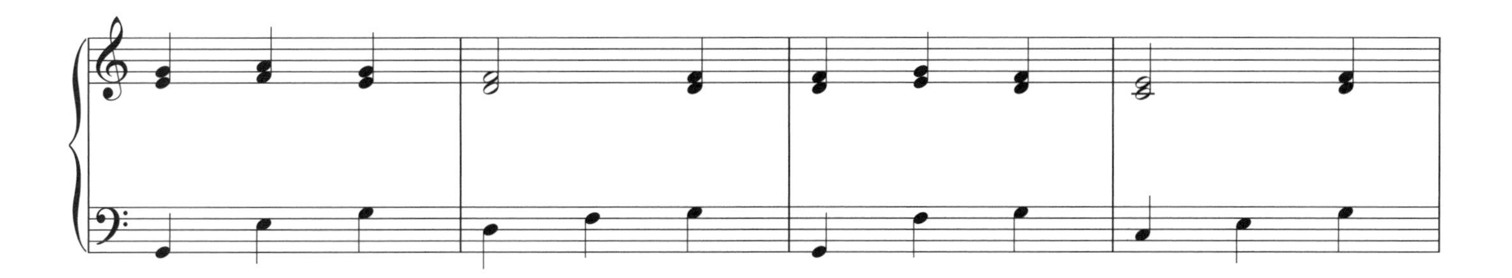

mf

mp
rit.

a tempo

mf

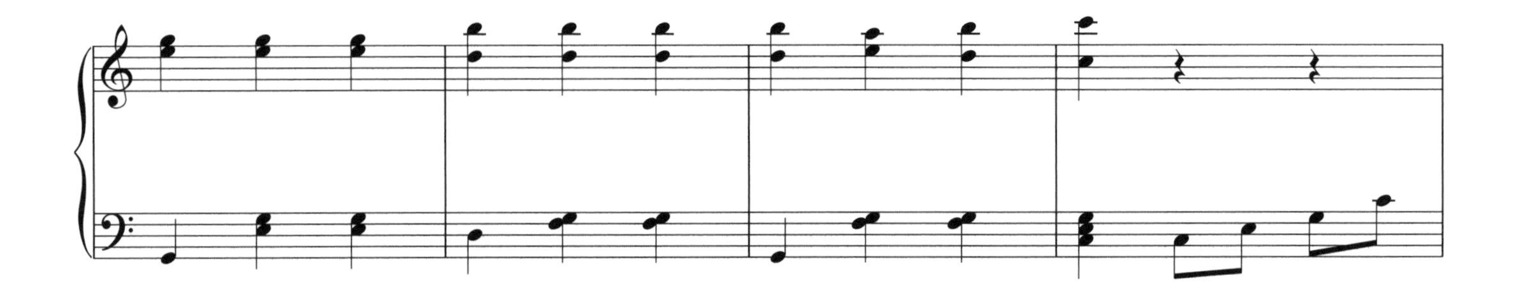

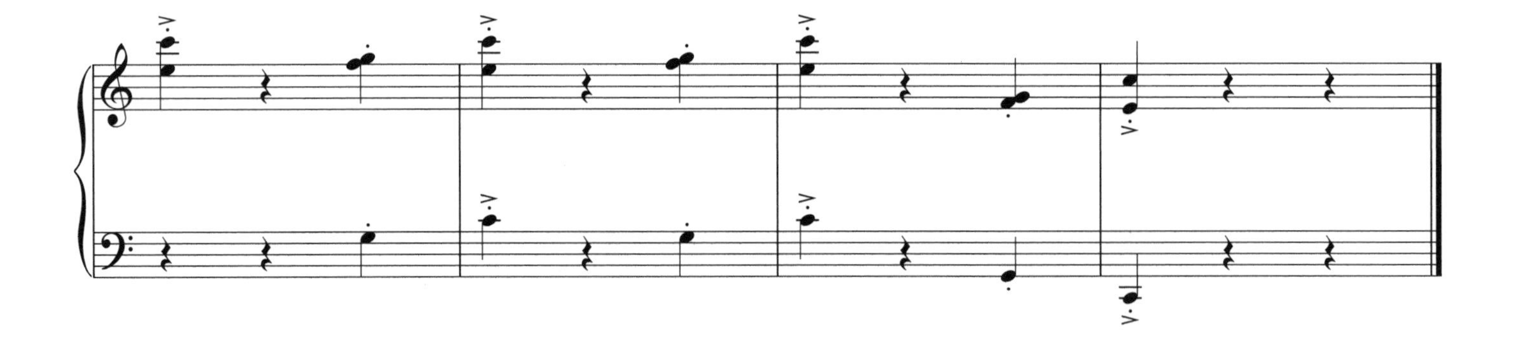

Traditional

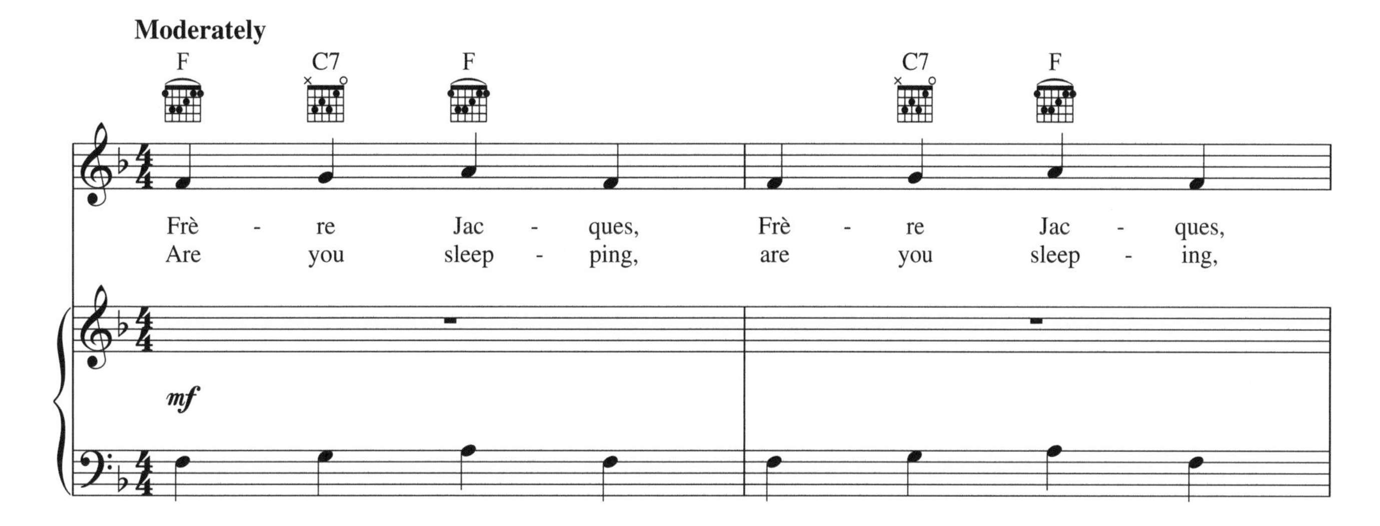

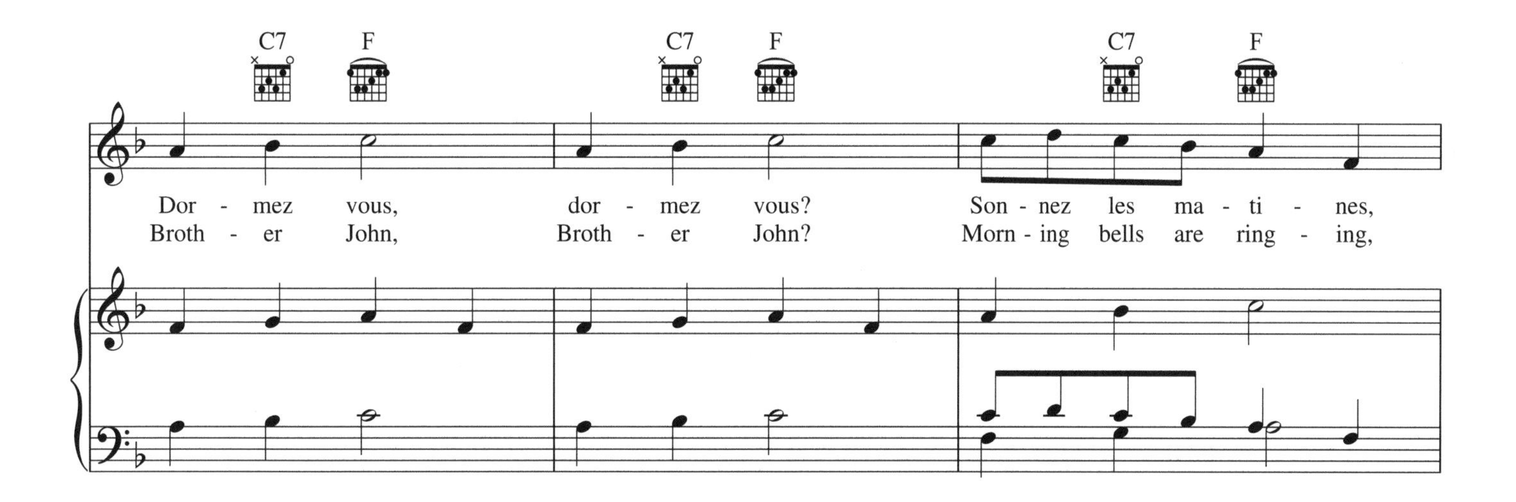

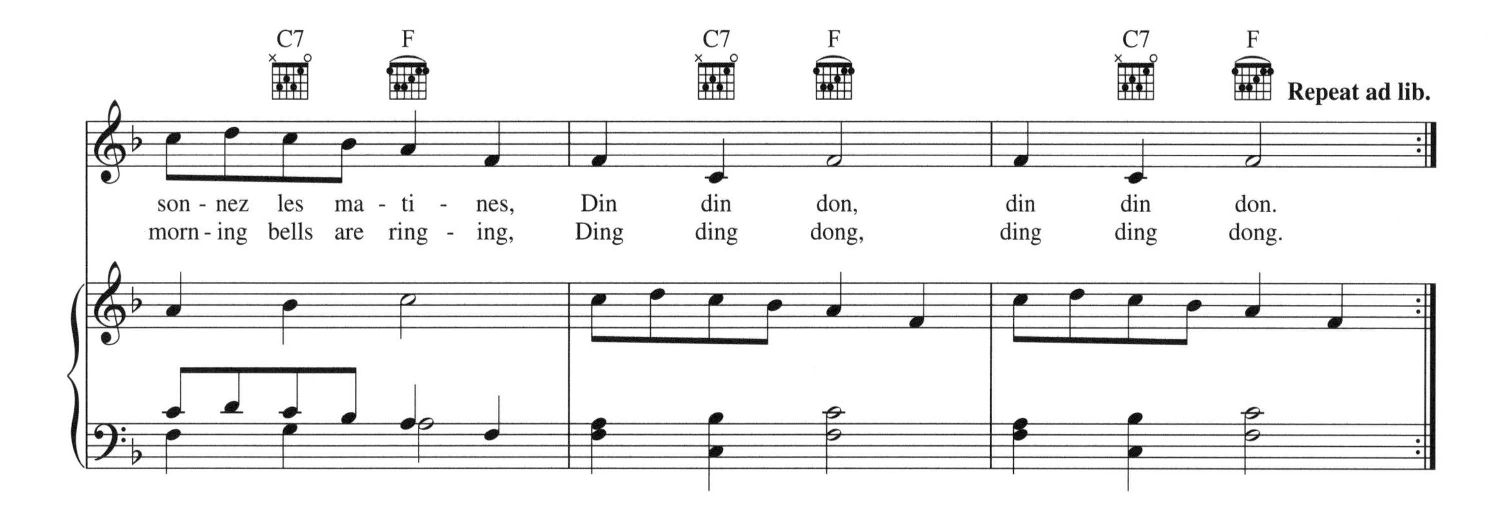

Dites-Moi
(Tell Me Why)

from SOUTH PACIFIC
Lyrics by Oscar Hammerstein II
Music by Richard Rodgers

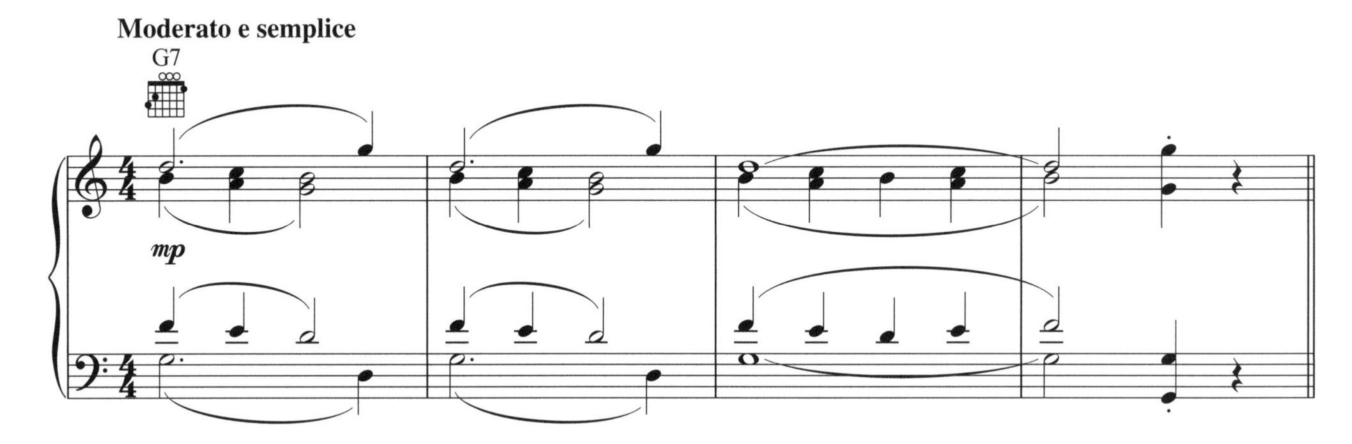

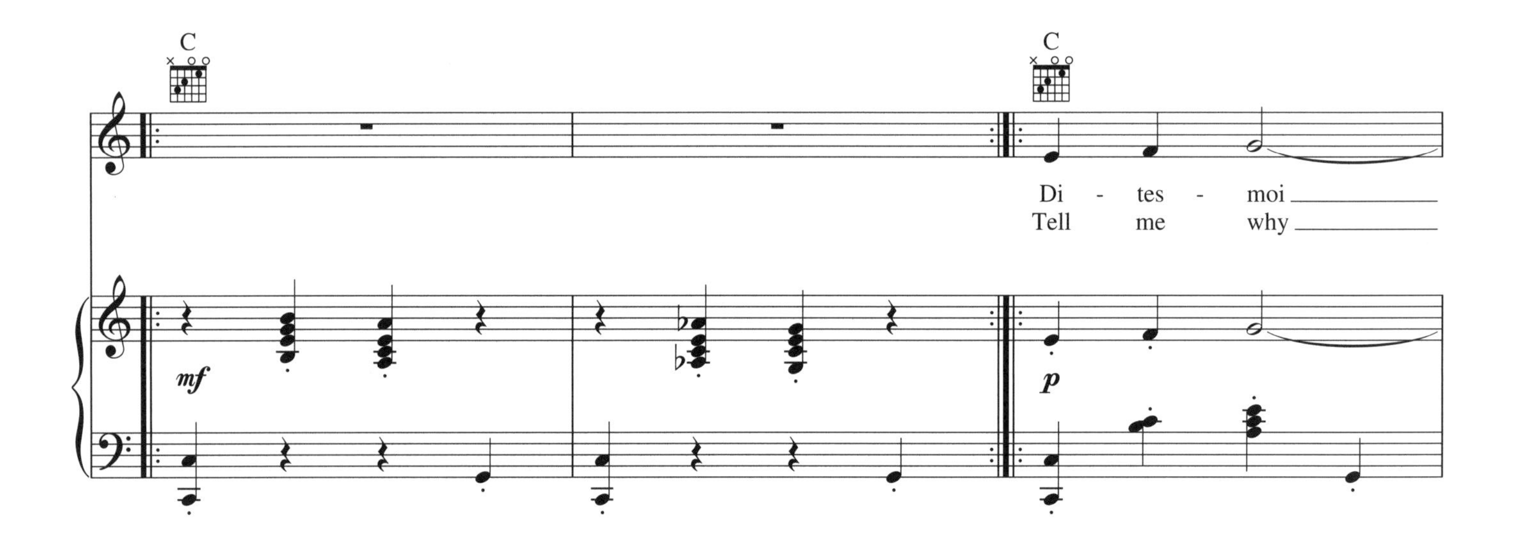

Di - tes - moi
Pour - quoi
La vie est
Tell me why
We fly
on clouds a -

C
gai?
Di - tes - moi
Pour - quoi,
bove
Can it be
that we

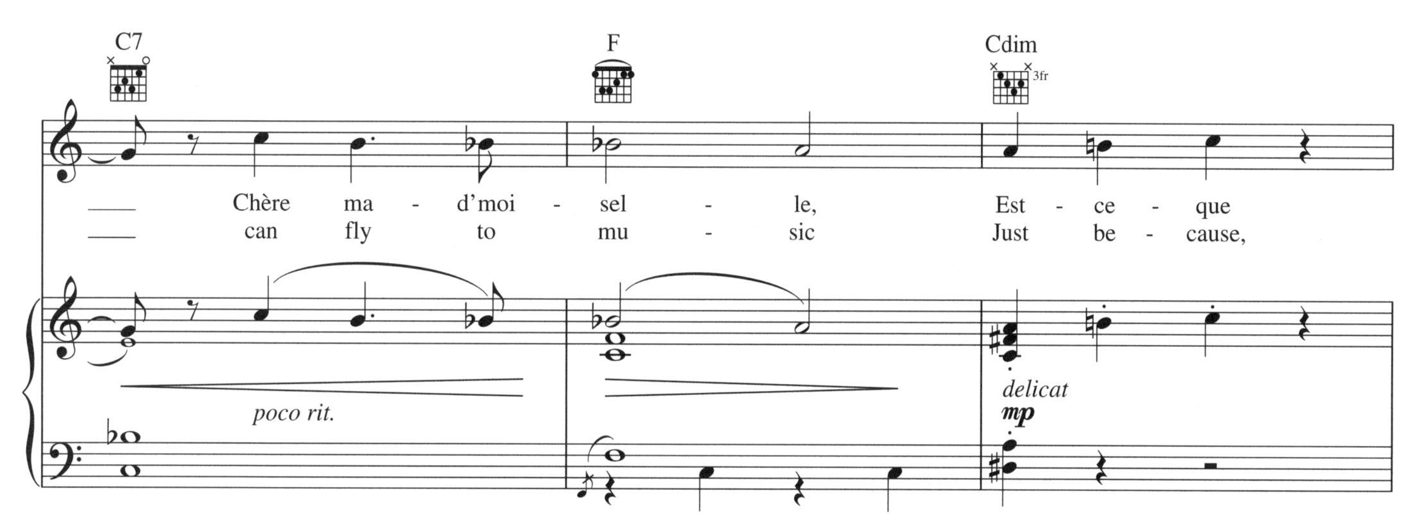
C7
F
Cdim
3fr
Chère ma - d'moi - sel - le,
Est - ce - que
can fly to mu - sic
Just be - cause,
poco rit.
delicat
mp

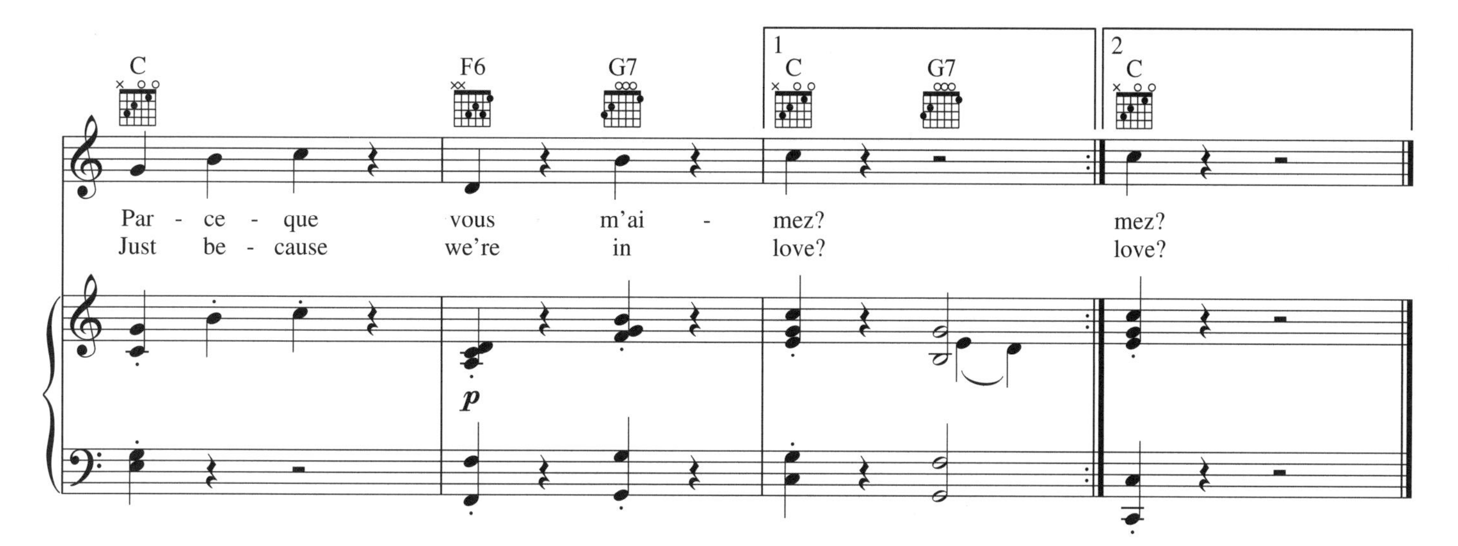
C
F6
G7
1
C
G7
2
C
Par - ce - que vous m'ai - mez?
mez?
Just be - cause we're in love?
love?
p

Do-Re-Mi

from THE SOUND OF MUSIC
Lyrics by Oscar Hammerstein II
Music by Richard Rodgers

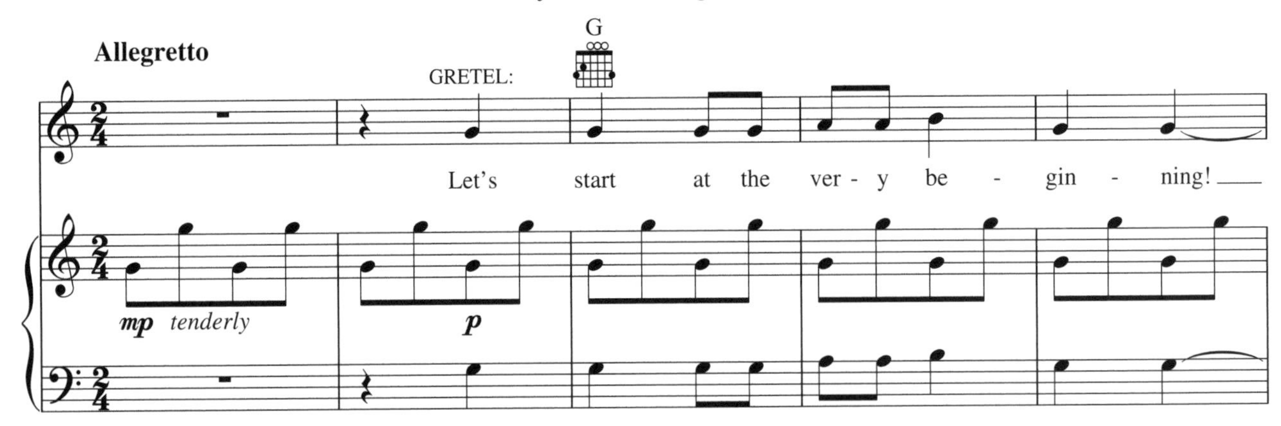

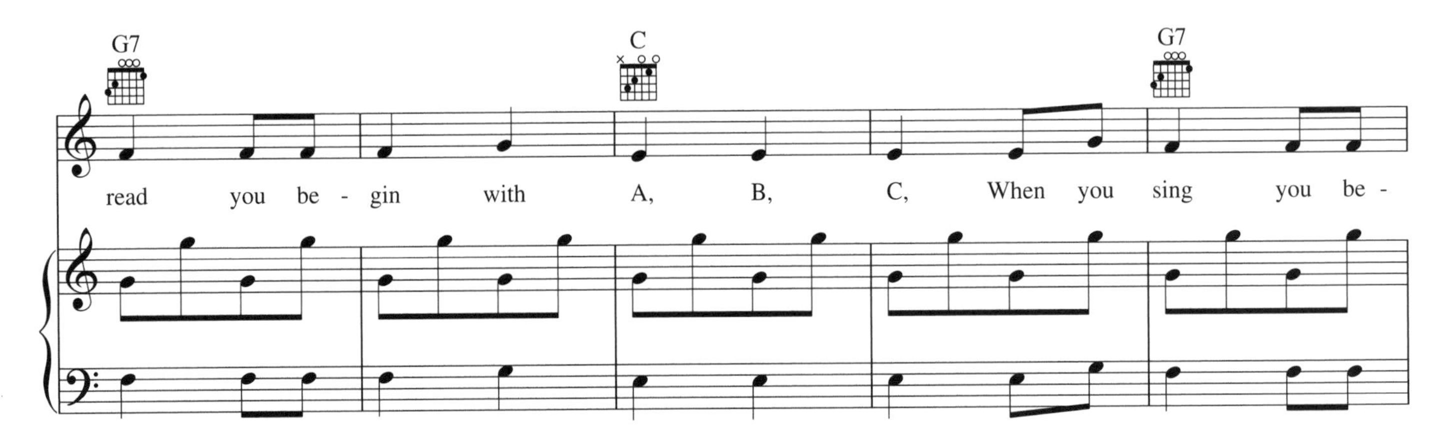

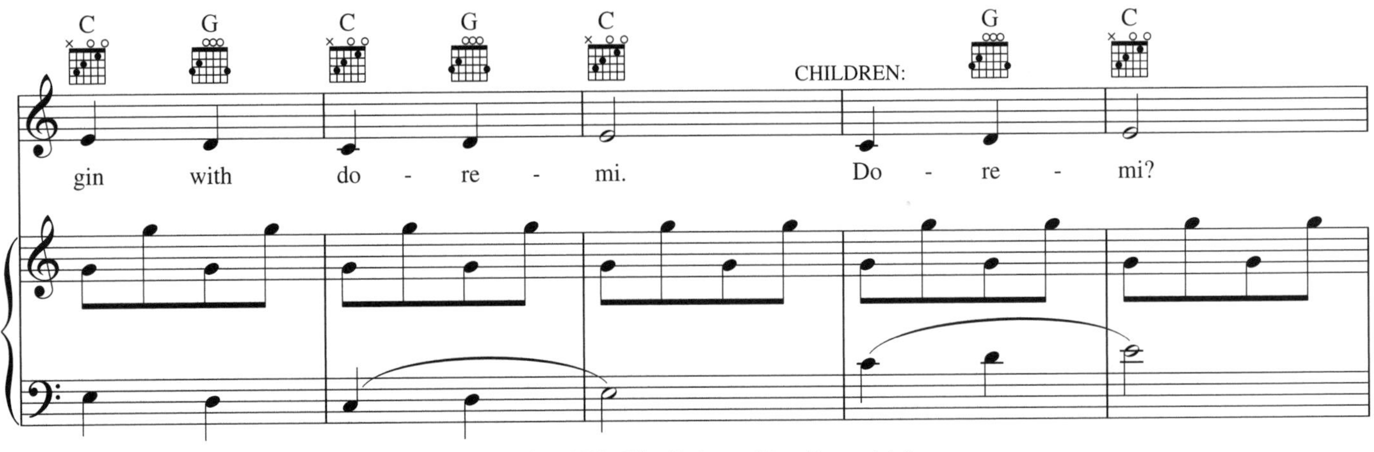

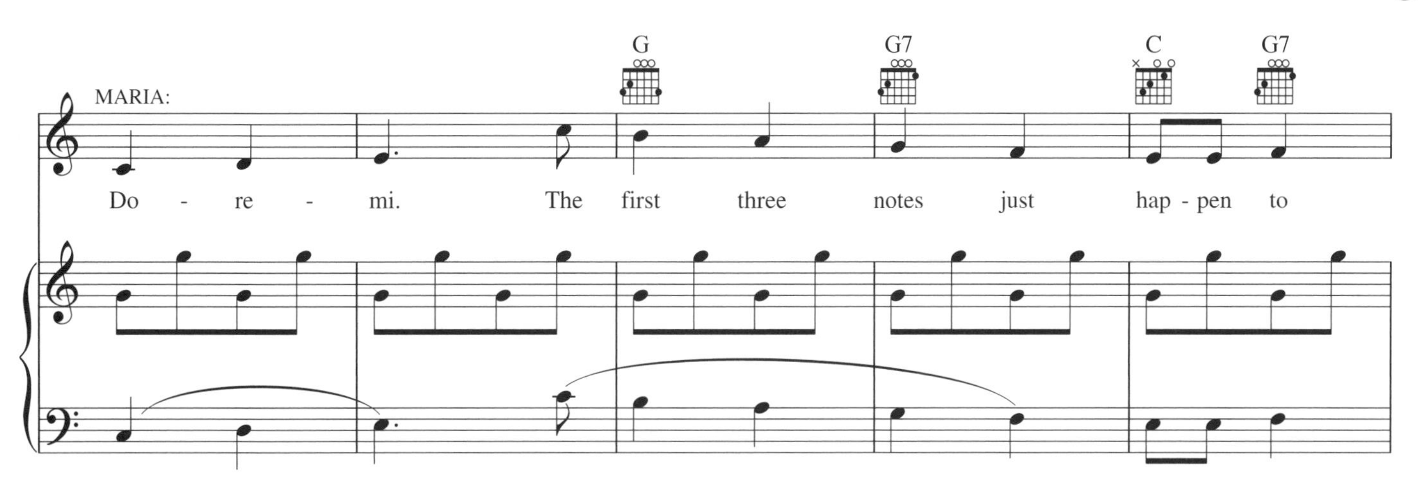
G
G7
C
G7
MARIA:
Do - re - mi. The first three notes just hap - pen to

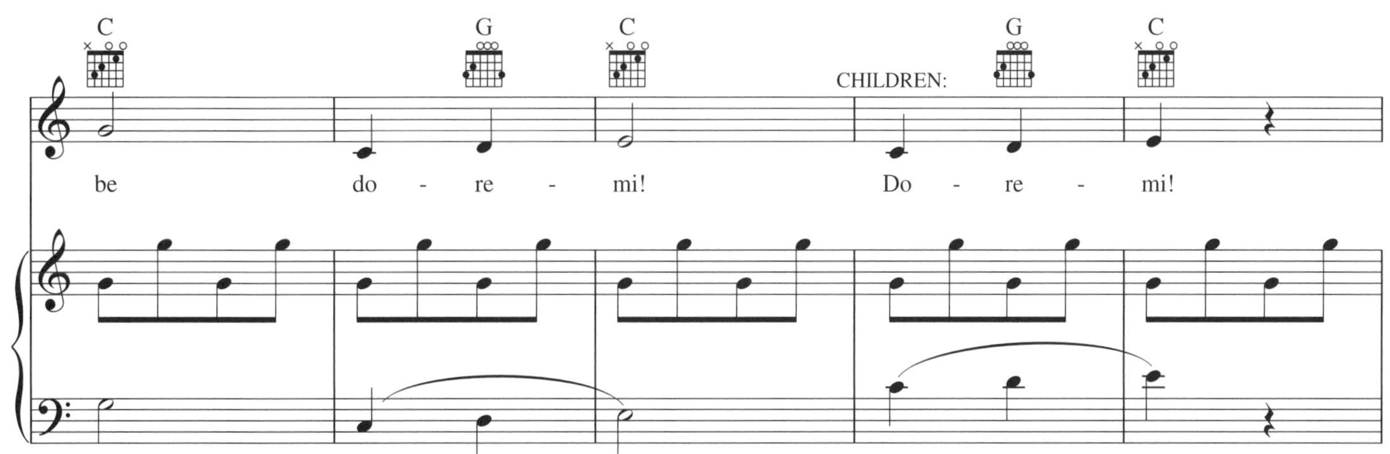
C
G
C
G
C
CHILDREN:
be do - re - mi! Do - re - mi!

G7
C
G7
MARIA:
(Spoken:)
Do - re - mi - fa - so - la - ti
All right, I'll make
it easier. Listen:
mf

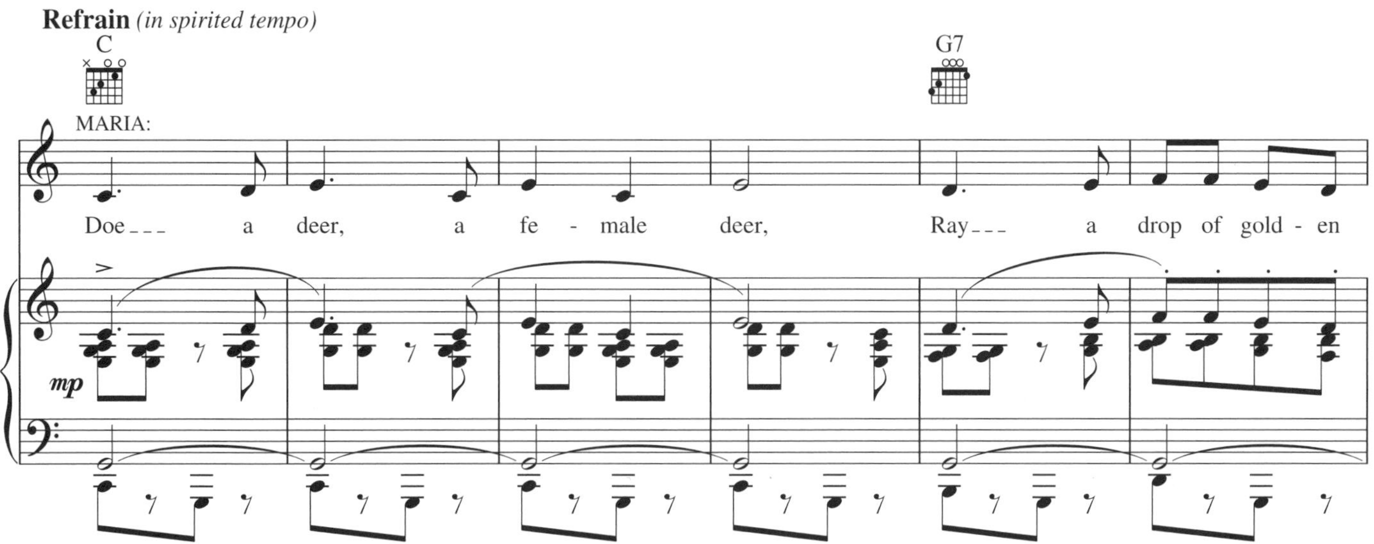
Refrain (in spirited tempo)
C
G7
MARIA:
Doe a deer, a fe - male deer, Ray a drop of gold - en
mp

G9
G7
C
sun,
Me
a
name
I
call
my
-
self,
G9
C/E
C7
Far
a
long, long
way
to
run.
Sew
a
nee - dle
pull-ing
poco a poco cresc.

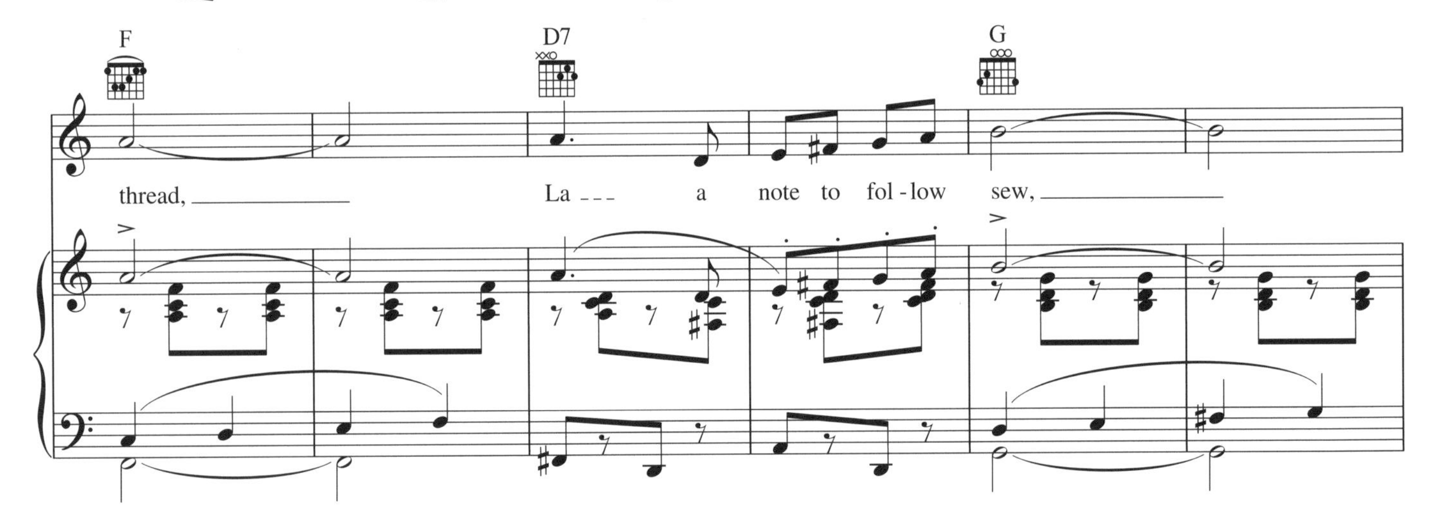
F
D7
G
thread,
La
a
note
to
fol - low
sew,

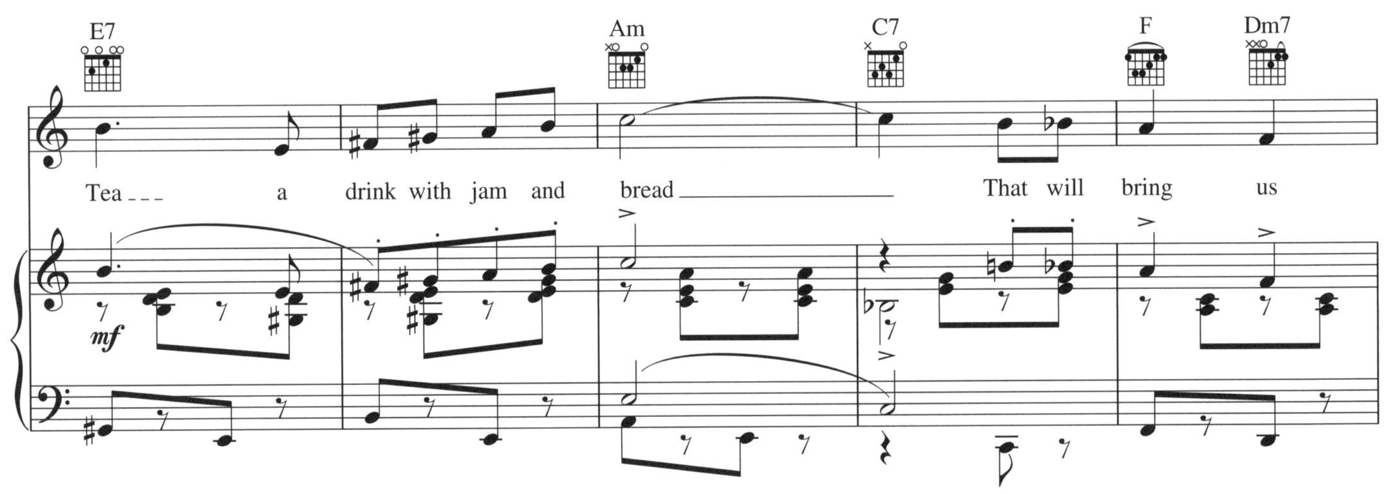
E7
Am
C7
F
Dm7
Tea
a
drink
with
jam
and
bread
That
will
bring
us
mf

G7
C
G
C
back to do - oh - oh - oh! (Guitar) A deer, a fe - male
p
CHILDREN: (spoken)
G7
MARIA:
G9
G7
CHILDREN:
deer, Do! (Guitar) A drop of gold - en sun, Re!
C
MARIA:
CHILDREN:
G9
MARIA:
(Guitar) A name I call my - self Mi! (Guitar) A
G9
C/E
C7
CHILDREN:
MARIA: (sung)
CHILDREN:
long, long way to run, Fa! So! A nee - dle pull - ing
poco a poco cresc.

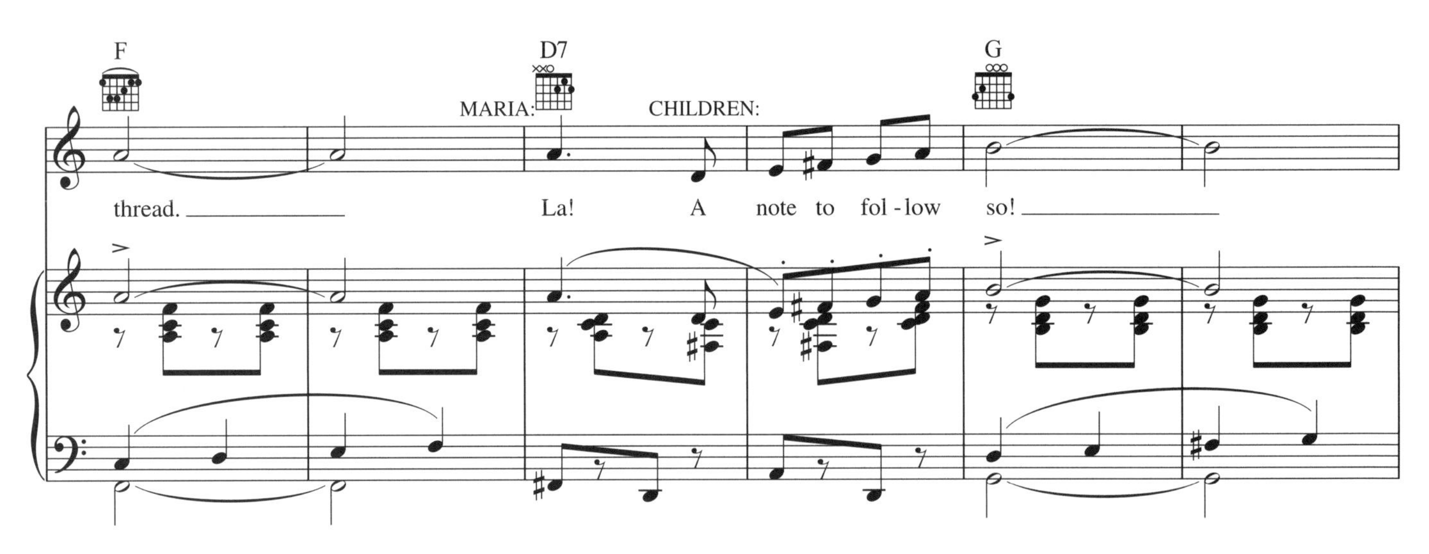
F
D7
G
MARIA:
CHILDREN:
thread.
La!
A
note to fol - low
so!

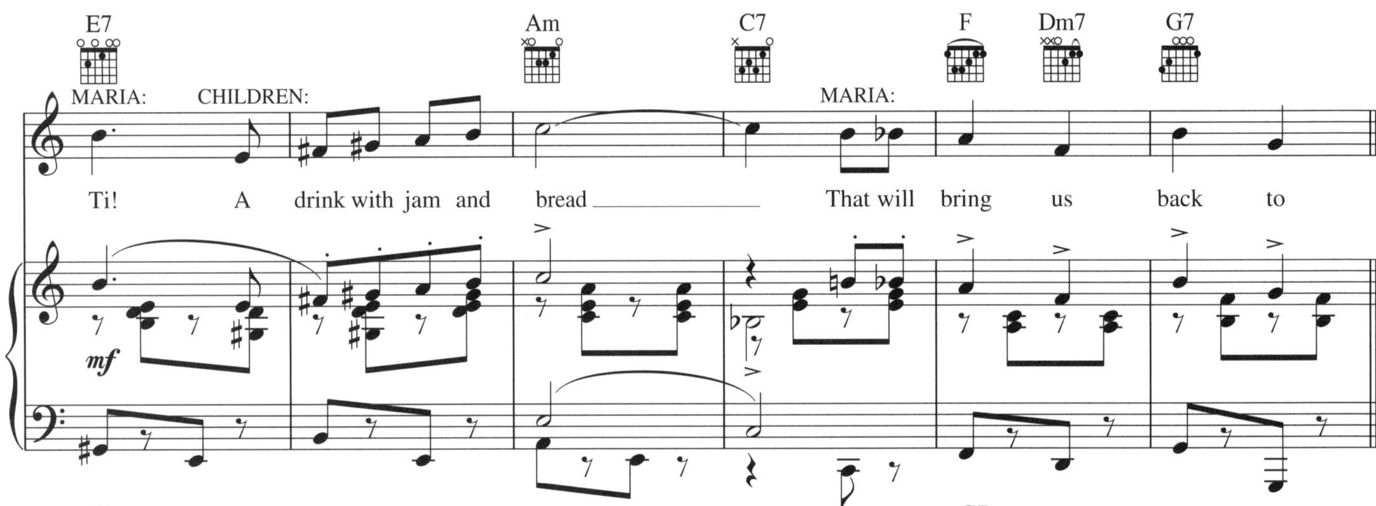
E7
Am
C7
F
Dm7
G7
MARIA:
CHILDREN:
MARIA:
Ti!
A
drink with jam and
bread
That will
bring
us
back
to
mf

C
G7
ALL:
Doe
a
deer,
a
fe - male
deer,
Ray
a
drop of gold - en
mf

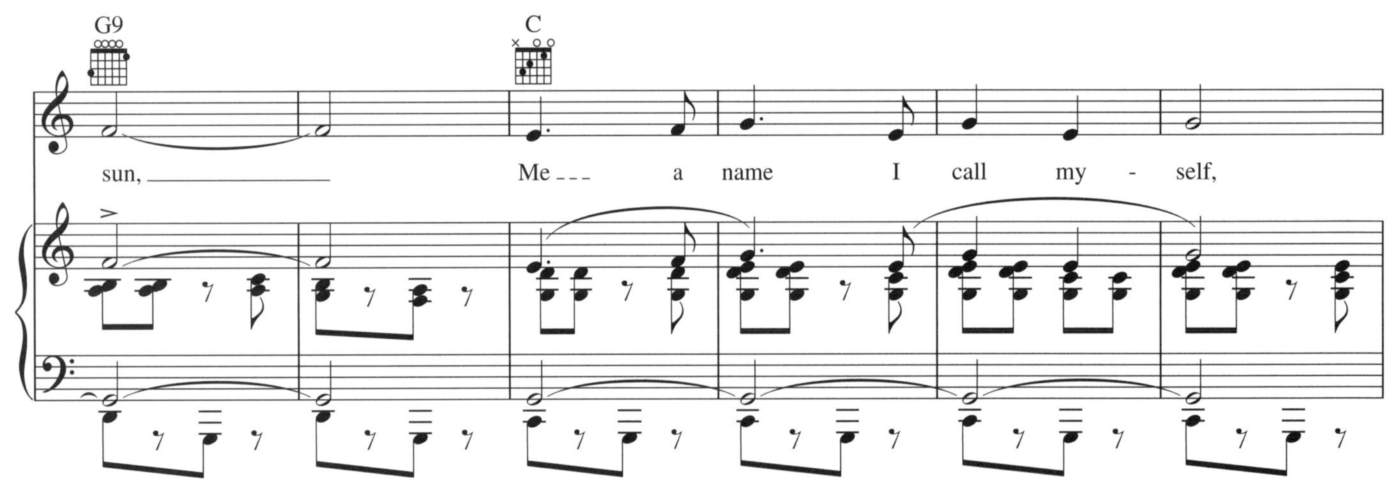
G9
C
sun,
Me
a
name
I
call
my - self,

G9
C/E
C7
Far - - - a long, long way to run.
Sew - - - a nee - dle pull - ing
poco a poco cresc.

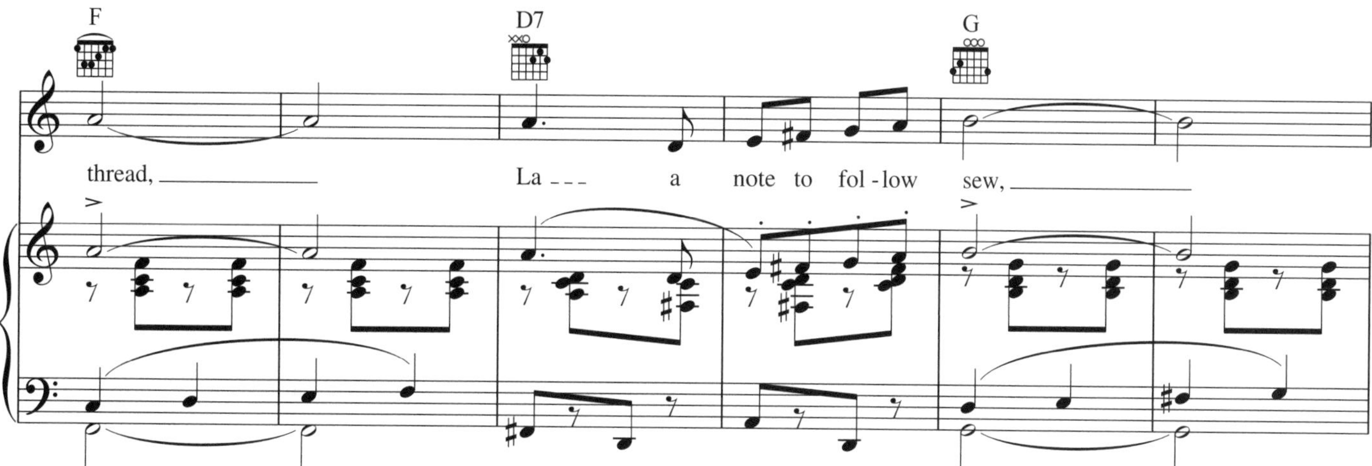
F
D7
G
thread,
La - - - a note to fol - low sew,

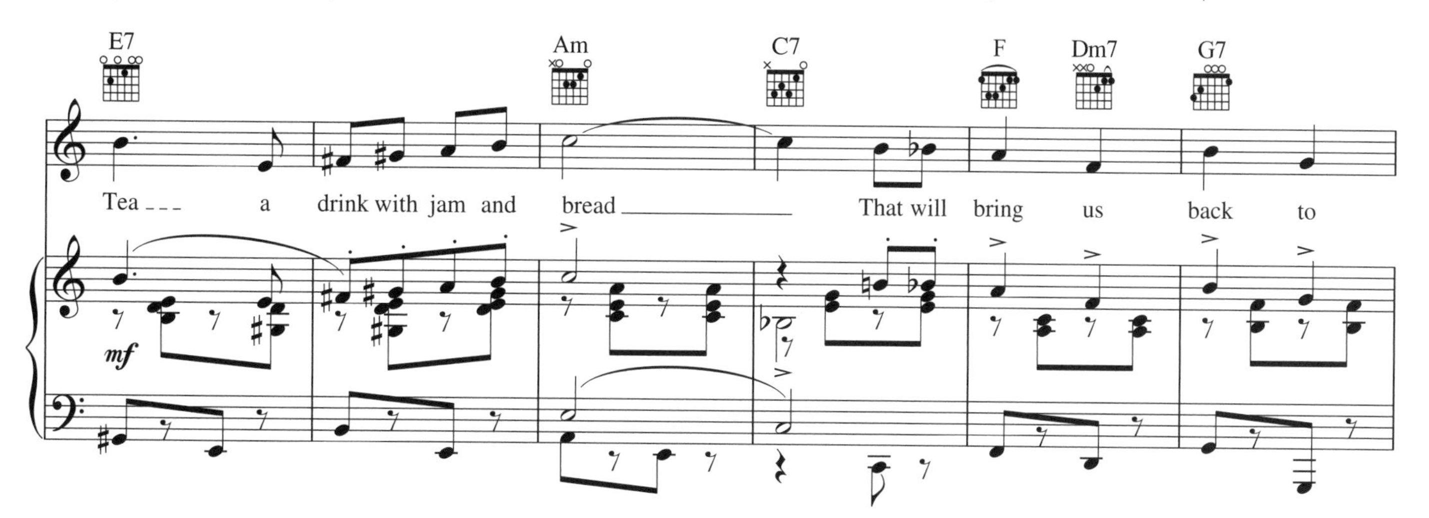
E7
Am
C7
F
Dm7
G7
Tea - - - a drink with jam and bread
That will bring us back to
mf

C
C7
F
F/E
Dm7
G7
C
doe!
Do - re - mi - fa - so - la - ti - do!
f

For He's a Jolly Good Fellow

Traditional

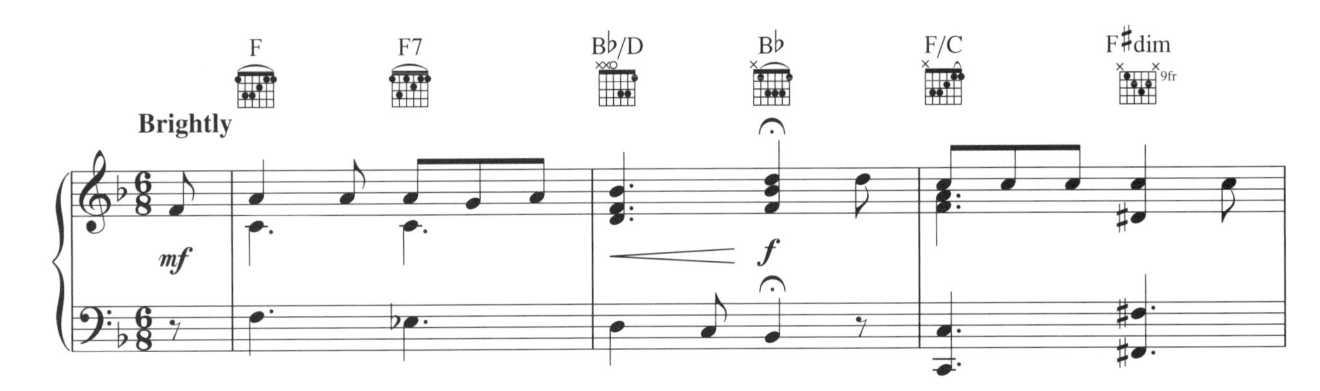

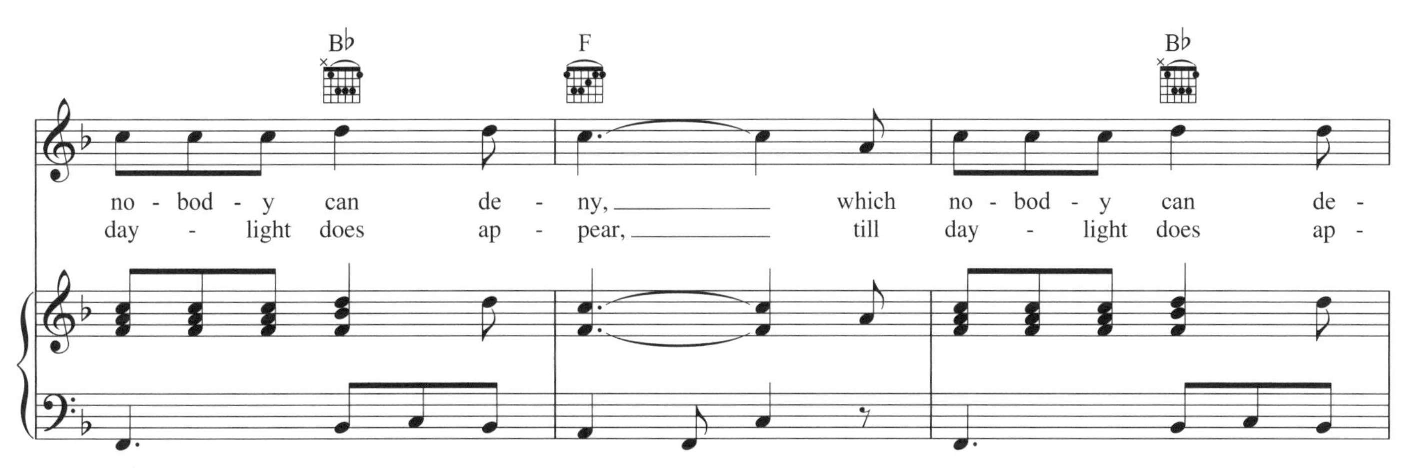
B♭
F
B♭
no - bod - y can de - ny, which no - bod - y can de -
day - light does ap - pear, till day - light does ap -

F
B♭
F
ny. For he's a jol - ly good fel - low, for
pear. We won't go home un - til morn - ing, we

C7
F
F7
he's a jol - ly good fel - low. For he's a jol - ly good
won't go home un - til morn - ing. We won't go home un - til

B♭
C7
1
F
2
F
fel - low, which no - bod - y can de - ny. We
morn - ing, till day - light does ap - pear.

Getting to Know You

from THE KING AND I
Lyrics by Oscar Hammerstein II
Music by Richard Rodgers

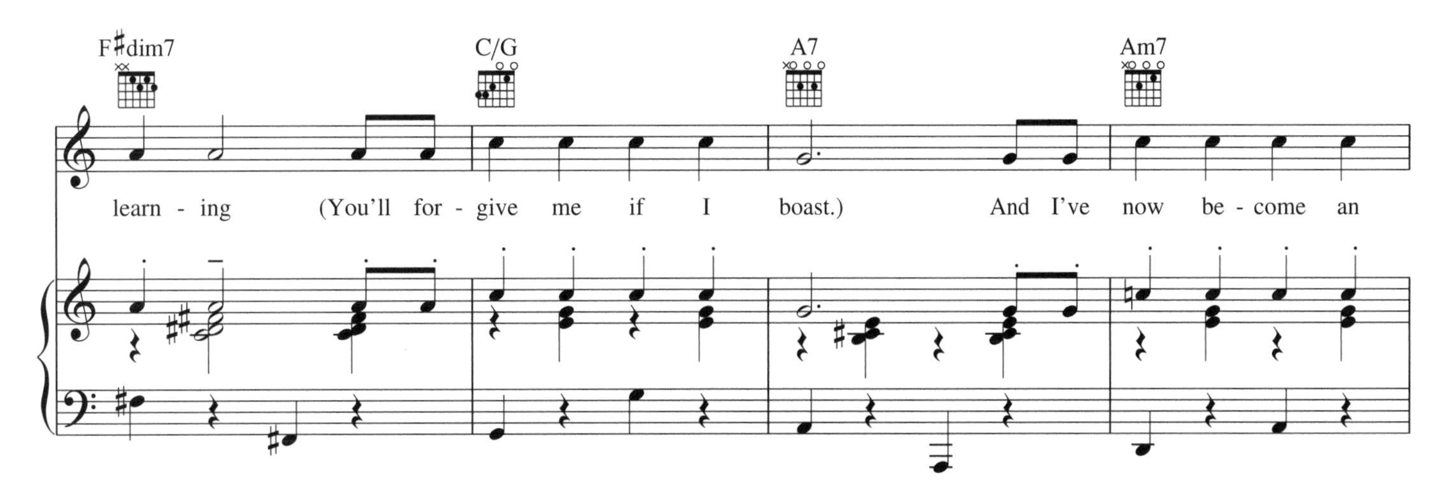
F♯dim7
C/G
A7
Am7
learn - ing (You'll for - give me if I boast.) And I've now be - come an

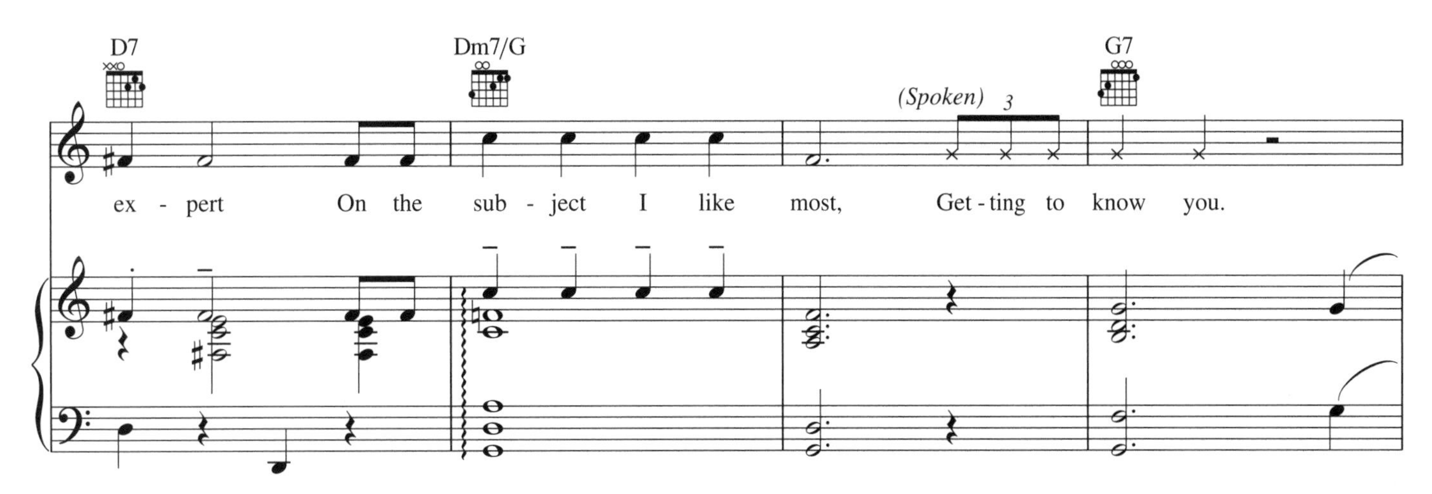
D7
Dm7/G
G7
(Spoken)
ex - pert On the sub - ject I like most, Get - ting to know you.

Refrain (gracefully and not fast)

C
Dm7
G7
Get - ting to know you, get - ting to know all a - bout you
mp
tranquillo

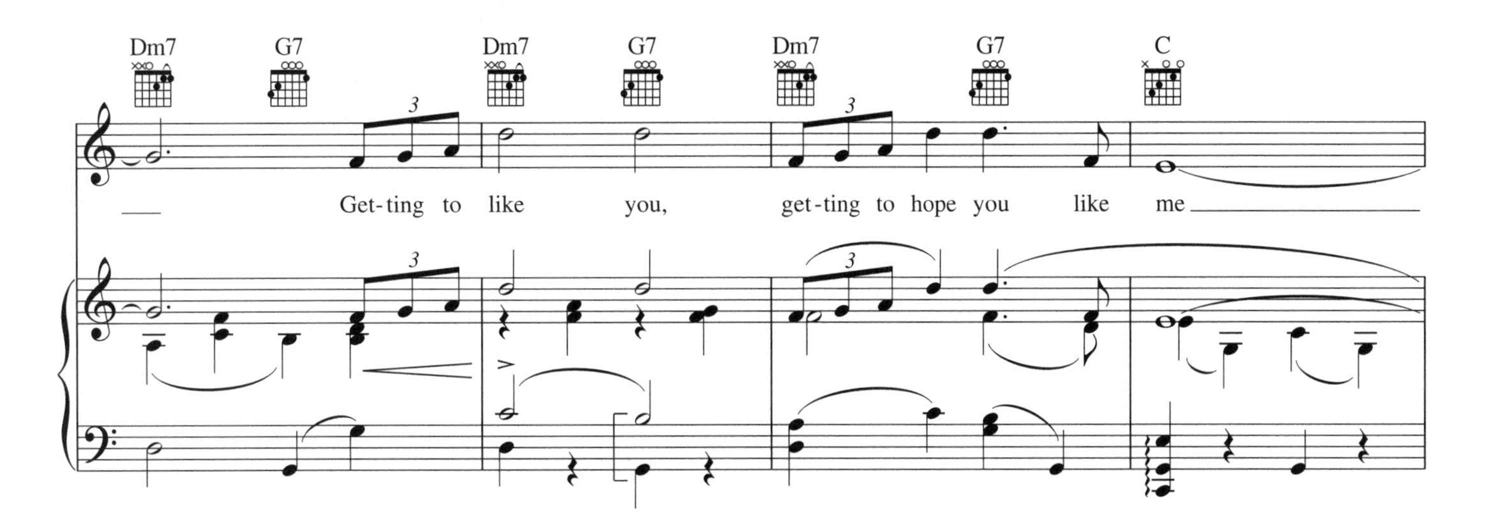
Dm7
G7
Dm7
G7
Dm7
G7
C
Get - ting to like you, get - ting to hope you like me

Fmaj7
F6
Get-ting to know you, Put-ting it my way, but nice - ly

F+
F
Am7
D7
Dm7/G
You are pre - cise - ly My cup of tea!
cresc.
mf

G7
C
Dm7
G7
Get-ting to know you, get-ting to feel free and eas - y
f
p

Dm7
G7
Dm7
G7
Dm7
G7
C7
When I am with you, get-ting to know what to say.

Fmaj7
F6
Dm7
G7
Have-n't you no - ticed? Sud-den-ly I'm bright and
Cmaj7
C7
F
C
Dm7
G7
breez - y Be - cause of all the beau-ti-ful and new
poco a poco cresc.
C(add9)
Am7
D7
Am7
D7
Dm7
G7
things I'm learn-ing a-bout you day by
C
G7
day. Get-ting to
C
F
C
day.

from the Television Series THE ROY ROGERS SHOW

Words and Music by Dale Evans

Slow and tenderly

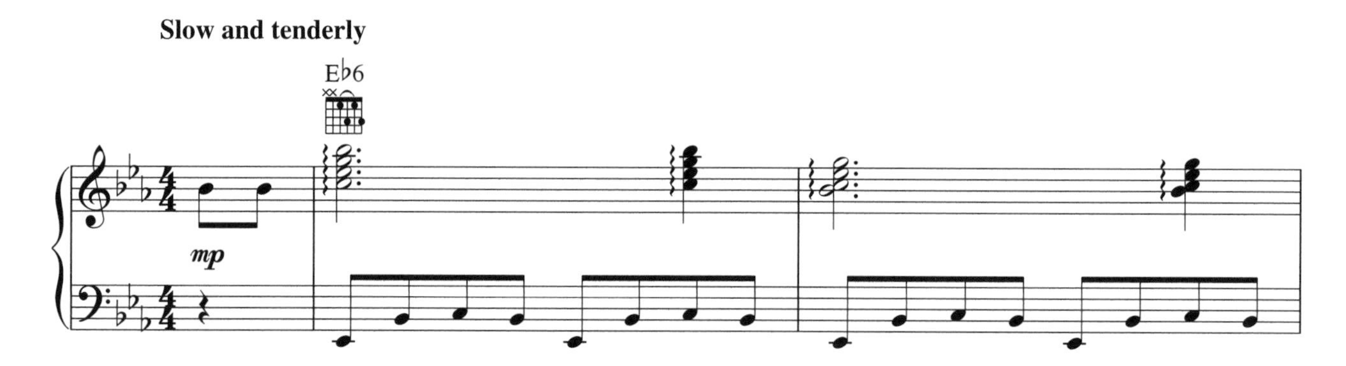

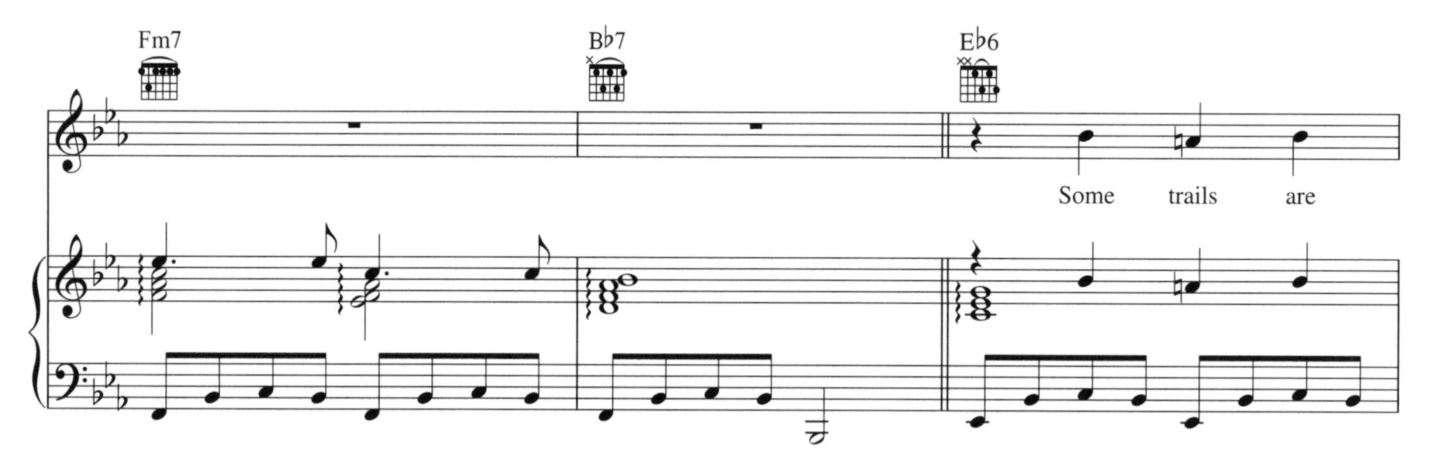

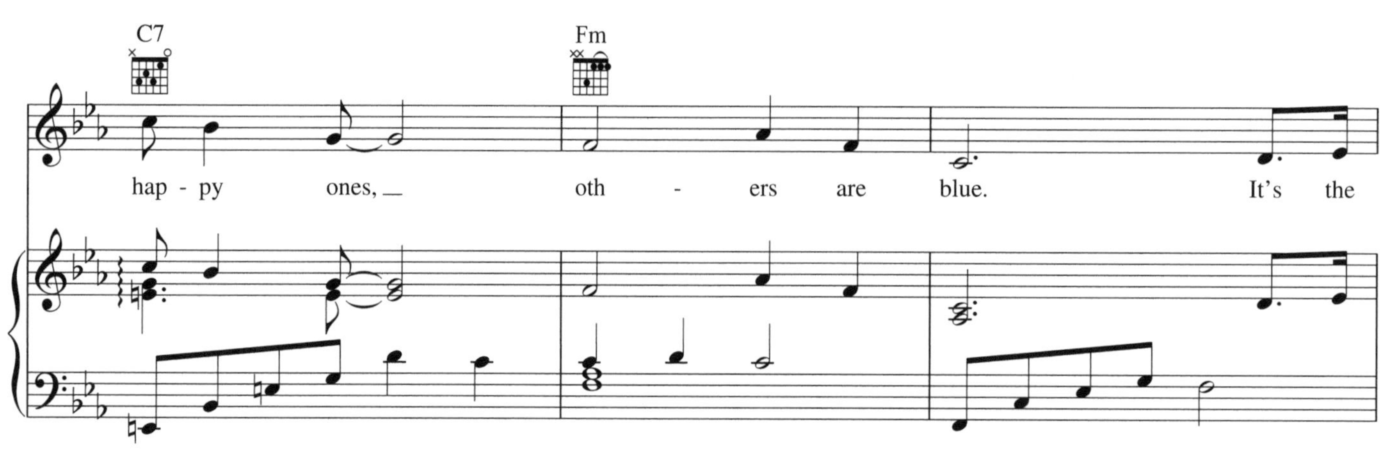

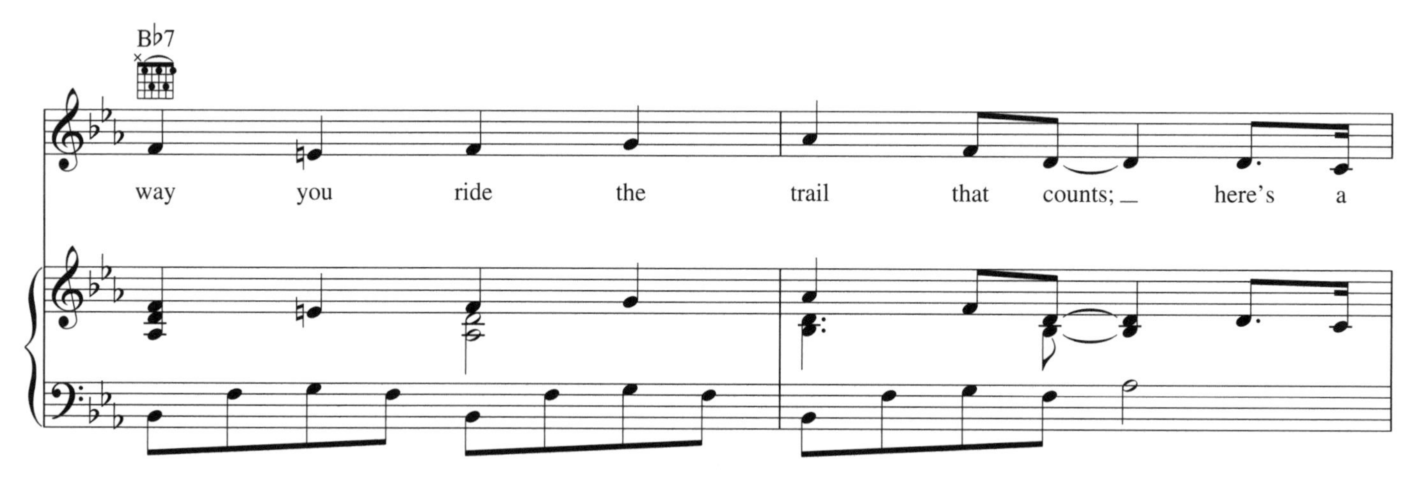

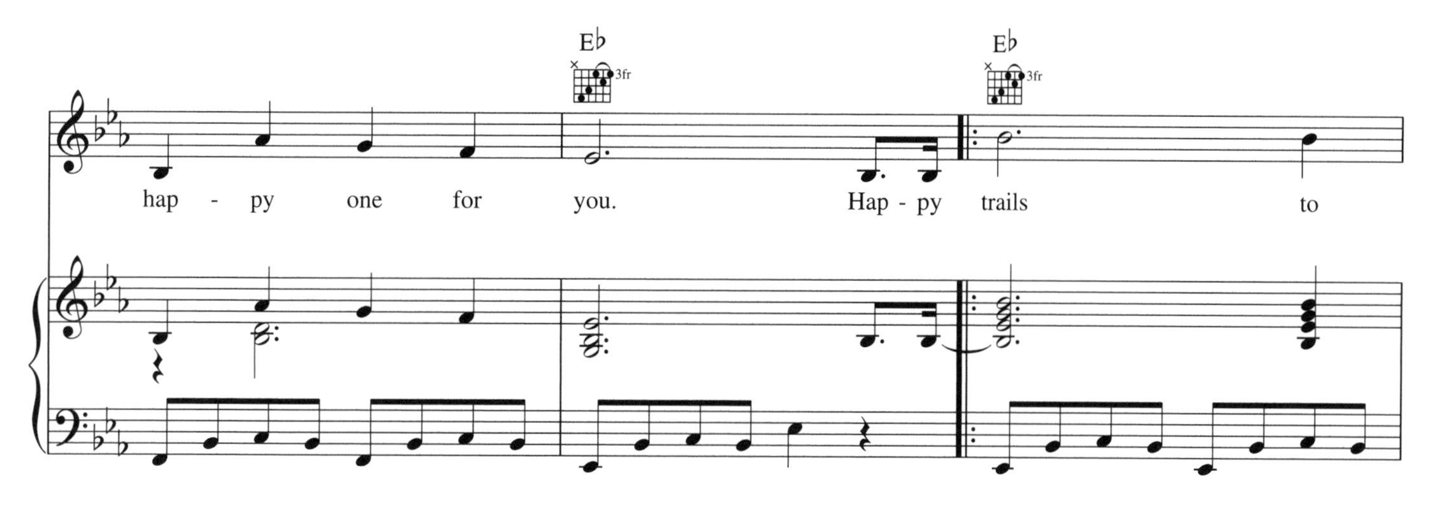
E♭
3fr
E♭
3fr
hap - py one for you.
Hap - py trails to

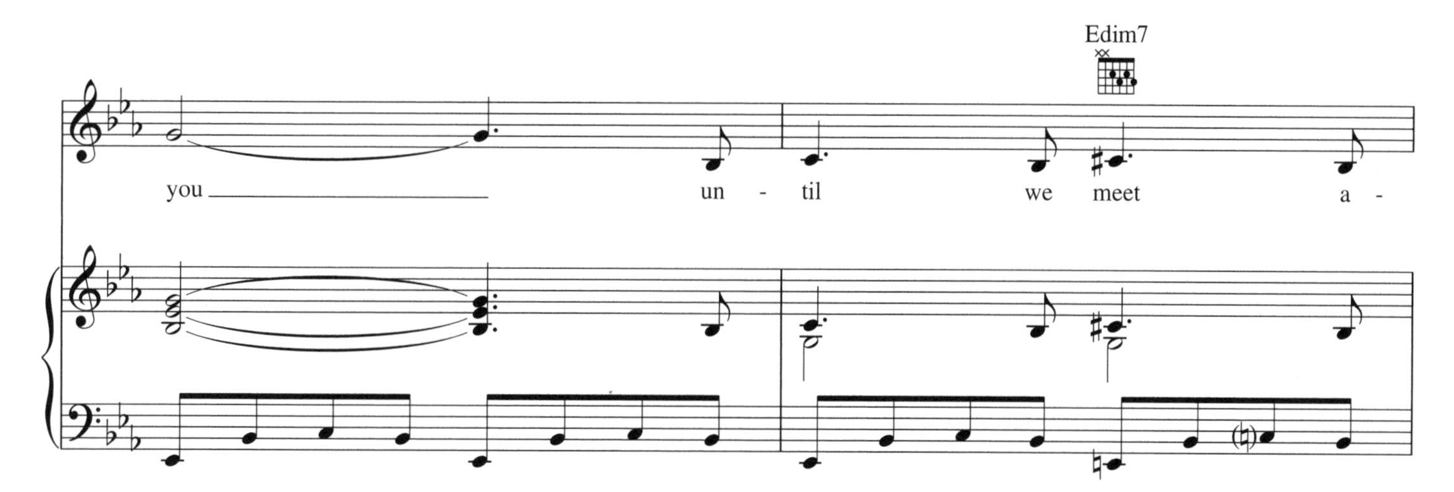
Edim7
you
un - til we meet a -

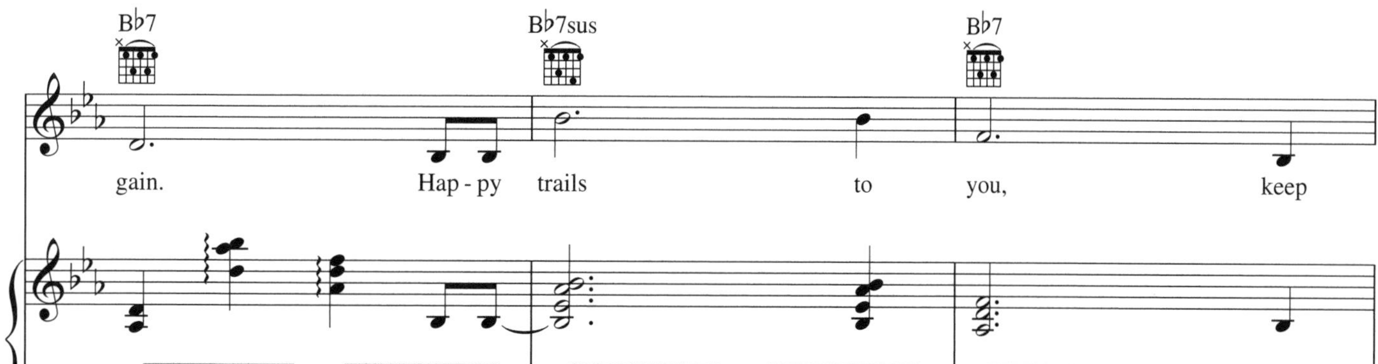
B♭7
B♭7sus
B♭7
gain.
Hap - py trails to you, keep

B♭7♯5
6fr
E♭(add9)
6fr
E♭
3fr

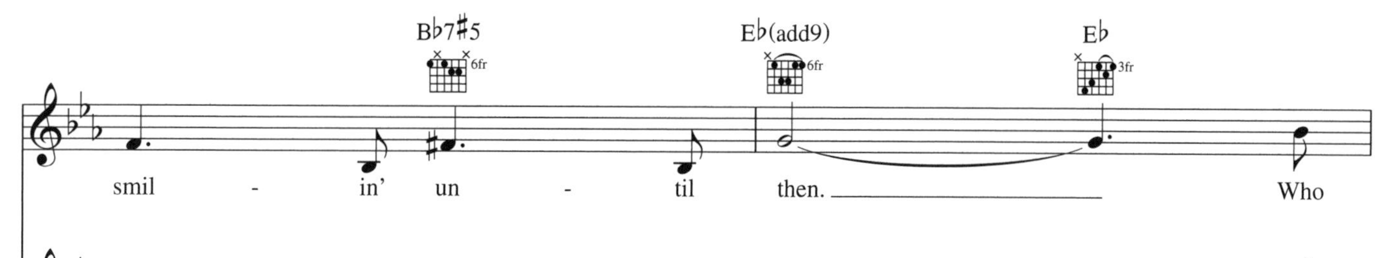
smil - in' un - til then.
Who

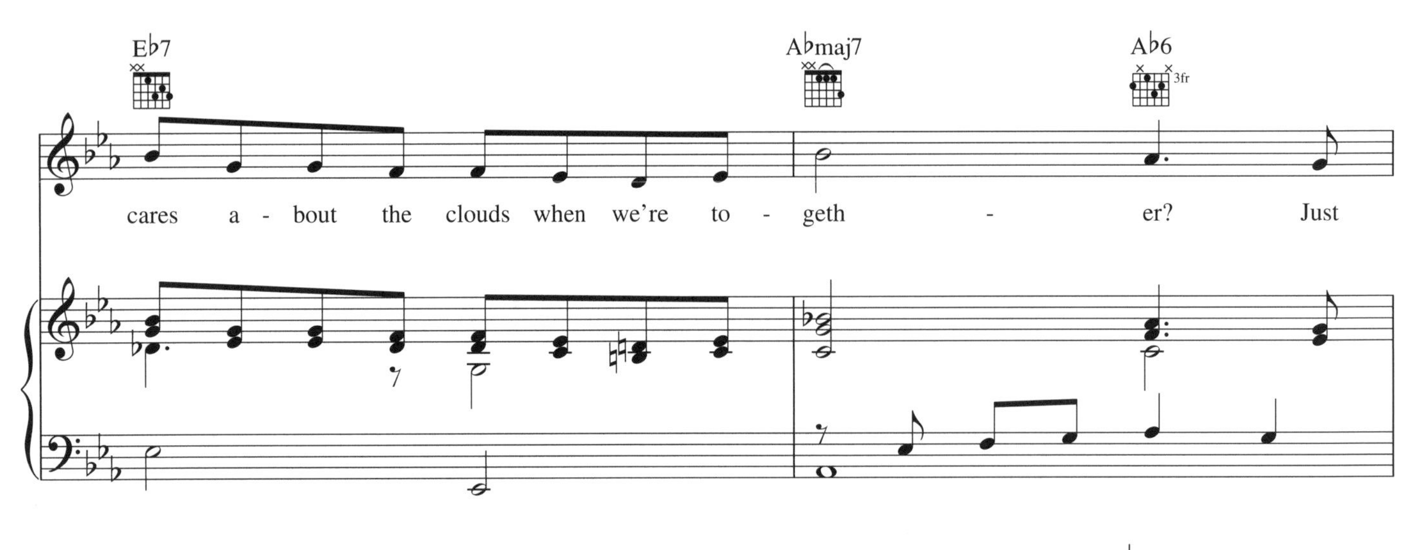
Eb7
Abmaj7
Ab6
3fr
cares a - bout the clouds when we're to - geth - er? Just

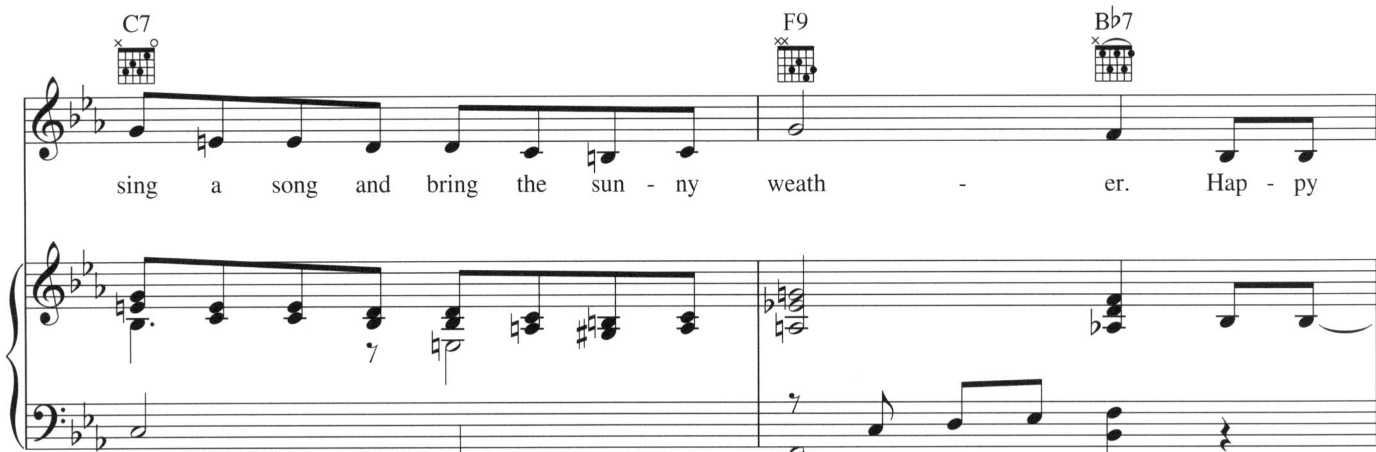
C7
F9
Bb7
sing a song and bring the sun - ny weath - er. Hap - py

Eb
3fr
Bbm6
6fr
C7
Fm
Bb7
trails to you till we meet a -

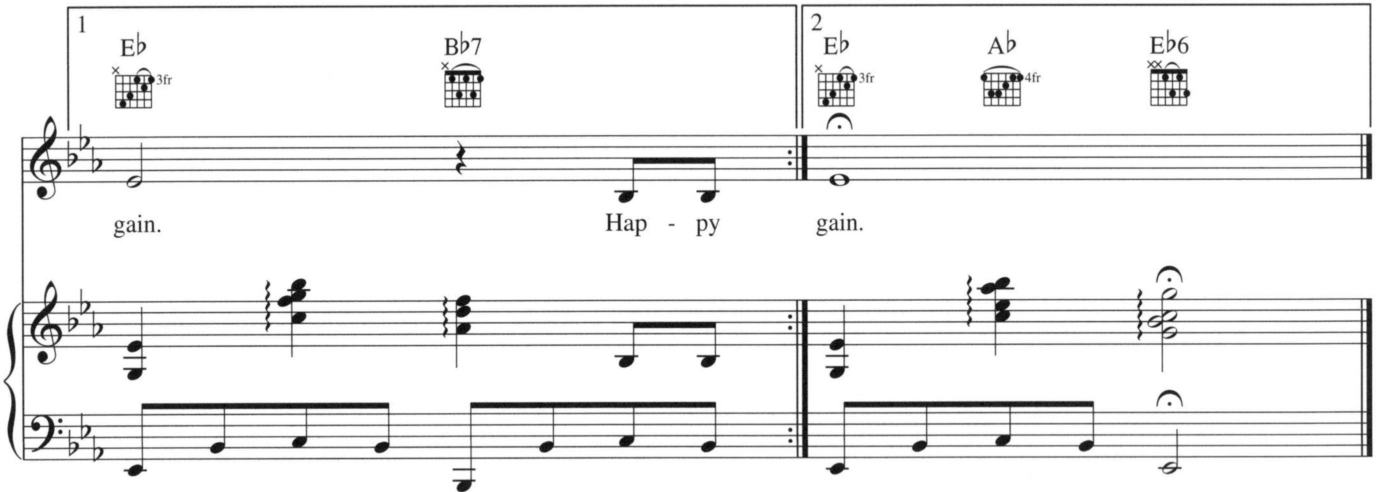
1
Eb
3fr
Bb7
2
Eb
3fr
Ab
4fr
Eb6
gain. Hap - py gain.

Home on the Range

Lyrics by Dr. Brewster Higley
Music by Dan Kelly

F
F7
B♭
B♭m
sel - dom is heard a dis - cour - ag - ing word, and the
stood there a - mazed and ___ asked as I gazed, if their

F/C
C7
F
skies are not cloud - y all day. ___
glo - ry ex - ceeds that of ours. ___

Chorus

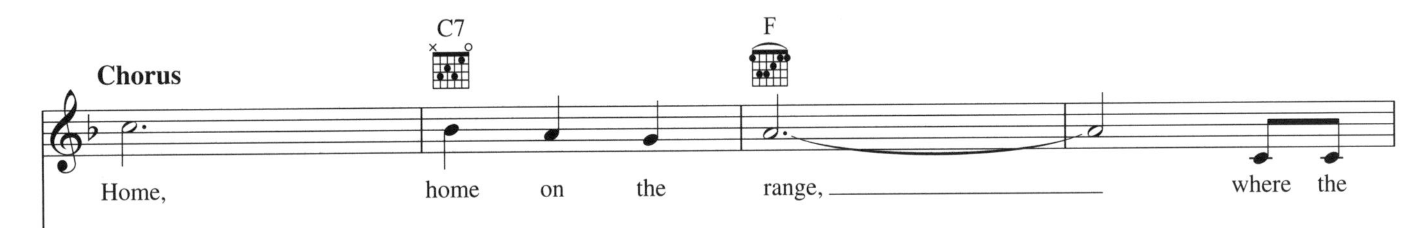
C7
F
Home, home on the range, ___ where the

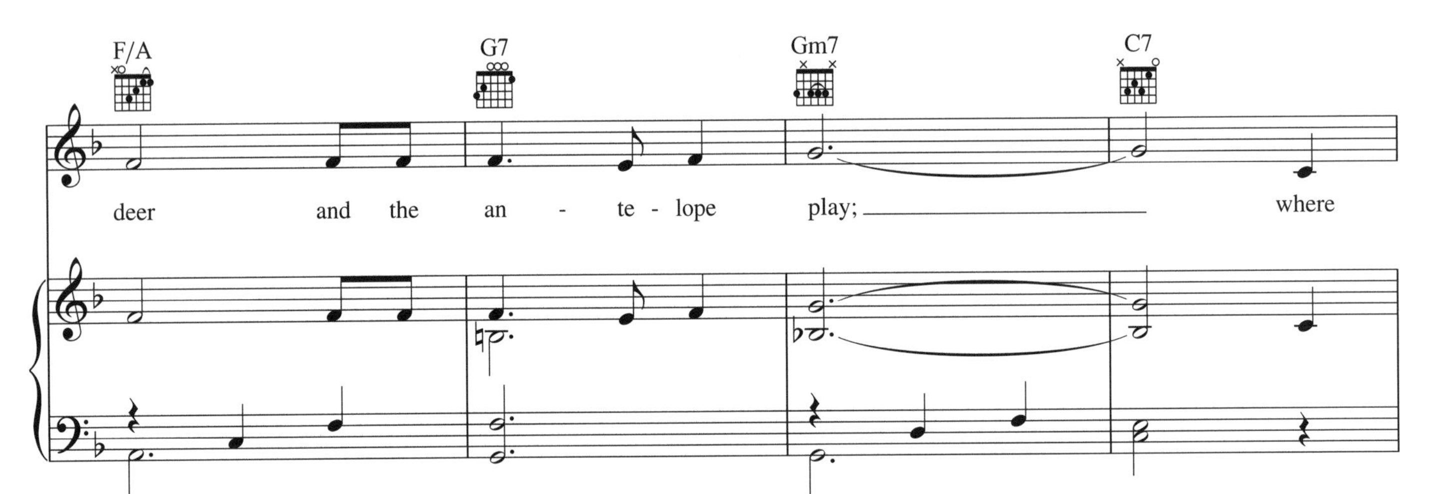
F/A
G7
Gm7
C7
deer and the an - te - lope play; ___ where

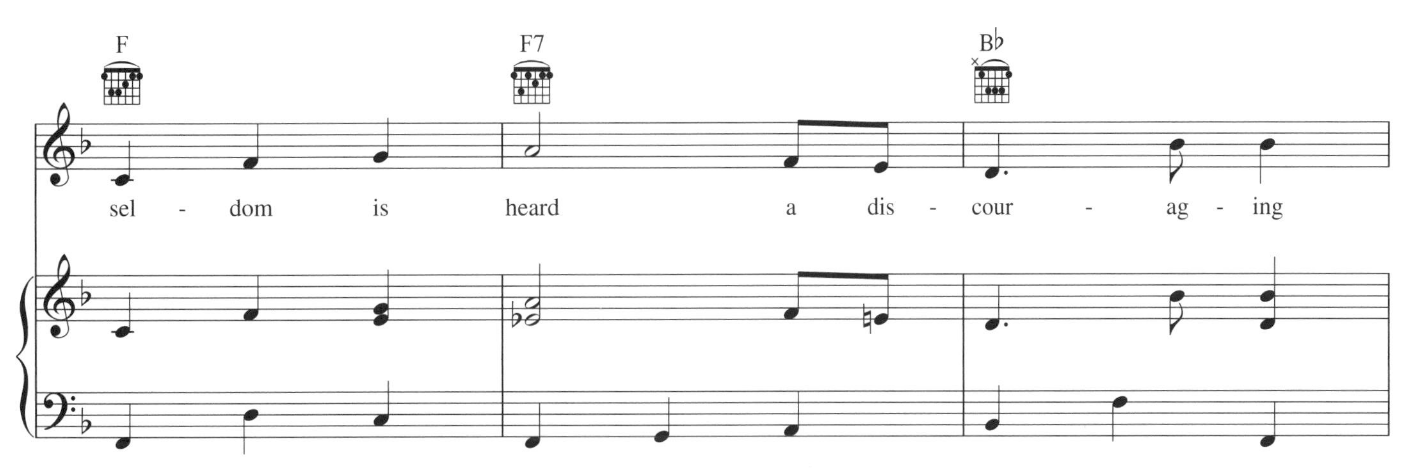

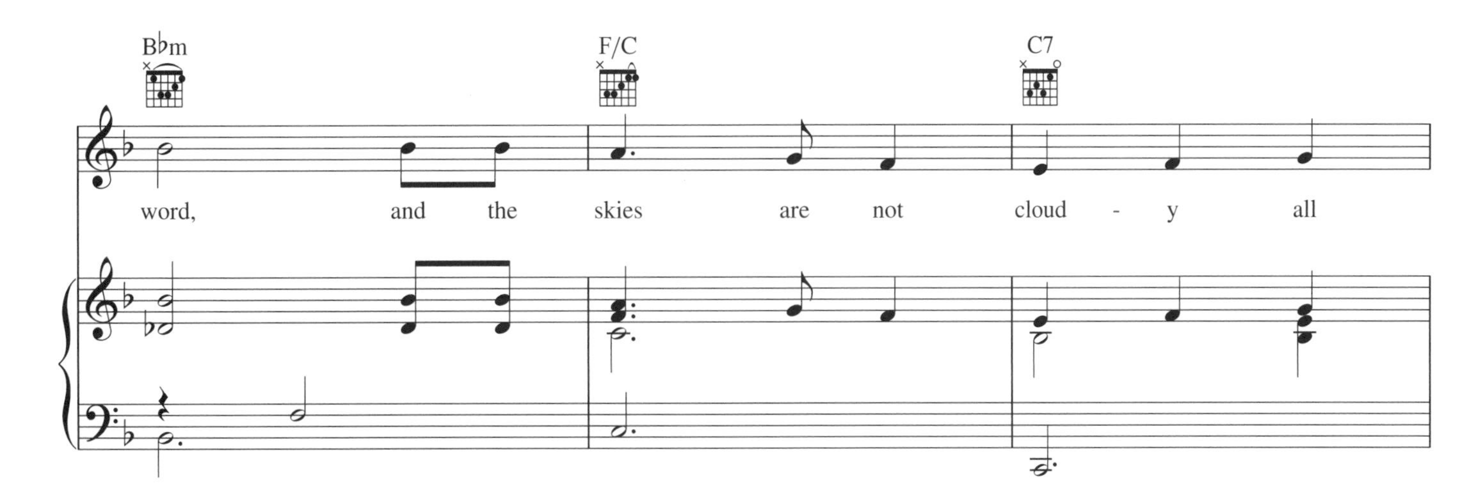

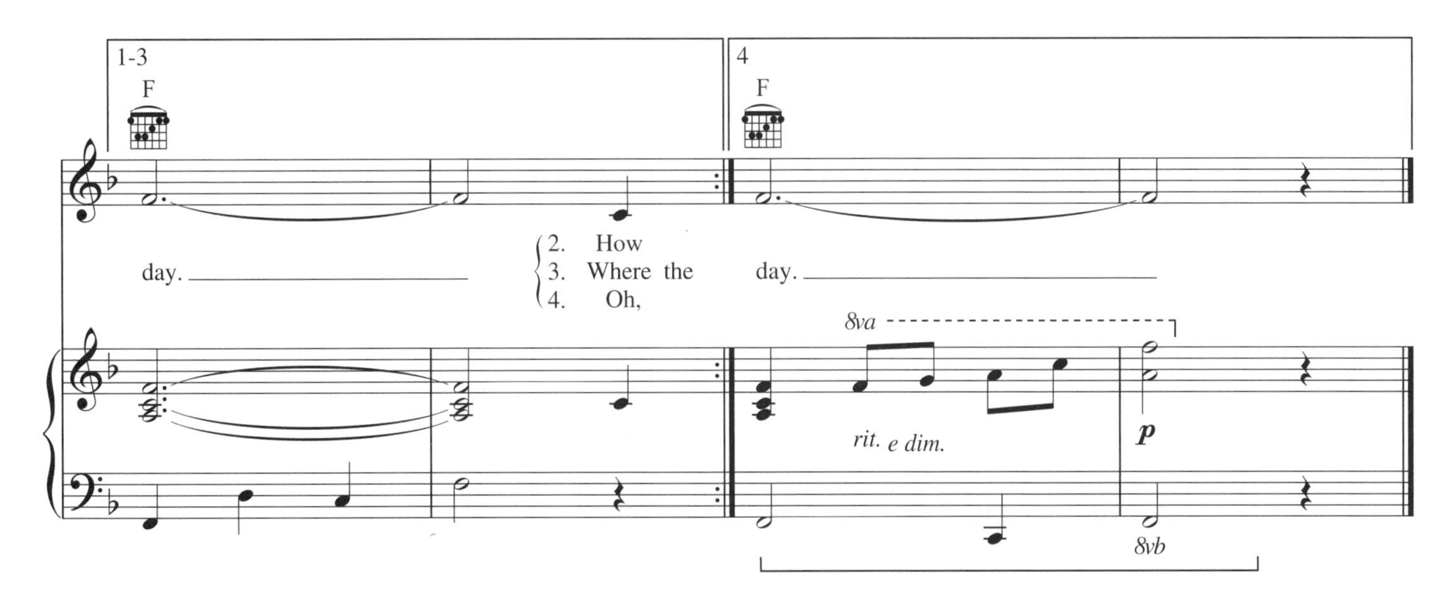

Additional Lyrics

3. Where the air is so pure and the zephyrs so free,
   And the breezes so balmy and light;
   Oh, I would not exchange my home on the range
   For the glittering cities so bright.
   Chorus

4. Oh, give me a land where the bright diamond sand
   Flows leisurely down with the stream,
   Where the graceful white swan glides slowly along,
   Like a maid in a heavenly dream.
   Chorus

Heart and Soul
from the Paramount Short Subject A SONG IS BORN
Words by Frank Loesser
Music by Hoagy Carmichael
Moderately, not too fast
F
Dm7
Gm7
C7
Dm7
G9
9fr
mf
Freely
B♭/C
C13
2fr
Gm7/C
F
F♯dim7
I've let a pair of arms en - slave me oft
Gm
3fr
C7
F6
Gm7/C
times be - fore, but more than just a thrill you
F
G7
Gm7/C
C7
gave me, yes more, much more.

Moderately, lightly rhythmical

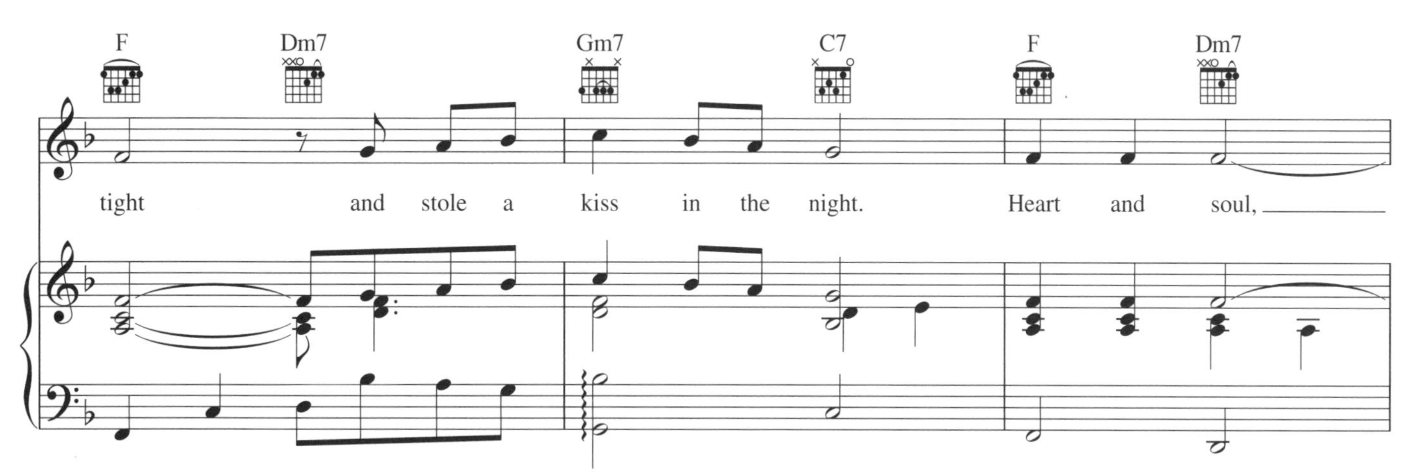

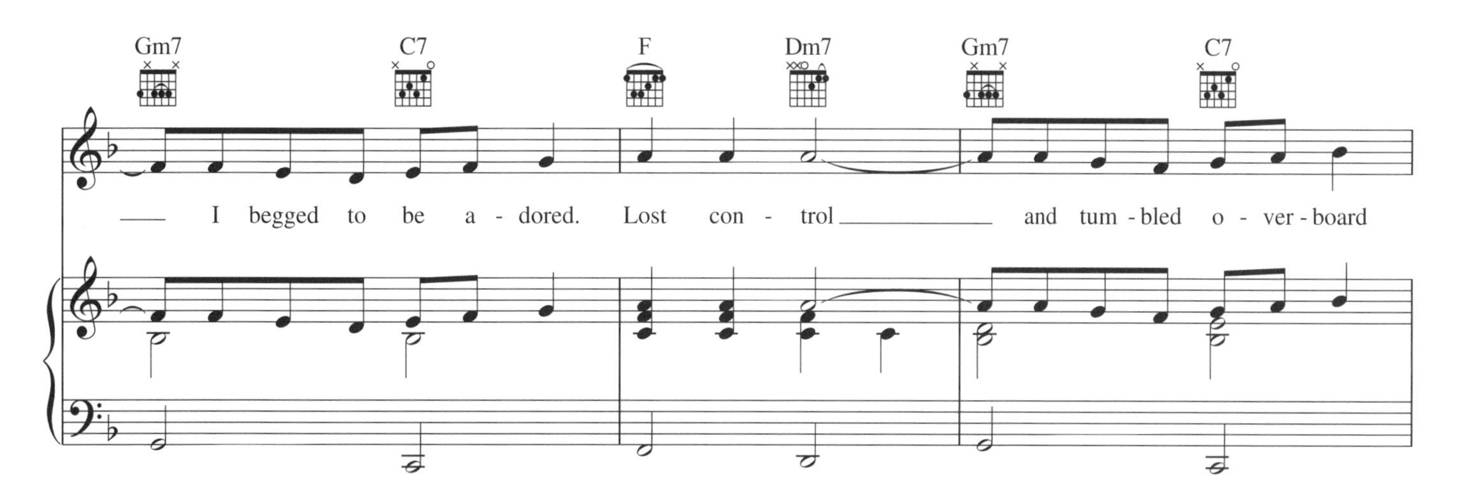

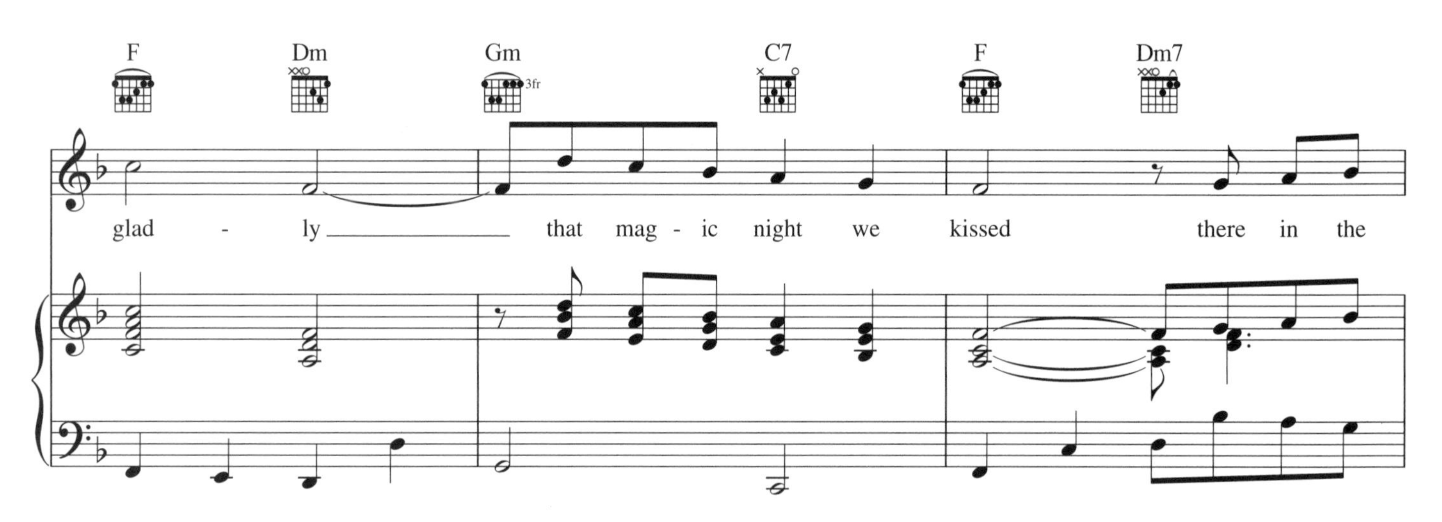
F
Dm
Gm
3fr
C7
F
Dm7
glad - ly that mag - ic night we kissed there in the

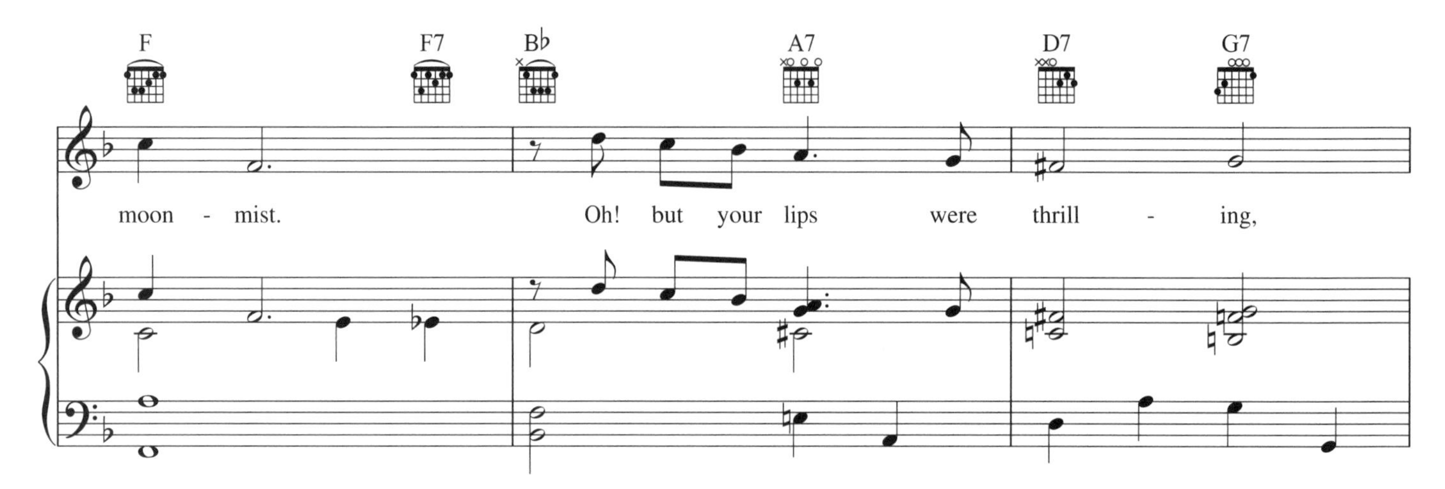
F
F7
B♭
A7
D7
G7
moon - mist. Oh! but your lips were thrill - ing,

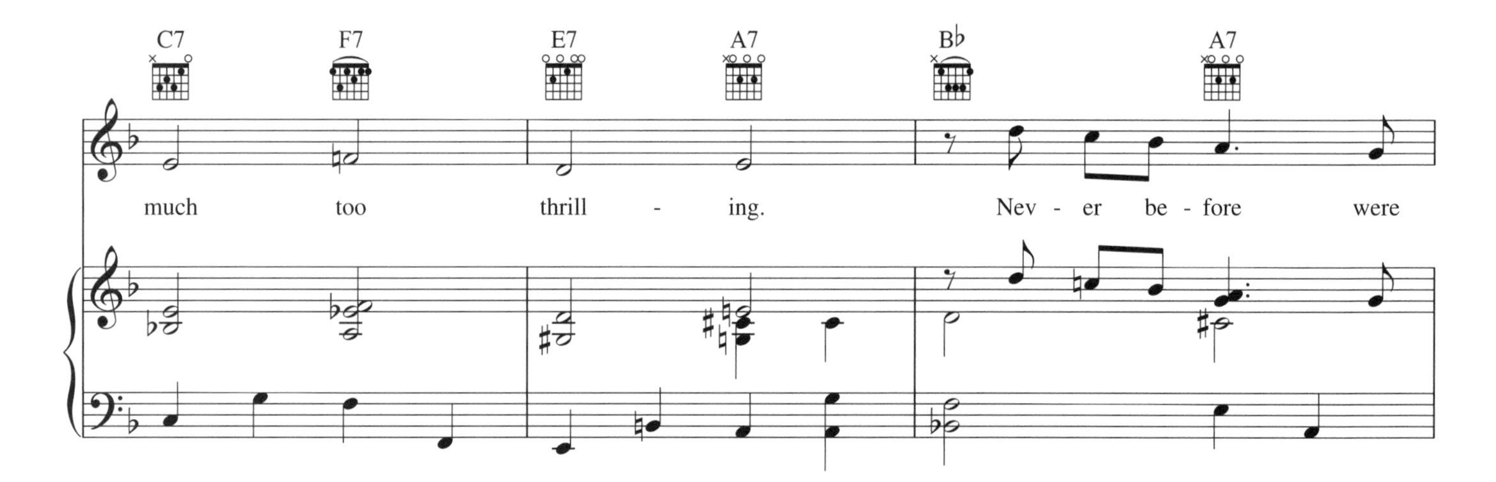
C7
F7
E7
A7
B♭
A7
much too thrill - ing. Nev - er be - fore were

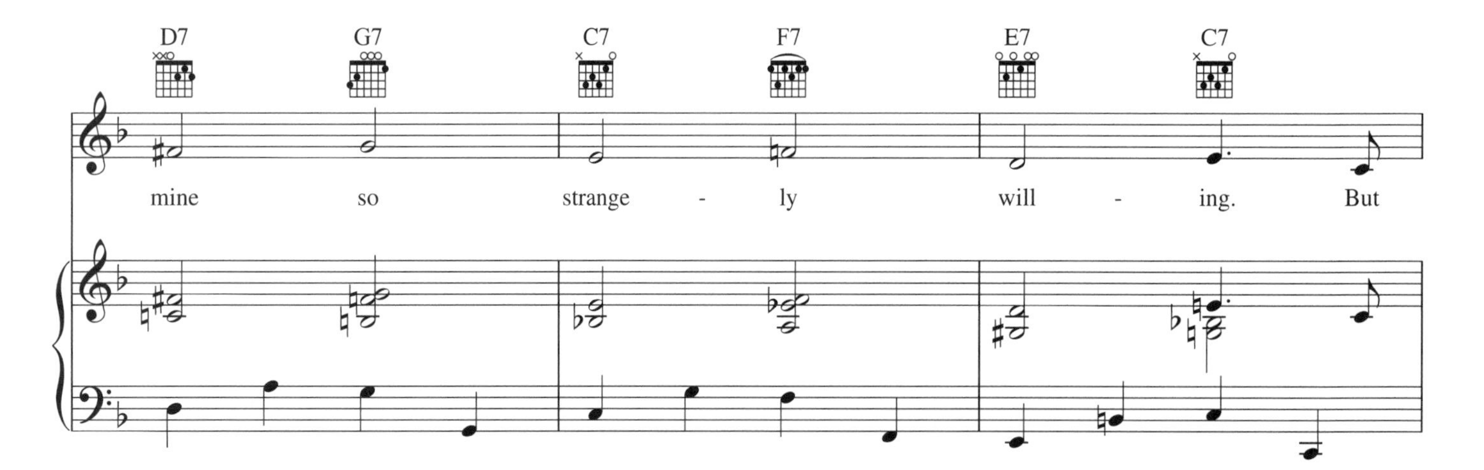
D7
G7
C7
F7
E7
C7
mine so strange - ly will - ing. But

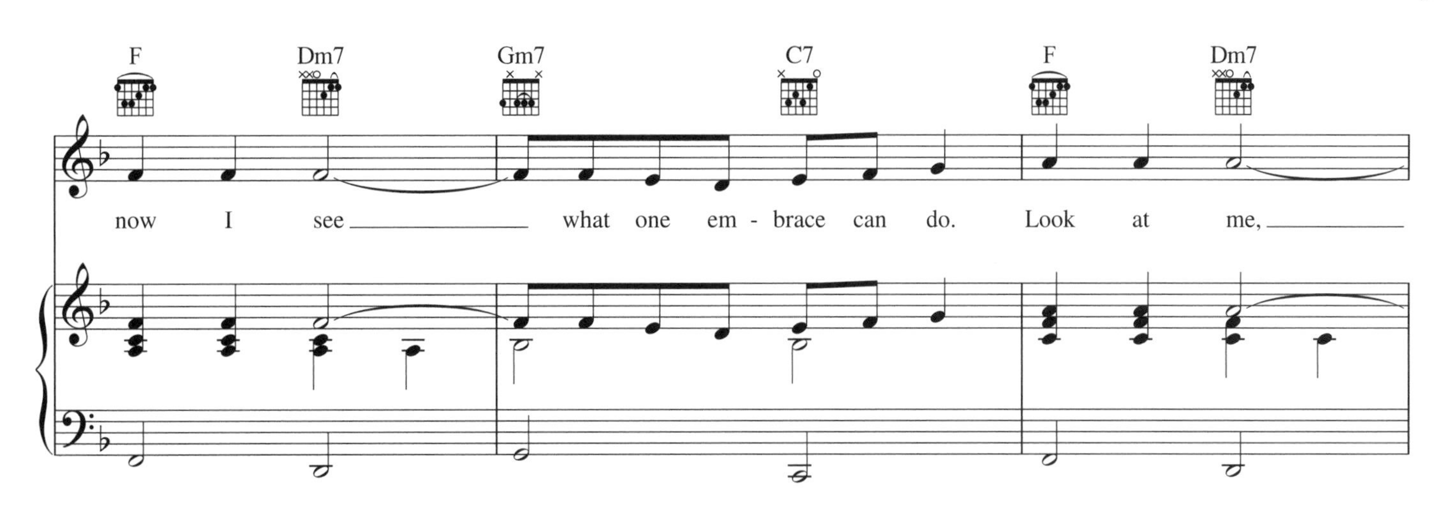
F
Dm7
Gm7
C7
F
Dm7
now I see what one em - brace can do. Look at me,

Gm7
C7
F
Dm
Gm7
C7
it's got me lov - ing you mad - ly; that lit - tle kiss you

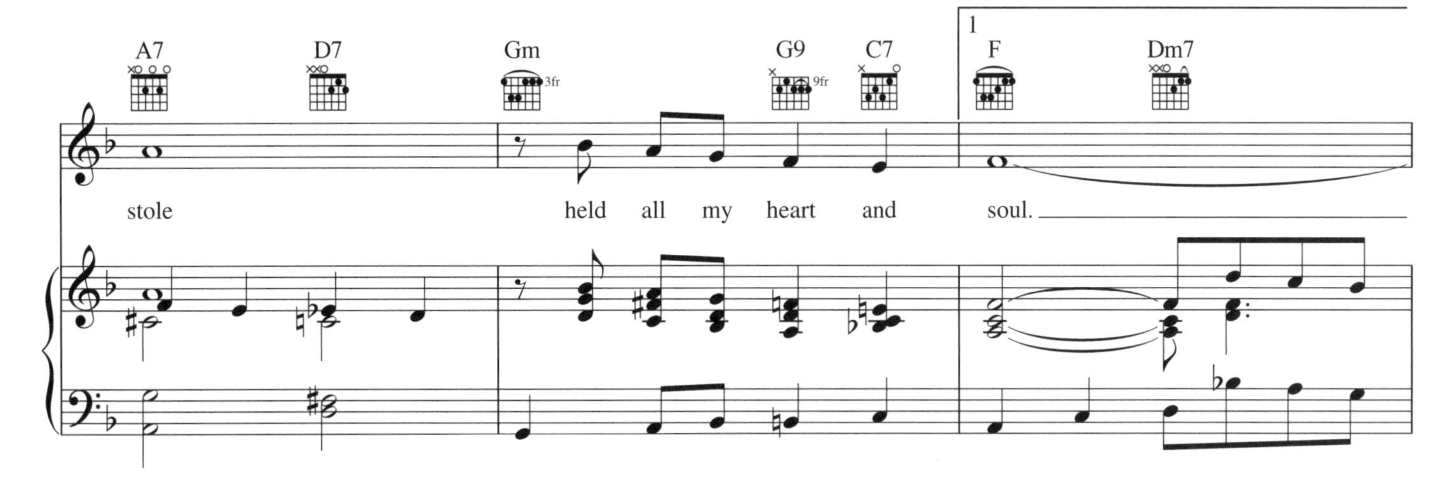
A7
D7
Gm
G9
C7
1
F
Dm7
stole held all my heart and soul.

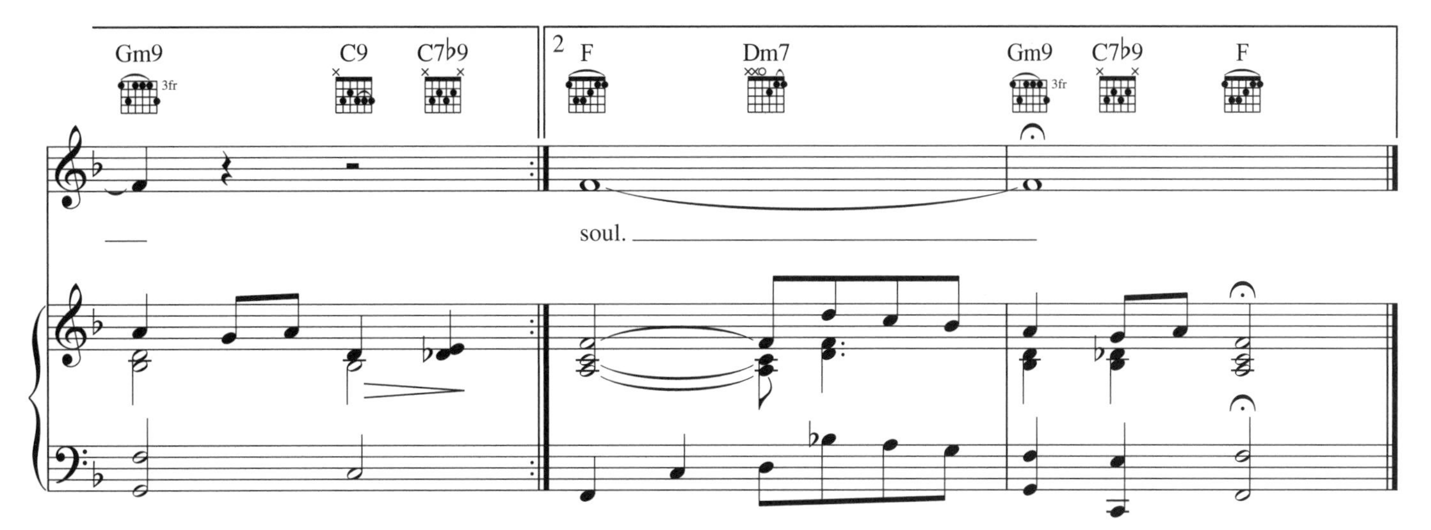
Gm9
C9
C7♭9
2
F
Dm7
Gm9
C7♭9
F
soul.

The Hokey Pokey

Words and Music by Charles P. Macak, Tafft Baker and Larry LaPrise

Additional Lyrics

4. Hey, you put your left hand in,
   You put your left hand out.
   You put your left hand in,
   And you shake it all about.
   Chorus

5. Hey, you put your right shoulder in,
   You put your right shoulder out.
   You put your right shoulder in,
   And you shake it all about.
   Chorus

6. Hey, you put your left shoulder in,
   You put your left shoulder out.
   You put your left shoulder in,
   And you shake it all about.
   Chorus

7. Hey, you put your right hip in,
   You put your right hip out.
   You put your right hip in,
   And you shake it all about.
   Chorus

8. Hey, you put your left hip in,
   You put your left hip out.
   You put your left hip in,
   And you shake it all about.
   Chorus

9. Hey, you put your whole self in,
   You put your whole self out.
   You put your whole self in,
   And you shake it all about.
   Chorus

How Much Is That Doggie in the Window

Words and Music by Bob Merrill

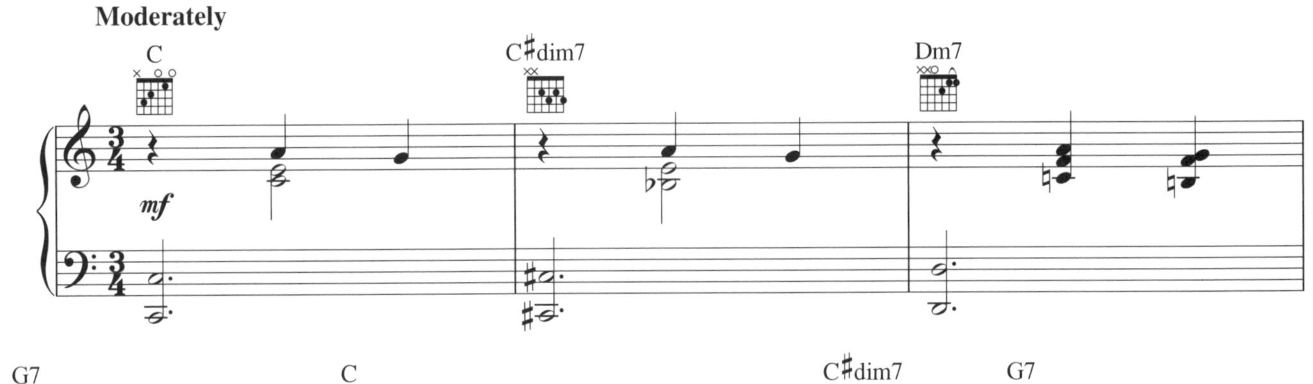

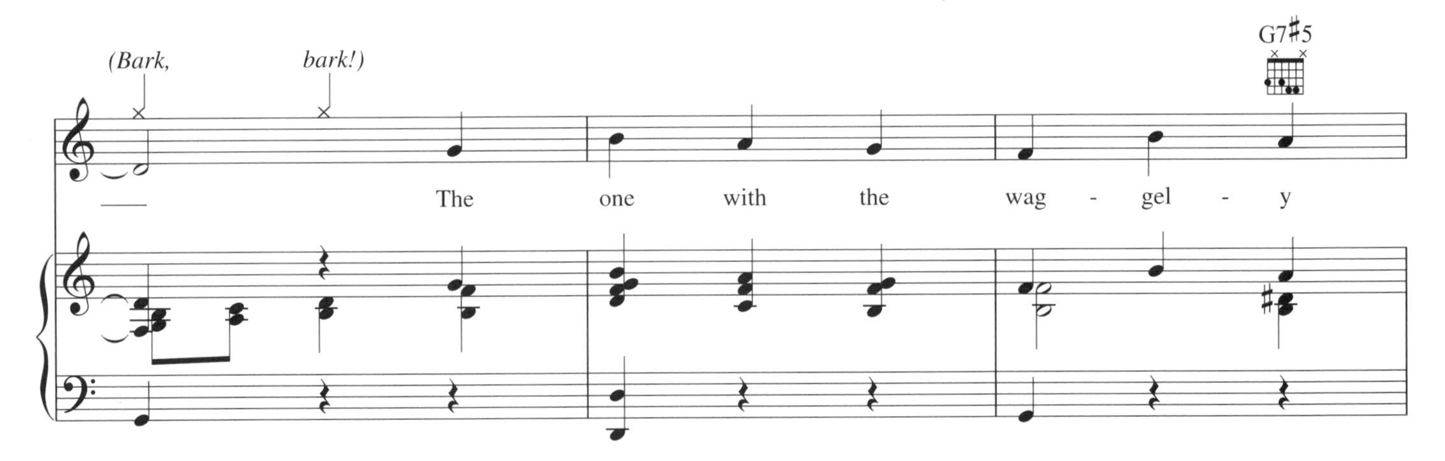

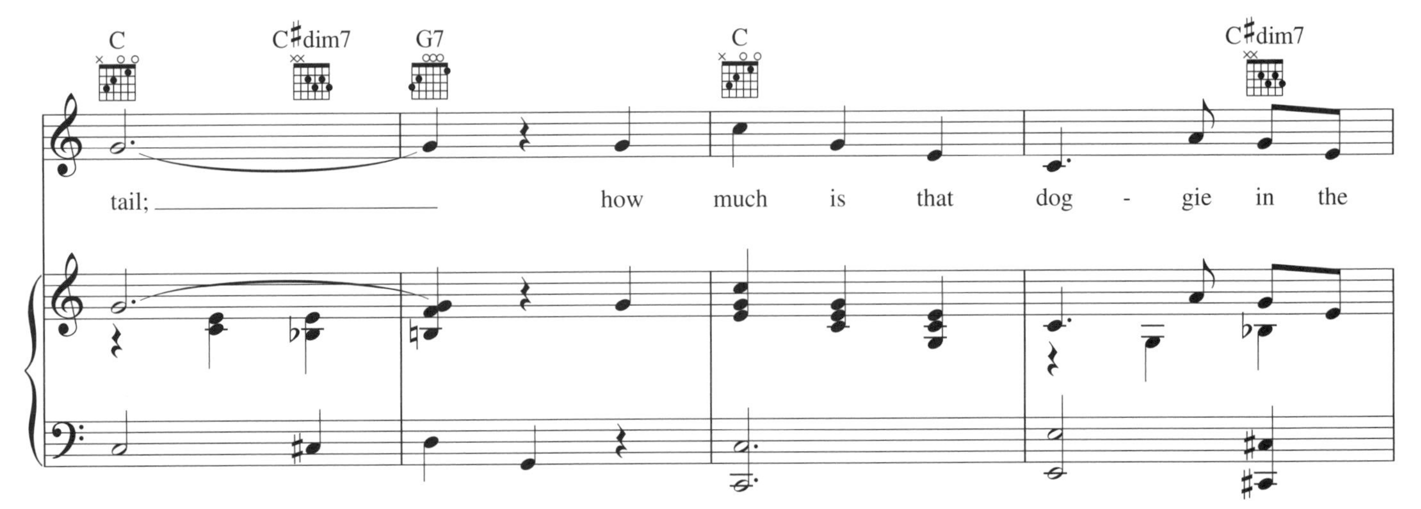

G7
(Bark, bark!)
win - dow? I do hope that
C
F/G
G7
dog - gie's for sale.
I
I
C
C#dim7
G7
must take a trip to Cal - i - for - nia and
read in the pa - pers there are rob - bers with
G7#5
C
C#dim7
G7
leave my poor sweet - heart a - lone. If
flash - lights that shine in the dark; my

C
C♯dim7
G7
he has a dog he won't be lone - some, and the
love needs a dog - gie to pro - tect him and
dog - gie will have a good home. How
scare them a - way with one
1
C
F/G
G7
2
C
F7
B♭7
bark. I
E♭
3fr
Edim7
B♭7
don't want a bun - ny or a kit - ty. I

Bb7#5
6fr
Eb
3fr
Edim7
don't want a par - rot that talks,

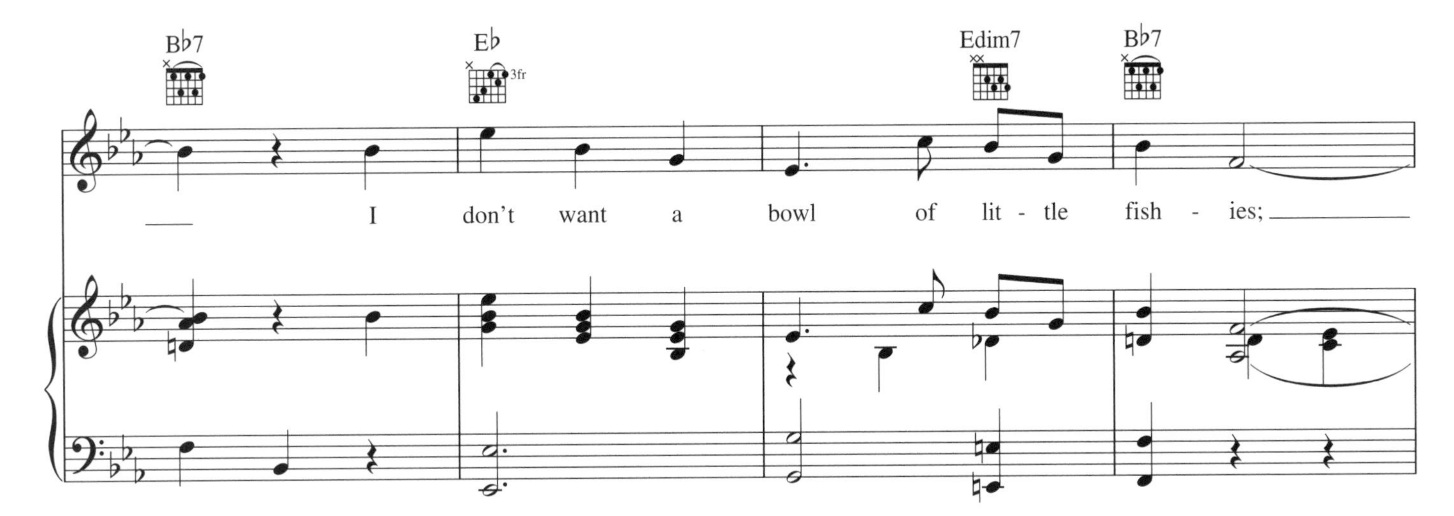
Bb7
Eb
3fr
Edim7
Bb7
I don't want a bowl of lit - tle fish - ies;

he can't take a gold - fish for

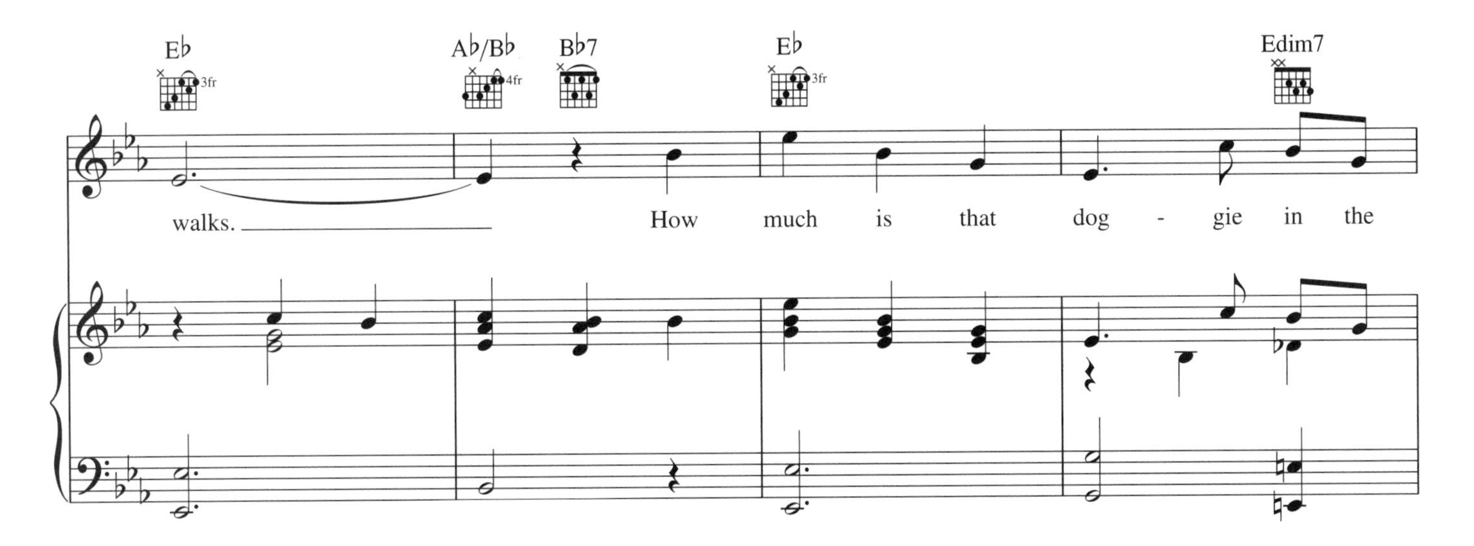
Eb
3fr
Ab/Bb
4fr
Bb7
Eb
3fr
Edim7
walks. How much is that dog - gie in the

B♭7
(Bark, bark!)
win - dow?
The one with the
B♭7♯5
E♭
Edim7
B♭7
E♭
wag - gel - y tail;
how much is that
Edim7
B♭7
(Bark, bark!)
dog - gie in the win - dow?
I

E♭
B♭7
E♭
do hope that dog - gie's for sale.

I Whistle a Happy Tune

from THE KING AND I
Lyrics by Oscar Hammerstein II
Music by Richard Rodgers

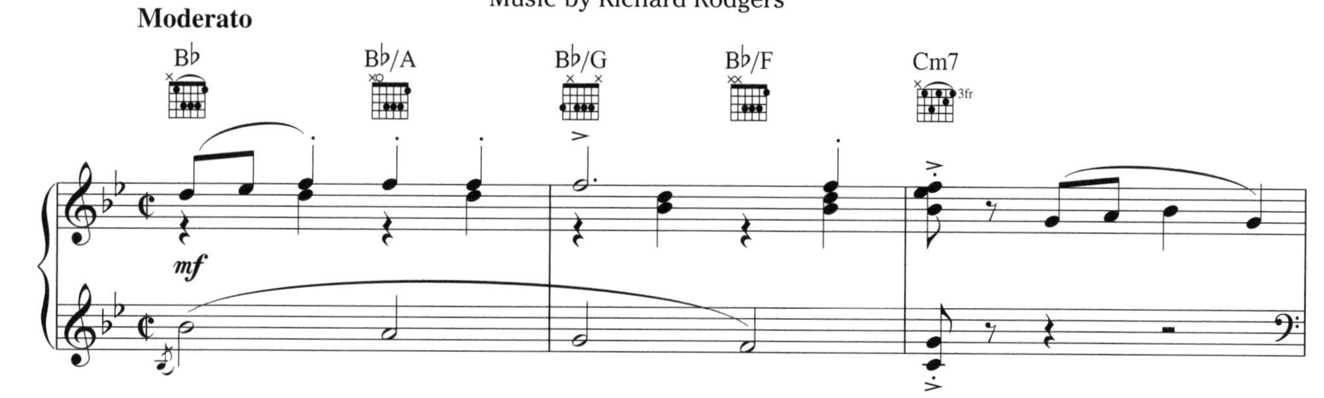

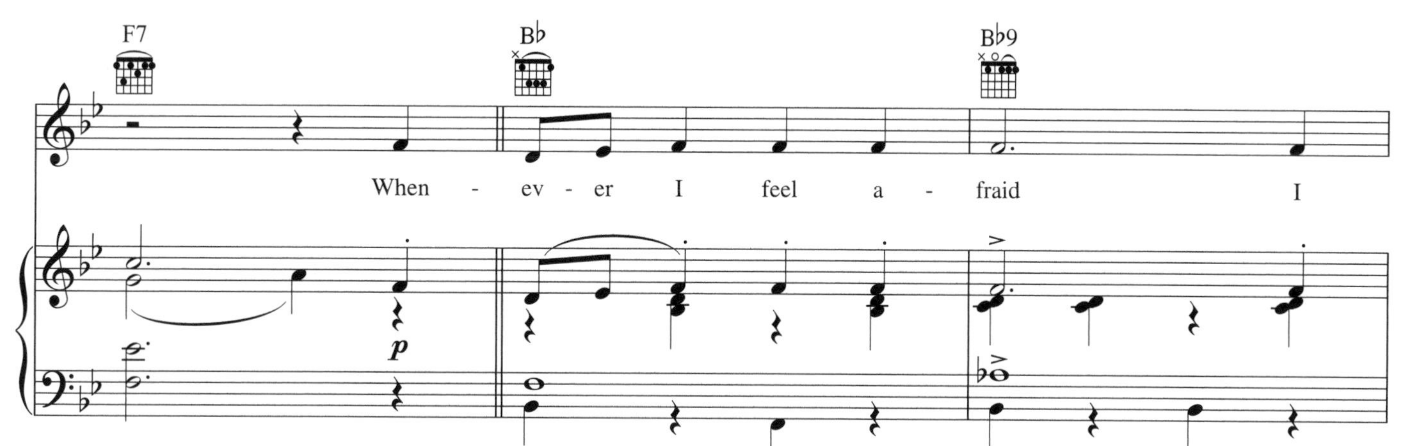

B♭(add9)
6fr
B♭
B♭maj7
B♭6
B♭
fraid. While shiv - er - ing in my
B♭9
E♭
3fr
E♭maj7
3fr
E♭6
shoes I strike a care - less pose And
F7
F7♯5
B♭
N.C.
whis - tle a hap - py tune, And no one ev - er
F7
B♭6
B♭
Cm7/B♭
6fr
B♭/D
knows I'm a - fraid. The re -
mp

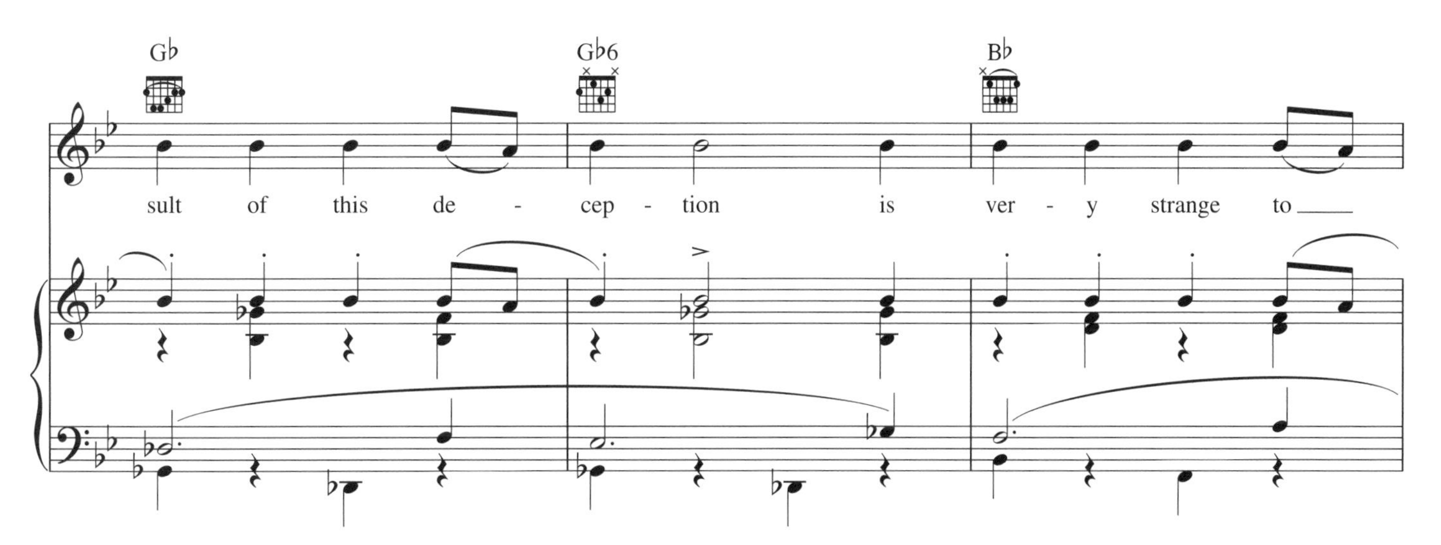
G♭
G♭6
B♭
sult of this de - cep - tion is ver - y strange to

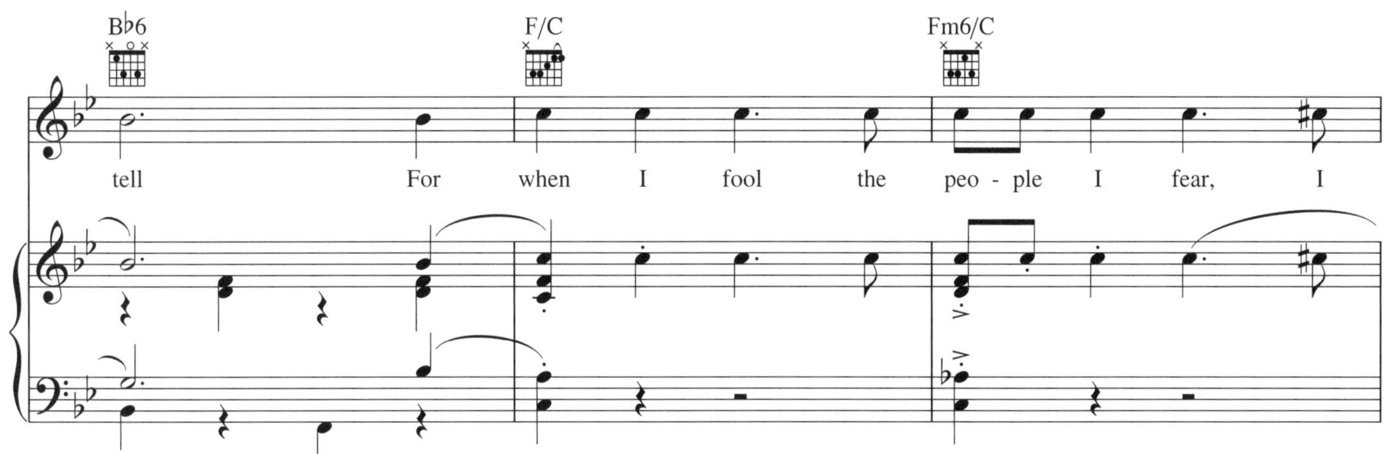
B♭6
F/C
Fm6/C
tell For when I fool the peo - ple I fear, I

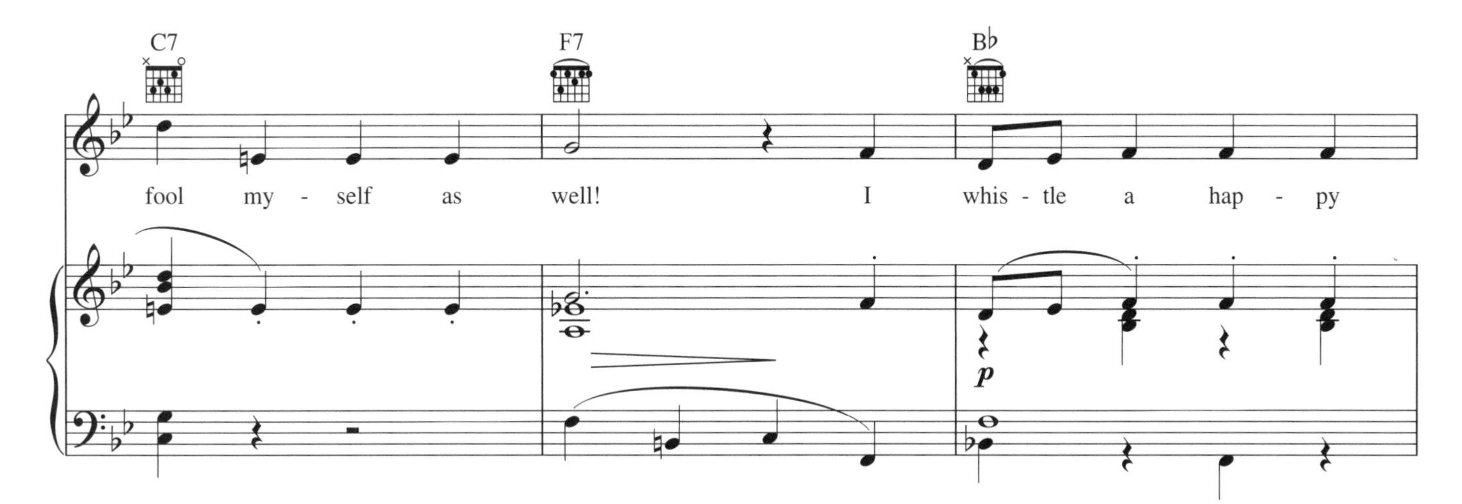
C7
F7
B♭
fool my - self as well! I whis - tle a hap - py

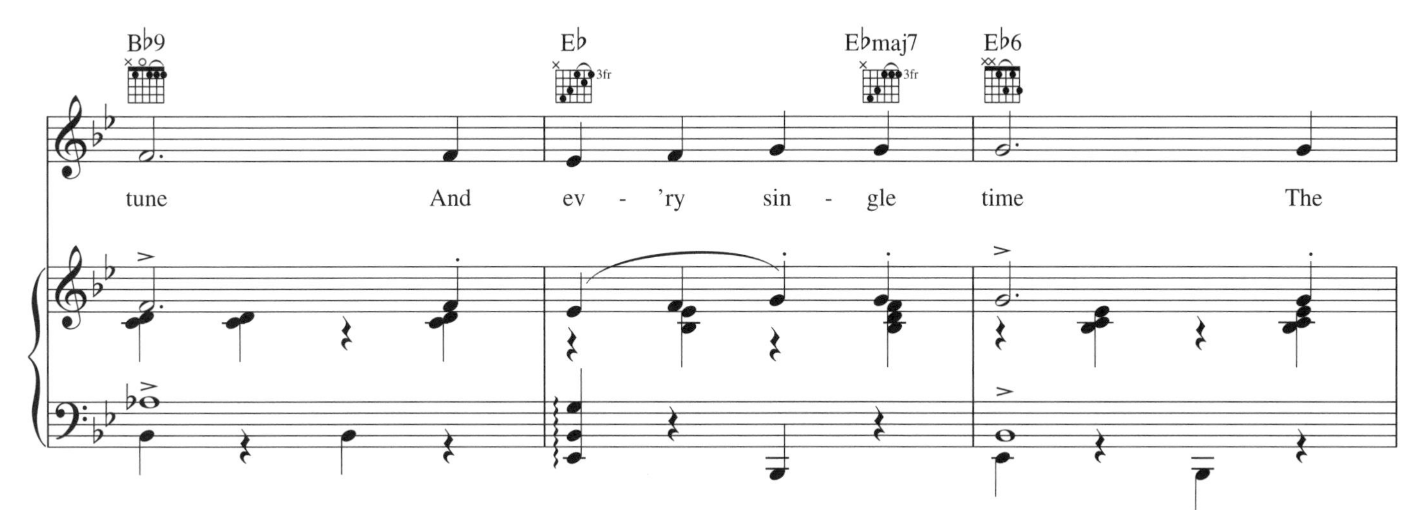
B♭9
E♭
E♭maj7
E♭6
tune And ev - 'ry sin - gle time The

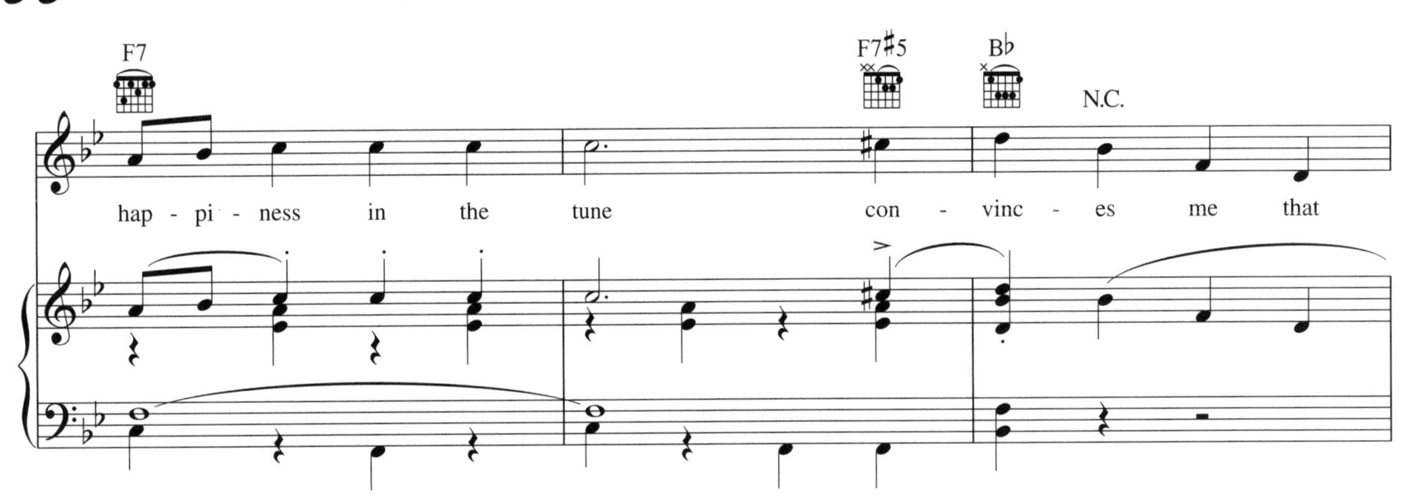
F7
F7♯5
B♭
N.C.
hap - pi - ness in the tune con - vinc - es me that

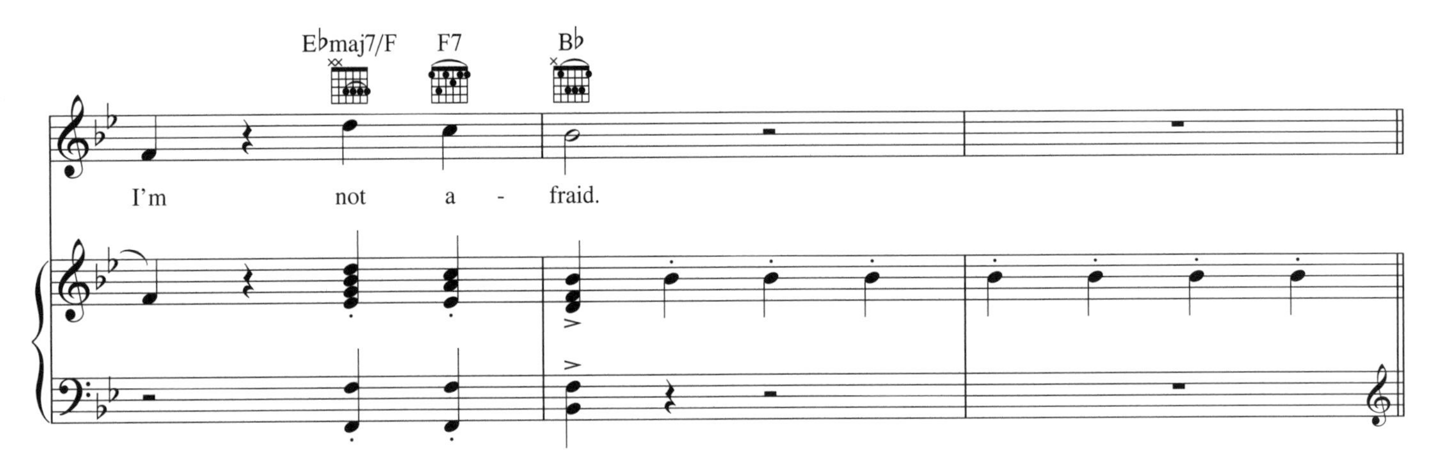
E♭maj7/F
F7
B♭
I'm not a - fraid.

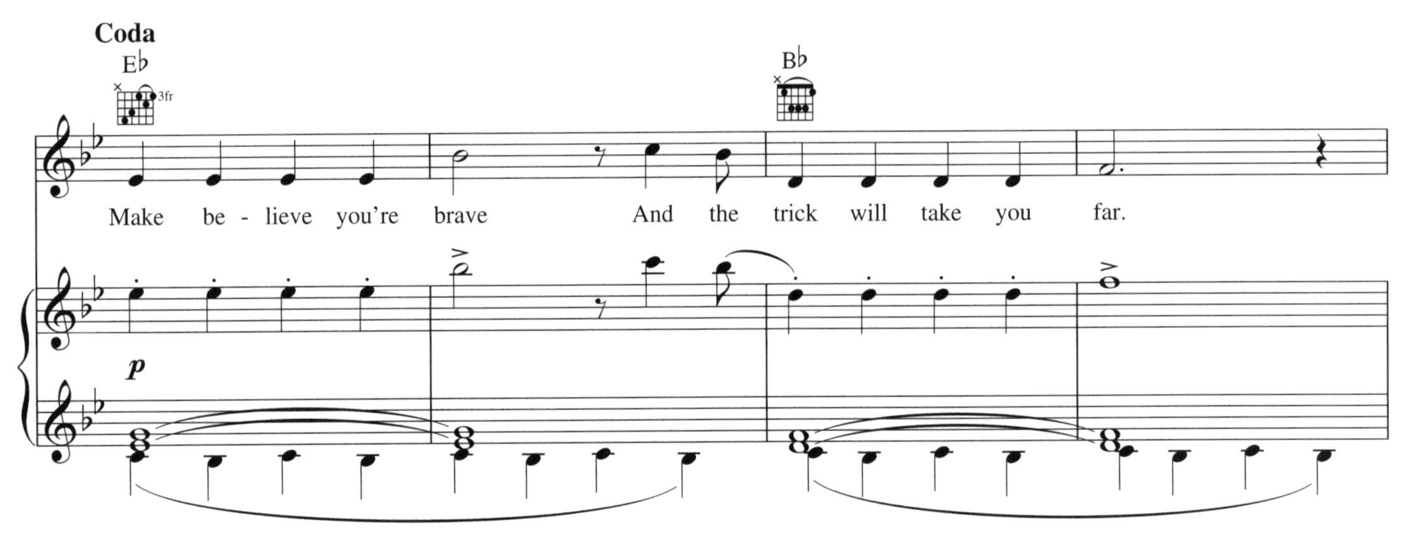
Coda
E♭
3fr
B♭
Make be - lieve you're brave And the trick will take you far.
p

E♭
3fr
B♭
You may be as brave as you make be - lieve you

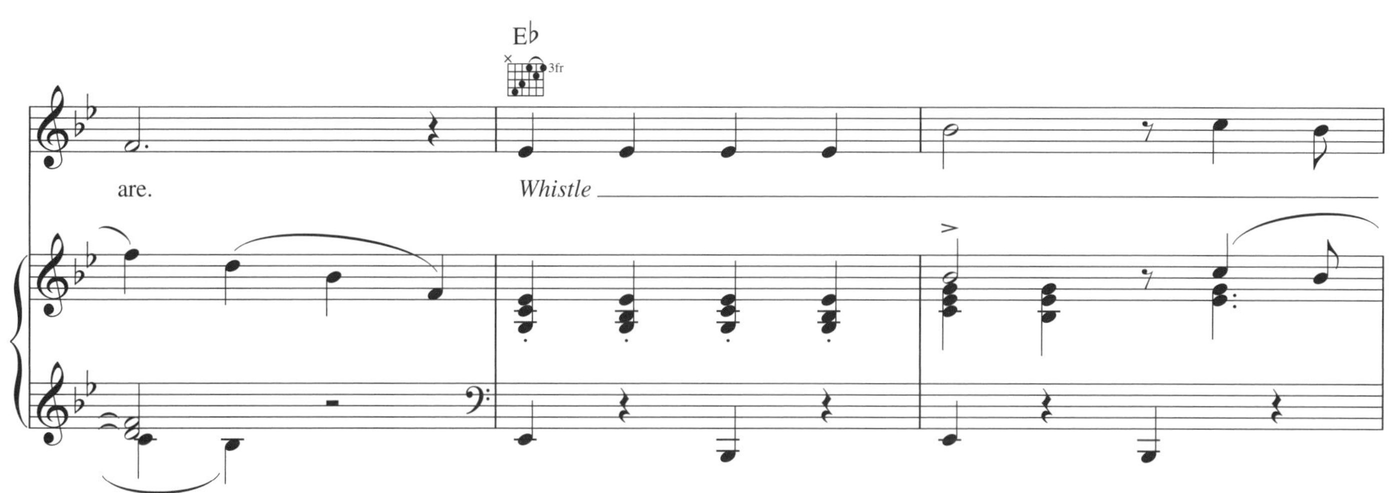
E♭
3fr
are.
Whistle

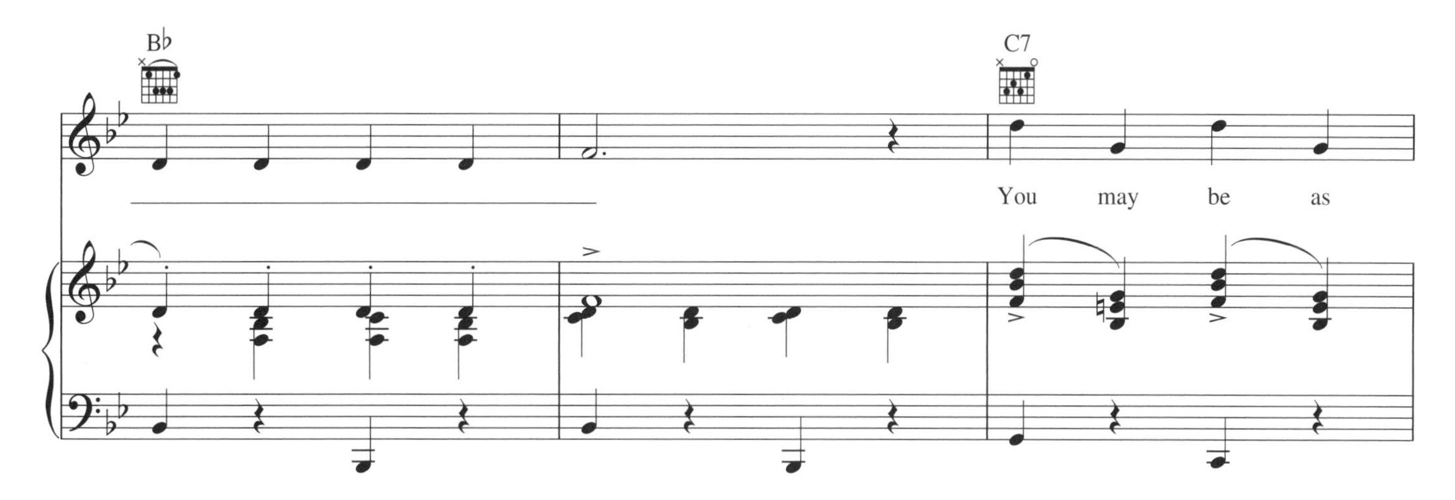
B♭
C7
You may be as

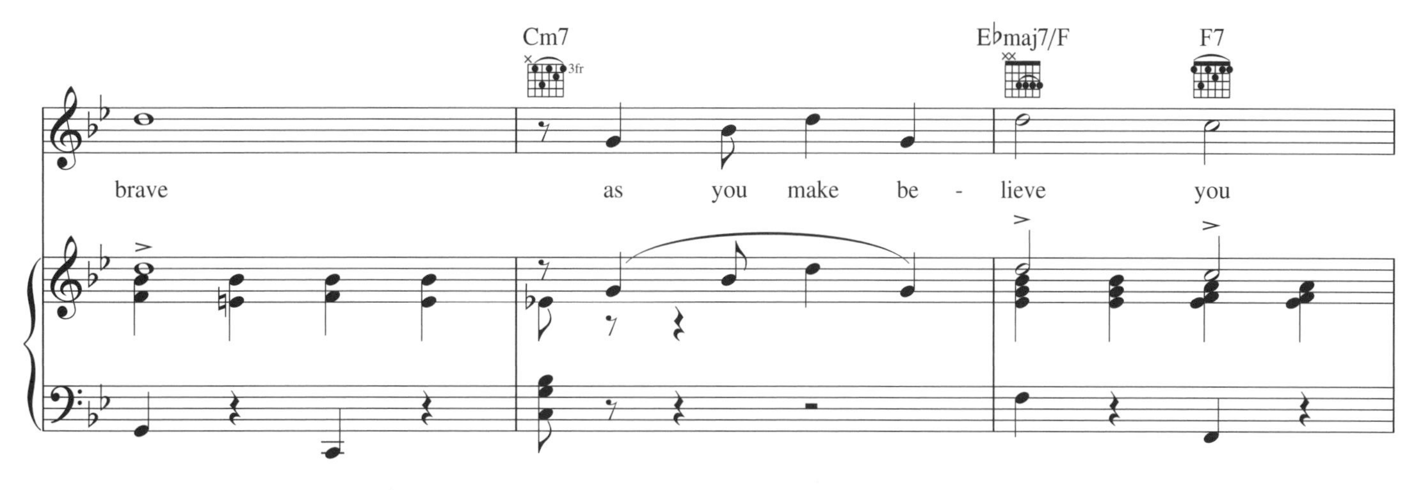
Cm7
3fr
E♭maj7/F
F7
brave
as you make be - lieve you

B♭
are.
8va
pp
p

(I Scream-You Scream-We All Scream For) Ice Cream

Words and Music by Howard Johnson, Billy Moll and Robert King

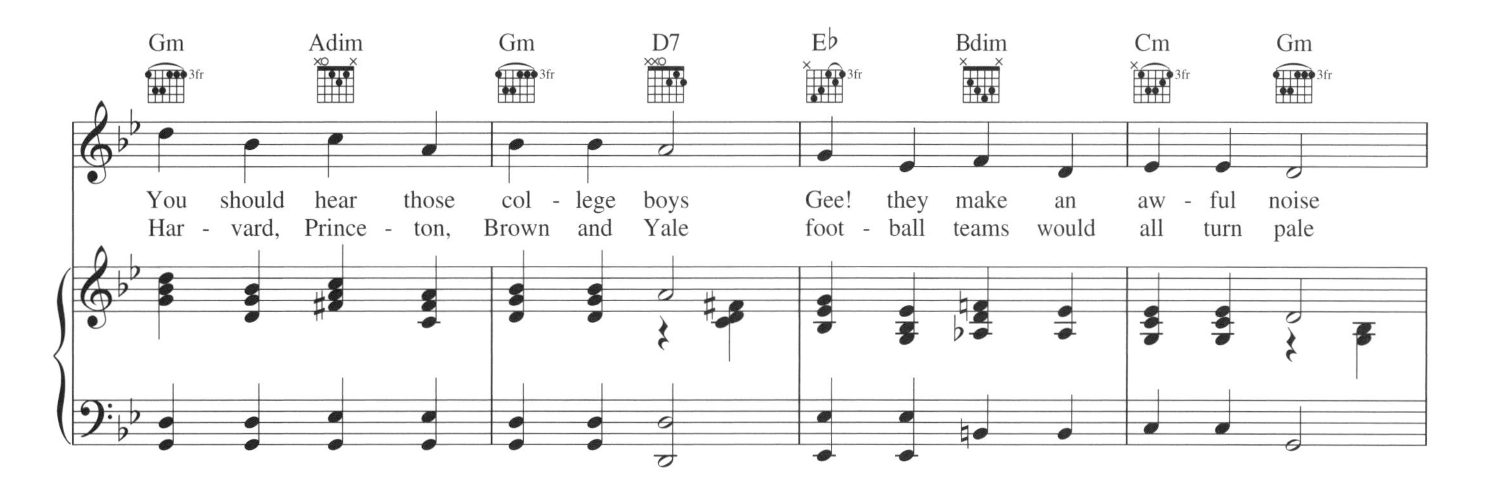
Gm Adim Gm D7 E♭ Bdim Cm Gm
You should hear those col - lege boys Gee! they make an aw - ful noise
Har - vard, Prince - ton, Brown and Yale foot - ball teams would all turn pale

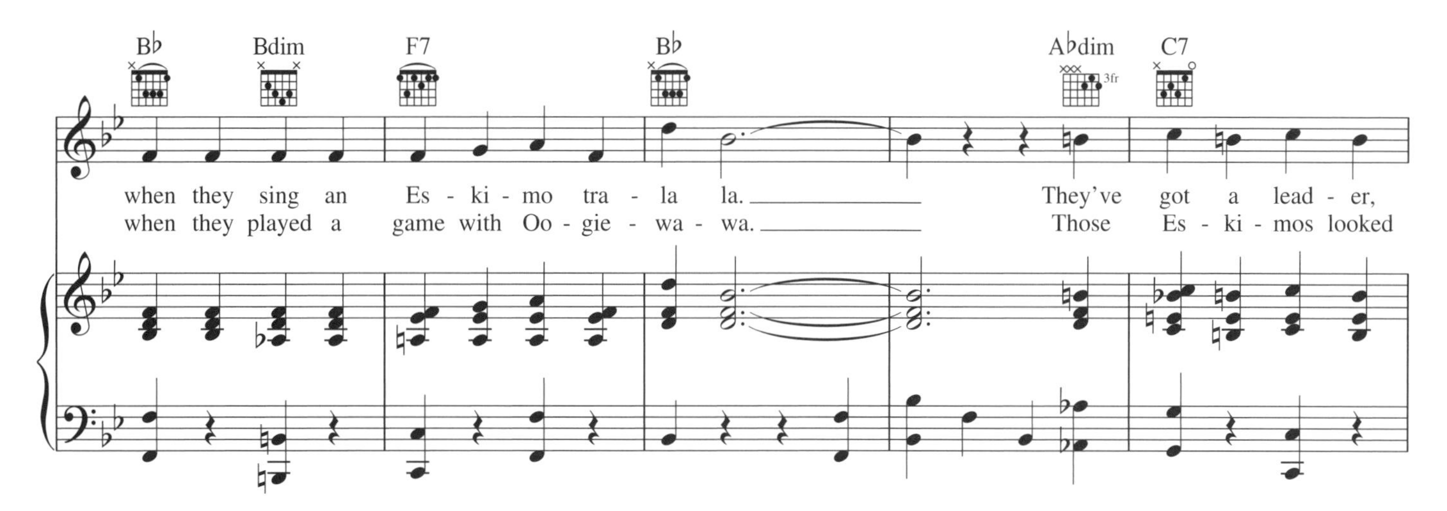
B♭ Bdim F7 B♭ A♭dim C7
when they sing an Es - ki - mo tra - la la. They've got a lead - er,
when they played a game with Oo - gie - wa - wa. Those Es - ki - mos looked

F F♯dim C7
big cheer-lead - er, oh! what a guy, he's got a fro - zen face, just like an
might - y tough when they took the field and peo - ple said "Ah!" there's a team that

F7 Gm Adim Gm D7 E♭ Bdim
Es - ki - mo pie. When he says, "Come on, let's go," tho' it's for - ty -
nev - er will yield. Then mid gore and fly - ing fur Just to show how

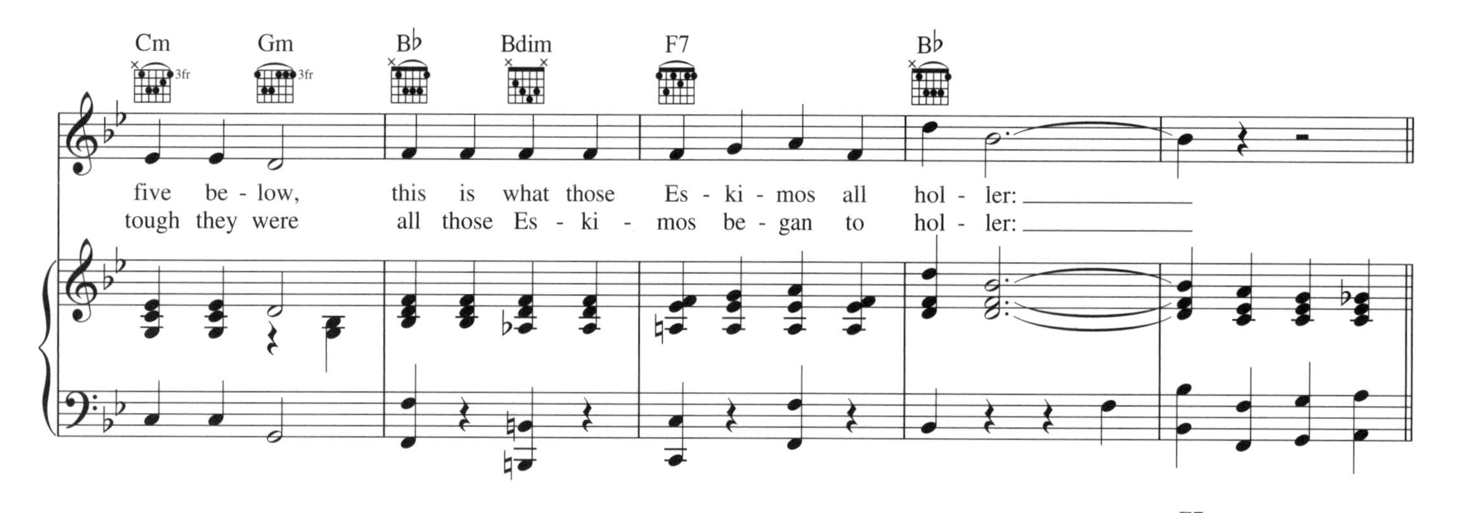
Cm Gm B♭ Bdim F7 B♭
3fr 3fr
five be - low, this is what those Es - ki - mos all hol - ler:
tough they were all those Es - ki - mos be - gan to hol - ler:

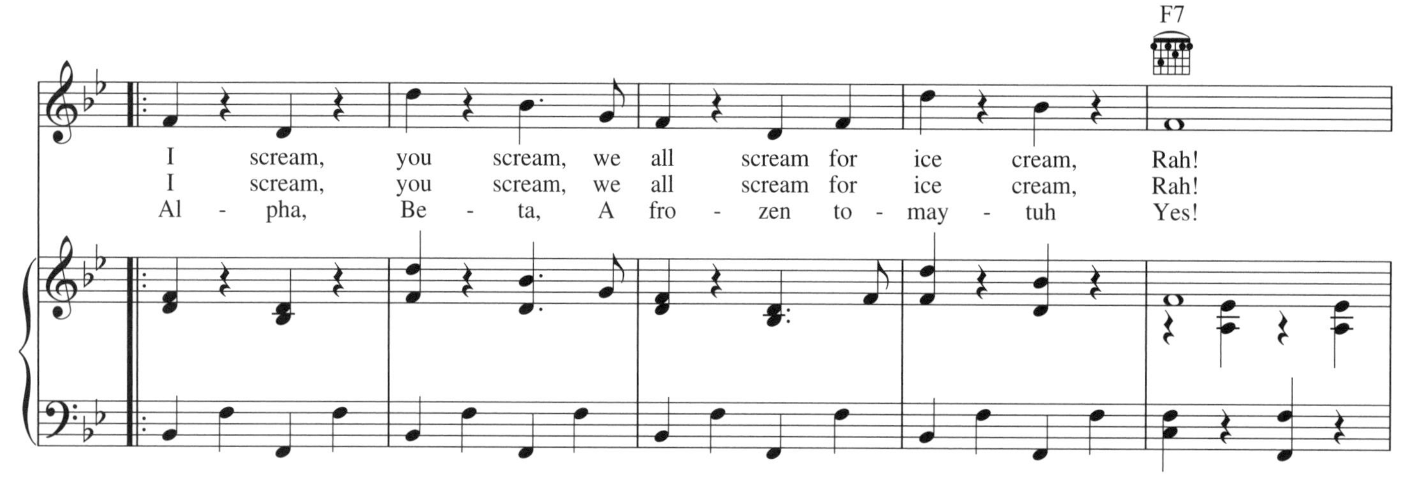
F7
I scream, you scream, we all scream for ice cream, Rah!
I scream, you scream, we all scream for ice cream, Rah!
Al - pha, Be - ta, A fro - zen to - may - tuh Yes!

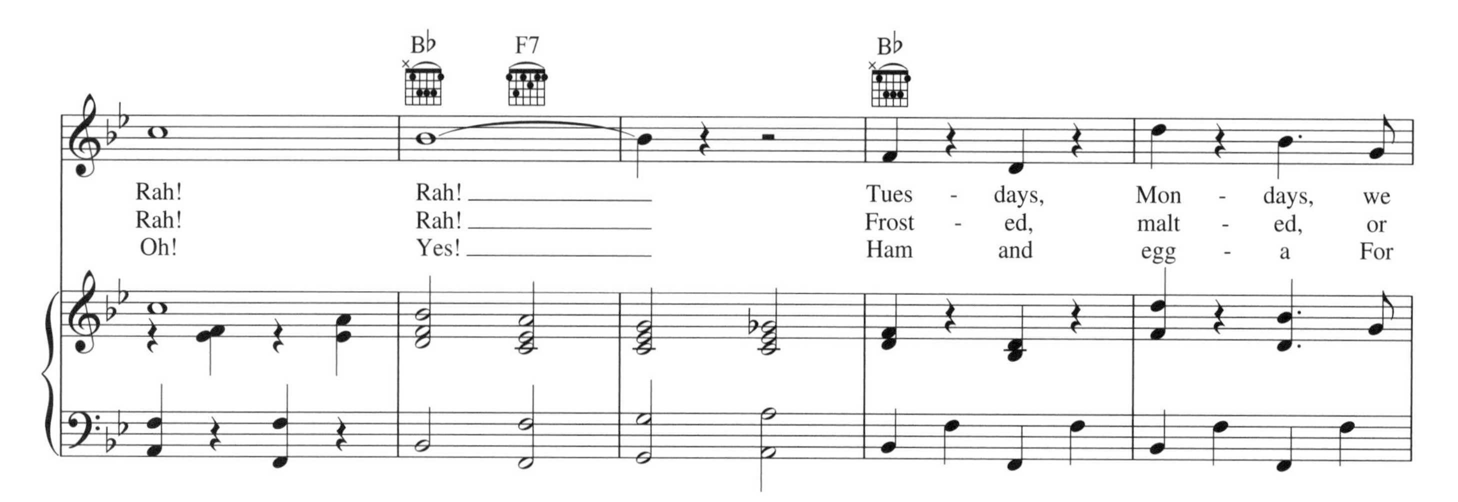
B♭ F7 B♭
Rah! Rah! Tues - days, Mon - days, we
Rah! Rah! Frost - ed, malt - ed, or
Oh! Yes! Ham and egg - a For

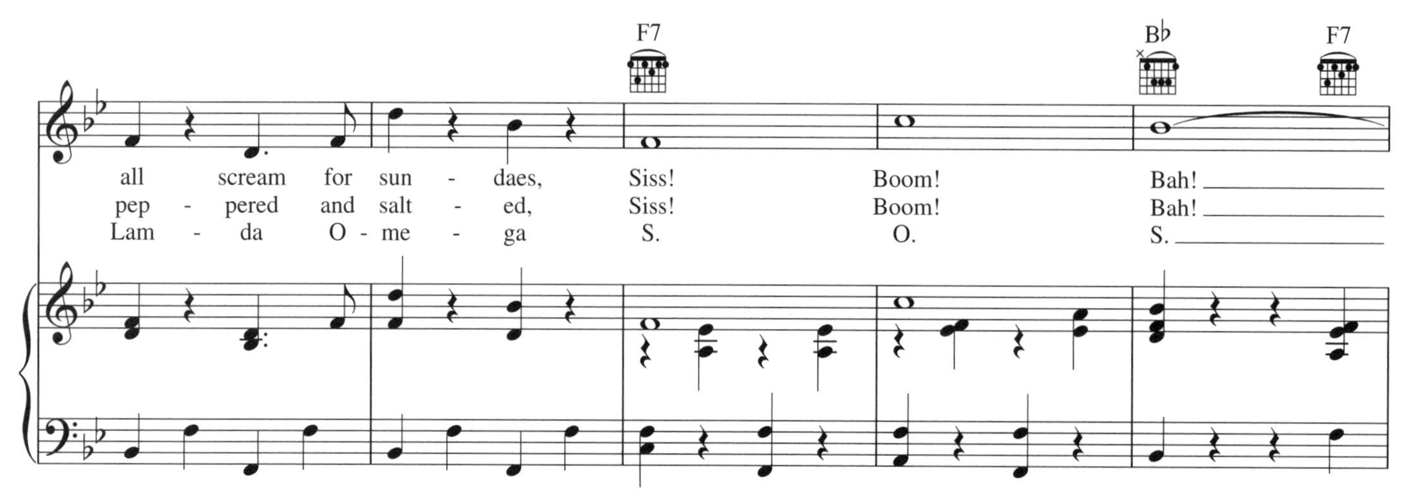
F7 B♭ F7
all scream for sun - daes, Siss! Boom! Bah!
pep - pered and salt - ed, Siss! Boom! Bah!
Lam - da O - me - ga S. O. S.

B♭
B♭7
E♭
E♭m
B♭
A♭dim
Boo - la Boo - la Sas - pa - ROO - la If you've got
Oh! Spu - mo - ni Oh! Tor - to - ni And con - fi -
A - B - C - ses X - Y - Z - ses But in the
C7
F7
B♭
Choc - o - LET We'll take Va - NOO - la I scream,
den - tial - ly, Oh! oh! Ba - lo - ney I scream,
win - ter - time No B. V. D. - ses Ketch - up,
F7
you scream, we all scream for ice cream, Rah! Rah!
you scream, we all scream for ice cream, Rah! Rah!
mus - tard On fresh cher - ry cus - tard Ice Cream
B♭
1,2
3
Rah!
Rah!
Pi. Rah!
fz

Performance Notes

A-Tisket A-Tasket (page 6)

"A-Tisket A-Tasket" is not only a traditional nursery rhyme, it's also a pop-culture phenomenon. After the legendary singer Ella Fitzgerald released a jazzy interpretation of the song in 1938, "A-Tisket A-Tasket" was referenced in everything from a Triscuit commercial to rap songs like "Ham n' Eggs," by A Tribe Called Quest and "Without Me," by Eminem.

This arrangement in the key of C major has some jazzy harmonies. Chords like C♯dim7 (C♯-E-G-B♭) and Dm7 (D-F-A-C) add color to the arrangement. Pay attention to the roadmap: After you've reached the repeat sign at the first ending, go back to the repeat sign in bar 3 and play through the second ending, skipping the first ending. Then, at the indication *D.S. al Coda (dal segno al coda,* meaning "from the sign to the coda"), find the sign back at bar 3. Start there, and play until you get to the indication *To Coda,* where you'll skip to the indented system marked *Coda* and proceed with the remaining two bars.

The Addams Family Theme (page 10)

The mid-1960s television program *The Addams Family* centered on the antics of a bizarrely supernatural extended family — Gomez, Morticia, Uncle Fester, and all the rest. Equally strange was the theme song, driven by a spooky harpsichord and punctuated with finger snaps.

"The Addams Family Theme" is arranged here in B♭ major. The key to playing the song properly is accurately playing the eighth note *triplets,* three evenly spaced eighth notes in one beat, as indicated by a three above the beam. To get a feel for these rhythms, try counting "trip-uh-let, trip-uh-let," and so on when you play through certain parts of the song, like the first eight bars. And don't forget to snap! Wherever you see the X-shaped noteheads on beats 2 and 3, take your hands off the keys and snap your fingers forcefully, as indicated by the *accent* marks (>).

Alley Cat Song (page 7)

With words by Jack Harlen and music by Frank Bjorn, "Alley Cat Song" is a fun song enjoyed by children and adults alike for some four decades. Great interpretations of this classic tune include those by Peggy Lee and Holly Cole, among other vocalists.

Presented here in the easy key of C major, "Alley Cat Song" has got some rhythmic activity to which you should pay close attention. The song is in *cut time,* as indicated at the beginning by the "C" with a vertical line through it. (¢) Feel this meter by counting in half notes, two per bar, rather than quarter notes. Also, the tune has a *swing feel.* To achieve this jazzy feel, wherever you see a pair of eighth notes, play the first note longer than the second, almost as if you're playing a dotted eighth note followed by a 16th note.

Alouette (page 12)

The traditional folk song "Alouette" was originally sung by French fur traders, who found that it inspired them to paddle their boats at a brisker pace as they worked. The lyrics, which detail the systematic removal of feathers from a skylark, might seem unsuitable for children. But with its gentle and simple melody, the song is now commonly used in the classroom as a lesson in anatomical vocabulary for young children.

Play "Alouette," shown here in the key of F, gently and in cut time. Note that the next-to-last bar should be repeated as desired, each time substituting a new body part as depicted in the footnote. When you get to the final bar, you'll see the direction *D.C. al Fine.* At that spot, go back to the very beginning, then play until you see the indication *Fine* (ending) above the double bar line.

Any Dream Will Do (page 14)

"Any Dream Will Do" comes from the Andrew Lloyd Webber musical *Joseph and the Amazing Technicolor Dreamcoat,* based on the Biblical story of Joseph. In the song, a narrator tells the story of Joseph to a group of children, encouraging them to become dreamers. Fittingly, the song was first heard as performed by a group of students at London's Colet Court preparatory school.

Although "Any Dream Will Do" is shown here in the simple key of C major, you might find some of the rhythms in the piano accompaniment tricky. If you experience any difficultly, just take things very slowly and *subdivide:* count "One-ee-and-uh, two-ee-and-uh, three-ee-and-uh, four-ee-and-uh," and so on. In the bass clef of bar 5, for example, the note C will fall on beat 1 and on the "uh" of beat 2. Luckily, once you've got this rhythm down, the bass line of the entire piece should fall into place.

Bein' Green (page 24)

"Bein' Green" is one of a handful of great songs that were first heard on the children's television program *Sesame Street.* The tune was sung by Kermit the Frog, who initially laments his greenness, but at the end of the song accepts it. "Bein' Green" has penetrated pop culture. The song's been covered by a number of great vocalists; Ray Charles, Van Morrison, and Diana Ross are among the most noteworthy, and it inspired the expression, "It's not easy being green," often heard from forlorn folks.

The at-times gloomy "Bein' Green" is arranged here in the decidedly happy key of B♭ major. The song has got lots of jazzy rhythms and *accidentals* (sharps and flats), so be sure to take things slowly when learning it. You might even try playing each hand separately at first. Throughout, enjoy the complex harmony. Chords like B♭maj7 (B♭-D-F-A), G7♭9 (G-B-D-F-A♭), and Gm(maj7) (G-B♭-D-F♯) lend sophistication to this children's song.

The Bible Tells Me So (page 21)

In the 1950s, the singing cowboy/cowgirl husband-and-wife team of Roy Rogers and Dale Evans were the stars of *The Roy Rogers Show,* a television program many children and their parents found delightful. Evans was an accomplished songwriter; she wrote one of the duo's most popular tunes of that period, "The Bible Tells Me So," which continues to remind listeners to "have faith, hope, and charity."

"The Bible Tells Me So" is arranged here for you in the key of G major, in cut time. This is a country-and-western song, so when you're playing the left-hand part, think about the sound that an upright bass makes: "oom-pah, oom-pah," and so on. To achieve the proper rhythmic feel, make sure to silence the bass notes as indicated by the rests, which often occur on beats 2 and 4. One more thing: In the next-to-last measure of the piece, the marking *rall.,* short for *rallentando,* means to gradually play the music more slowly until the end.

Bingo *(page 28)*

"Bingo," not to be confused by the game of chance played in senior citizens' centers throughout the U.S., is a children's song of murky origin. In a performance of this fun number, a dog's name, Bingo, is initially spelled out in full. On the first repetition, the B is replaced by a clap, and on subsequent repeats, the remaining letters follow suit one at a time until only claps remain.

The first thing you'll notice about "Bingo," played in the key of G major, is that it's in 2/4 time — two quarter notes per bar. So, instead of counting "One, two, three, four," as you would in 4/4, simply count "One, two," and so on throughout. And although not written this way in the notation, be sure to play the repeated section six times, each time deleting the appropriate letter (– INGO, – – NGO, – – – GO, and so on) and clapping your hands instead.

The Brady Bunch *(page 30)*

The Brady Bunch, a television program about a big, blended family, wasn't all that acclaimed during its initial primetime run, from 1969 to 1974. But through syndication, subsequent motion pictures, and other spinoffs, it became one of television's all-time biggest phenomena, claiming rabid fans throughout the world. At the same time, its lively theme song also became wildly popular.

Arranged for you here beginning in the key of G major, "The Brady Bunch" is sung first by the boys of the family. The girls then respond before the groups converge. Because there is some overlap between the lyrics of the boys and girls, this tune is best sung by two or more singers. Another thing to consider is the song's *modulation.* Several bars after the second ending, the basic chord progression remains the same, but is moved up a step, to the key of A♭ major, which adds a bit of intensity. Take things slowly here so that your fingers don't get tripped up by the key change.

"C" Is for Cookie *(page 34)*

"'C' Is for Cookie" is another great song from *Sesame Street,* this one performed, of course, by Cookie Monster. The blue furry creature has become more cognizant of nutrition since he first sang the song on a 1972 episode. He's even appeared in a rap video promoting the importance of fruits and vegetables. Nonetheless, "'C' Is for Cookie" remains one of *Sesame Street's* most popular numbers.

Shown here in the jazzy key of E♭ major, "'C' Is for Cookie" is a *ragtime* number. Ragtime is syncopated dance music, a precursor to jazz that was at its most popular in the late 1800s and early 1900s. Throughout the notation you'll see a bunch of *slash* chords. When you see this type of chord, the letter to the right of the chord represents the lowest note. For instance, in bar 9 the symbol E♭/G calls for an E♭ triad (E♭–G–B♭) with a G in the bass. This makes for a smooth transition in the bass line to the next bar's first chord, A♭.

The Candy Man (page 36)

The original *Willy Wonka and the Chocolate Factory* (1971), based on the 1964 Roald Dahl novel *Charlie and the Chocolate Factory,* is one of the most popular children's films ever made. Among other great songs, the movie features the wonderful number "The Candy Man," sung by Aubrey Woods as Bill the candy store owner. Later, Sammy Davis, Jr. scored the biggest hit of his entire singing career with this fun tune.

"The Candy Man" is written here in the key of E♭ major, containing three flats, so it might be a good idea to take things slowly when learning this number. Crucial to making the song sound bright and snappy is crisply articulating the rhythms, so subdivide if needed, counting "One-ee-and-uh, two-ee-and-uh, three-ee-and-uh, four-ee-and-uh," and so on, throughout. In the most prominent rhythm — the dotted eighth followed by a 16th note — the latter value will always fall on an "uh."

Casper the Friendly Ghost (page 40)

Casper, a pudgy, benevolent apparition, was the protagonist of *Casper the Friendly Ghost,* an animated cartoon that debuted in 1945. Casper went on to appear in numerous comic books, as well as television shows and films, many of which featured the original theme song, with words by Mack David and music by Jerry Livingston.

Although "Casper the Friendly Ghost" begins here with a C minor chord, it is actually in the bright and easy key of C major. The arrangement is fairly straightforward, but the notation might contain some symbols with which you're unfamiliar. In the bass clef of bar 3 is a type of *tremolo* sign: As indicated by the three slanted parallel lines, rapidly alternate between the lower and higher A♭ notes for the duration of the measure. Also, in the treble clef of bar 4 (and elsewhere) are 16th-note *grace notes,* to be played very quickly before the B on beat 1. Feel free to omit the grace notes if they're too difficult to play.

The Chicken Dance (page 42)

Not to be confused with the 1950s R&B dance fad of a similar name, "The Chicken Dance" is a song composed by Werner Thomas, a Swiss accordionist. Thomas played his song, originally called "The Duck Dance," at local gigs in restaurants and hotels during the 1960s. Now some five decades later, "The Chicken Dance," and its accompanying dance, which mimics the physicality of a rooster, has become popular throughout the world.

"The Chicken Dance," shown here in C, has two beats per measure, so when you're playing it, think of an "oom-pah" sound, or the rhythm of a typical polka band or accordion accompaniment. Although not indicated in the sheet music, a typical performance of the song starts moderately and gradually increases in tempo. Be sure to notice the indication *glissando* (abbreviated gliss.) in the *Coda.* As depicted by the angled line, quickly slide your finger up the white keys beginning on the middle C and ending two octaves higher at the beginning of the final measure.

Chim Chim Cher-ee (page 45)

The 1964 Disney movie musical *Mary Poppins* yielded a handful of wonderful songs, one of which, "Chim Chim Cher-ee," had the distinction of winning an Oscar. The song found quite a wide audience. It became a favorite not just of children, but of jazz musicians as well; legends like the saxophonist John Coltrane and the singer/trumpeter Louis Armstrong both recorded fine interpretations of "Chim Chim Cher-ee."

Arranged here in the key of C minor, "Chim Chim Cher-ee" is a light waltz. So, when you play it count, "one, two, three, one, two, three," throughout, emphasizing the first beat of each bar. Imagine that you're performing the song for an elegant, old-fashioned dance. One of the reasons jazz musicians find this tune so appealing is that it's got some pretty slick harmony for a children's song. Chords like G7♭9 (G-B-D-F) and Am7♭5 (A-C-E♭-G) lend a sophisticated sound. These chords tend to incorporate notes outside of the key, so when you're learning the song remember to scan ahead for the accidentals that might trip you up.

Chopsticks (page 50)

The very simple and extremely popular piano piece known today as "Chopsticks" was originally called "The Celebrated Chop Waltz." It was composed in 1877 by the British teenager Euphemia Allen under the pseudonym Arthur de Lulli. She gave the piece its fun name because she intended it to be played by striking the piano keys with a chopping motion.

"Chopsticks" is typically played as shown here, in the key of C major. One of the reasons for the composition's popularity is that it's within the reach of even the most inexperienced pianist. So, given that the actual notes will probably come easily to you, this arrangement offers a good opportunity to concentrate on articulation and dynamics. As indicated in bar 4 by the hairpin lines, for instance, crescendo from soft (*p*) to loud (*f*). In bar 5, the *fermata* sign (𝄐) calls for you to hold the notes for an unspecified duration, as long as you'd like.

Dites-Moi (Tell Me Why) (page 54)

South Pacific, the 1949 musical by Richard Rodgers and Oscar Hammerstein II, is widely considered one of the masterpieces of its genre. Some of the songs, such as "Some Enchanted Evening" and "Younger Than Springtime" have become standards for both adults and children. While not as celebrated as these numbers, "Dites-Moi (Tell Me Why)," also from *South Pacific,* is a very satisfying tune to sing and play.

To make "Dites-Moi," (notated here in C major) sound expressive, you'll want to carefully observe all the articulation markings. As indicated by the *slurs* (the curved lines above and below the notes), smoothly connect those notes without separation. Where you see a *staccato* marking (a dot above or below a notehead), play the notes short and separated, the opposite of the notes with slurs. Also, be sure to follow the dynamic markings throughout the arrangement.

Do-Re-Mi (page 56)

"Do-Re-Mi" is another wonderful children's song from a musical. It was first heard in the original 1959 production of Rodgers & Hammerstein's *The Sound of Music,* which chronicled the lives of the von Trapp family, who fled Nazi persecution in Austria. In the musical, the charismatic governess, Maria, enters the family and teaches the children to love music, especially through the song "Do-Re-Mi." These days, the tune is often used to teach young music students the notes of the major scale.

"Do-Re-Mi" is in the key of C major. It is to be played *Allegretto;* lively and fast. You might have noticed that the piece starts off with a sort of unresolved sound. This is due to the incorporation of what is known as the V or *dominant* chord, in this case G, for a handful of measures. The V chord tends to resolve to the *tonic,* or I chord, in this case C, which first provides resolution in bar 13.

For He's a Jolly Good Fellow (page 62)

The melody of "For He's a Jolly Good Fellow" originated from the French folk song "Marlborough s'en va-t-en guerre" ("Marlborough Has Left for the War," 1709), which purportedly became popular when a nurse began singing it as a lullaby to one of Marie Antoinette's children. By around 1870 in New York, the tune was known as "We Won't Go Home till Morning." Now, many years later, "For He's a Jolly Good Fellow" is used to celebrate milestones in life, a birthday, or other significant events.

Arranged here in the key of F major, "For He's a Jolly Good Fellow" is in 6/8 time; that's six eighth notes per bar, so count, "*One*-two-three, *four*-five-six," emphasizing the first and fourth beats while keeping those eighth notes bouncing along. You can also think of 6/8 as having two strong beats per bar.

Frère Jacques (Are You Sleeping?) (page 53)

Known in English as "Brother John" or "Brother Peter," "Frère Jacques (Are you Sleeping?)" is a traditional nursery rhyme most often sung in French. These days it is used both as a French lesson for young children and a music lesson, often on the recorder.

"Frère Jacques," arranged here in F major, is a very short song. It's only eight bars long, to be repeated as desired. With its straightforward rhythms and lack of accidentals, the song's quite easy to play on the piano. One small detail: In the bass clef of bars 5 and 6, on beat 3, the note A is represented both as an quarter note and a half note simply to show that the same note is part of two different voices (or layers) in the music, so play the A only once each time.

Getting to Know You (page 64)

"Getting to Know You" is another great show tune by Rodgers & Hammerstein. It comes from the 1951 musical *The King and I,* in which a schoolteacher named Anna becomes acquainted with the children and the wives of the King of Siam. The song became both a children's standard as well as a pop vocal gem, sung by Bing Crosby, Dinah Shore, and other entertainers.

Arranged here in cut time and in the key of C major, "Getting to Know You" has some music symbols that might be new to you. In bar 3, for example, the squiggly line on beat 3 calls for you to quickly roll the chord from the lowest note to the highest. The short, slanted parallel lines in the next measure are a *caesure,* or grand pause. Lift your hands from the keyboard and take a breath before continuing. And in bar 6, on beat 2, as indicated by the *tenuto* mark, play the chord with a bit of emphasis, such that it sounds separate from beats 1 and 4.

Happy Trails (page 68)

Like "The Bible Tells Me So," "Happy Trails" also comes from the television series *The Roy Rodgers Show* and was written by Rogers' wife, Dale Evans. The song, which appeared in the closing credits of the program, became immensely popular on its own and has since been covered by a diverse array of artists, including everyone from the hard rock group Van Halen to the bluegrass band Nickel Creek.

A slow and tender number, "Happy Trails" is shown here in the key of E♭ major. The use of an E♭6 chord gives the song a particularly wistful quality. In case you're curious, an E♭6 chord is an E♭ triad (E♭-G-B♭) with an added 6th (C). To best appreciate the special sound of this chord, simply try omitting the note C when you encounter it, and then compare that with the sound of the chord with the added sixth.

Heart and Soul (page 74)

With words by Frank Loesser and music by Hoagy Carmichael, "Heart and Soul" was written in 1938 and became a pop hit the following year. Because of the song's catchy simplicity, it is now a piano staple, particularly for those whose acquaintance with the instrument is extremely casual.

Although "Heart and Soul" is commonly played as a duet in the key of C major, it is arranged here for one pianist in the original key of F major. Note that in a typical performance of the song, the first 12 bars are often omitted. The music starting on the second page probably sounds very familiar to you. That's because the song contains a chord progression, I–vi–ii–V (in this case, F–Dm7–Gm7–C7), that became the backbone of so many pop and rock songs!

The Hokey Pokey (page 78)

"The Hokey Pokey" is a traditional song with an accompanying dance that peaked in popularity in British and Irish dance halls in the 1940s. An American version became popular the following decade, not long after it was recorded by a group known as the Ram Trio. Although originally a form of adult entertainment, "The Hokey Pokey" is now a staple at children's parties.

Shown here in the key of F major, "The Hokey Pokey" is fairly easy to play on the piano. To make it really come alive, though, pay close attention to the rhythms, and in particular, the rests. In the first bar, for instance, make sure that the chord is silenced on the "and" of beat 3, continuing on with only the right hand melody until the second bar, where the same rhythm pattern is repeated. One more thing: On the last page, you'll see two X noteheads, which call for the notes to be shouted, not sung.

Home on the Range (page 71)

"Home on the Range" enjoys a special distinction in this collection — it's the only official state song, that of Kansas. The tune started out as a poem that one Dr. Brewster M. Higley wrote in the early 1870s. The poem became a song, and settlers, cowboys, and other traveling types spread it throughout the United States. "Home on the Range" is now one of the great American patriotic songs, as well as a popular number for children.

A moderate waltz, "Home on the Range" is arranged for you here in F major. Most of the music falls squarely within the key, with the occasional exception of the note B♮, which lends a slightly funky flavor to the proceedings. In the last two bars are some symbols that might be new to you. As indicated by the *8va* and *8vb* signs, play the music an octave higher and an octave lower respectively, than written. Also, as directed by the Italian words *rit. e dim.,* play more slowly and quietly at the final ending.

How Much Is That Doggie in the Window (page 80)

An adaptation of an older Victorian music hall song, "How Much Is That Doggie in the Window" was written by Bob Merrill in 1952. The following year, the song saw a hit in pop singles by Patti Page in the United States and Lita Rose in Great Britain. Today the tune has the tendency to annoy adults, but it remains a favorite with children.

Although "How Much Is That Doggie in the Window" starts off in the easy key of C major, on the last system of the third page it *modulates* (changes key) to the more difficult key of E♭. You may want to learn each of these sections separately before combining them, making sure to transition smoothly between the keys. Another thing to note: The song makes good use of a *diminished seventh* chord — C♯dim7 (C♯-E-G-B♭) in the key of C, and Edim7 (E-G-B♭-D♭) in the key of E♭. This more intense chord is most often used to transition between gentler chords.

(I Scream — You Scream — We All Scream For) Ice Cream (page 90)

The classic college song "(I Scream — You Scream — We All Scream For) Ice Cream" was composed by the songwriter Howard Johnson in 1927 and recorded the following year by the banjoist/bandleader Harry Reser and his Six Jumping Jacks. Now more than 80 years later, the song is a favorite of children everywhere clamoring for their favorite frozen dessert.

"Ice Cream," shown here in the key of B♭ major, is in a lively cut time, so think of an "oom-pah" sound in the bass when you're playing through the arrangement. And for a convincing rhythmic effect, be sure to observe the rests on beats 2 and 4 where indicated in the left-hand part. Note, too, that the *fz (forzando)* symbol in bar 8 and in the last bar calls for you to play the chord with sudden emphasis.

I Whistle a Happy Tune (page 85)

"I Whistle a Happy Tune" is another great song from *The King and I.* In the musical, the teacher, Anna, sings it to her son, encouraging him not to be afraid as they serve the intimidating King of Siam. Originally sung by Gertrude Lawrence, the bright and optimistic song has been covered by everyone from Marvin Gaye to Frank Sinatra.

Shown here in the key of B♭ major, "I Whistle a Happy Tune" has got some fancy chord work, along with several different rhythmic layers, notated with opposing stems in both clefs. Because of this, you may want to try learning the hands separately before combining everything. Also, be sure to closely observe the many different articulation markings; staccatos, accents, and slurs, that occur throughout.

I'm Popeye the Sailor Man (page 110)

Popeye, the fictional sailor hero who encourages impressionable young children to eat spinach, debuted in his first comic strip way back in 1918. But it wasn't until the early 1930s that "I'm Popeye the Sailor Man," the extremely catchy theme song he's since been closely associated with, appeared.

What makes "I'm Popeye the Sailor Man," written here in the key of E♭ major, so special actually eludes musical notation. In the original theme song, the voice of Popeye is wonderfully idiosyncratic, with a strange accent, gravelly tone, and imperfect intonation. So, to make the most out of this arrangement, be sure to listen to the original song and try to emulate Popeye's mannerisms, especially the strange sound effects, not shown here, that he inserts between vocal phrases. Pay particular attention to the ways in which Popeye mispronounces certain words, perhaps due to the ever-present pipe in his mouth.

If You're Happy and You Know It (page 118)

"If You're Happy and You Know It" is a traditional children's tune, thought to have originated from a Latvian folk song. Although the version most schoolchildren know today is credited to the songwriter Alfred B. Smith (1916–2001), the song has been adapted for many other languages and can even be heard sung in Japanese in a memorable scene from the comedy *The 40-Year-Old Virgin.*

"If You're Happy and You Know It" is shown here in the key of F in 6/8 time. (For instructions on how to count that meter, see the notes to "For He's a Jolly Good Fellow.") The music should be easy enough to tackle, just be sure not to lose the beat when you transition between playing the piano and clapping, tapping, or nodding. Also, you may enjoy substituting some common variations for, "then your face will surely show it." Typical substitutions include, "and you really want to show it" and "then you really ought to show it."

It's a Small World (page 115)

It's a Small World is the name of a delightful ride that debuted at the 1964 World's Fair and is now a permanent fixture at Disney theme parks. In the ride, dolls of various nationalities sing a song whose theme is world peace. The tune, written by the brothers Richard and Robert Sherman, was originally a ballad, but to strike a more optimistic tone, they increased the tempo to match the style of a *roundelay,* a short, simple song with a catchy refrain. Fittingly, it was recorded by young people in studios around the world and soon became one of the most popular children's songs of all time.

"It's a Small World" is in the key of F major and is to be taken at a march tempo. So, when you're playing the song on the piano, imagine the sounds made by a festive marching band during a parade. Your left hand should sound like a tuba and a bass drum; your right hand like a group of woodwinds. Because the song is all about global unity, you might enjoy singing it in a language other than English. A quick Google search should reveal a translation for the language of your choice.

Kum Ba Yah (page 120)

Sometimes spelled "Kumbayah," "Kum Ba Yah" is a traditional spiritual written in the 1930s, perhaps on the coast of South Carolina. The title, originally written in the Gulla language, translates to "come by here." The song became popular during the folk era, when it was recorded by legends like Pete Seeger and Joan Baez. Some fifty years later, it is still heard frequently around the campfire.

Arranged in the key of C major and containing no accidentals, "Kum Ba Yah" is easy enough to play on the piano. Because this song is more of a strummer, though, you might want to bust out that old acoustic guitar to play it. Using the chord frames shown above the notation, try strumming a simple eighth-note pattern with alternating upstrokes and downstrokes. If you have trouble playing the F chord, you could sing the music a step higher than written, and play basic open D, G, and A7 chords in the place of C, F, and G7. Instead of C/G, simply play an open D chord and include the open A string.

Linus and Lucy (page 124)

In 1964 the pianist and composer Vince Guaraldi released a recording called *Jazz Impressions of a Boy Named Charlie Brown.* One of the most notable tunes on the album was "Linus and Lucy," named, of course, after the siblings in Charles M. Schulz's *Peanuts* cartoon. Not only did the composition find its way onto most *Peanuts* television specials, it also became a great jazz standard.

"Linus and Lucy" is shown here in the original key of A♭ major. The most important part of the tune is the groovy bass line, with its wide intervals and syncopated rhythm, so it might be a good idea to first learn the left hand part before tackling the entire tune. To get into the groove, make sure that you're playing an A♭ on the "ands" of beats 3 and 4. Also, when you get to the end of the third page, where you see the indication for a swing feel, don't forget to play the first eighth note longer than the second, as explained in the notes for "Alley Cat."

The Marvelous Toy (page 121)

Tom Paxton is one of the most significant of all folk singer-songwriters, and many of his tunes hold special appeal for children. One such song, "The Marvelous Toy," became a hit in 1963 for the Chad Mitchell Trio and was subsequently covered by such folk stars as John Denver and Peter, Paul, and Mary.

Arranged here in C, "The Marvelous Toy" has a simple verse-chorus structure that is repeated four times, so in learning the song you essentially get four sections for the price of one! Notice the small cue-sized notes that occur throughout the vocal staff. No, these aren't to be sung by miniature vocalists, rather they're to be played only on certain repeats. For example, in bar 5, the small C is only sung the fourth time, and corresponds to the word "have."

Michael Row the Boat Ashore (page 130)

"Michael Row the Boat Ashore" is an old African-American spiritual, first heard during the American Civil War, which has become a children's classic. Like many spirituals, the song has also been a favorite of folk singers, including the Highwaymen, Lonnie Donegan, and Pete Seeger, among many others.

A typical interpretation of "Michael Row the Boat Ashore," written here in the key of C, has a bit more syncopation than is notated. It might be fun for you to first learn the song in a straightforward way as written. Then, check out some recorded versions and try to incorporate some of the more complicated rhythms you hear. On the first system, for instance, instead of singing the syllable "shore" on beat 1 in the second bar, you might anticipate the beat by singing "shore" on the "and" of beat 4, tied into bar 2.

Mickey Mouse March (page 132)

Many Baby Boomers grew up with *The Mickey Mouse Club* television show, which was broadcast on weekday afternoons from 1955 to 1959. And many Baby Boomers (whether they like to admit it or not) have been unable to forget the show's attention-grabbing theme song, with its bright march tempo and spelling-lesson chorus.

Although the "Mickey Mouse March," presented here in the key of F major, appears to be a pretty simple number, it makes use of some pretty slick harmonic devices. In bars 9-10, for instance, the chords change while the melody note stays the same. A *common tone* is being used here. The note F is found in all four chords: F (F-A-C-F), F/E♭ (E♭-A-F), B♭/D (D-B♭-F), and B♭m/D♭ (D♭-B♭-F). Placing the F in the top of each chord makes for a very smooth progression.

Old MacDonald (page 134)

Published in 1917, "Old MacDonald" is a traditional song about a farmer named MacDonald and the various animals to which he tends. The song has a fun structure in which a new animal is introduced in each verse, along with its characteristic sound. One of the most famous of all children's songs, "Old MacDonald" has been translated into many languages, including Egyptian Arabic.

There's a pretty good chance that you'll encounter no difficulties in sight-reading through "Old MacDonald," shown here in the key of F major. One of the most rewarding ways to learn music is by ear, and this song could potentially offer you a good chance to do so. If you're up for the task, check out some popular versions, like those by jazz singer Ella Fitzgerald and bluegrass band Flatt & Scruggs, and see if you can figure out what they're doing and incorporate some of their touches in your own interpretation.

On the Good Ship Lollipop (page 136)

First featured in the film *Bright Eyes,* "On the Good Ship Lollipop" was the signature song of the childhood actress Shirley Temple, who was all of 6 years old when it was released in 1934. The song was a huge hit; it sold more than half a million copies in sheet music form, which was as popular then as MP3s are now. A fun fact: the Good Ship Lollipop was actually an *airship,* or airplane, as that vehicle is known today.

Although "On the Good Ship Lollipop" is written here in the easiest of keys, C major, there are some accidentals here and there that you might find a bit difficult to sing. If, for instance, you find yourself leaning toward an F♮ instead of an F♯ at the end of bar 4, make sure to play an F♯ on the piano for reference. Isolate that spot until you can sing the F♯ perfectly before moving on.

Over the River and Through the Woods (page 139)

"Over the River and Through the Woods" first appeared in 1884 as a poem written by Lydia Maria Child, a novelist and teacher. In the poem, Child reflects on visiting her grandfather's house for Thanksgiving, but the song is now just as often sung by children at Christmas time.

Shown here in the key of C, "Over the River and Through the Woods" is in 6/8 time and should be played and sung with a feeling of two beats per measure. If this presents any problems for you, start by counting the piece with a regular 6/8 feel, six beats per measure. Then, after you're comfortable with the rhythms, remove those "extra" beats, tapping your foot perhaps, on just the first and fourth eighth note of each bar. Also, when you're playing the piece, try to kind of bounce along — think of the movement made by a horse-drawn sleigh — to get the jolly, energetic feel this tune requires.

Peter Cottontail (page 140)

"Peter Cottontail" was written by the team of Steve Nelson and Jack Rollins — the same songwriters who brought you "Frosty the Snow Man," "Here Comes Santa Claus," and "Rudolph the Red-Nosed Reindeer." Although "Peter Cottontail" was originally written as an Easter song, Nelson and Rollins later retooled the song with some year-round lyrics; both versions are shown in the arrangement here.

Be sure to play "Peter Cottontail," appearing here in the key of C major, with a light and playful touch. Actually try to capture the feel of a rabbit hopping down a trail when you're working on the song. A notational explanation: In bar 1, the text *L.H.* indicates that the down stemmed treble clef notes should be played by the left hand until (in bar 2) a slanted line directs you to the bass clef.

Puff the Magic Dragon (page 148)

One of the most beloved of all folk songs, "Puff the Magic Dragon" was first recorded by Peter, Paul, and Mary in 1962. Although considered by many to be about an illicit substance enjoyed by certain adults, the song, which was based on a poem written by a 19-year-old college student named Lenny Lipton, is actually about a loss of childhood innocence.

Although "Puff the Magic Dragon," shown here in A major, sounds pretty good on the piano, it begs to be played on guitar. If you've got a six-string, follow the chord frames and try strumming a basic rhythm in each bar. Better yet, try playing the chords as arpeggios, as did Peter Yarrow and Paul Stookey, picking the individual notes with your fingers and letting them ring together.

The Rainbow Connection (page 143)

"The Rainbow Connection" was first heard in the opening credits of the *The Muppet Movie* (1979), as sung by Kermit the Frog (Jim Henson). Reaching #25 on the *Billboard Hot 100* in November 1979, the song became the only hit ever by an amphibian, and an ever-popular inspirational song for children.

In the original recording of "The Rainbow Connection," which kicks off here in the key of A major, Kermit the Frog accompanies himself on the banjo. So, when you play this arrangement's bass clef chords, think of that instrument and try to get a banjo-like sound, kind of chunky and without a lot of sustain. Note that at the end of the third page the song modulates up a half step, to B♭ major. Learn the B♭ section separately if needed.

Row, Row, Row Your Boat (page 152)

"Row, Row, Row Your Boat" is the quintessential children's song. It was first published in English in 1852, but with a melody that was quite different from the one we know today, first recorded in 1881. The song's deceptively simple lyrics can be taken literally by children or figuratively by adults, as a metaphor for the difficult choices one makes in life.

Although not shown in the notation, "Row, Row, Row Your Boat" is often sung as a round. If you'd like to try this at home, you'll need at least two singers. Here's how it works: The first person will sing the first line alone. After that, the first singer will continue into the second line and beyond while the second singer starts the first line. Repeat the entire song as desired, with the first singer always a line ahead of the second. Then, the song will end like it began, but with the second person singing the final line alone.

Sesame Street Theme (page 154)

Since 1969, "Sesame Street Theme" has been heard at the beginning of the show. The hip original recording featured the jazz harmonica great Toots Thielemans jamming along with a mixed children's choir. Through several other arrangements, including a calypso setting, "Sesame Street Theme" has become not just a beloved children's song, but one of the most memorable themes in the history of television.

"Sesame Street Theme" is in the key of C, but because the melody makes extensive use of the note B♭, it appears in the key signature. To play the truncated version heard at the beginning of the show, run through the music through bar 16, then go back to the repeat sign at bar 5. Play the music through bar 15, and end the song by repeating bars 14–15 as desired (without the tie on the C). One thing to note: If it seems like you've heard the music in bars 5-16 somewhere else, it's because they're based on the classic 12-bar blues form.

Sing (page 160)

"Sing" is another great song from *Sesame Street,* sung by human cast members (and sometimes, special celebrity guests) along with Muppets. The song became an easy listening and pop hit through early 1970s recorded by Barbra Streisand and the Carpenters. It is now one of the most played songs on *Sesame Street.*

"Sing" is written here in the key of B♭ major. At the beginning of the song, the indication *With pedal* calls for you to use the rightmost pedal, the sustain pedal, with your right foot. As you've probably noticed, this pedal allows for all the notes on the piano to sustain after the keys have been lifted. In playing "Sing," don't keep the pedal depressed throughout. Instead, experiment with holding the pedal for a vocal phrase or so at a time, so that only the desired notes ring together.

Splish Splash (page 157)

"Splish Splash" is a late 1950s tune recorded and co-written by the popular singer Bobby Darin. This fun song, which references characters from other songs of the era, like "Peggy Sue" and "Golly Miss Molly," became one of Darin's greatest hits, as well as one of the all-time classic rock songs.

Play "Splish Splash," shown here in the key of B♭, with a moderate but driving beat. Remember, it's a rock song. The song's melody is simple but expressive due to the occasional use of a *blue note,* the flatted third, D♭. This simple alteration makes everything sound down and dirty; try singing the melody with a D♮ instead to hear the difference. Note that the blue note D♭ is also part of one of the song's chords, E♭9 (E♭-G-B♭-D♭-F).

SpongeBob SquarePants Theme Song (page 164)

Created by the marine biologist and animator Stephen Hillenburg, *SpongeBob SquarePants* is a children's television series that centers around the underwater exploits of the goofy main protagonist, a sea sponge who's employed as a fry cook. Following the show's 1999 debut, its nautical-sounding theme song quickly became very popular with children — and *some* of their parents.

"SpongeBob SquarePants Theme Song," depicted here in the key of G major, makes excellent use of a style known as *call and response.* In this technique, long heard in African musical cultures and later appropriated by blues, R&B, and rock musicians, a leader sings a line and a group replies. In our theme song, the leader, Painty the Pirate, sings lines and the kids respond by shouting in unison, indicated here with X-shaped noteheads.

Supercalifragilisticexpialidocious (page 166)

"Supercalifragilisticexpialidocious" is a word that Richard and Robert Sherman invented when they were writing the music for the Walt Disney film *Mary Poppins.* The word, according to the movie, is to be used when one "has nothing to say." The brothers Sherman, though, had plenty to say in their song of the same name, which became an instant children's classic.

Take "Supercalifragilisticexpialidocious" at a bright and lively tempo. To make the most of this arrangement, you might try incorporating details from the original, sung by Julie Andrews and Dick Van Dyke, that aren't in the notation. In the first verse, for instance, see if you can imitate the way Andrews half sings and half speaks some of the phrases. Also, the original version starts a step lower than written here and modulates up a half step, to B major, in the third verse and another half step, to C, in the following verse, so you might try transposing the sheet music to those other keys.

Take Me Out to the Ball Game (page 171)

Neither the lyricist Jack Norworth nor the composer Albert Von Tilzer had any interest in baseball and had in fact never even attended a game when they wrote "Take Me Out to the Ball Game" in 1908. Yet, the song became a smash hit that year and went on to become the unofficial anthem of baseball, often song during the seventh-inning stretch of a game.

It should be fairly easy for you to play this arrangement of "Take Me Out to the Ball Game, written in B♭ major. So, for fun you might try inventing your own version, as you might've done with "Old MacDonald." For some ideas, check out any of the great interpretations that have been recorded throughout the years — everything from the bluesy version sung by Jerry Lee Lewis in the 1960s to the Yiddish version sung by Mandy Patinkin in the late '90s.

This Land Is Your Land (page 174)

Written by Woody Guthrie in 1940, "This Land Is Your Land" is one of America's best-known folk songs. Although many folks have interpreted the song as patriotic, it was actually a cynical response to Irving Berlin's "God Bless America." Nonetheless, many generations of children have enjoyed singing along to "This Land Is Your Land."

Perhaps more than any other song in this collection, "This Land Is Your Land," shown here in G major, screams for an acoustic guitar accompaniment. The song should be very easy to play; it's only got four chords, all open: C, G, D, and D7. If you decide to tackle the song on guitar, flatpick a single bass note on each beat 1 and 3, and on beats 2 and 4 toss in a pair of eighth-note strums on the upper strings.

Three Little Fishies (Itty Bitty Poo) (page 176)

Saxie Dowell was a jazz/pop bandleader and singer-songwriter from North Carolina who was at his most prolific in the 1930s and 1940s. His most well-known piece is "Three Little Fishies (Itty Bitty Poo)." A catchy song about our finned friends containing novel pronunciation of certain words, it was a big hit back when it was first recorded, in 1939, and is now a children's favorite.

Don't be intimidated by the density of this manuscript of "Three Little Fishes," written in the key of F major. Because the song is highly repetitive, once you've conquered bars 5-12, you'll essentially have learned the entire song. Be sure not to play the piece too stiffly. If you have trouble getting the song to swing, just check out the version recorded in 1939 by Hal Kemp and his orchestra.

Tomorrow (page 178)

Based on a comic strip about a young girl who escapes a vile orphanage on New York's Lower East Side, *Annie* opened on Broadway in 1977. In the musical's signature song, "Tomorrow," Annie strikes an optimistic note in spite of her difficult circumstances. More than 30 years later, the song continues to inspire many children, while grating on the nerves of a few parents.

Don't be intimated by the tricky-looking rhythms in "Tomorrow," shown here in F major. Just take things slow and subdivide. Start by counting, "One-ee-and-uh, two-ee-and-uh, three-ee-and-uh, four-ee-and-uh." In the first bar, the 32nd-note B will fall in between the "ee" and the "and" of "one;" the eighth-note C will fall on the "and;" and the last note of the measure will fall on the "uh" of beat four. If you take the time to break rhythms down in this manner, you'll get to the point where you'll be able to play them automatically on sight, without having to think about how they're divided.

When I'm Sixty-Four (page 182)

Paul McCartney wrote "When I'm Sixty-Four" when he was essentially himself still a child, at the age of 16. Although the song first appeared on 1967's masterpiece recording *Sgt. Pepper's Lonely Hearts Club Band,* the Beatles had been playing it in concert when their amplifiers over-heated for years. And although many in the Beatles' generation weren't big on "When I'm Sixty-Four," it now ranks among their most popular tunes, and is a great children's song, too.

It'd be possible for you to play this C major arrangement of "When I'm Sixty-Four" exactly as written but sound pretty unexpressive. So, before tackling the song you should check out the Beatle's original version, which has got a clarinet trio playing an infectiously swinging accompaniment. When you run through the piano arrangement, try to capture the phrasing you heard on the original, paying close attention to where notes in both the singing and accompaniment are accented and where they're cut off.

Won't You Be My Neighbor? (page 188)

For many years, Fred Rogers would introduce the children's television program *Mister Rogers' Neighborhood* by entering the set, changing into a cardigan, and singing "Won't You Be My Neighbor?" The show ended when Rogers died, in 2001. But the theme song, which pits a sophisticated jazz arrangement against childlike lyrics, remains a television favorite, a song for both adults and children.

At the beginning of "Won't You Be My Neighbor?" you'll notice that this arrangement, written in F major instead of the original key of C, is to be played as a medium *stride.* Stride is an early jazz piano style in which the left hand typically played bass notes on beats 1 and 3 and chords on 2 and 4. If you're unsure as to how stride is supposed to feel and sound, now would be a good time to check out the work of such jazz pioneers as James P. Johnson, Willie "The Lion" Smith, and Fats Waller. And don't forget to swing those eighth notes.

Yellow Submarine (page 190)

In a collection containing pop and rock songs that ended up as children's favorites, The Beatles' "Yellow Submarine" has got a special distinction: Paul McCartney actually initially conceived of this rock song as a children's story. Nonetheless, the song went to #1 on all the British rock charts shortly after its 1966 release.

Although "Yellow Submarine" was originally written in the key of G♭ major, we've arranged it here for you in the much easier key of G. If you're on a guitar and would like to play along with the recording, simply tune your guitar down a half step, to E♭-A♭-D♭-G♭-B♭-E♭, and strum the chords indicated in the notation. The Beatles' studio recording featured a bunch of nautical sound effects, including a submarine voice created by talking into a can, and bubble sounds made by blowing into a straw. This might sound wacky, but for extra fun try recreating these effects yourself — it'd be really entertaining to children.

Zip-A-Dee-Doo-Dah (page 194)

"Zip-A-Dee-Doo-Dah" was first heard in the 1946 Disney feature film *Song of the South.* That same year it won the Academy Award® for Best Original Song. The tune was then featured for many years as part of the opening for *The Wonderful World of Disney* television program. But testament to the song's durability is the stylistically wide array of covers that it has inspired, by everyone from the Jackson Five to Steve Miller.

Shown here in the key of B♭ major, "Zip-A-Dee-Doo-Dah" has a 32-bar AABA song form in which each section is eight bars long. What does that mean for you? It simply means that there's quite a bit less music to learn here than it would appear. After you've gotten down the first A section (bars 1–8), you've essentially tackled 75 percent of the song. Having a structural awareness of a piece makes learning music quicker and easier.

I'm Popeye the Sailor Man

Theme from the Paramount Cartoon POPEYE THE SAILOR
Words and Music by Sammy Lerner

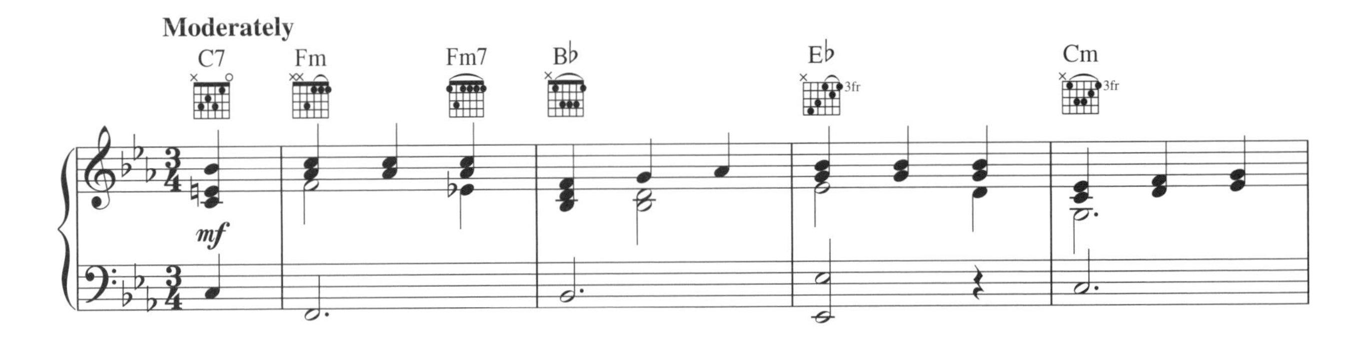

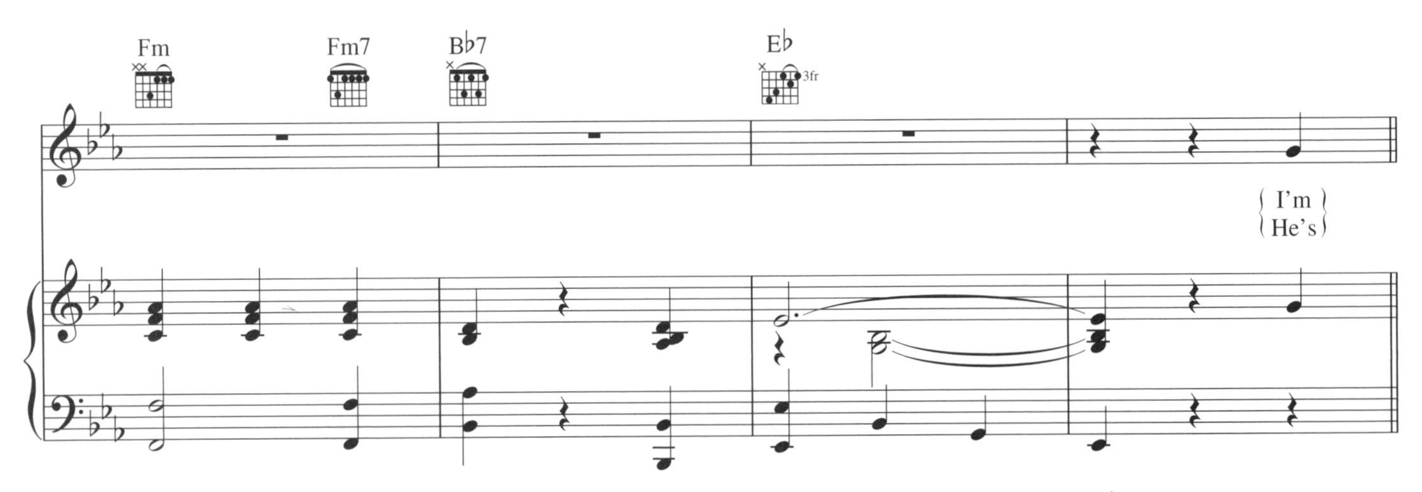

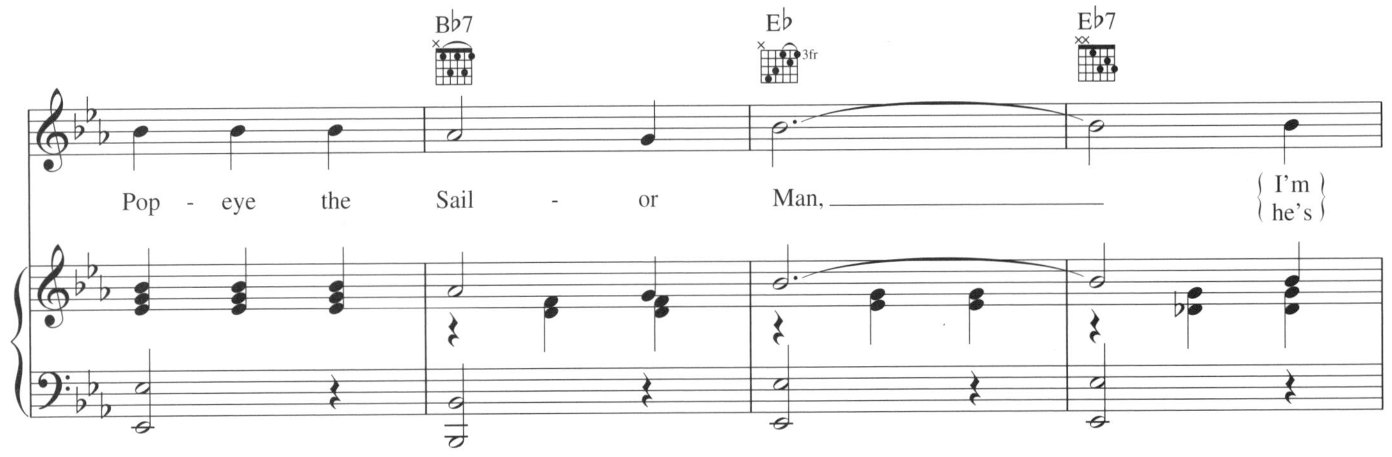

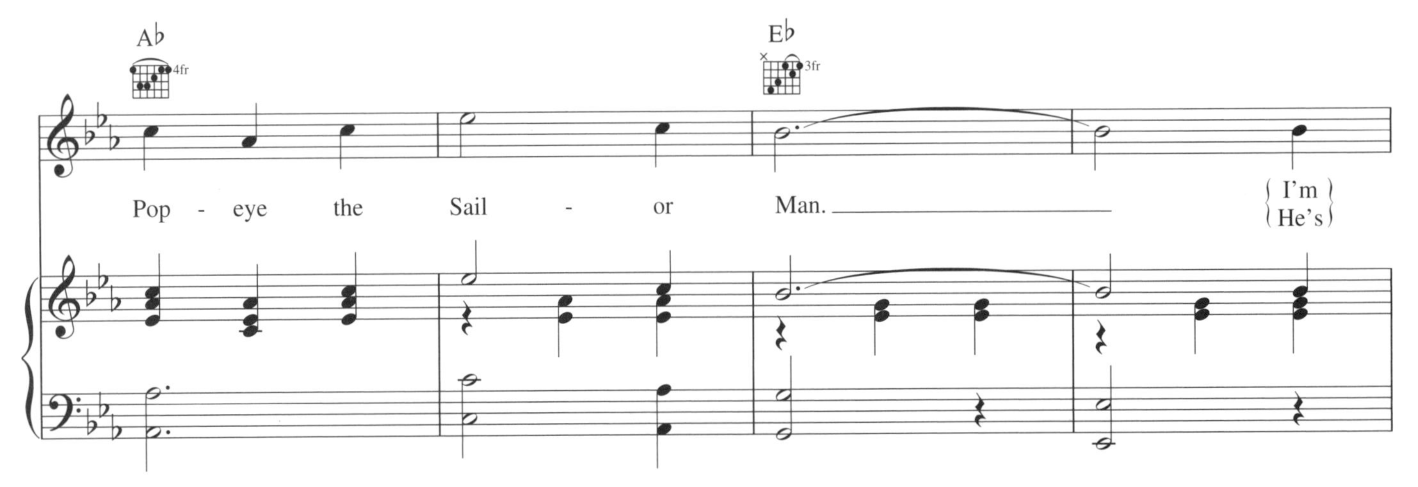

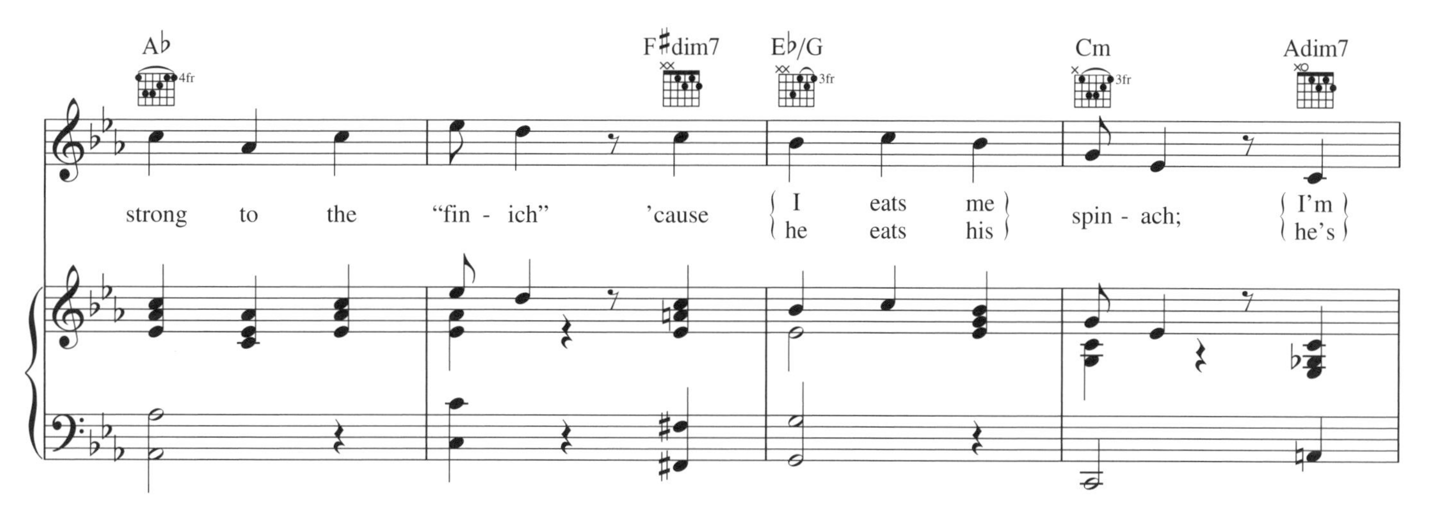
A♭
4fr
F♯dim7
E♭/G
3fr
Cm
3fr
Adim7
strong to the "fin - ich" 'cause
I eats me
he eats his
spin - ach;
I'm
he's

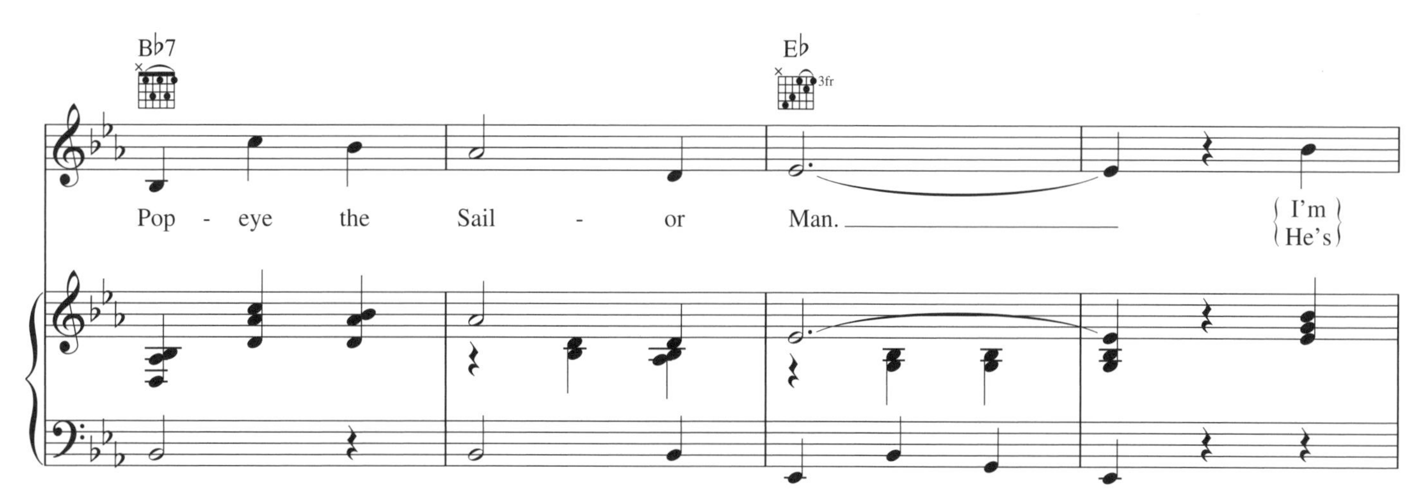
B♭7
E♭
3fr
Pop - eye the Sail - or Man.
I'm
He's

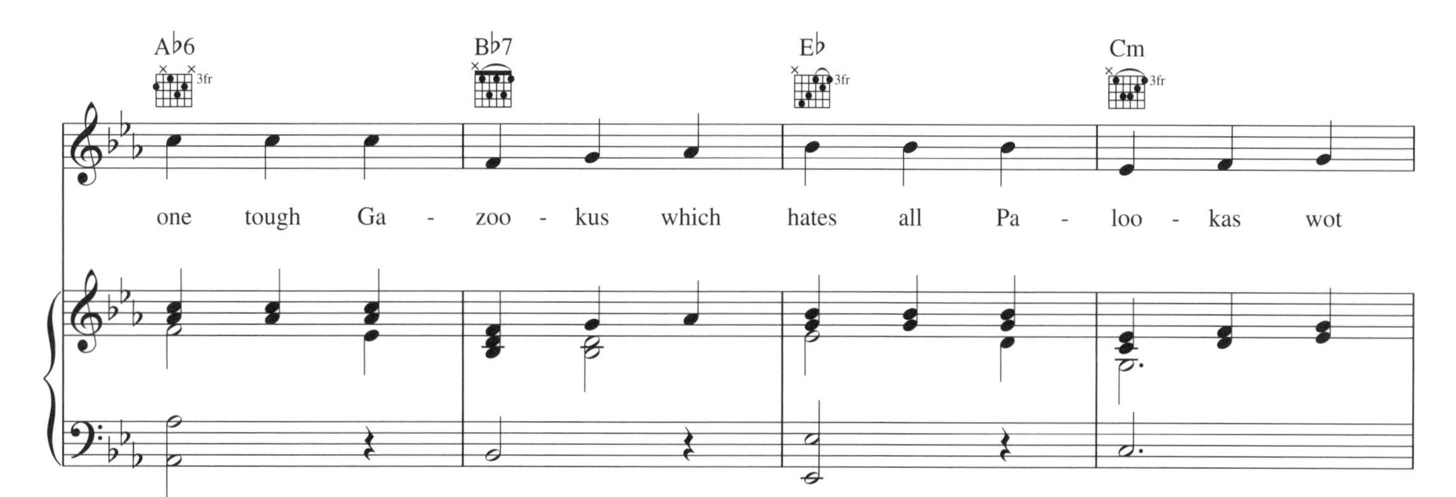
A♭6
3fr
B♭7
E♭
3fr
Cm
3fr
one tough Ga - zoo - kus which hates all Pa - loo - kas wot

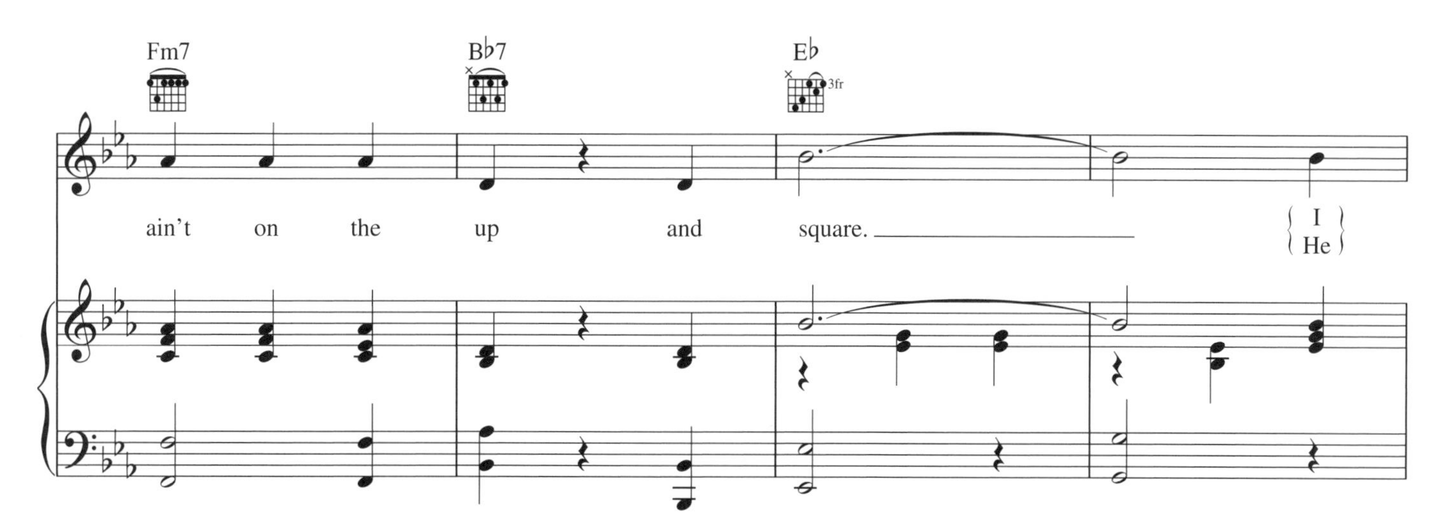
Fm7
B♭7
E♭
3fr
ain't on the up and square.
I
He

A♭6
B♭7
E♭
biffs 'em and buffs 'em an' al - ways out -
Cm
Fm7
B♭7
roughs 'em an' none of 'em gits no -
E♭
A♭
where.
If an - y - one
Fm7
F♯dim7
E♭/G
E♭
dass - es to risk { my his } "fisk" it's

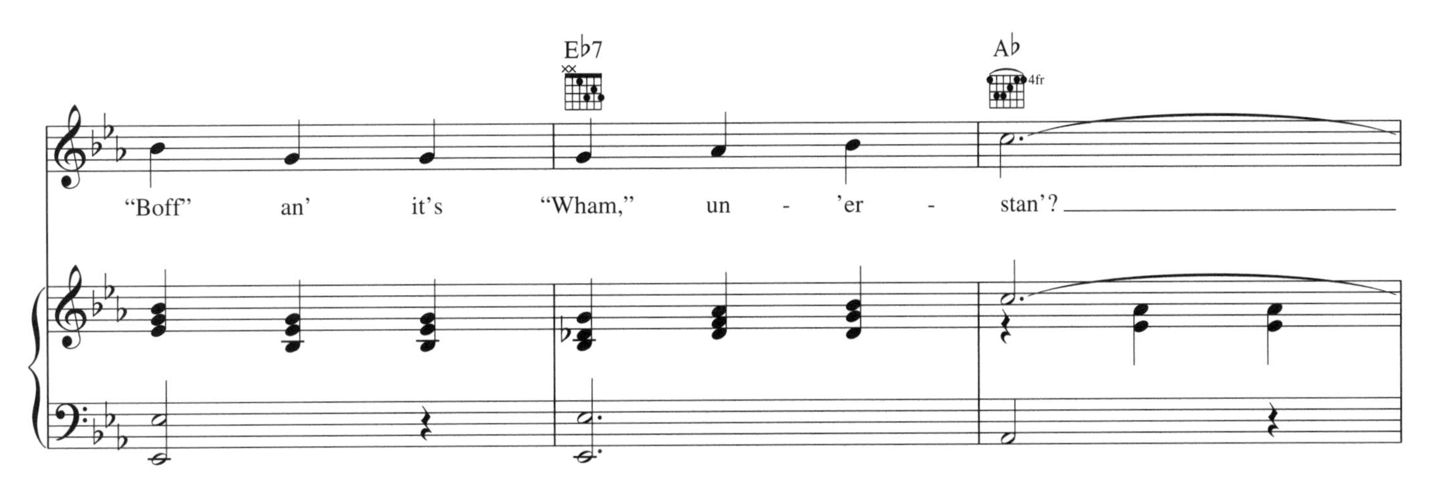
Eb7
Ab
4fr
"Boff" an' it's "Wham," un - 'er - stan'?

C7
Fm
Fm7
Bb7
So, keep "Good Be - hav - 'or," that's

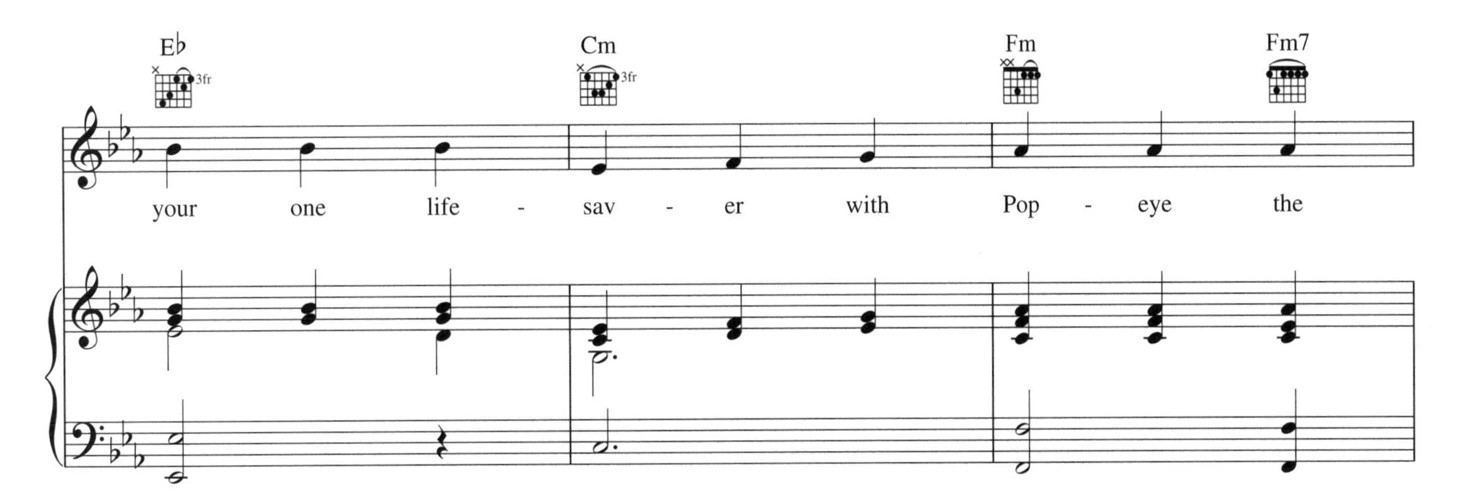
Eb
3fr
Cm
3fr
Fm
Fm7
your one life - sav - er with Pop - eye the

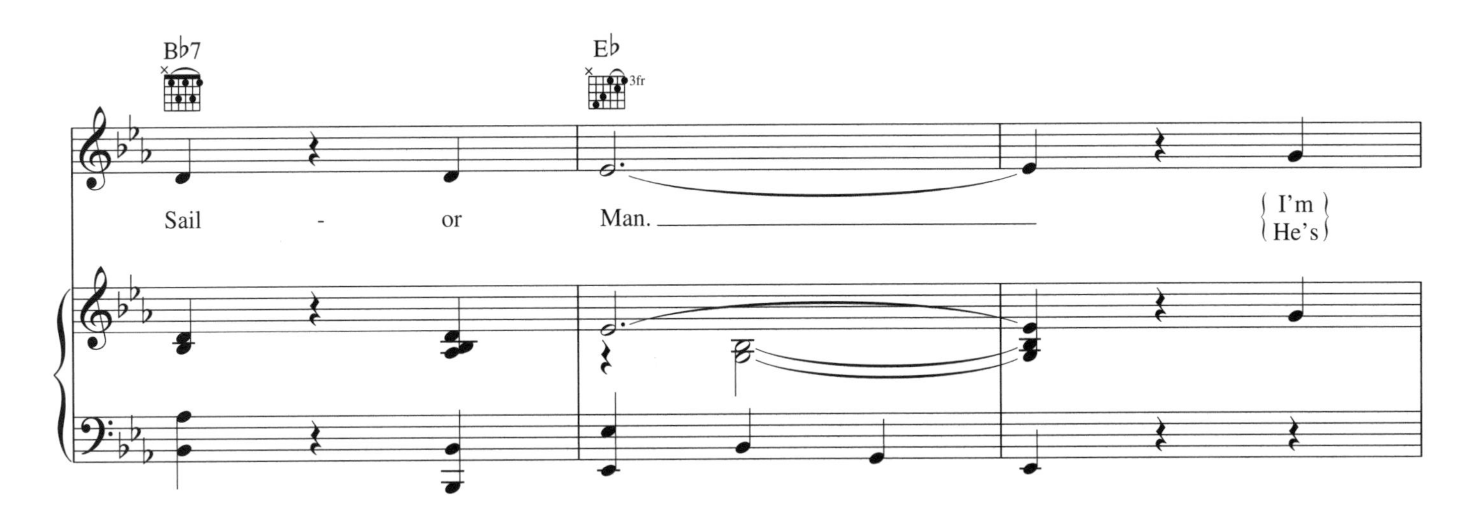
Bb7
Eb
3fr
Sail - or Man.
I'm
He's

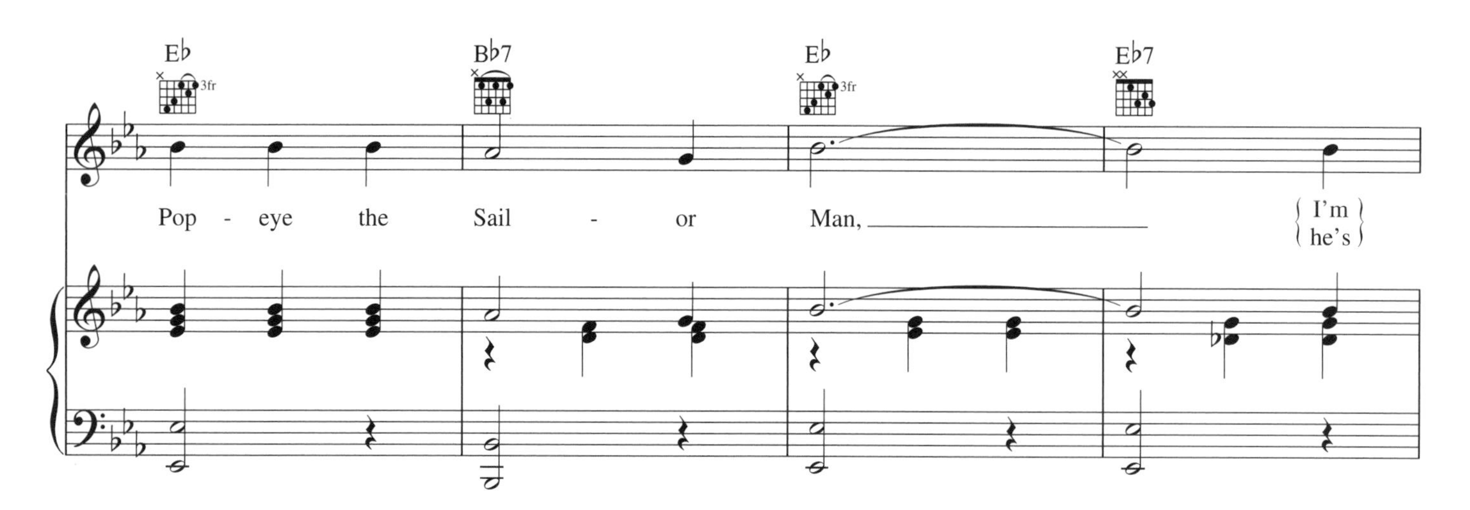
E♭
B♭7
E♭
E♭7
3fr
Pop - eye the Sail - or Man,
I'm
he's

A♭
E♭
4fr
3fr
Pop - eye the Sail - or Man.
I'm
He's

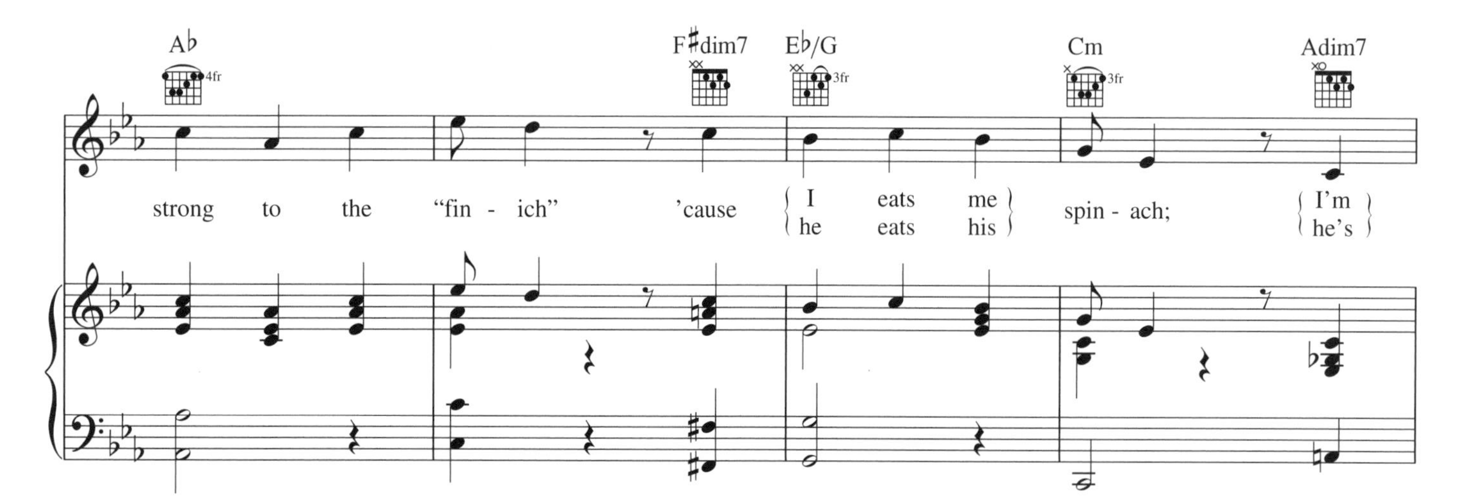
A♭
F♯dim7
E♭/G
Cm
Adim7
4fr
3fr
strong to the "fin - ich" 'cause
I eats me
he eats his
spin - ach;
I'm
he's

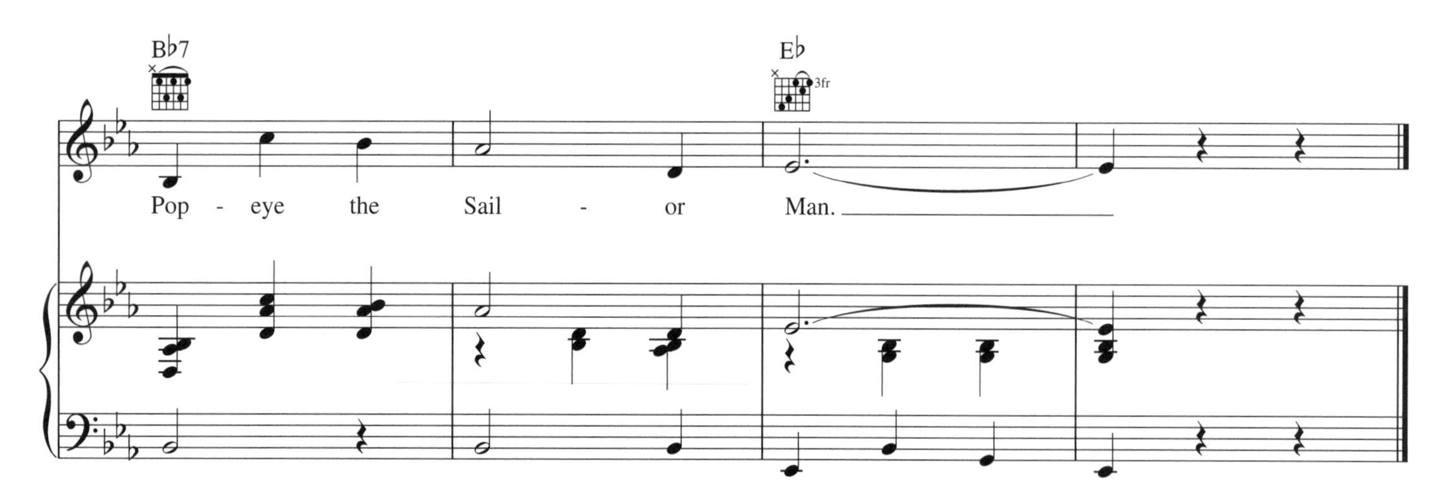
B♭7
E♭
3fr
Pop - eye the Sail - or Man.

It's a Small World

from "it's a small world" at Disneyland Park and Magic Kingdom Park
Words and Music by Richard M. Sherman and Robert B. Sherman

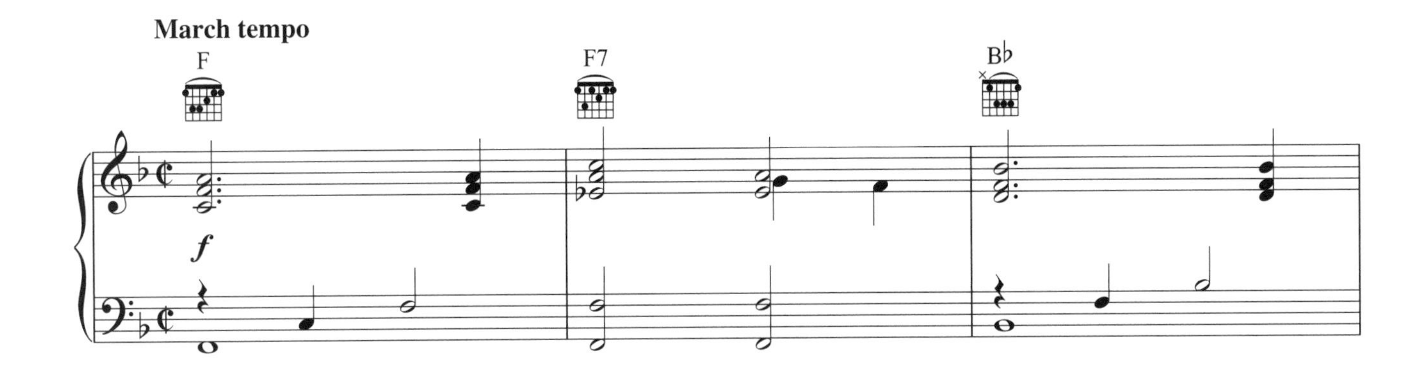

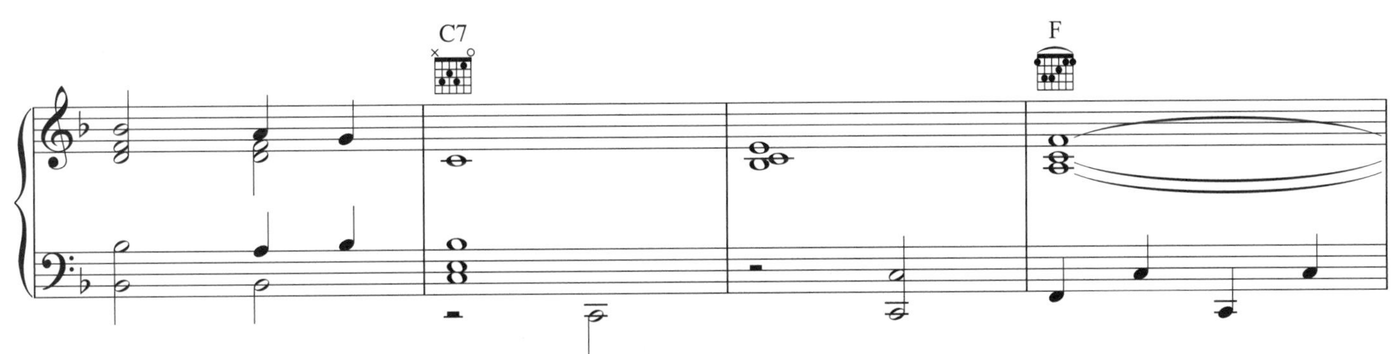

Fdim7
F
world of fears. There's so much that we
ev - 'ry - one. Though the moun - tains di -

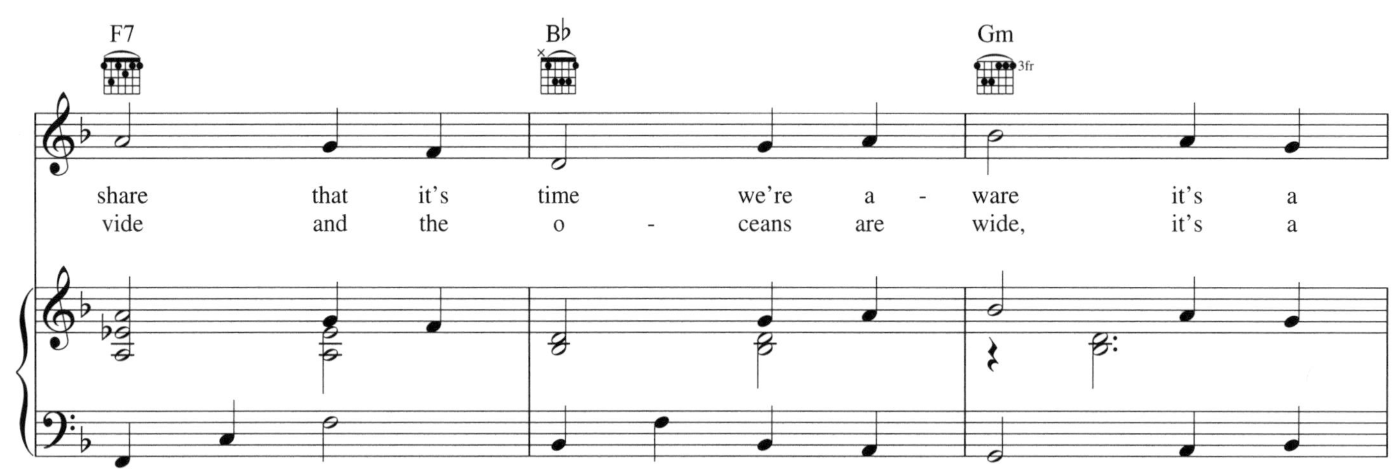
F7
B♭
Gm
3fr
share that it's time we're a - ware it's a
vide and the o - ceans are wide, it's a

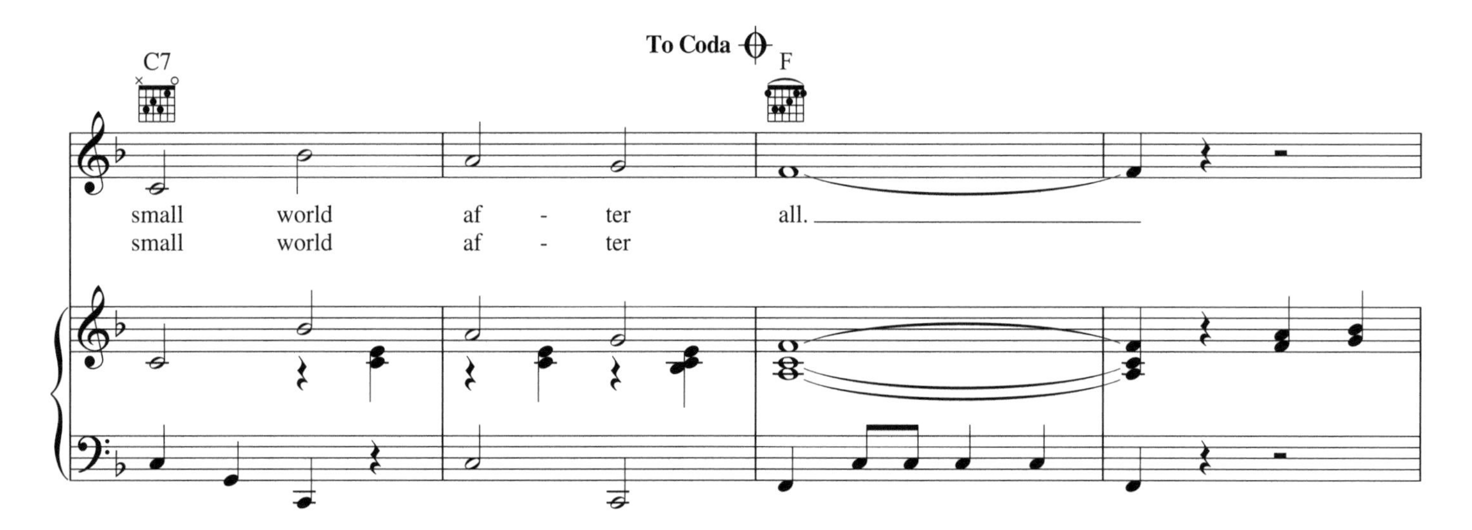
To Coda
C7
F
small world af - ter all.
small world af - ter

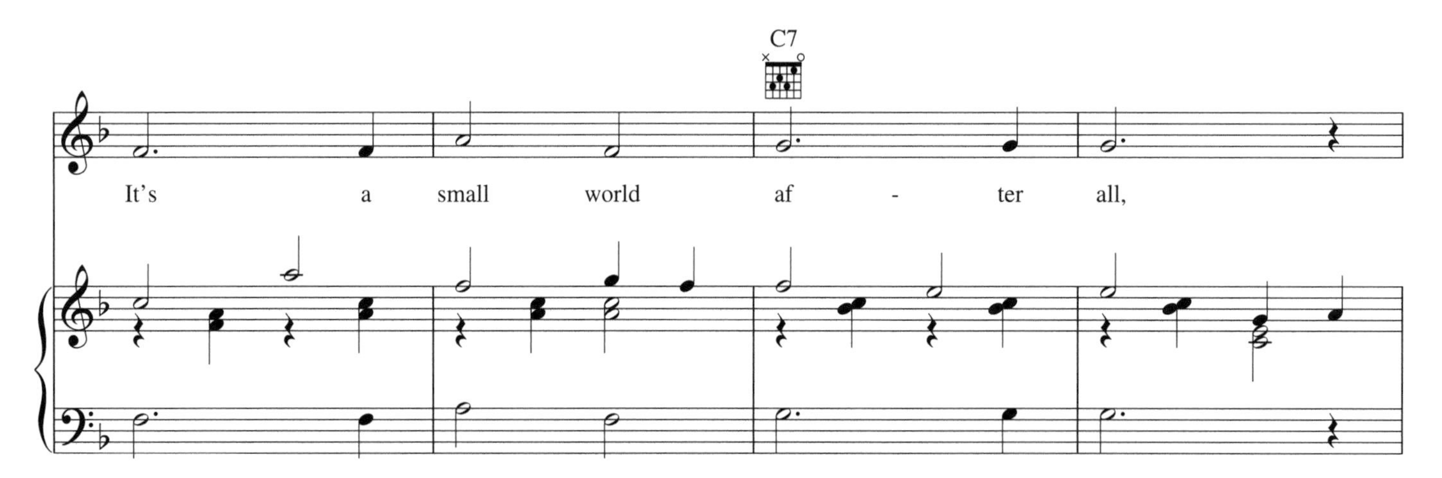
C7
It's a small world af - ter all,

F
it's a small world af - ter

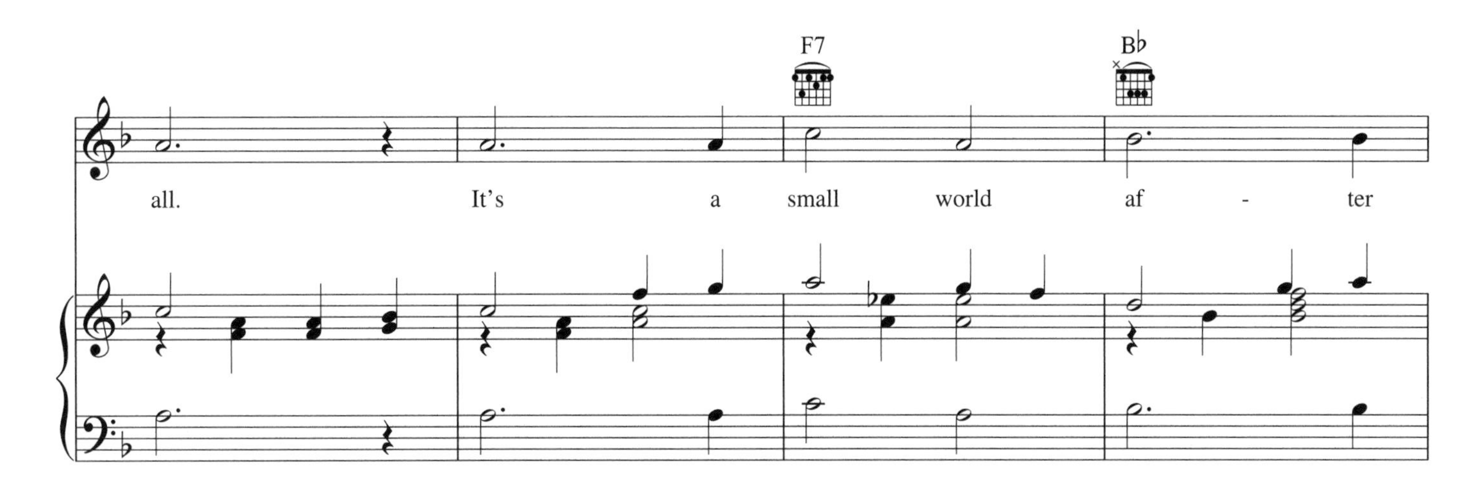
F7
B♭
all. It's a small world af - ter

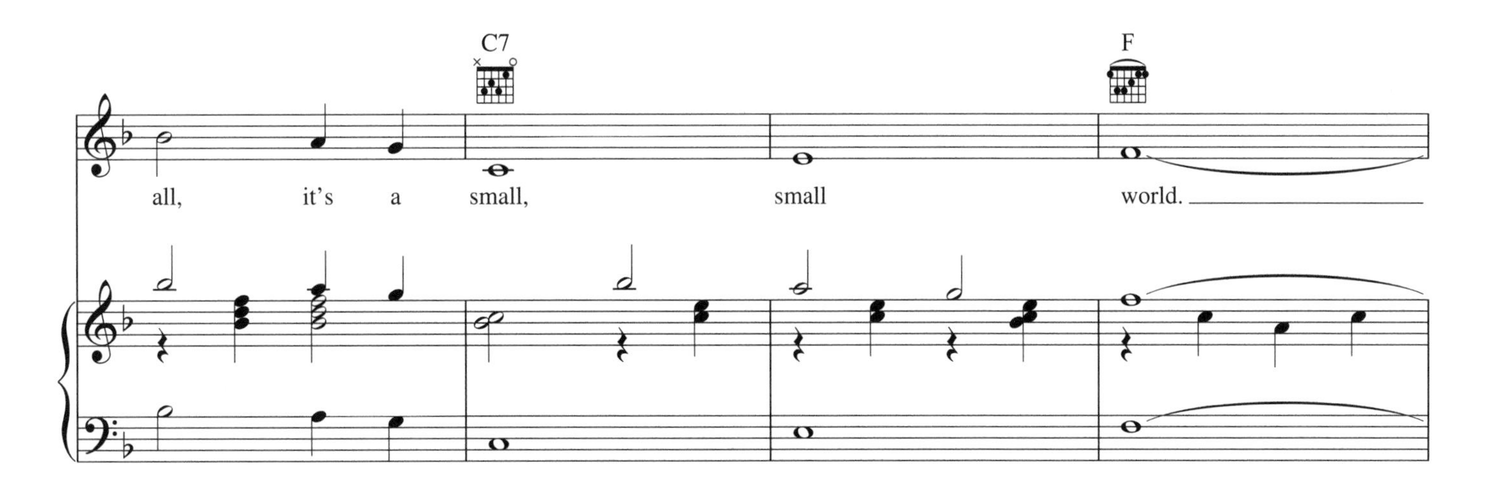
C7
F
all, it's a small, small world.

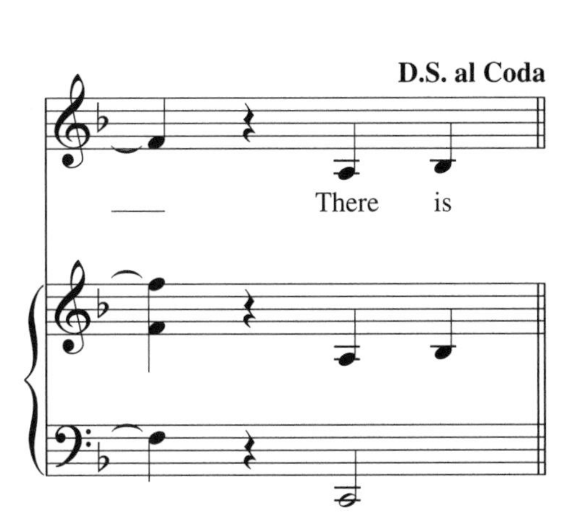
D.S. al Coda
There is

CODA
F
all.

If You're Happy and You Know It

Words and Music by L. Smith

F7
B♭
clap) If you're hap - py and you know it, then your
tap) If you're hap - py and you know it, then your
nod) If you're hap - py and you know it, then your

F
Gm7
C7
face will sure - ly show it. If you're hap - py and you know it, clap your
face will sure - ly show it. If you're hap - py and you know it, tap your
face will sure - ly show it. If you're hap - py and you know it, nod your

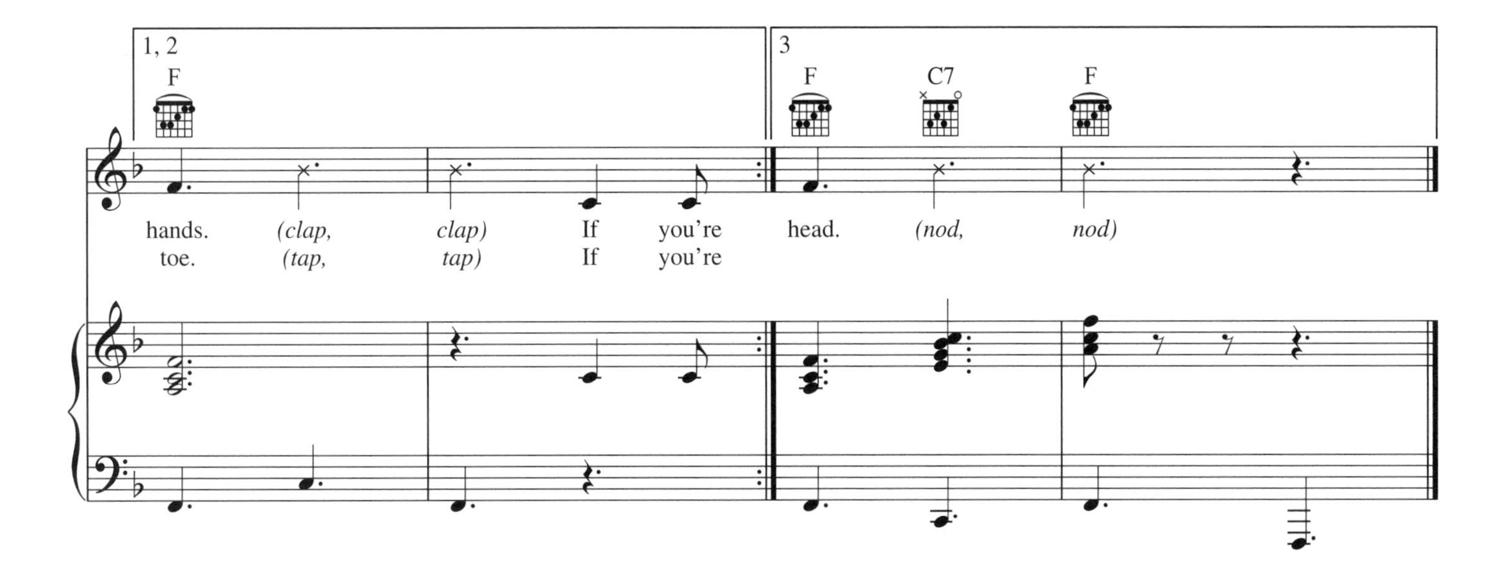
1, 2
F
3
F
C7
F
hands. (clap, clap) If you're head. (nod, nod)
toe. (tap, tap) If you're

Kum Ba Yah

Traditional Spiritual

The Marvelous Toy

Words and Music by Tom Paxton

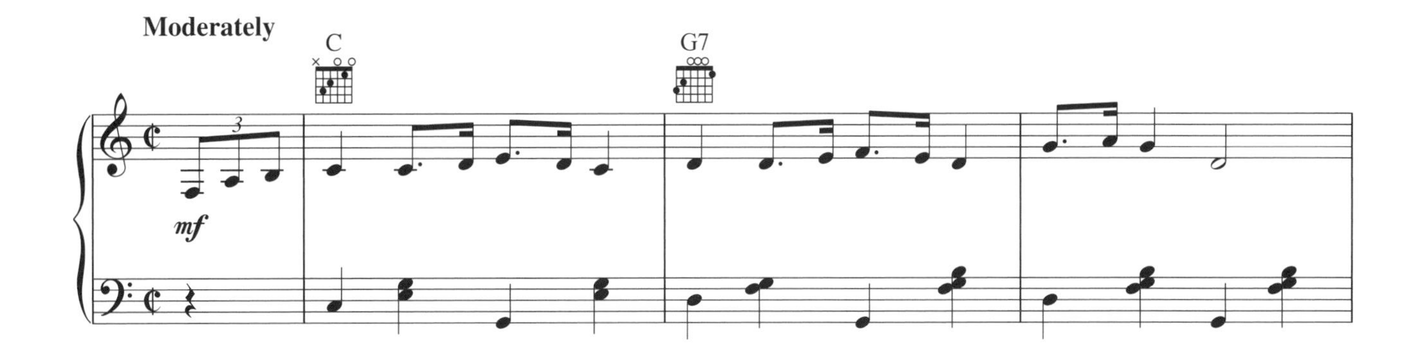

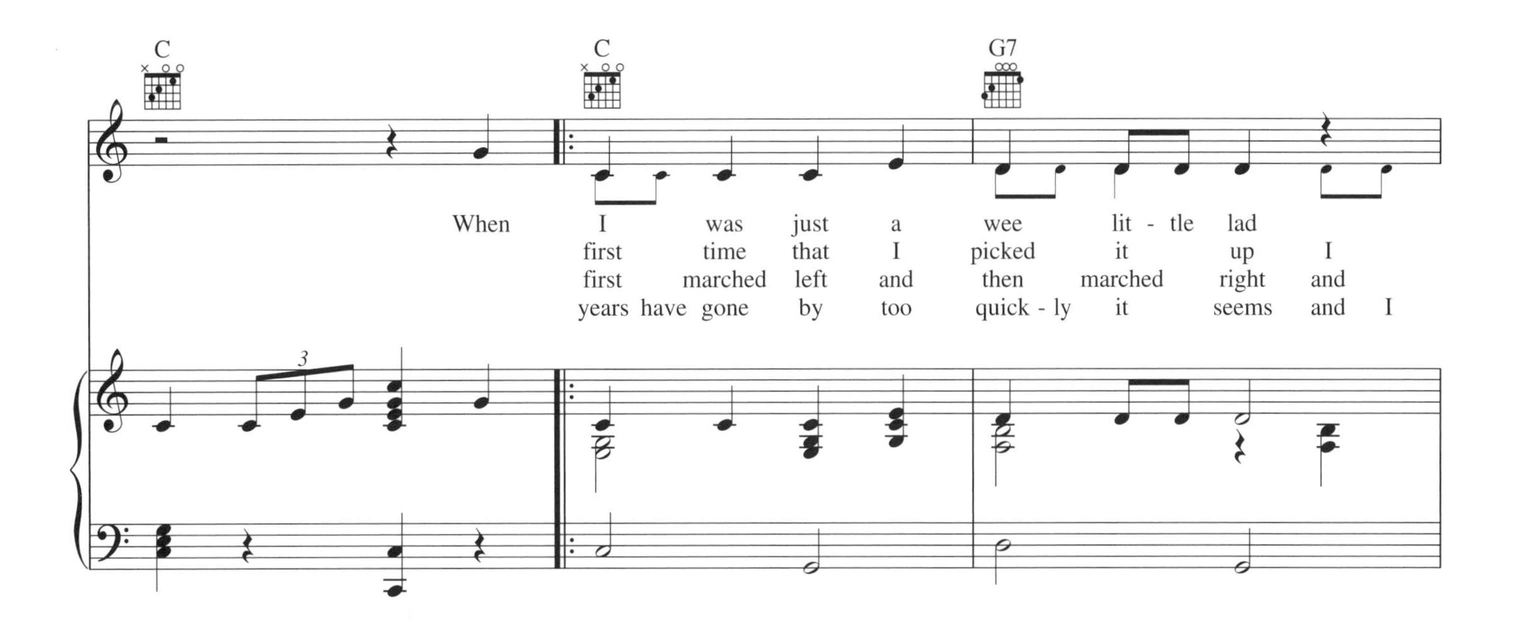

C
D7
G7
came one night, and gave to me a toy. A
two big but-tons that looked like big green eyes. I
it had gone, it was - n't e - ven there! I
gave to him my mar - v'lous lit - tle toy. His

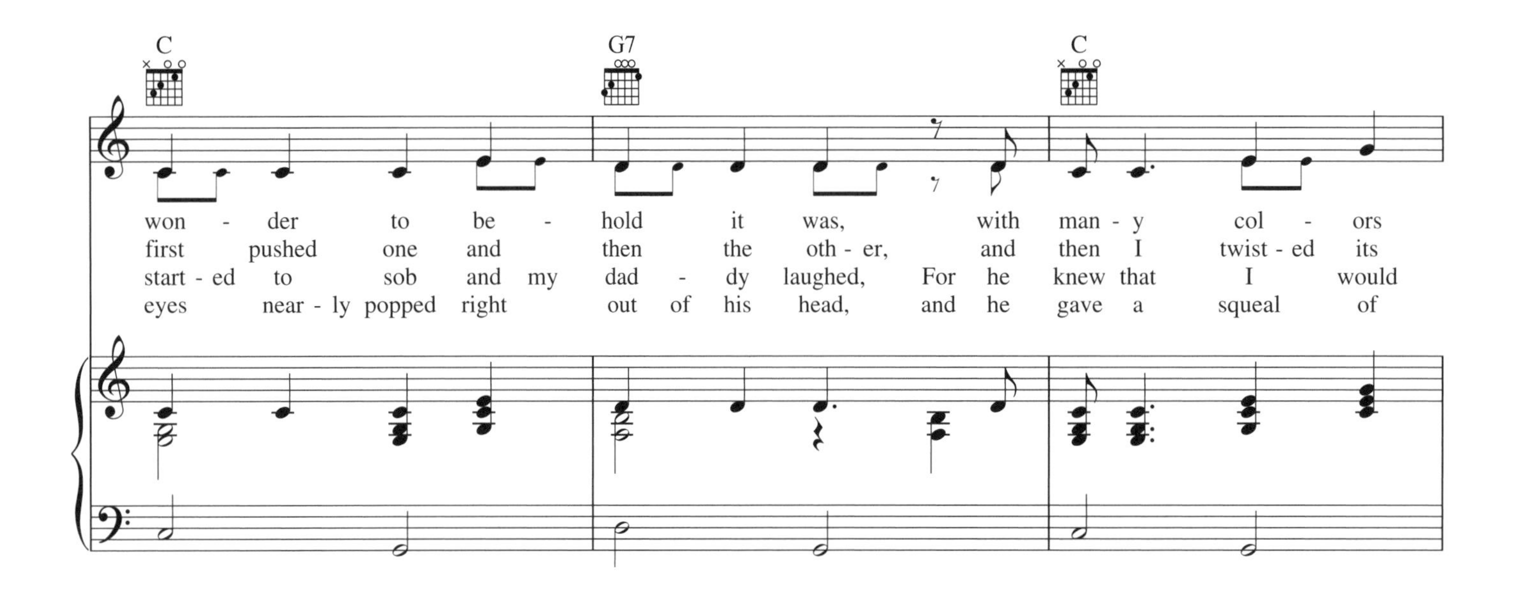
C
G7
C
won - der to be - hold it was, with man - y col - ors
first pushed one and then the oth - er, and then I twist - ed its
start - ed to sob and my dad - dy laughed, For he knew that I would
eyes near - ly popped right out of his head, and he gave a squeal of

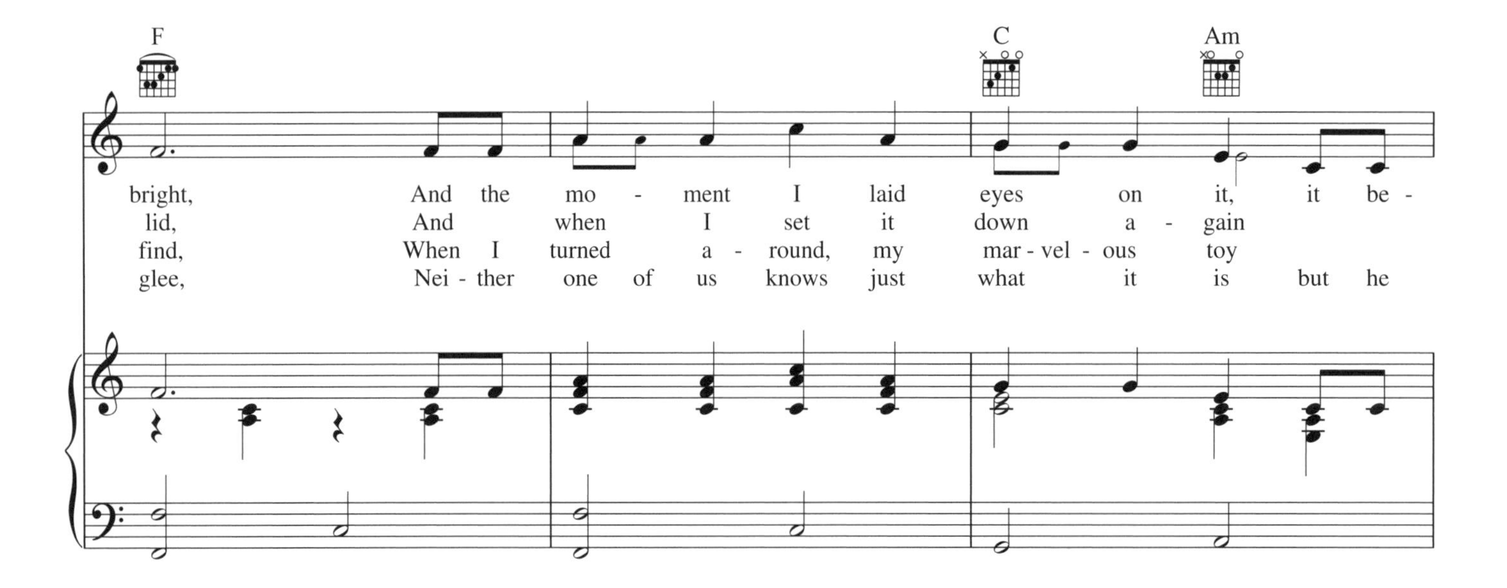
F
C
Am
bright, And the mo - ment I laid eyes on it, it be -
lid, And when I set it down a - gain
find, When I turned a - round, my mar - vel - ous toy
glee, Nei - ther one of us knows just what it is but he

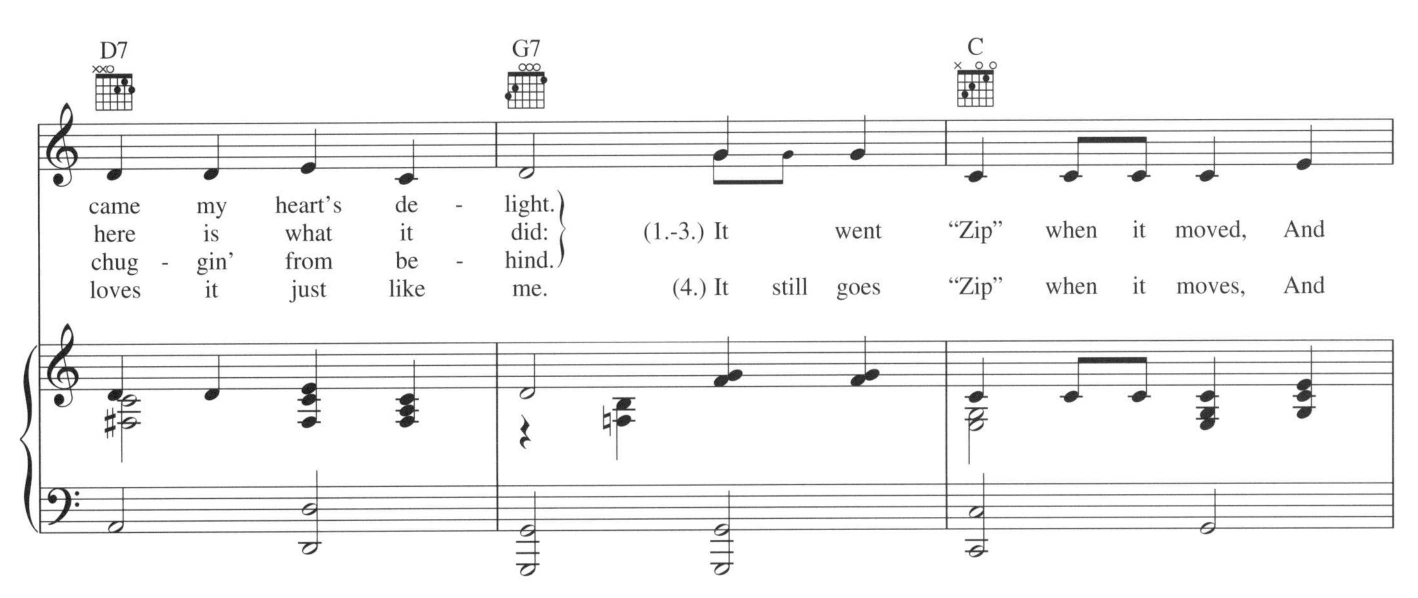
D7
G7
C
came my heart's de - light.
here is what it did:
chug - gin' from be - hind.
loves it just like me.
(1.-3.) It went "Zip" when it moved, And
(4.) It still goes "Zip" when it moves, And

G7
C
F
"Bop" when it stopped, And "Whirr" when it stood still.
"Bop" when it stops, And "Whirr" when it stands still.
I nev - er knew just

C
G7
1–3
C
G7
4
C
what it was and I guess I nev - er will.
The
It
Well, the
will.

G7
C
3

Linus and Lucy

By Vince Guaraldi

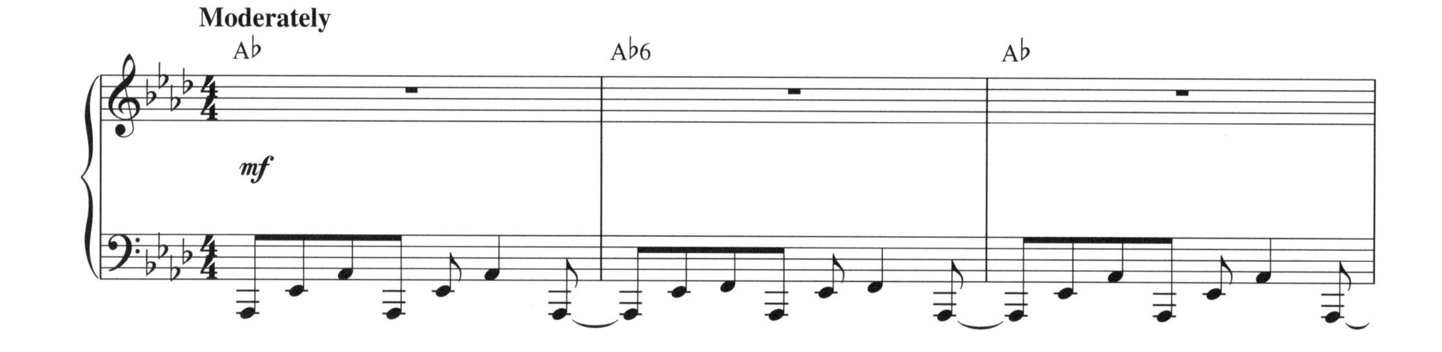

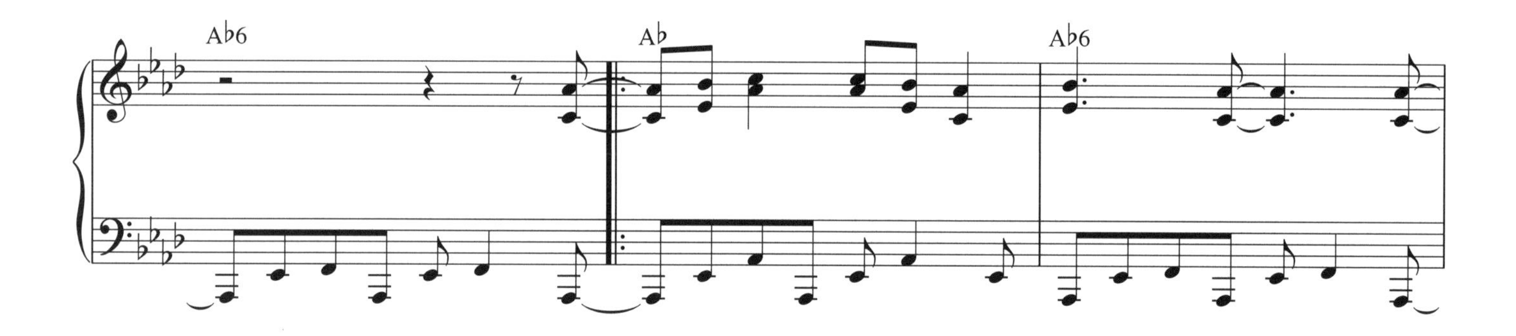

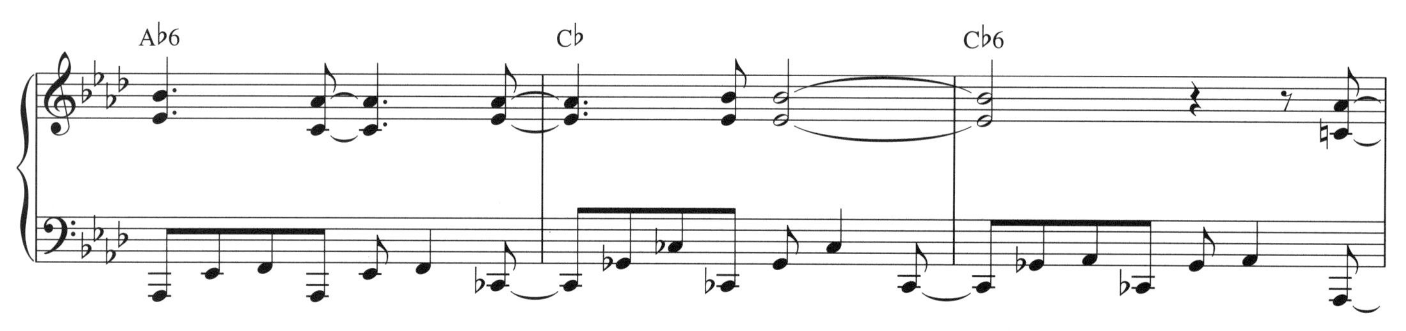

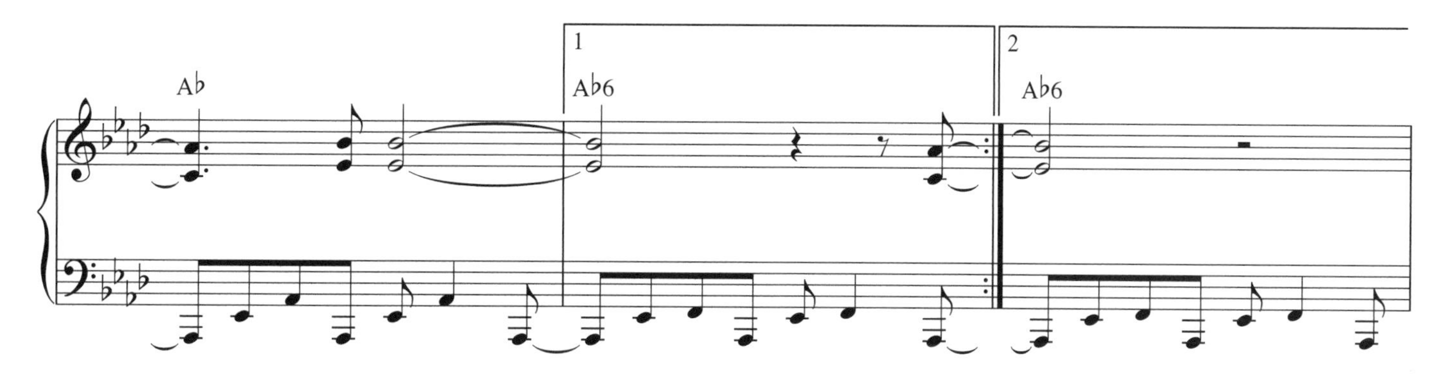
1
2
A♭
A♭6
A♭6

D♭
E♭
D♭
E♭

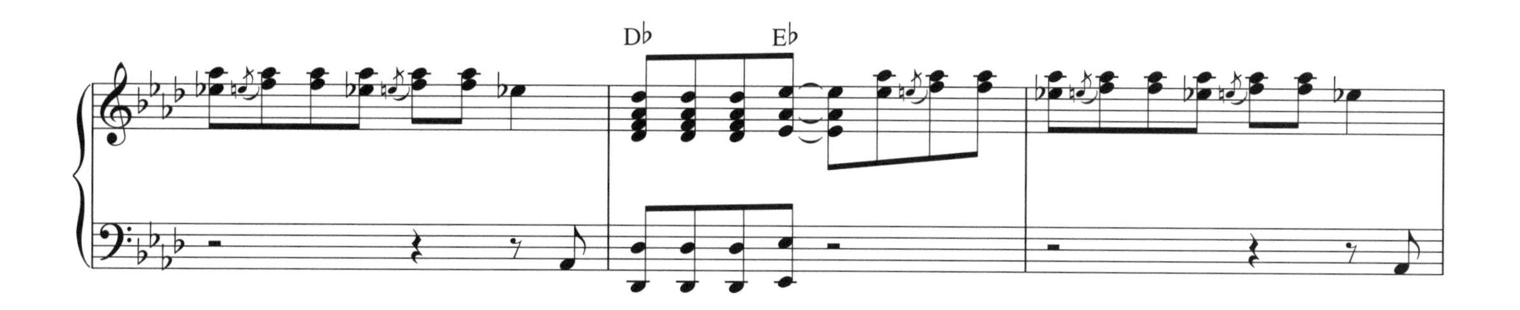
D♭
E♭

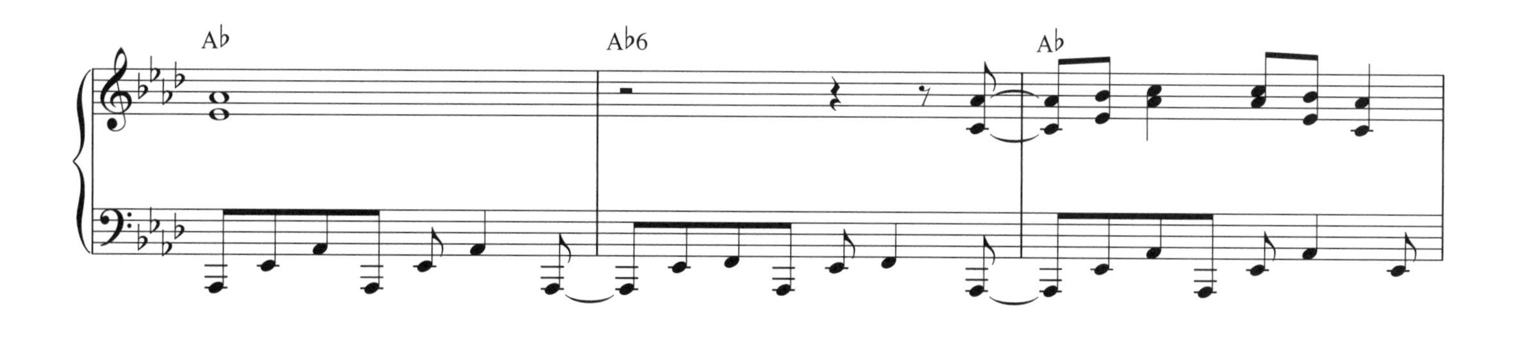
A♭
A♭6
A♭

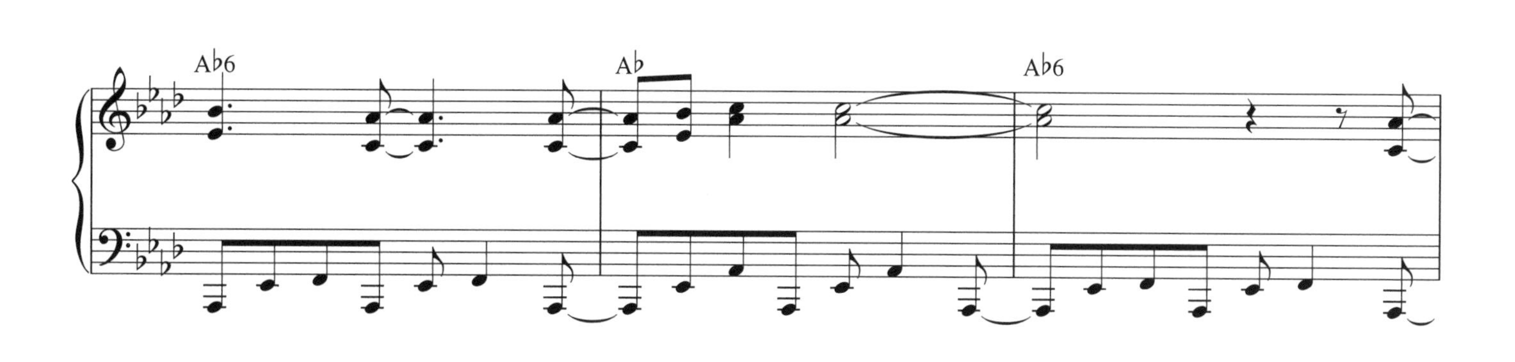
A♭6
A♭
A♭6

A♭
A♭6
C♭

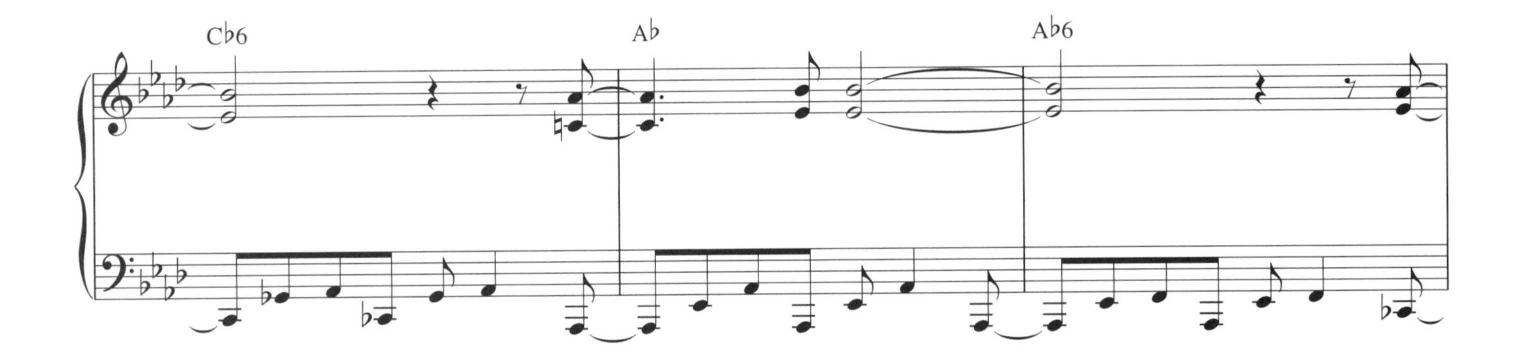
C♭6
A♭
A♭6

C♭
C♭6
A♭

A♭6
Swing feel
E♭7

D♭7

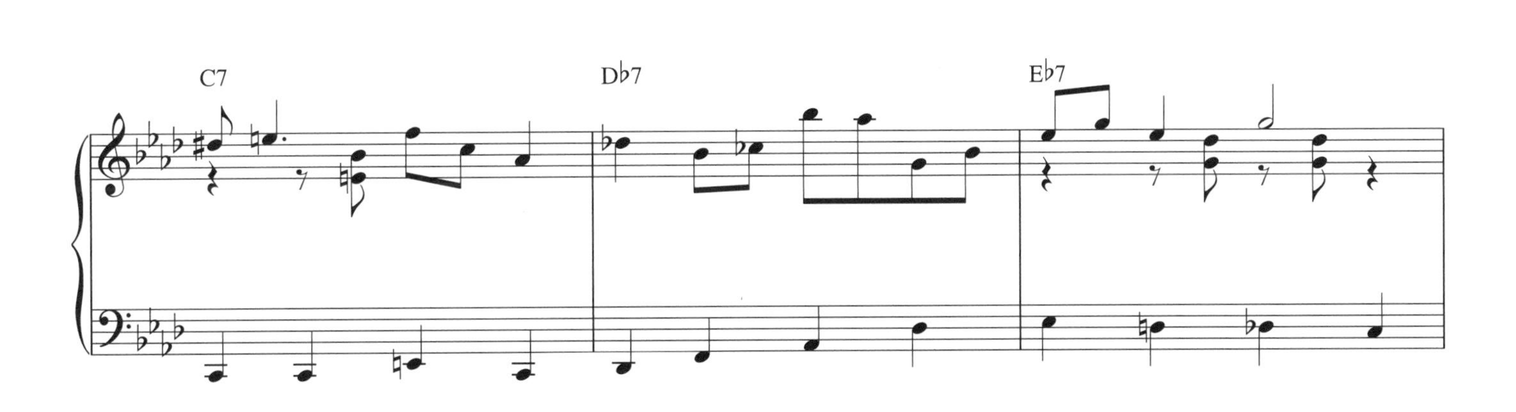
C7
D♭7
E♭7

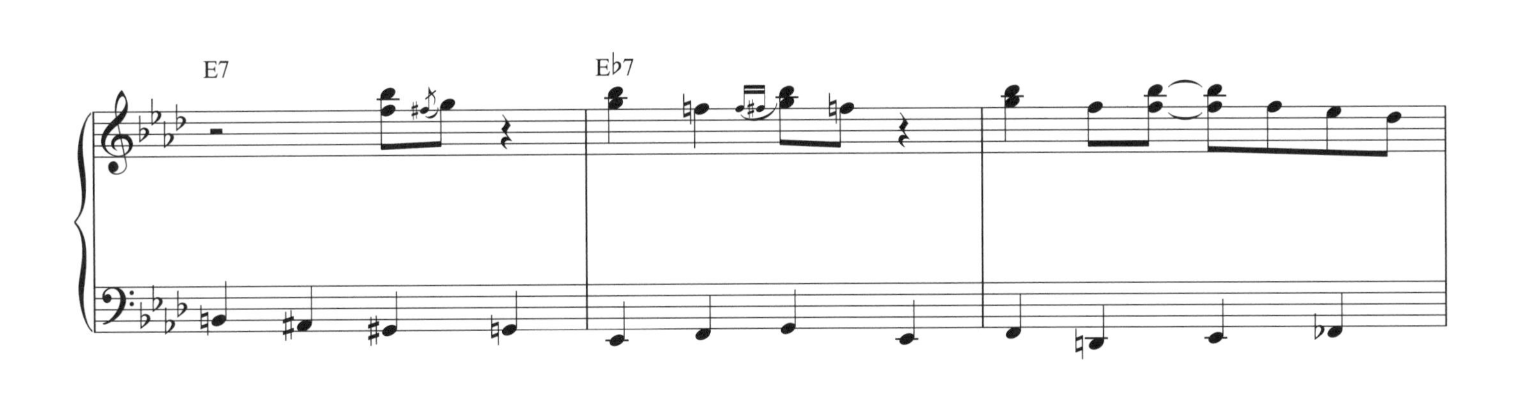
E7
E♭7

D♭7

C7
D♭7
D7

Original Tempo (♩♩ = ♩♩)
E♭7
A♭
A♭6

A♭
A♭6
A♭

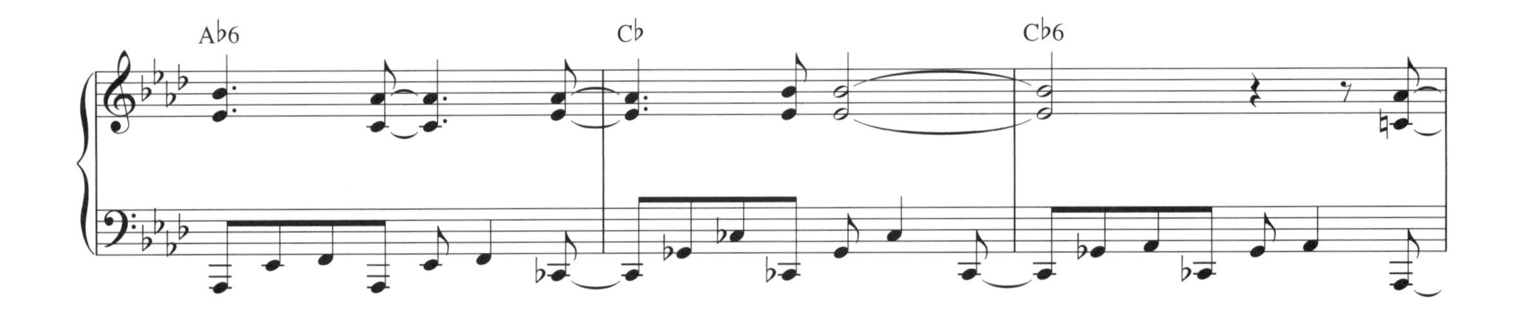
A♭6
C♭
C♭6

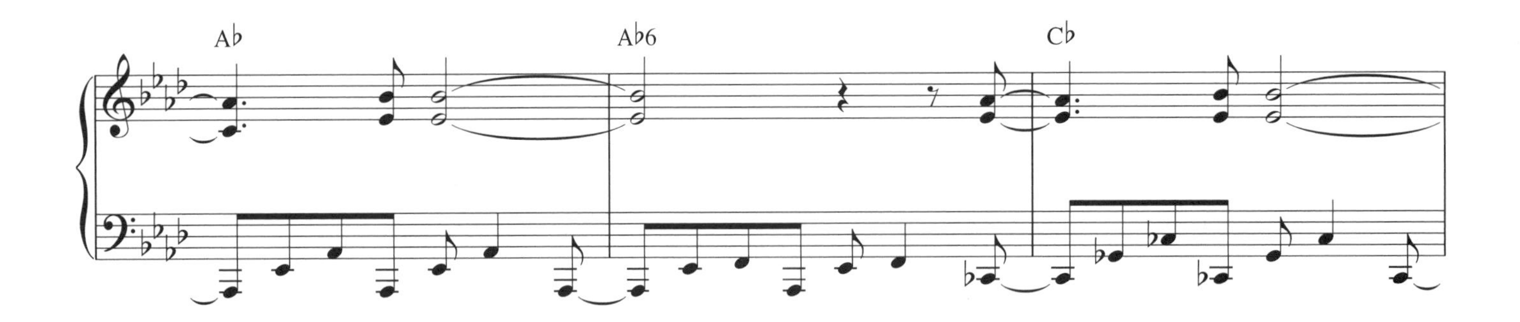
A♭
A♭6
C♭

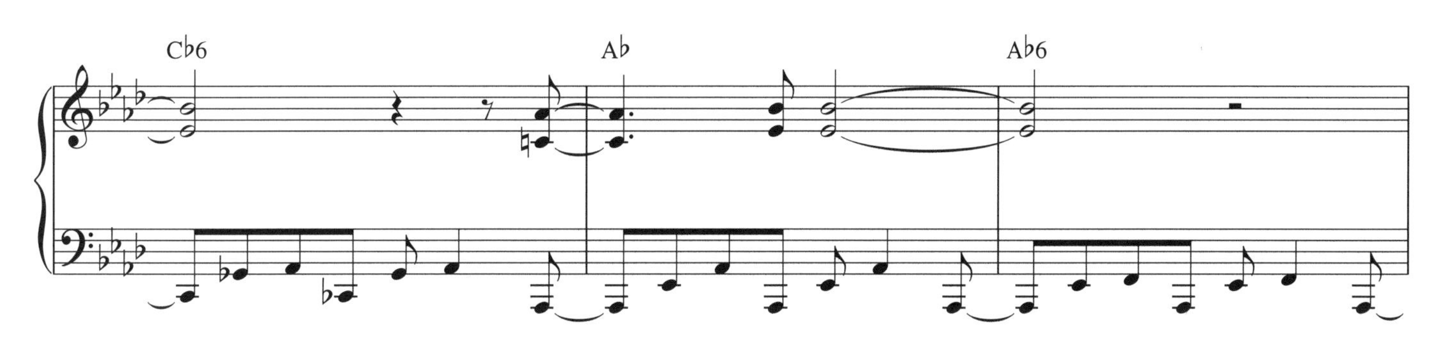
C♭6
A♭
A♭6

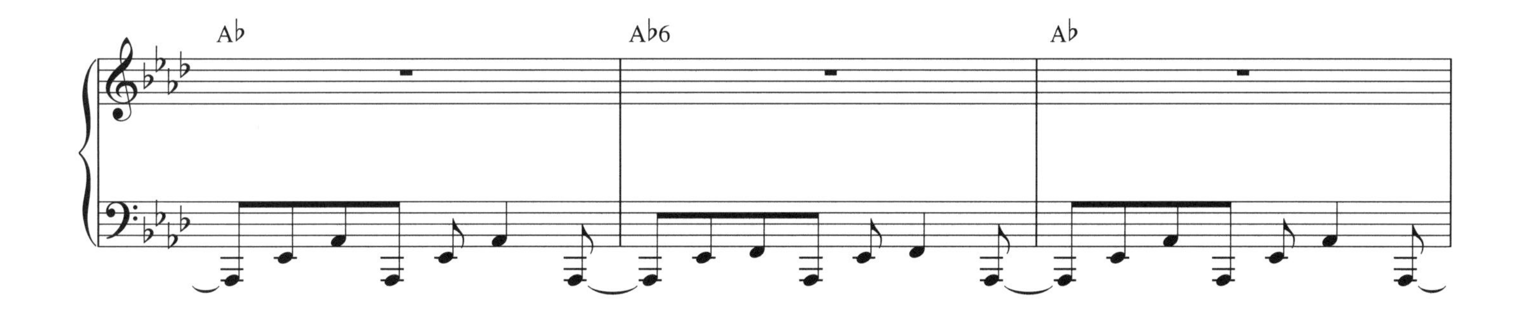
A♭
A♭6
A♭

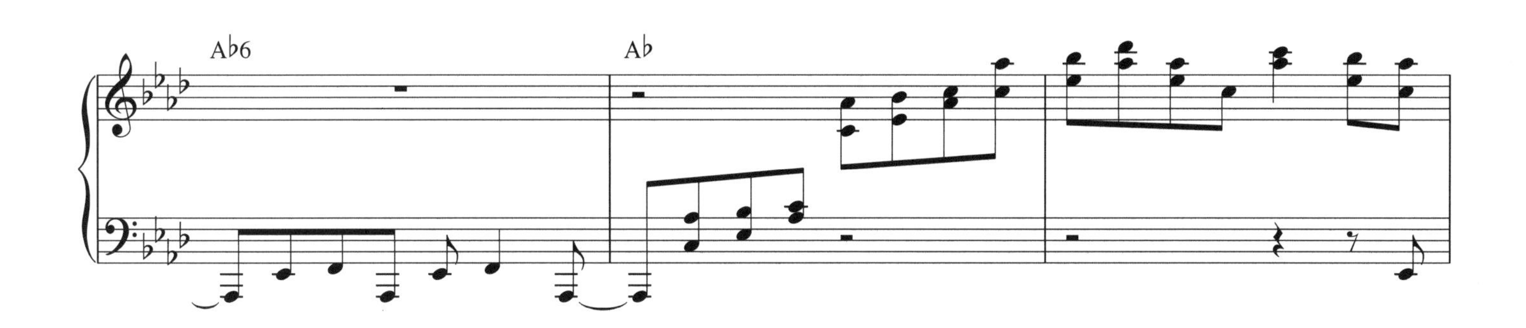
A♭6
A♭

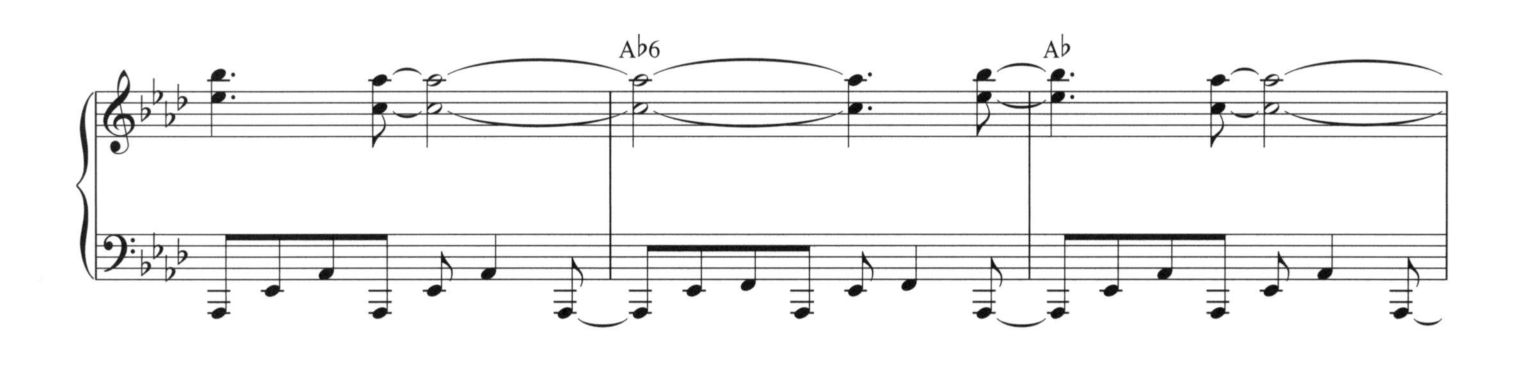
A♭6
A♭

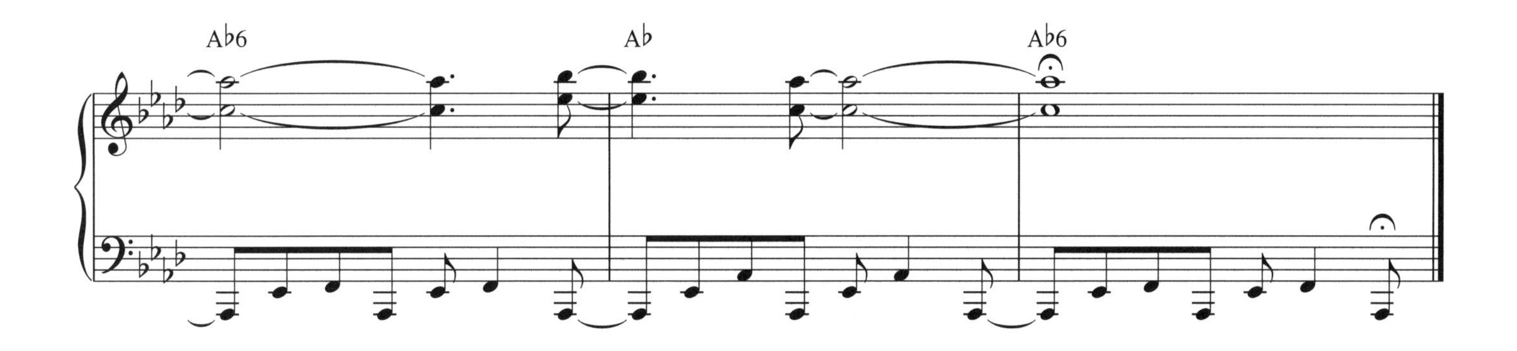
A♭6
A♭
A♭6

Michael Row the Boat Ashore

Traditional Folksong

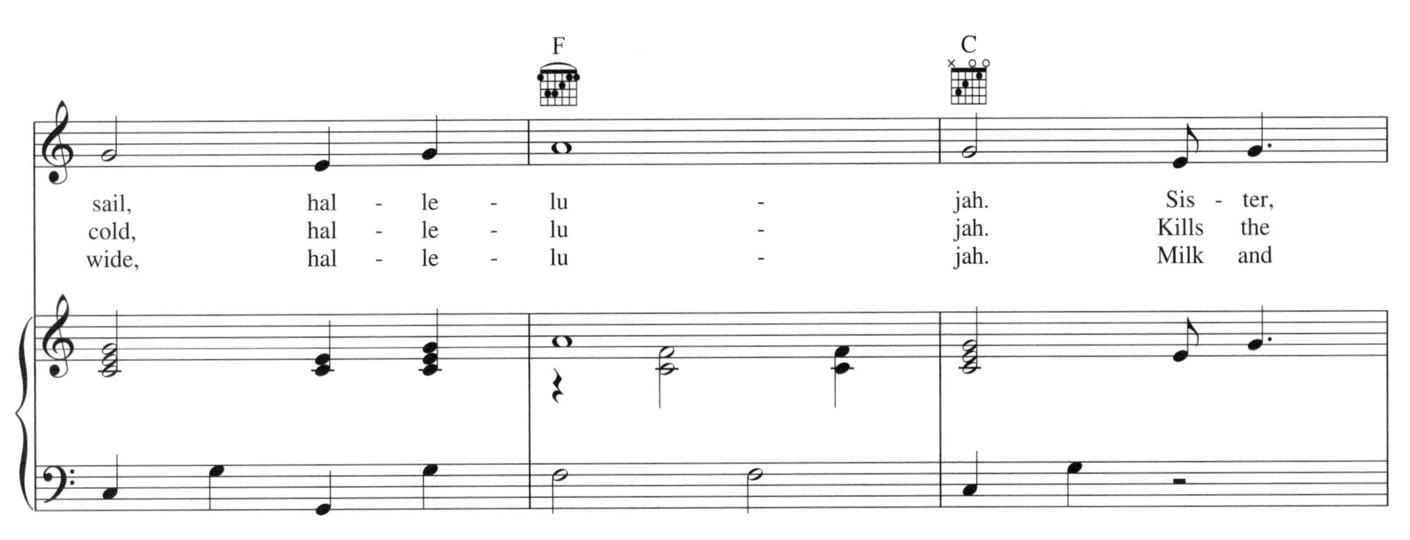
F
C
sail, hal - le - lu - jah. Sis - ter,
cold, hal - le - lu - jah. Kills the
wide, hal - le - lu - jah. Milk and

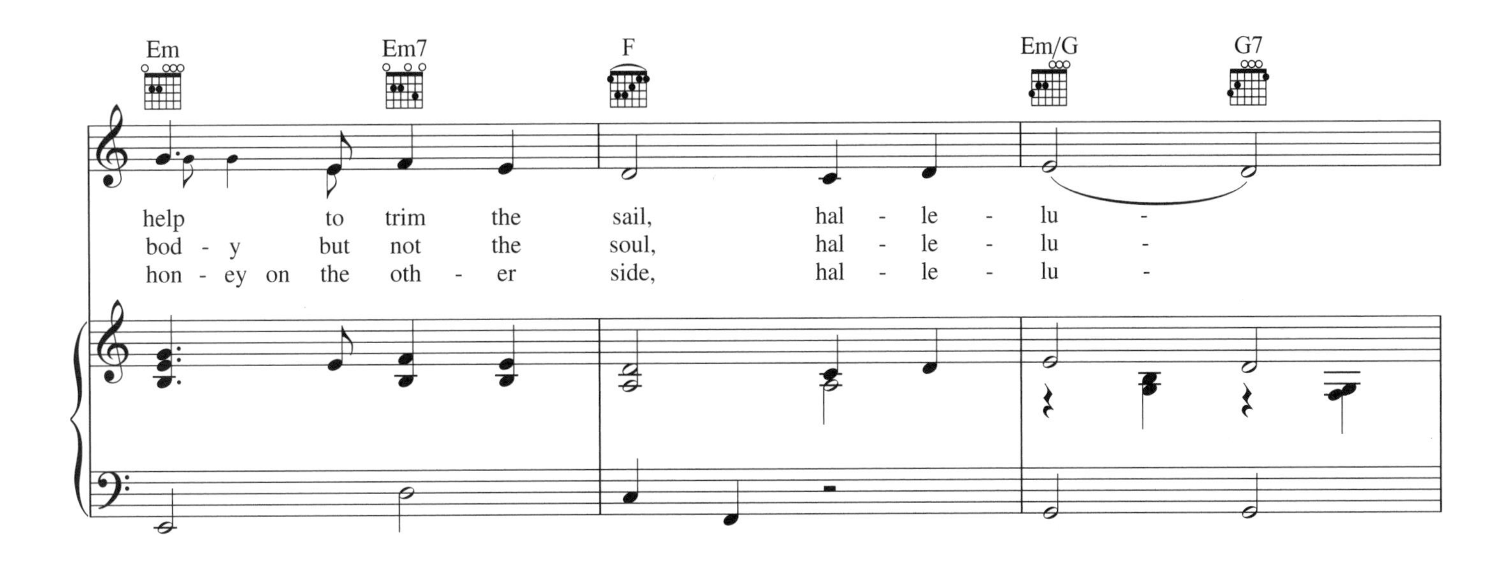
Em
Em7
F
Em/G
G7
help to trim the sail, hal - le - lu -
bod - y but not the soul, hal - le - lu -
hon - ey on the oth - er side, hal - le - lu -

1, 2
C
3
C
jah! Mi - chael, row ___ jah!
jah! Mi - chael, row ___

Mickey Mouse March

from Walt Disney's THE MICKEY MOUSE CLUB
Words and Music by Jimmie Dodd

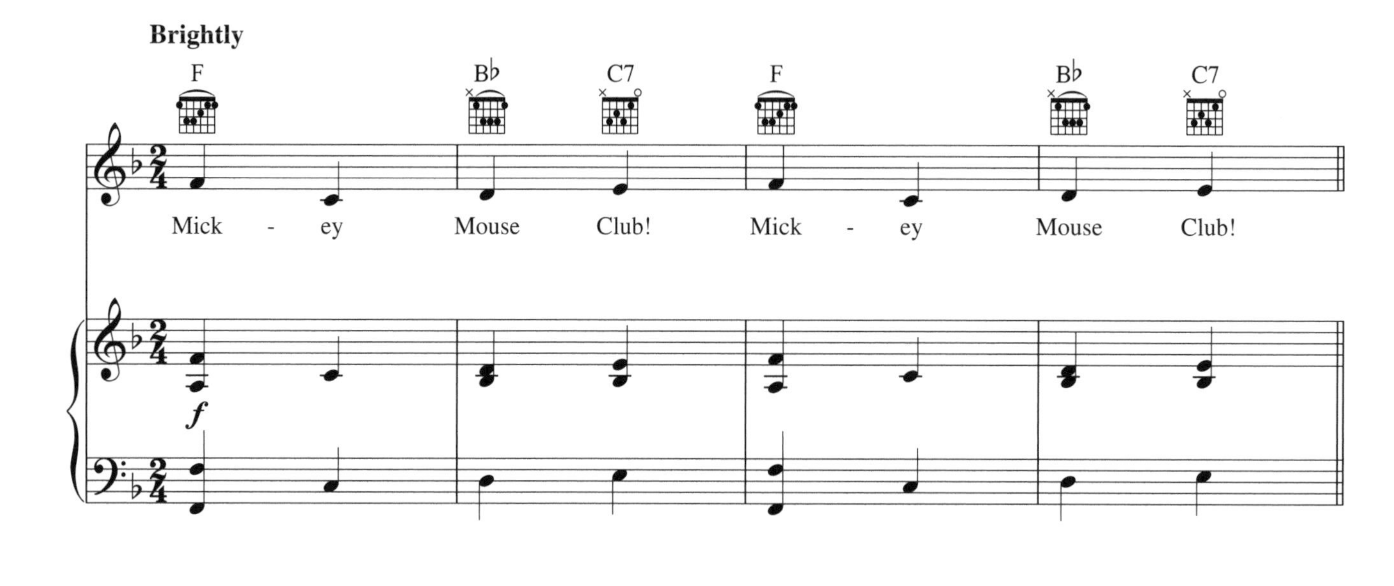

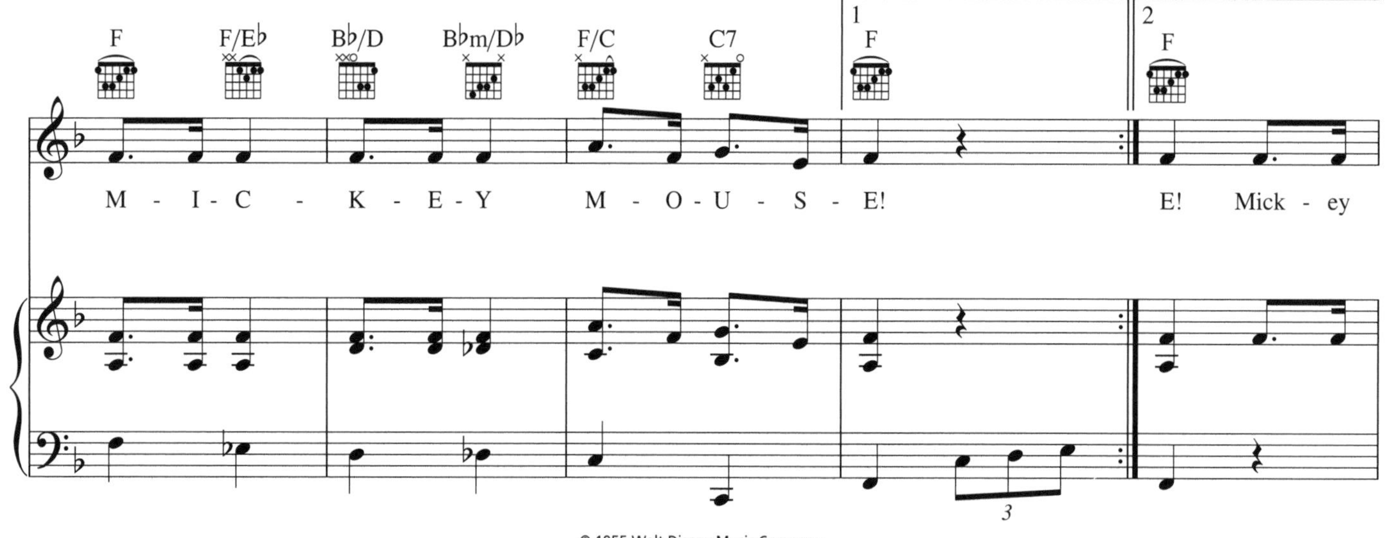

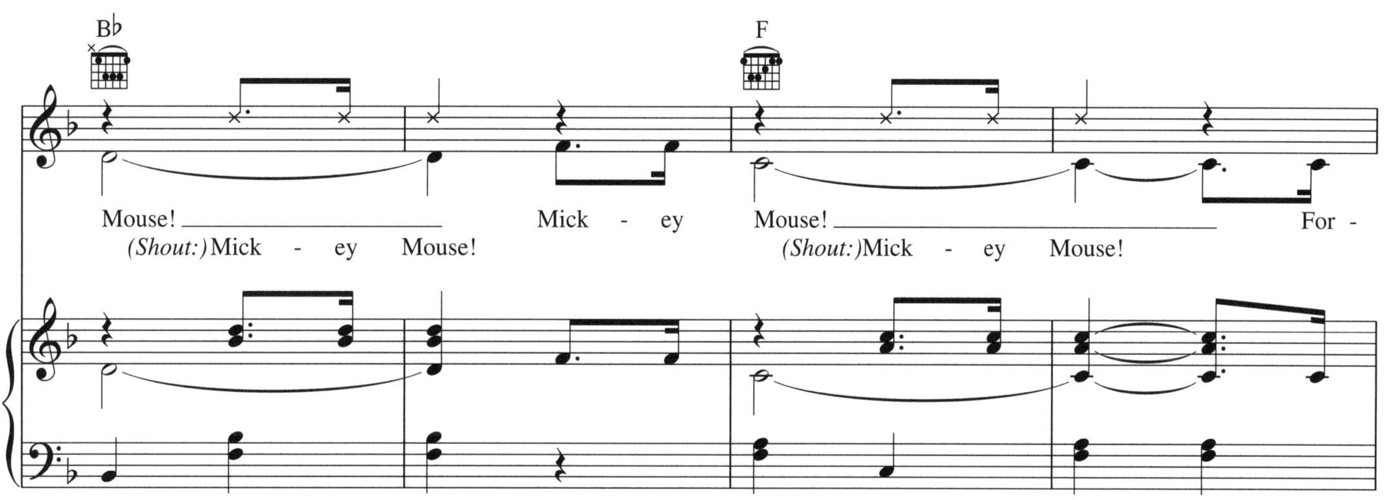
B♭
F
Mouse!
Mick - ey
Mouse!
For -
(Shout:) Mick - ey Mouse!
(Shout:) Mick - ey Mouse!

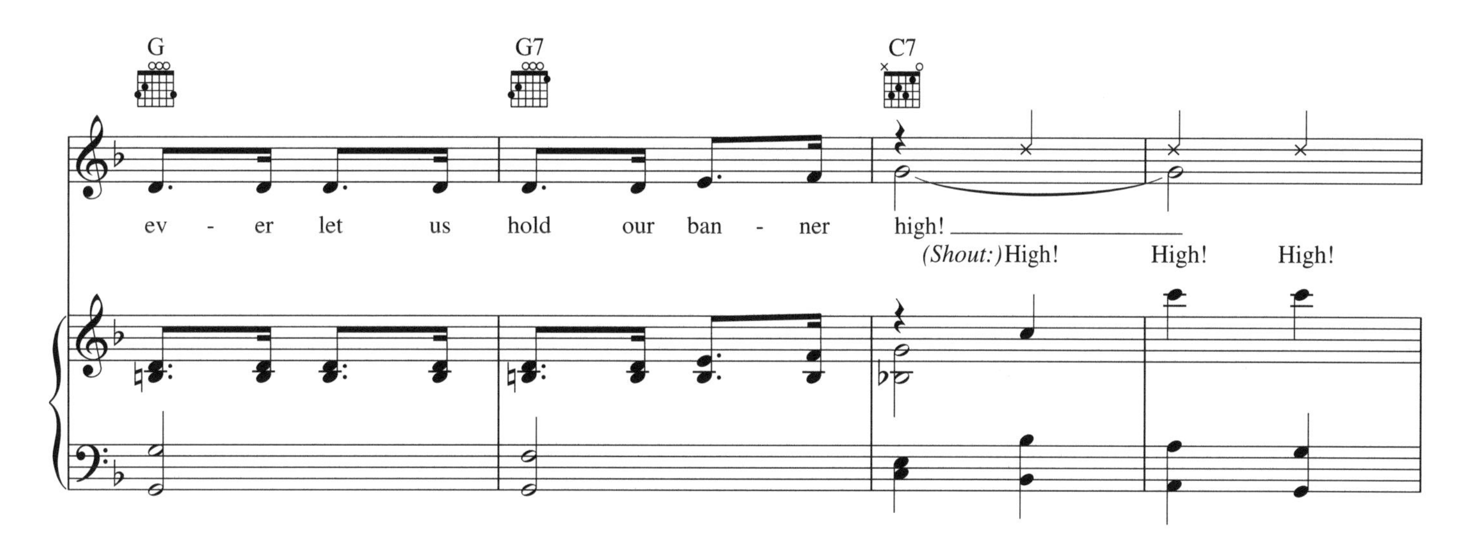
G
G7
C7
ev - er let us hold our ban - ner high!
(Shout:) High! High! High!

F
G7
C7
Come a - long and sing a song and join the jam - bo - ree!

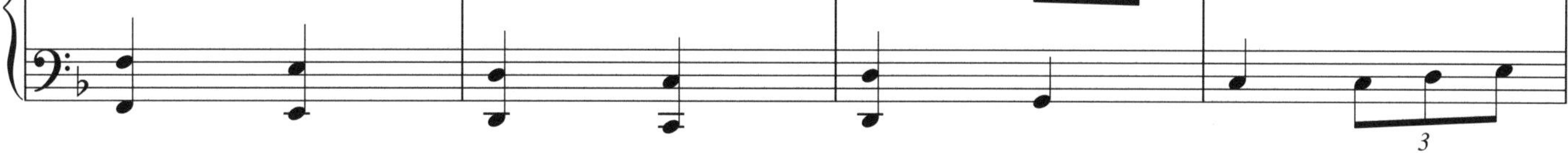
F
F7
B♭
B♭m
F
C7
F
M - I - C - K - E - Y M - O - U - S - E!

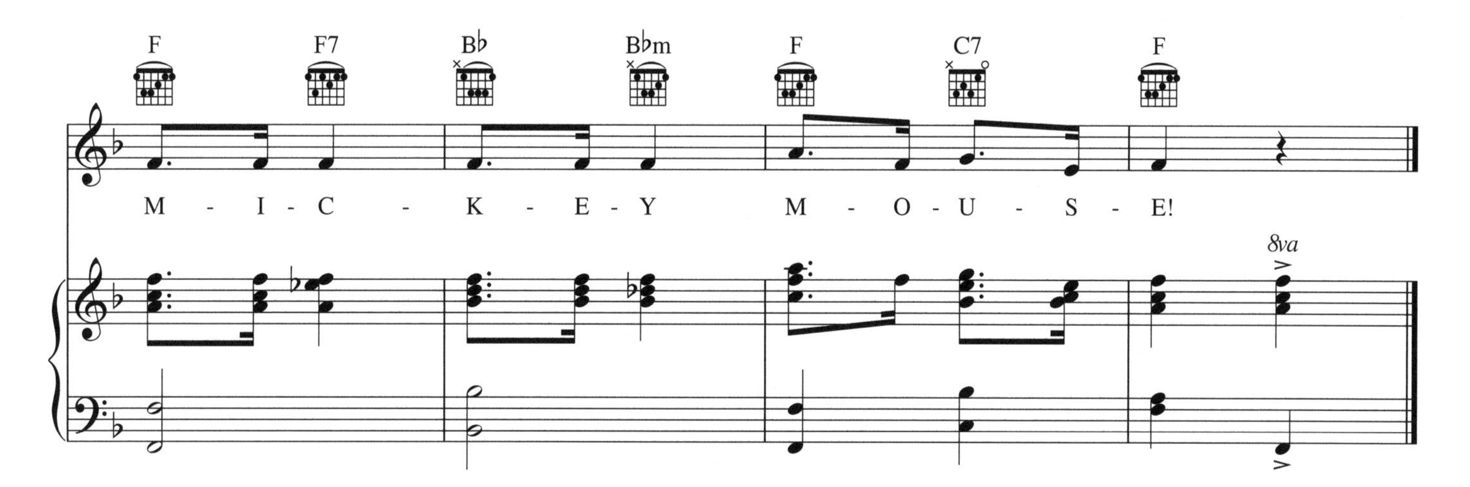
8va

Traditional Children's Song

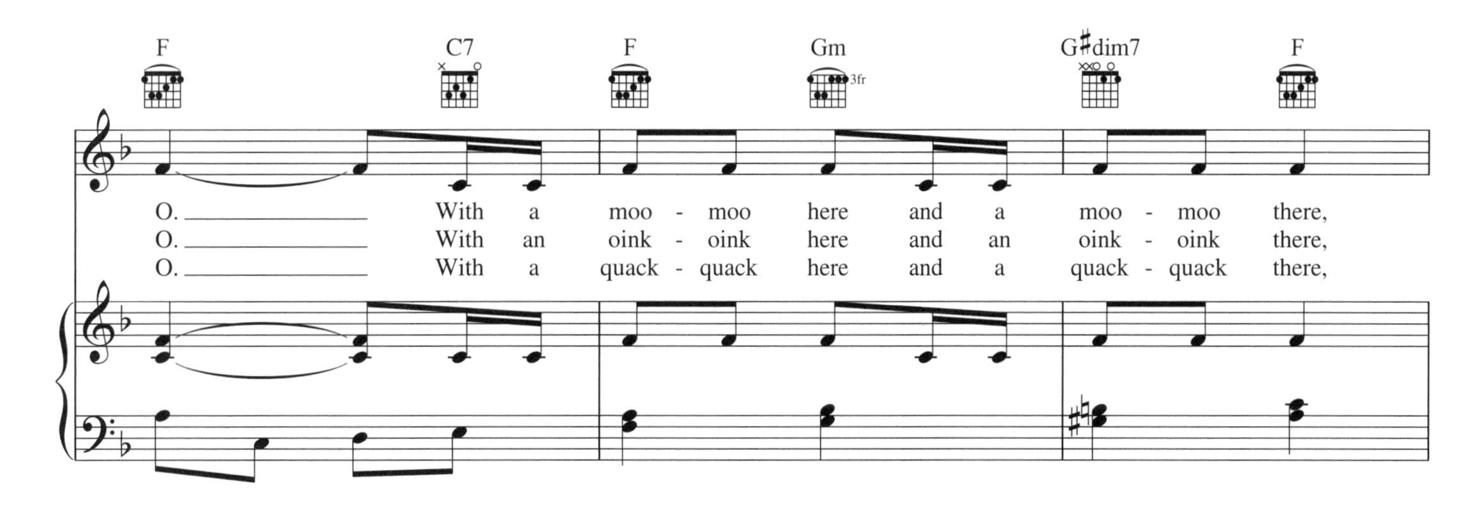

Additional Lyrics

4. Old MacDonald had a farm,
   E-I-E-I-O,
   And on his farm he had a horse,
   E-I-E-I-O,
   With a neigh-neigh here and a neigh-neigh there, etc.

5. Old MacDonald had a farm,
   E-I-E-I-O,
   And on his farm he had a donkey,
   E-I-E-I-O,
   With a hee-haw here and a hee-haw there, etc.

6. Old MacDonald had a farm,
   E-I-E-I-O,
   And on his farm he had some chickens,
   E-I-E-I-O,
   With a chick-chick here and a chick-chick there, etc.

On the Good Ship Lollipop

from BRIGHT EYES

Words and Music by Sidney Clare and Richard A. Whiting

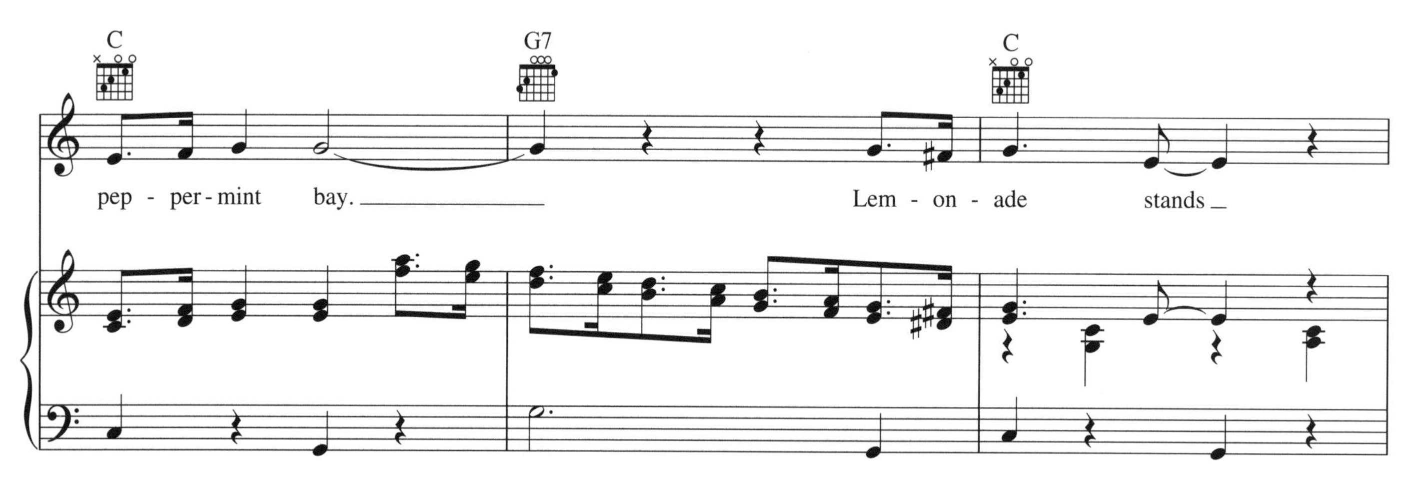

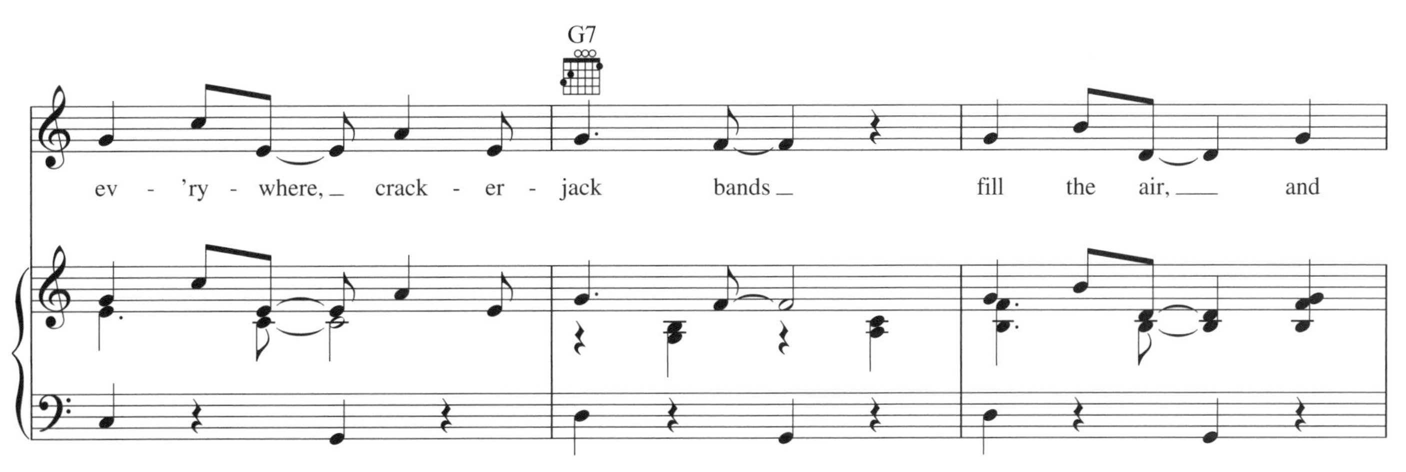
G7
ev - 'ry - where, crack - er - jack bands fill the air, and

C
there you are hap - py land - ing on a choc - o - late bar.

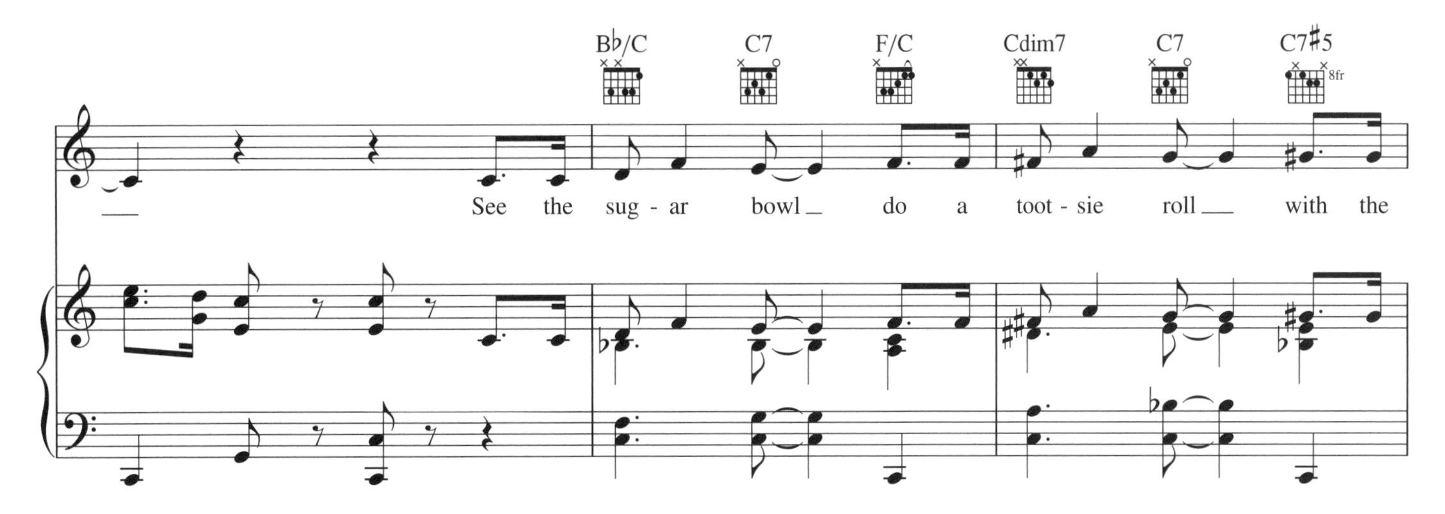
B♭/C C7 F/C Cdim7 C7 C7♯5
8fr
See the sug - ar bowl do a toot - sie roll with the

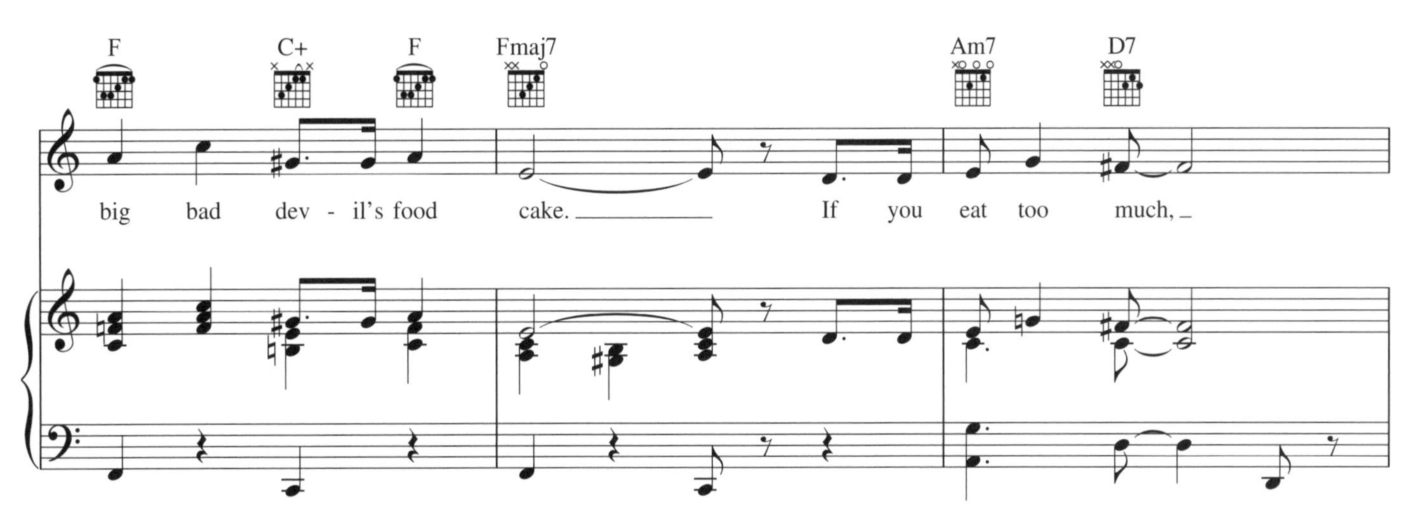
F C+ F Fmaj7 Am7 D7
big bad dev - il's food cake. If you eat too much,

Am9
D7
G
Adim7
G7♭9
G7
5fr
ooh! ooh! you'll a - wake with a tum - my ache. On the
C
G7
good ship, Lol - li - pop, it's a night trip in - to
bed you hop with this com - mand: "All a - board for
and dream a - way on the good ship,

1
2
C
G7
C
C6/9
Can - dy Land." On the Lol - li - pop!

Over the River and Through the Woods

Traditional

Peter Cottontail

Words and Music by Steve Nelson and Jack Rollins

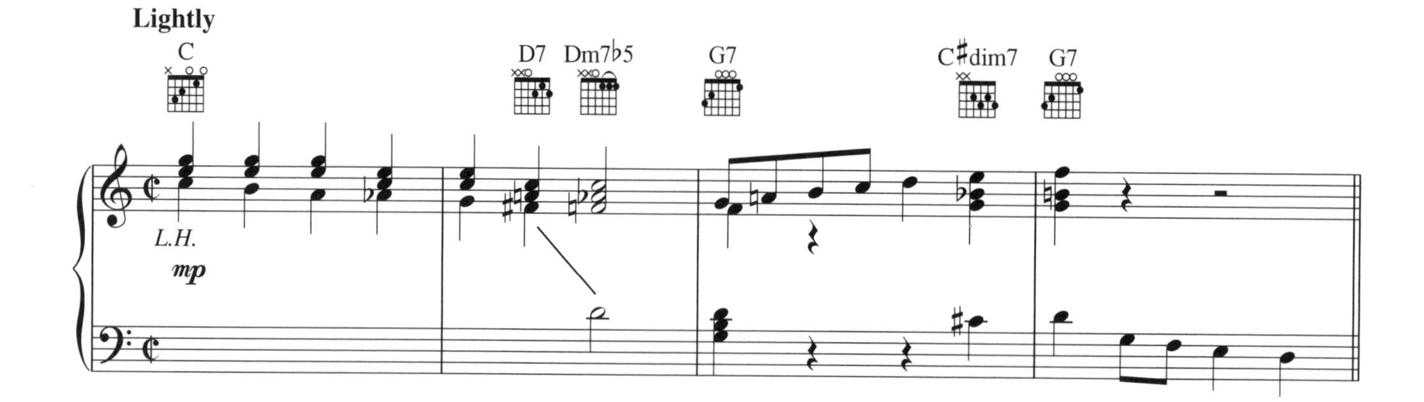

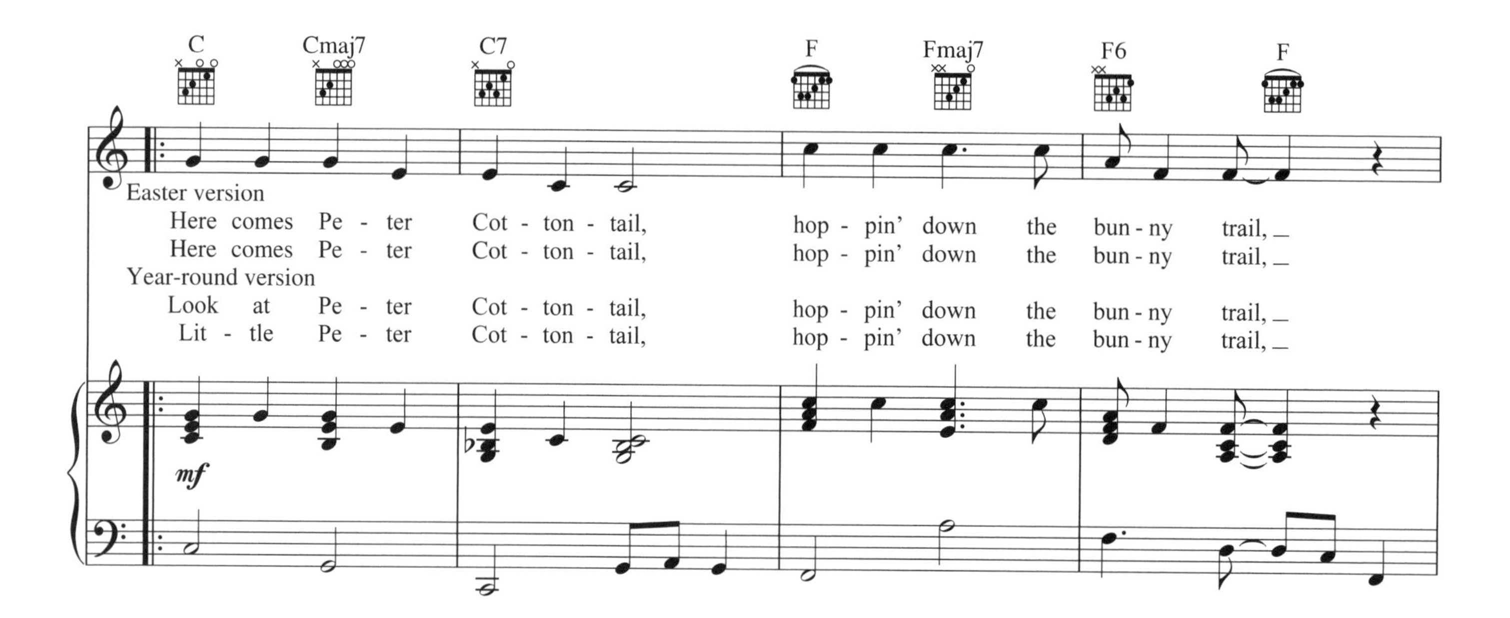

C Cmaj7 C7 F Fmaj7 F6 F
Bring - in' ev - 'ry girl and boy bas - kets full of Eas - ter joy,
"Try to do the things you should." May - be if you're ex - tra good,
He's the king of Bun - ny Land, 'cause his eyes are shin - y and
Some - thing told him it was wrong, Farm - er Jones might come a - long
G7 C♯dim7 G7 C F
things to make your Eas - ter bright and gay.
he'll roll lots of Eas - ter eggs your way.
he can spot the wolf a mile a - way.
and an aw - ful price he'd have to pay.
C C7 F F+ F6
He's got jel - ly beans for Tom - my, col - ored
You'll wake up on Eas - ter morn - ing and you'll
When the oth - ers go for clo - ver and the
But he knew his legs were fast - er so he
C C7 F F+
eggs for sis - ter Sue, there's an or - chid for your
know that he was there when you find those choc - 'late
big bad wolf ap - pears, he's the one that's watch - ing
nib - bled three or four, and he al - most met dis -

F6 Am D7 G G7#5
Mom - my and an Eas - ter bon - net, too. Oh!
bun - nies that he's hid - ing ev - 'ry where. Oh!
o - ver giv - in' sig - nals with his ears. And
as - ter when he heard that shot - gun roar. Oh,
C Cmaj7 C7 F Fmaj7
Here comes Pe - ter Cot - ton - tail, hop - pin' down the
Here comes Pe - ter Cot - ton - tail, hop - pin' down the
that's why folks in Rab - bit town feel so free when
that's how Pe - ter Cot - ton - tail hop - pin down the
F6 F G7/D C#dim7 G7/D G7
bun - ny trail; hip - pi - ty hop - pi - ty, Hap - py Eas - ter
bun - ny trail; hip - pi - ty hop - pi - ty, Hap - py Eas - ter
he's a - roun'; Pe - ter's help - in' some - one ev - 'ry
bun - ny trail lost his tail, but still he got a -
1 C C#dim7 Dm7 G7
day.
day.
2 C F C
day.
way.

The Rainbow Connection

from THE MUPPET MOVIE
Words and Music by Paul Williams and Kenneth L. Ascher

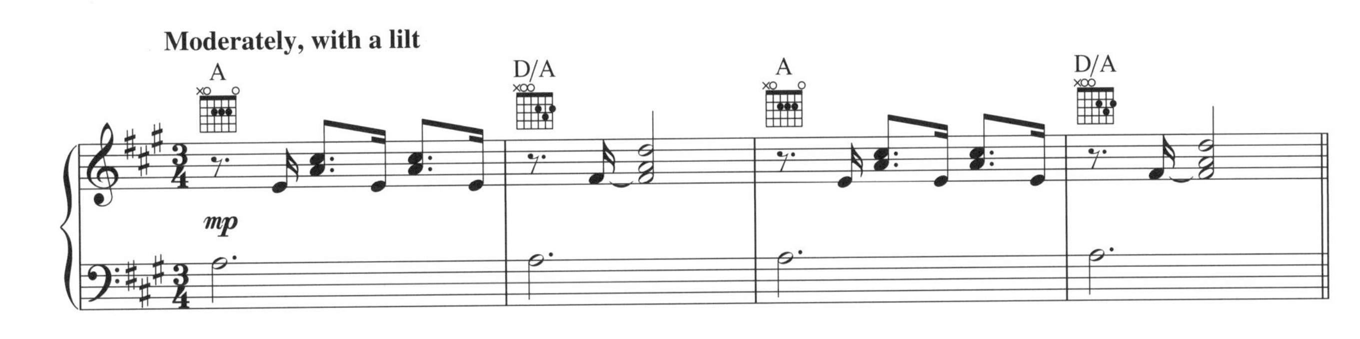

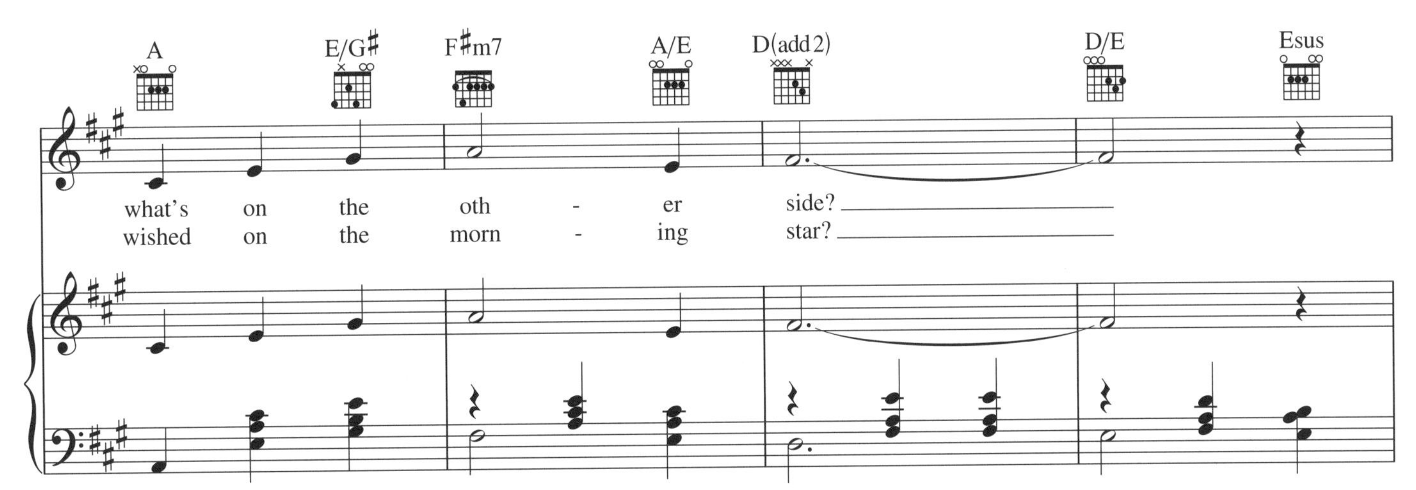

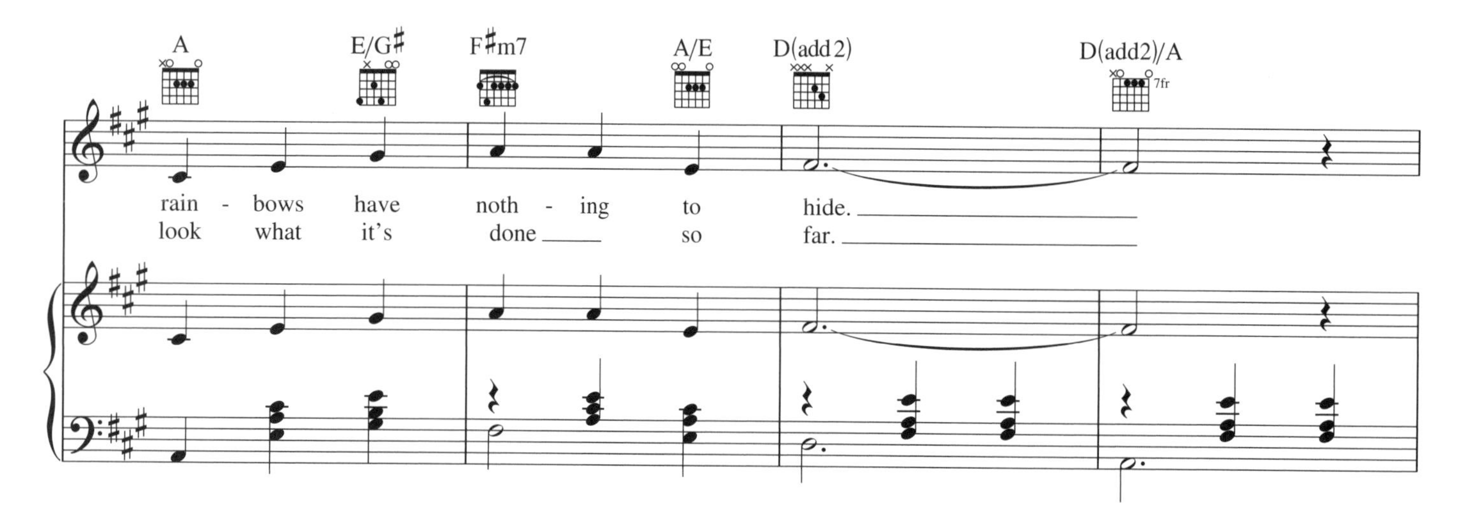
A
E/G#
F#m7
A/E
D(add2)
D(add2)/A
rain - bows have noth - ing to hide.
look what it's done so far.

Dmaj7
So we've been told, and some choose to be - lieve it.
What's so a - maz - ing that keeps us star - gaz - ing, and

G#m/C#
I know they're wrong; wait and see.
what do we think we might see?

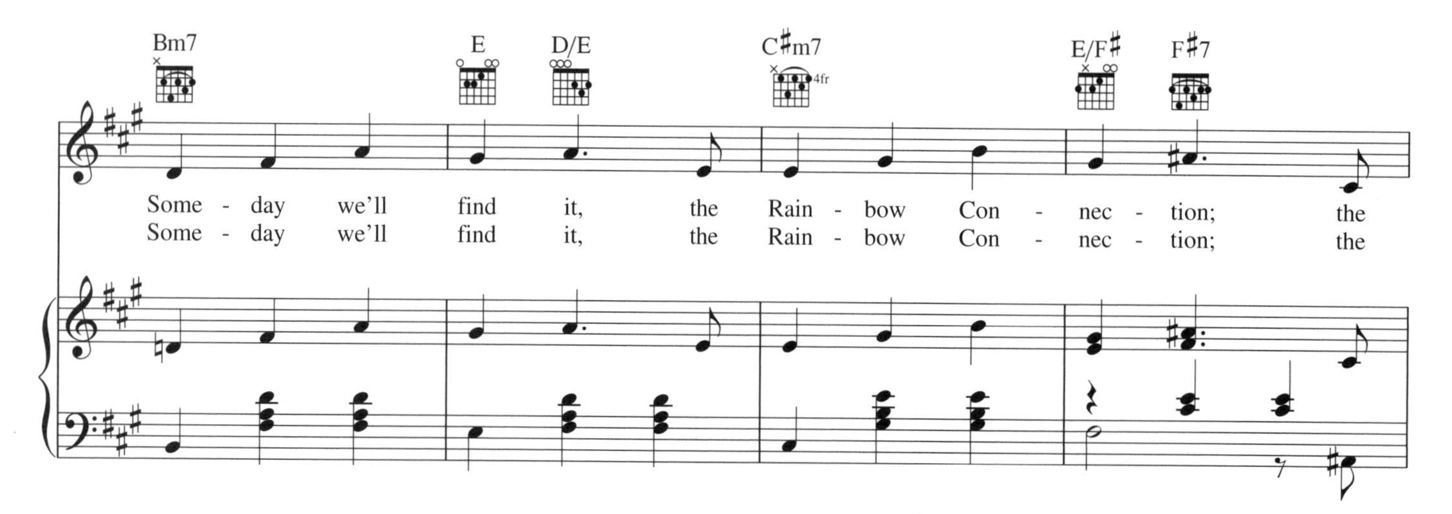
Bm7
E
D/E
C#m7
E/F#
F#7
Some - day we'll find it, the Rain - bow Con - nec - tion; the
Some - day we'll find it, the Rain - bow Con - nec - tion; the

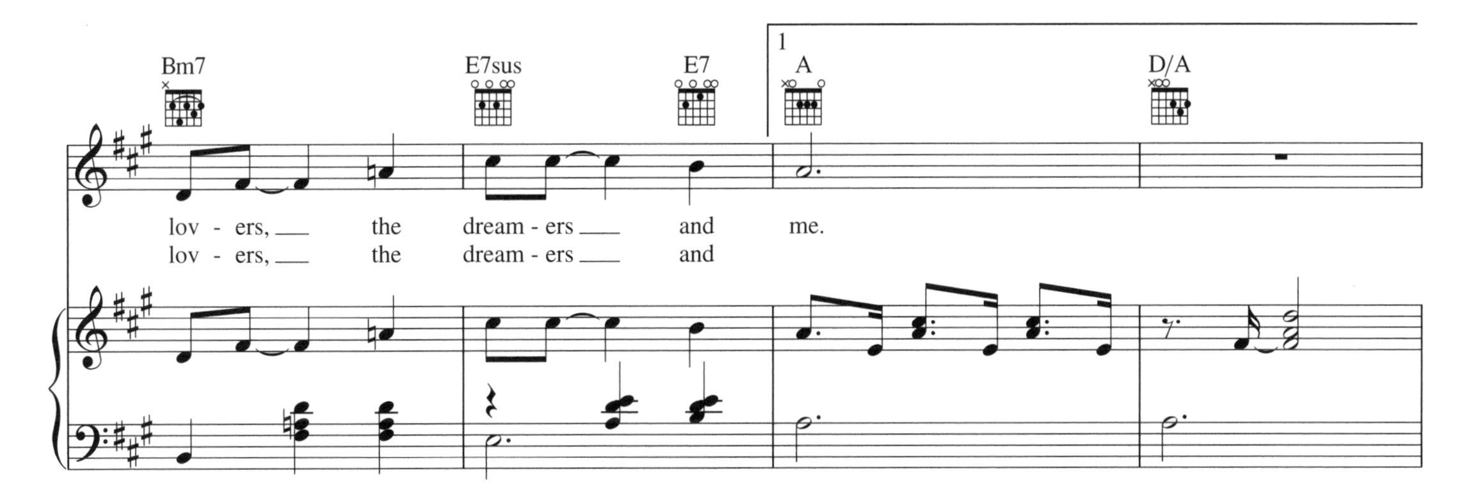
Bm7
E7sus
E7
1
A
D/A
lov - ers, the dream - ers and me.
lov - ers, the dream - ers and

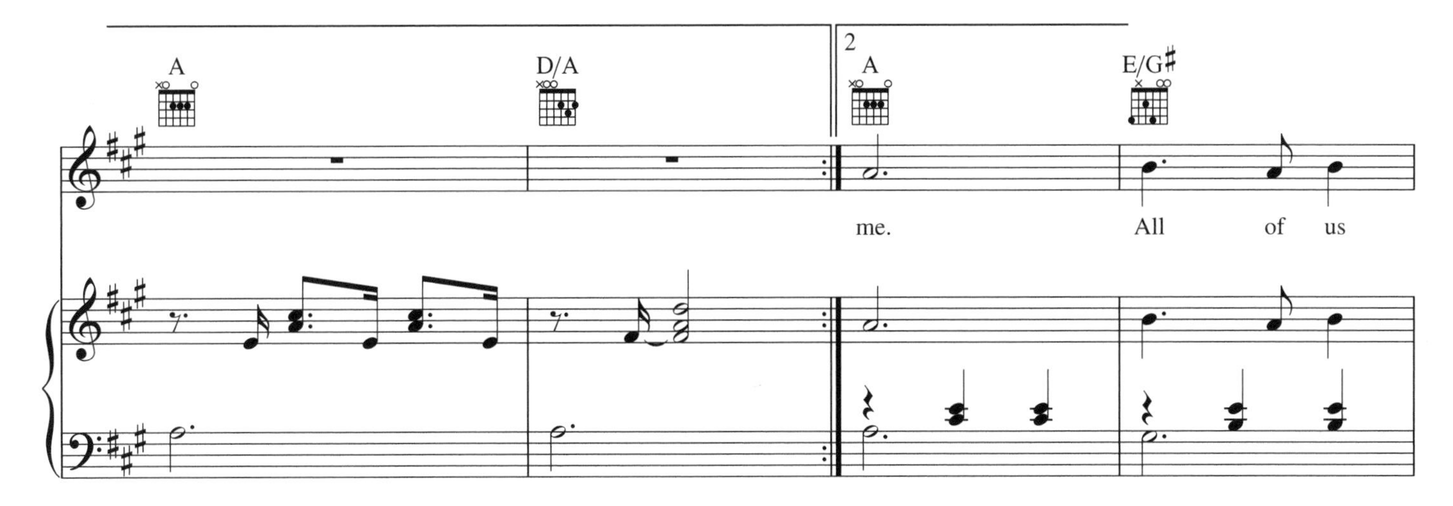
A
D/A
2
A
E/G♯
me. All of us

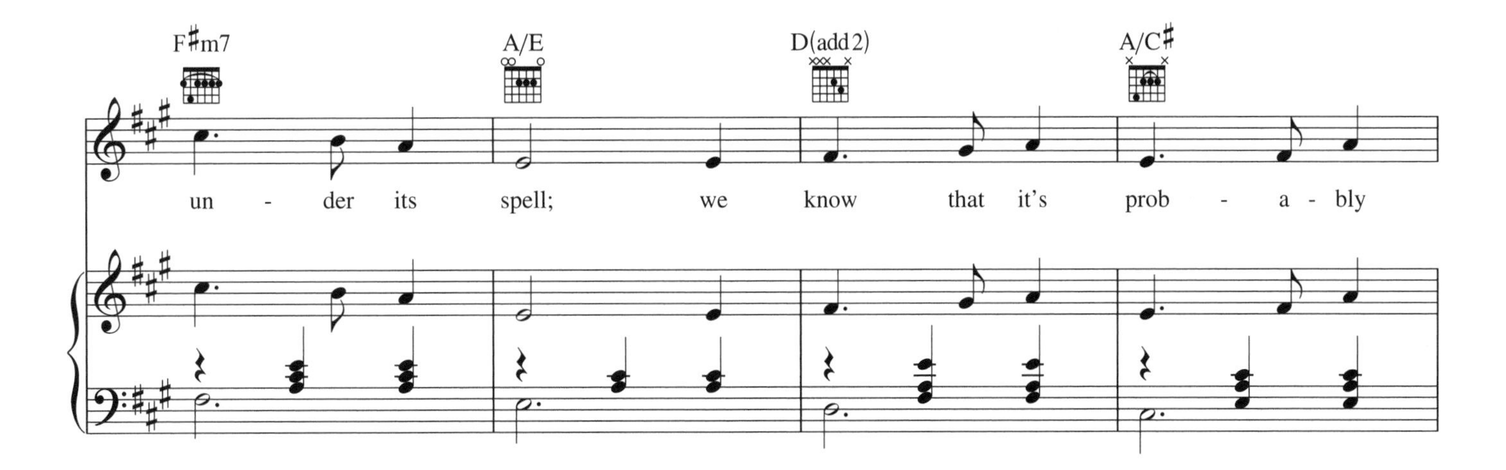
F♯m7
A/E
D(add2)
A/C♯
un - der its spell; we know that it's prob - a - bly

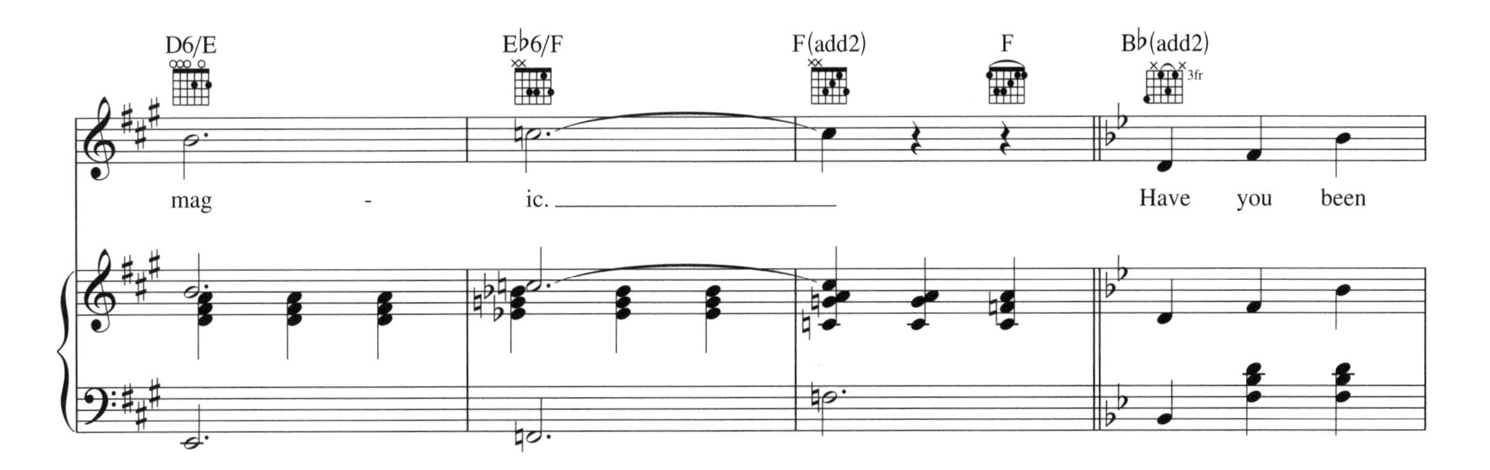
D6/E
E♭6/F
F(add2)
F
B♭(add2)
3fr
mag - ic. Have you been

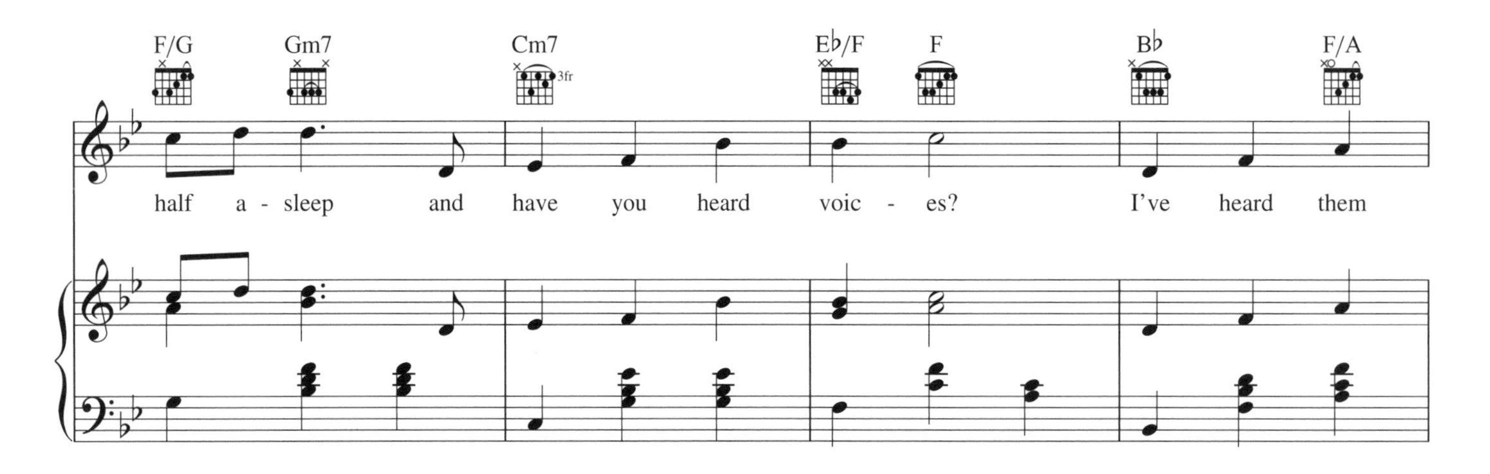
F/G
Gm7
Cm7
E♭/F
F
B♭
F/A
half a - sleep and have you heard voic - es? I've heard them

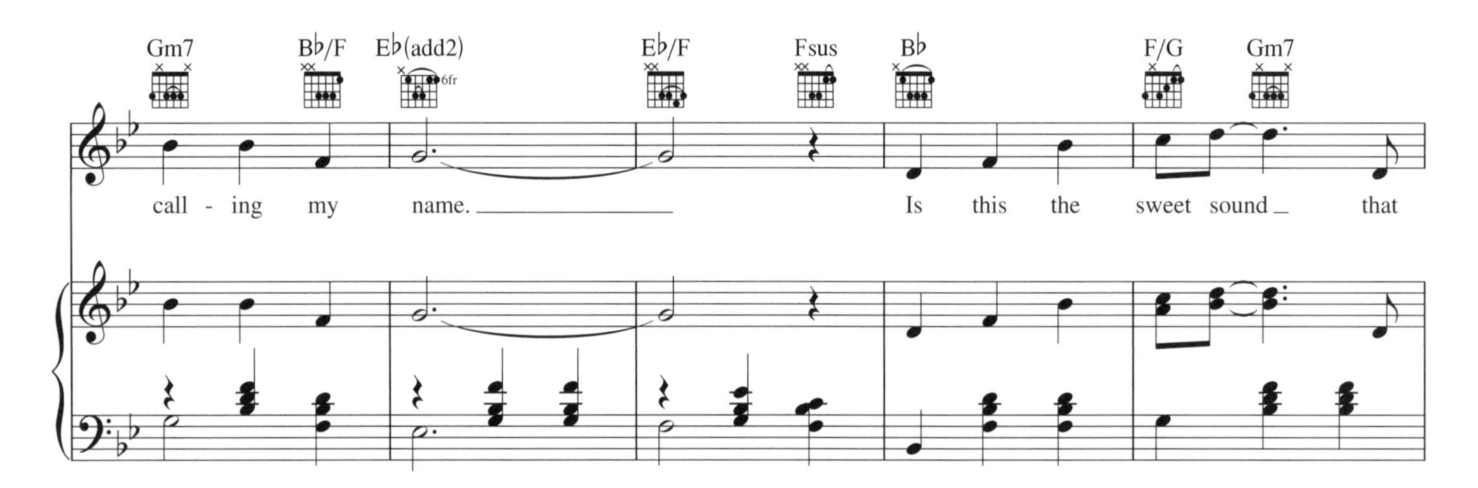
Gm7
B♭/F
E♭(add2)
E♭/F
Fsus
B♭
F/G
Gm7
call - ing my name. Is this the sweet sound that

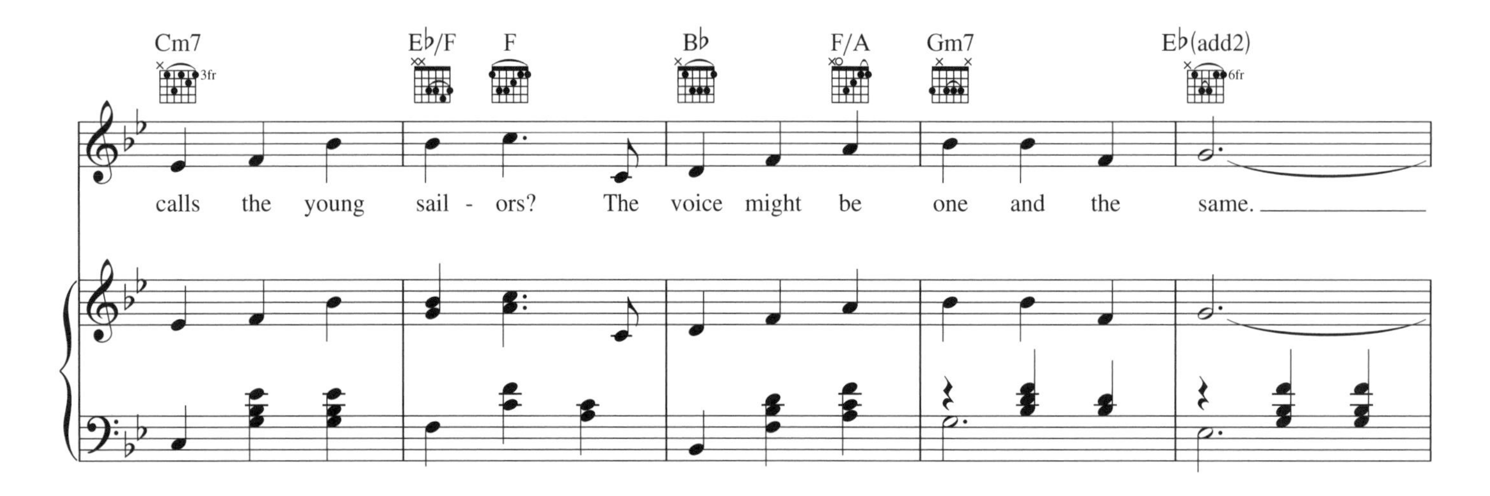
Cm7
E♭/F
F
B♭
F/A
Gm7
E♭(add2)
calls the young sail - ors? The voice might be one and the same.

E♭
E♭maj7
I've heard it too man - y times to ig -

Am/D
nore it. It's some - thing that I'm s'posed to be.
Cm7 F E♭/F Dm7 F/G G7
Some - day we'll find it, the Rain - bow Con - nec - tion; the
Cm7 F7sus F7 B♭ F/A Gm7
lov - ers, the dream - ers and me. La da da dee da da
B♭/F E♭(add2) E♭ Fsus F7 B♭
do la la da da da de da do.

Puff the Magic Dragon

Words and Music by Lenny Lipton and Peter Yarrow

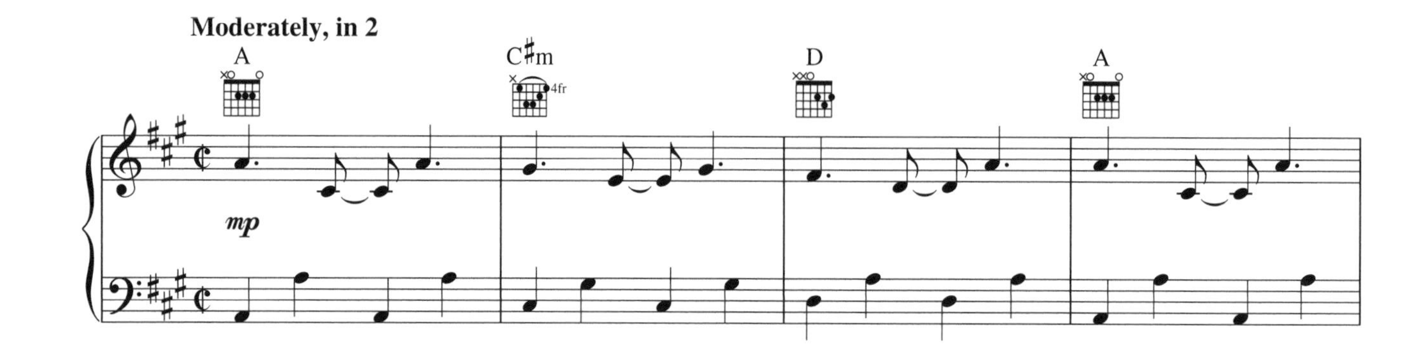

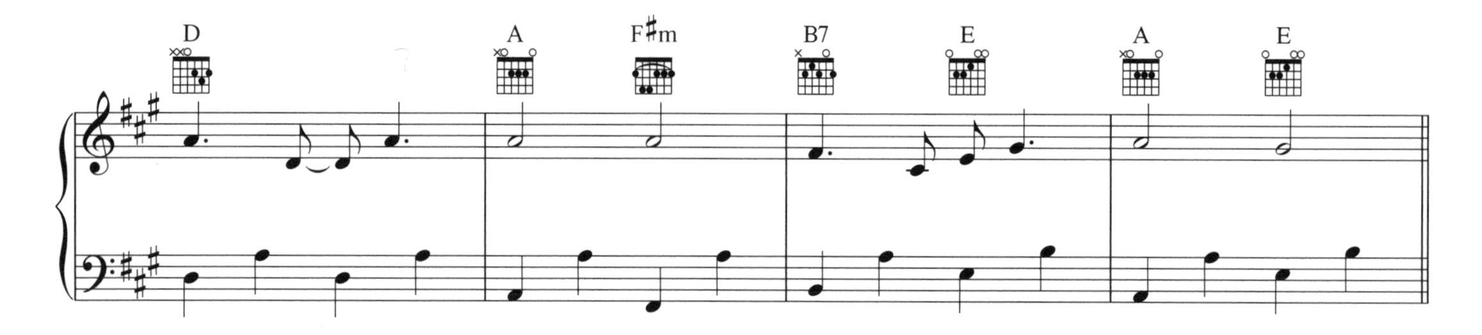

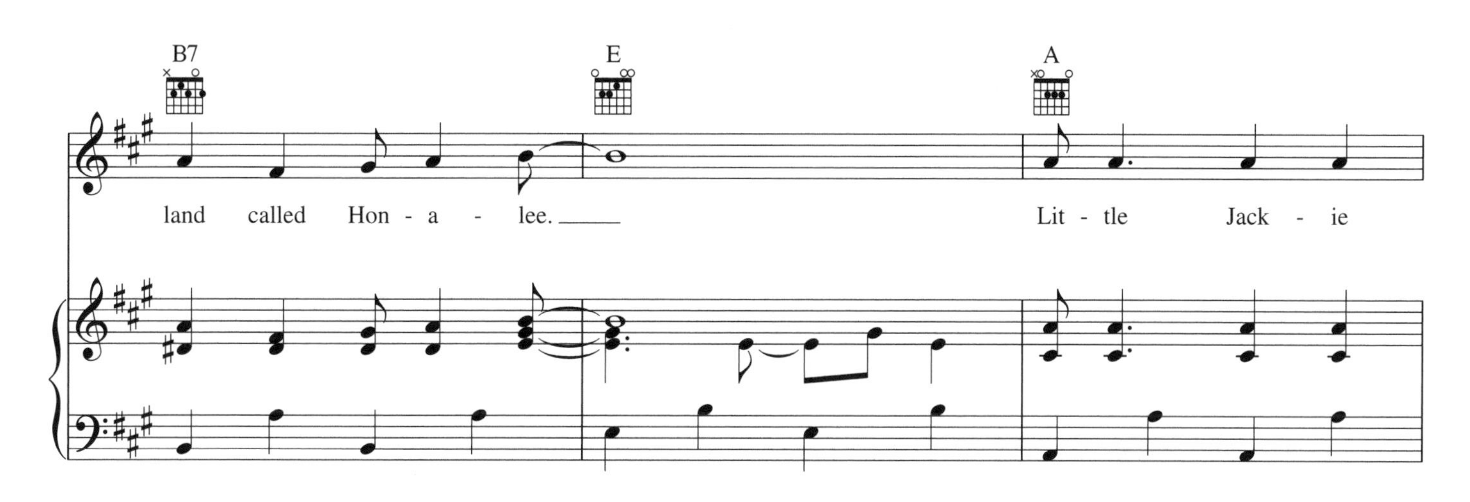
B7
E
A
land called Hon - a - lee.
Lit - tle Jack - ie

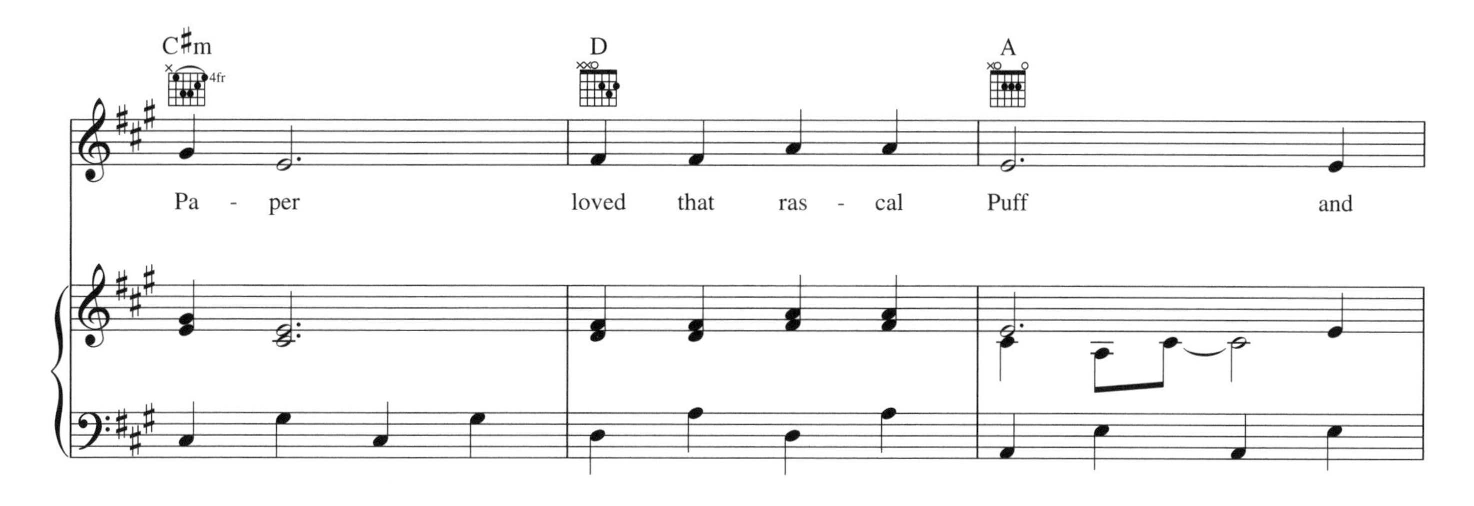
C♯m
4fr
D
A
Pa - per loved that ras - cal Puff and

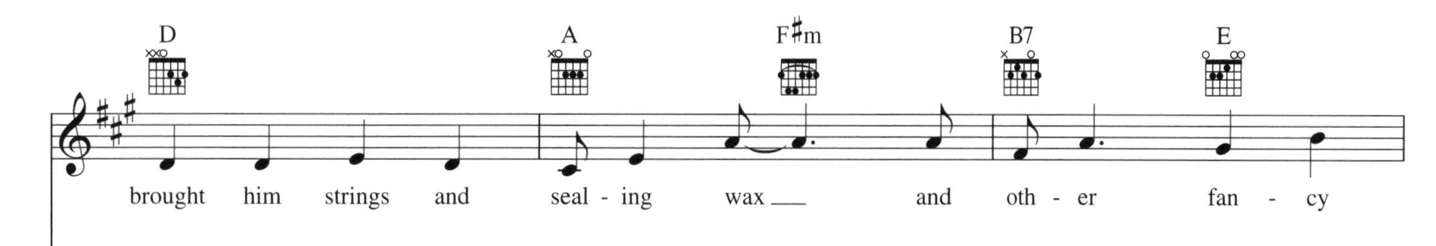
D
A
F♯m
B7
E
brought him strings and seal - ing wax and oth - er fan - cy

Chorus
A
E
A
C♯m
4fr
stuff. Oh! Puff the Mag - ic Drag - on

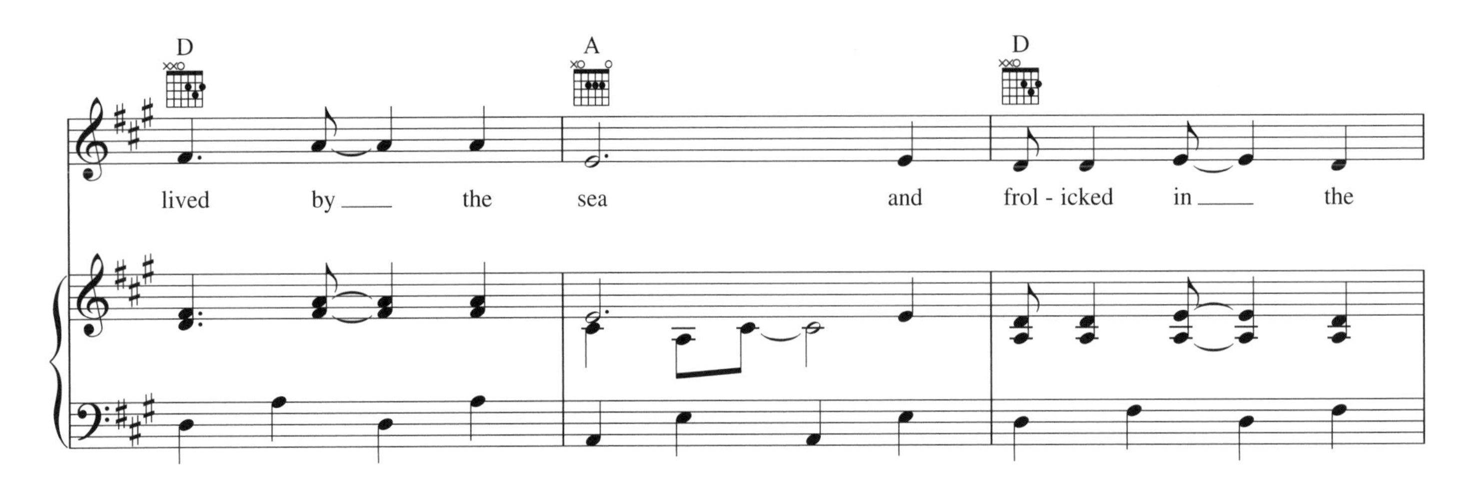
D
A
D
lived by the sea and frol - icked in the

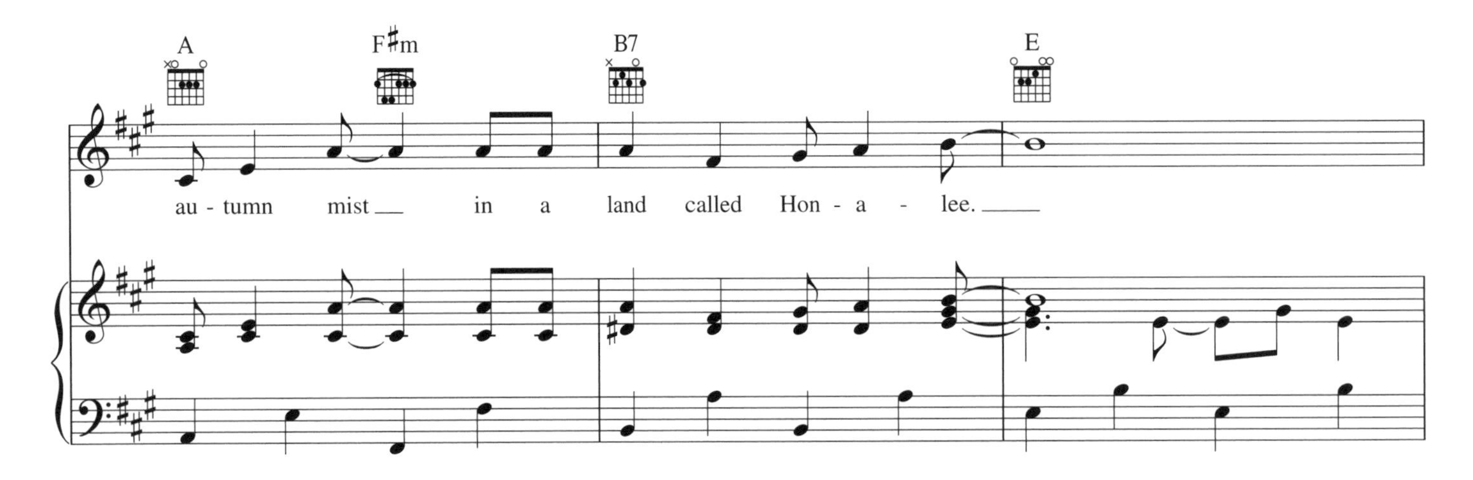
A
F♯m
B7
E
au - tumn mist in a land called Hon - a - lee.

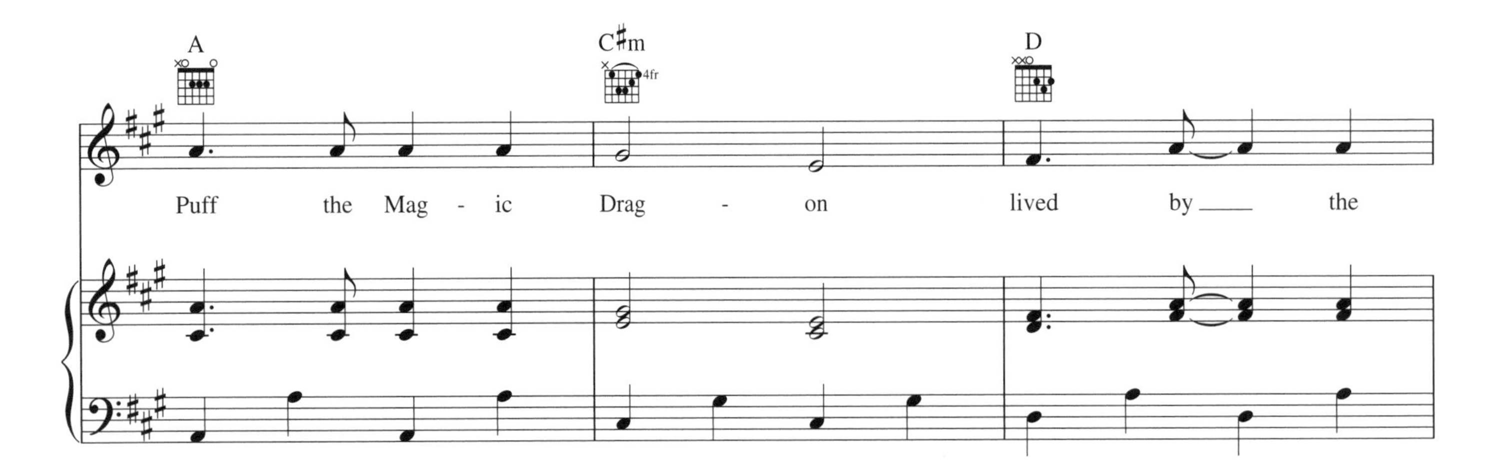
A
C♯m
4fr
D
Puff the Mag - ic Drag - on lived by the

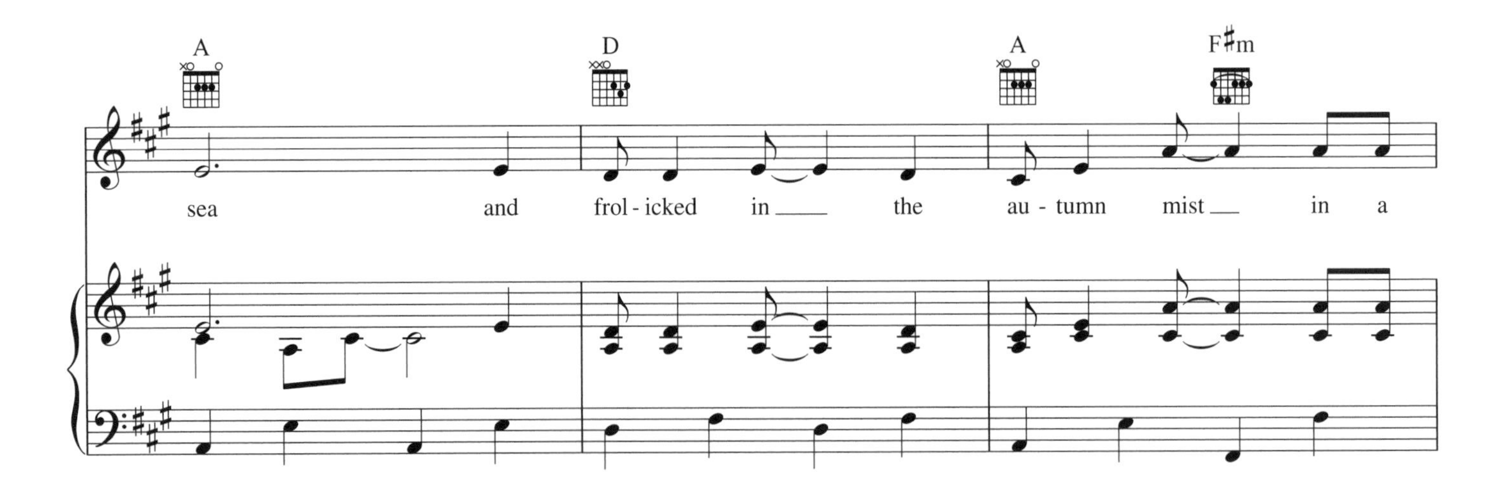
A
D
A
F♯m
sea and frol - icked in the au - tumn mist in a

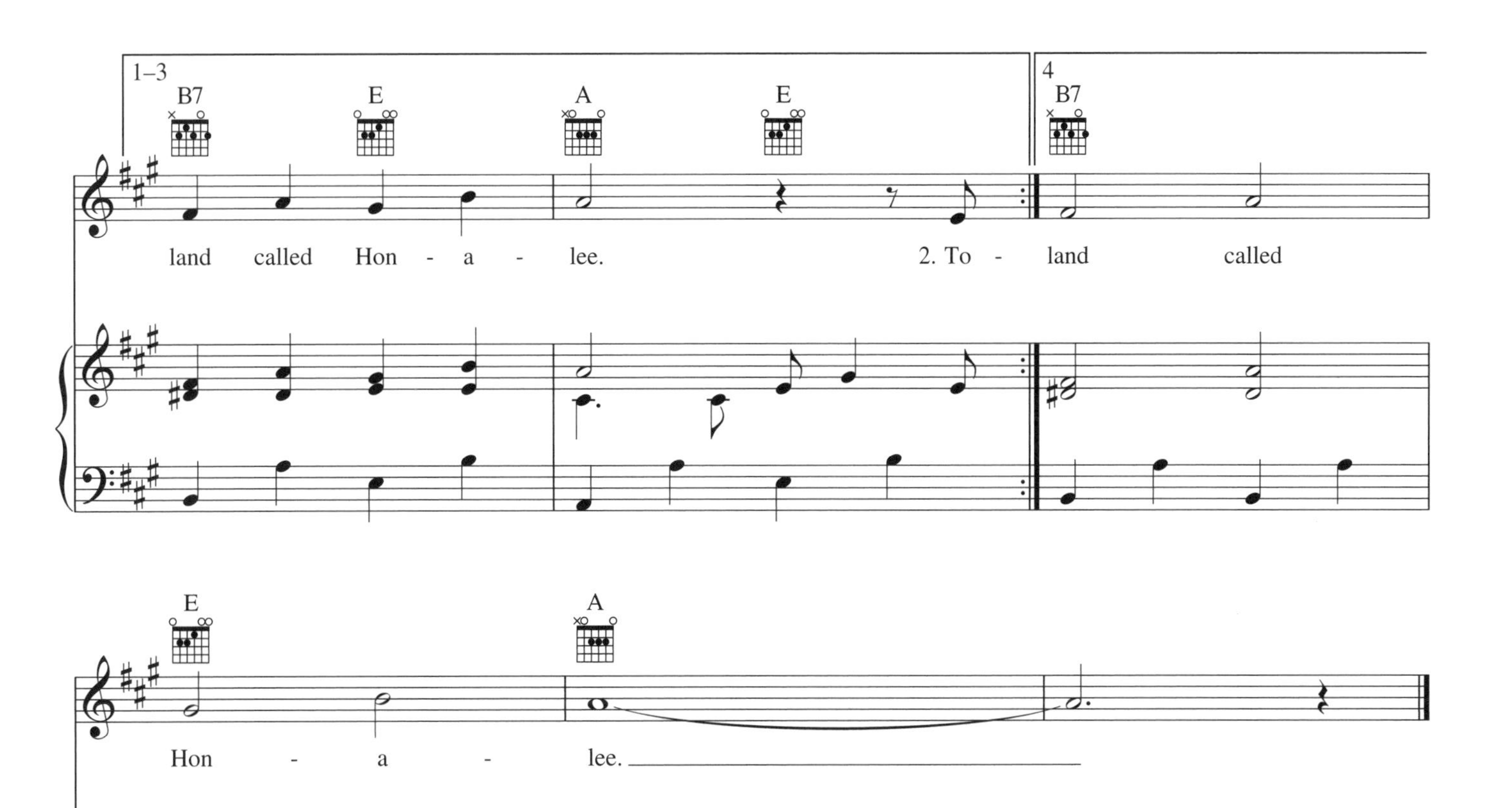

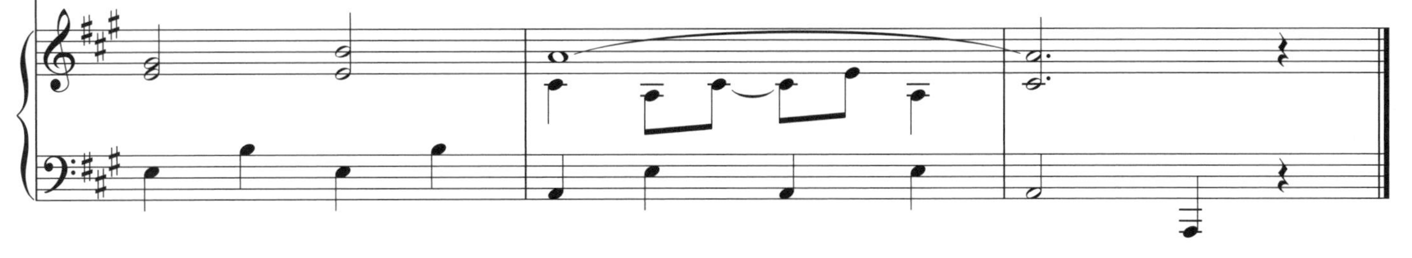

Additional Lyrics

2. Together they would travel on a boat with billowed sail.
Jackie kept a lookout perched on Puff's gigantic tail.
Noble kings and princes would bow when e'er they came.
Pirate ships would low'r their flags when Puff roared out his name. Oh!
(Chorus)

3. A dragon lives forever, but not so little boys.
Painted wings and giant rings make way for other toys.
One gray night it happened, Jackie Paper came no more,
And Puff that mighty dragon, he ceased his fearless roar.

4. His head was bent in sorrow, green tears fell like rain.
Puff no longer went to play along the Cherry Lane.
Without his lifelong friend, Puff could not be brave,
So Puff that mighty dragon sadly slipped into his cave. Oh!
(Chorus)

*THE RETURN OF PUFF

5. Puff the magic dragon danced down the Cherry Lane.
He came upon a little girl, Julie Maple was her name.
She'd heard that Puff had gone away, but that can never be,
So together they went sailing to the land called Honalee.
(Chorus)

Row, Row, Row Your Boat

Traditional

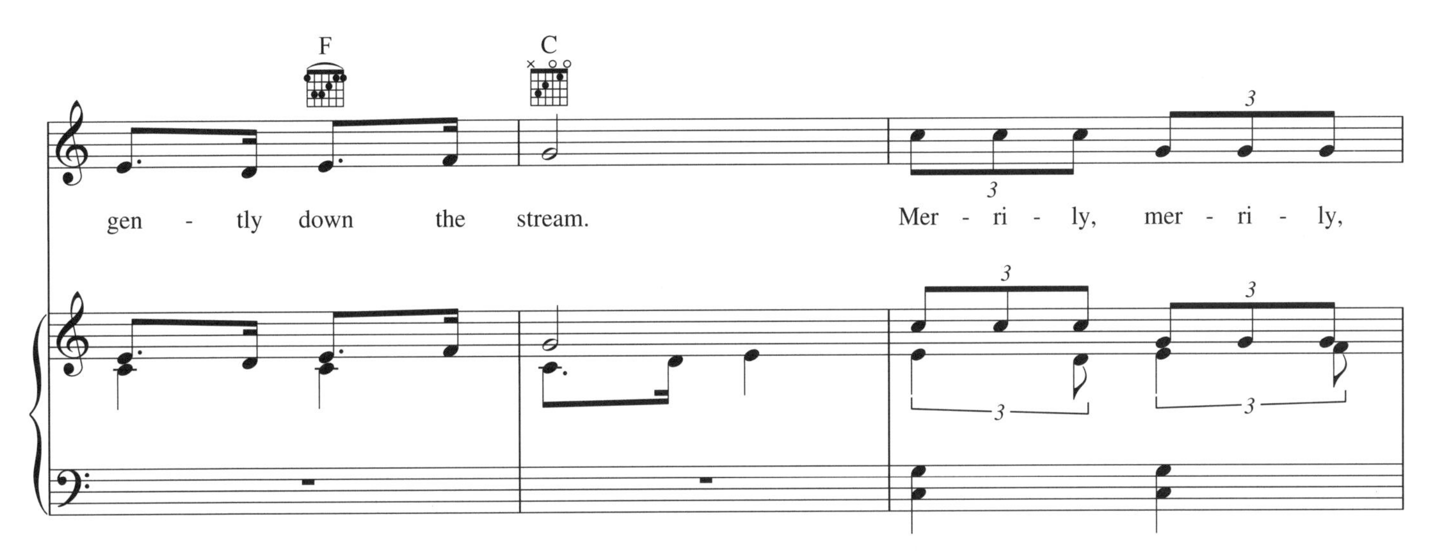
F
C
gen - tly down the stream.
Mer - ri - ly, mer - ri - ly,

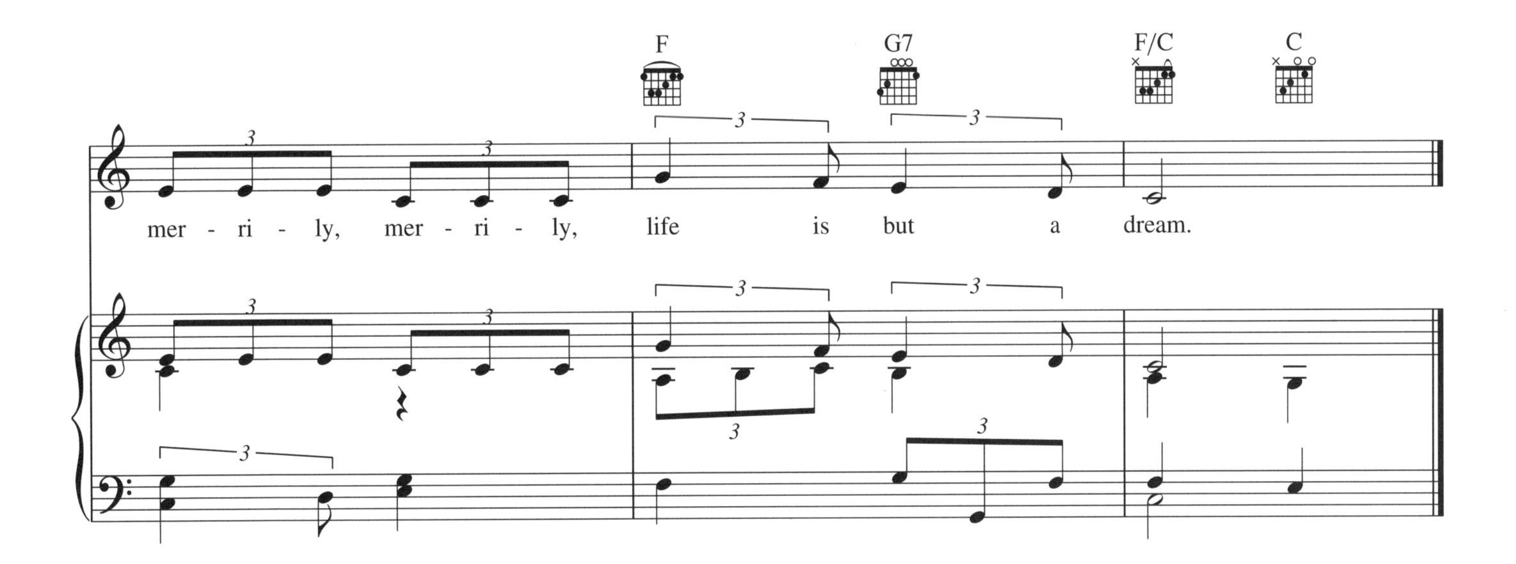
F
G7
F/C
C
mer - ri - ly, mer - ri - ly, life is but a dream.

Sesame Street Theme

Words by Bruce Hart, Jon Stone and Joe Raposo
Music by Joe Raposo

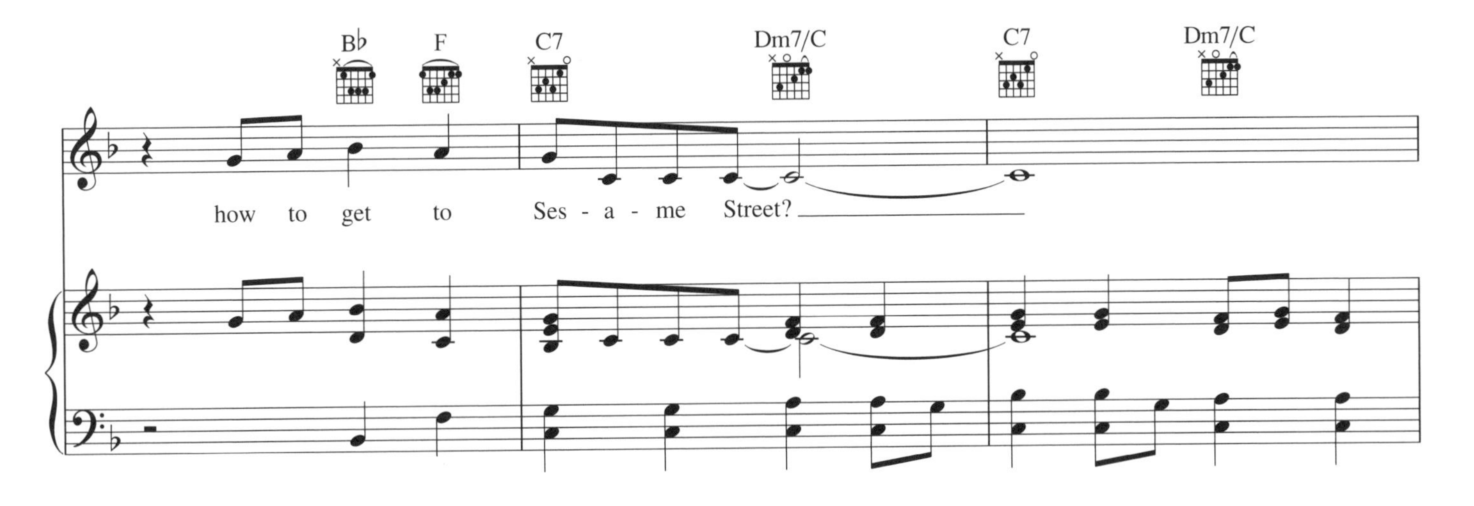
B♭
F
C7
Dm7/C
C7
Dm7/C
how to get to Ses - a - me Street?

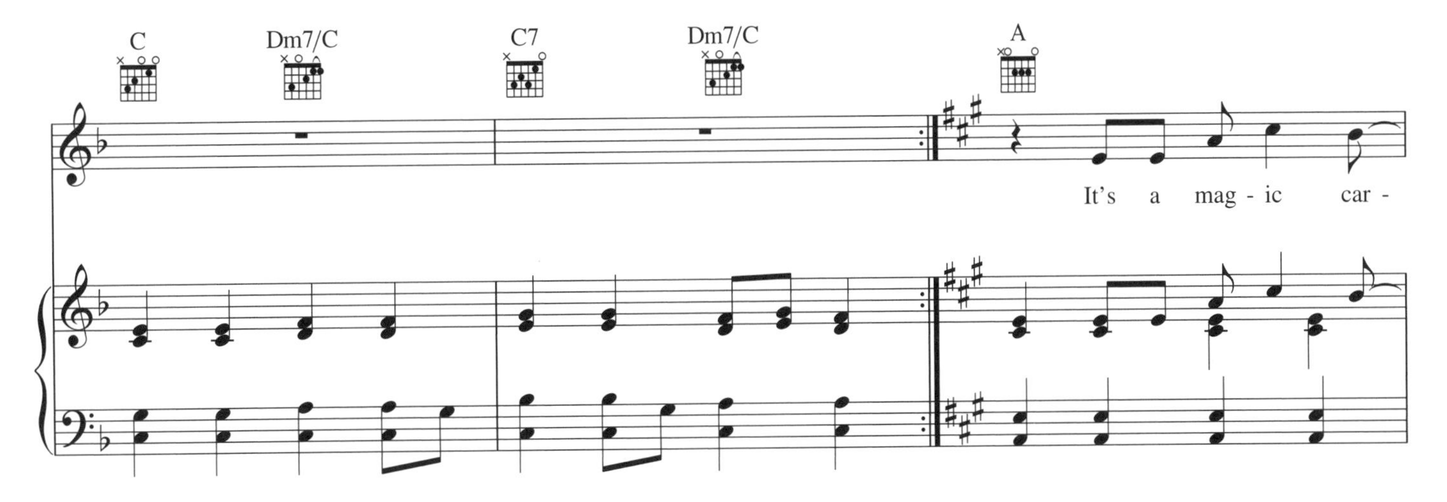
C
Dm7/C
C7
Dm7/C
A
It's a mag - ic car -

Bm7/A
E7/A
A
Bm7/A
E7
- pet ride.
Ev - 'ry door will o - pen wide to hap - py

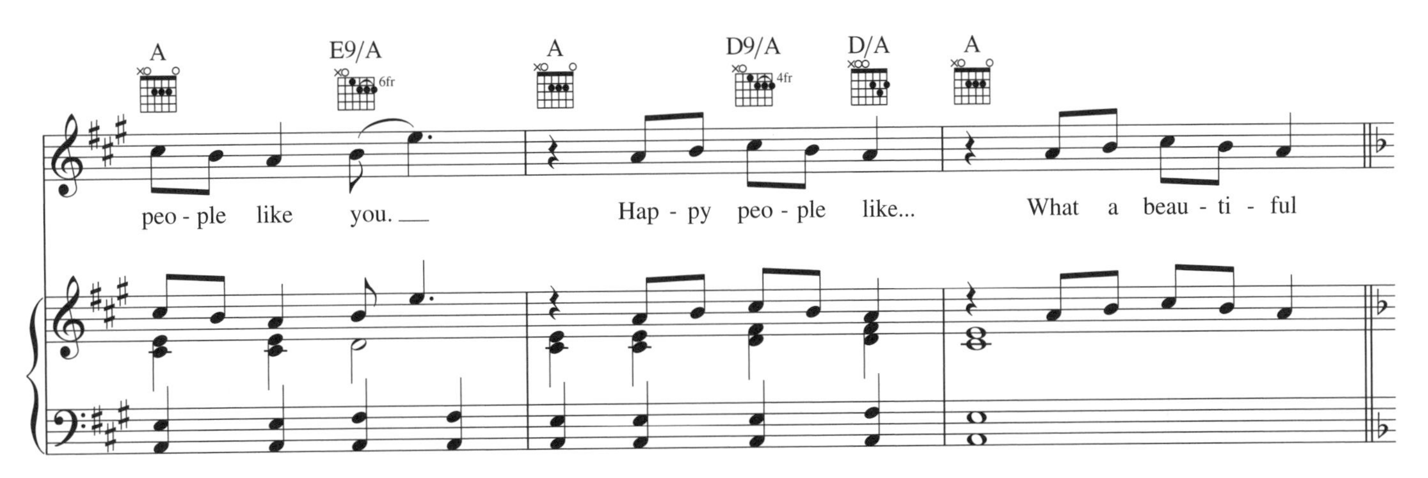
A
E9/A
6fr
A
D9/A
4fr
D/A
A
peo - ple like you.
Hap - py peo - ple like...
What a beau - ti - ful

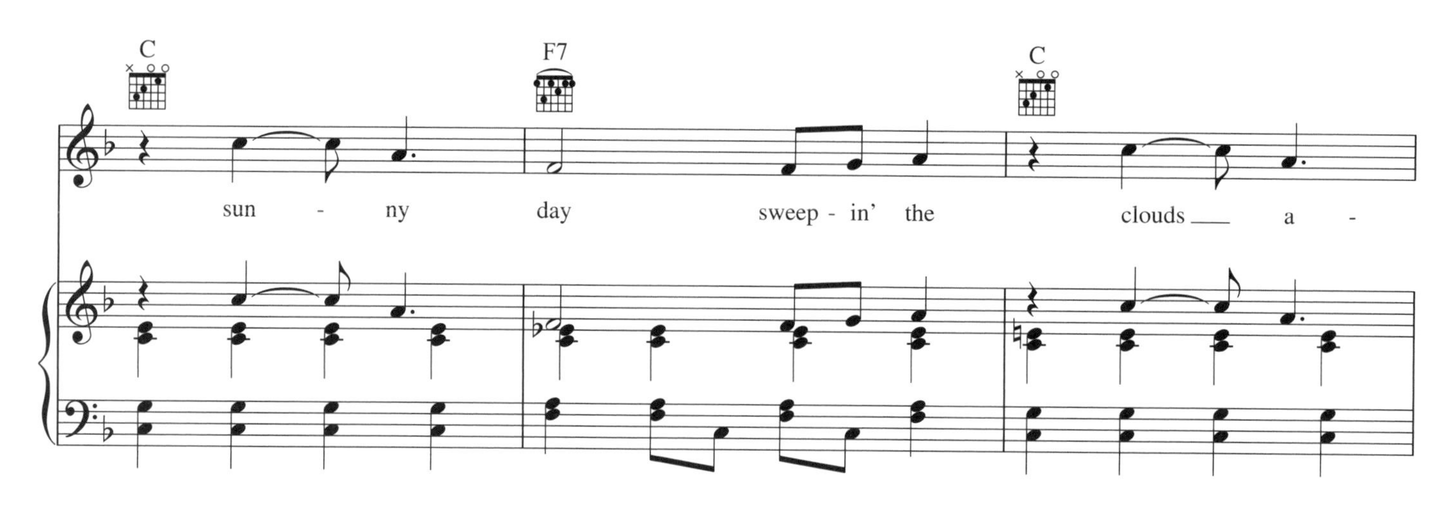
C
F7
C
sun - ny day sweep - in' the clouds a -

F7
C
F7
G7/D
Dm7
G7/D
way. On my way to where the air is sweet.

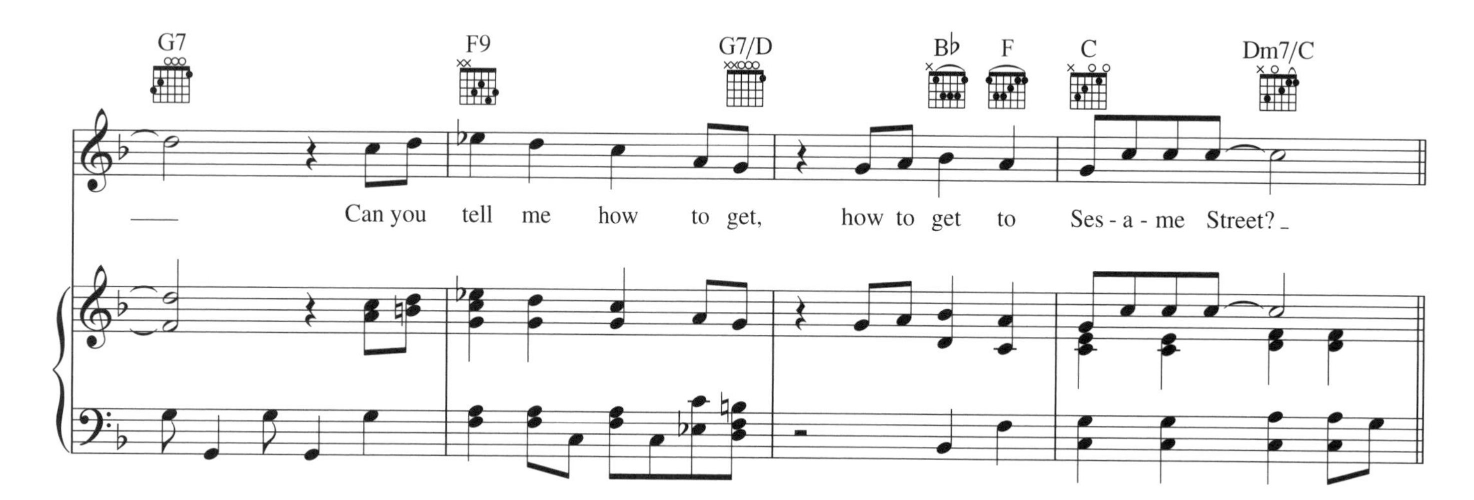
G7
F9
G7/D
B♭
F
C
Dm7/C
Can you tell me how to get, how to get to Ses - a - me Street?

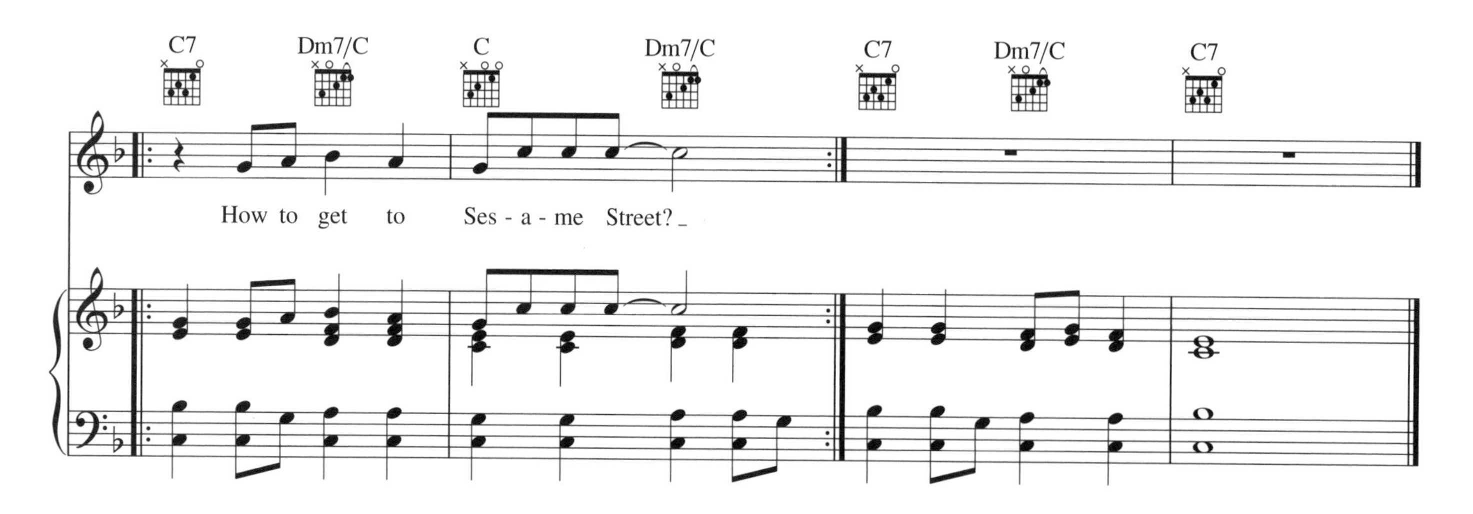
C7
Dm7/C
C
Dm7/C
C7
Dm7/C
C7
How to get to Ses - a - me Street?

Splish Splash

Words and Music by Bobby Darin and Murray Kaufman

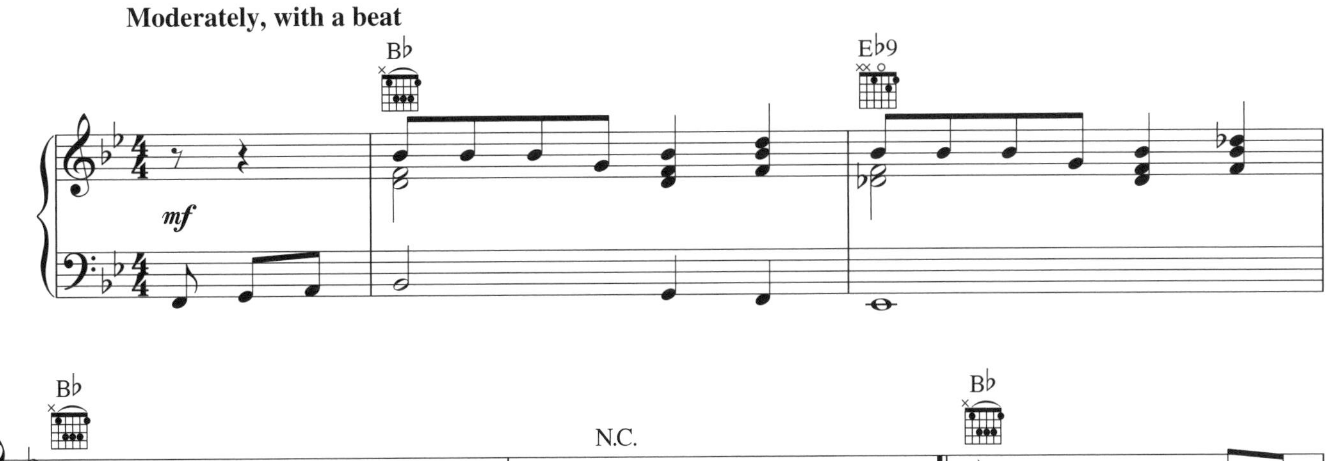

C7
F7
think - in' ev - 'ry - thing was all right. Well, I
teens had the danc - in' bug. There was
B♭
stepped out the tub, put my feet on the floor. I
Lol - li - pop with Peg - gy Sue. Good
E♭6
Edim7
F7
wrapped the towel a - round me and I o - pened the door, and then, a -
gol - ly, Miss Mol - ly was a - e - ven there, too. A - well, a -
B♭
F7
- splish splash, I jumped back in the bath. Well,
- splish splash, I for - got a - bout the bath. I

B♭
1
how was I to know there was a par - ty go - ing on?
went and put my danc - ing shoes
2
on. I was a - splish - in' and a - splash - in', I was a -
roll - in' and a - stroll - in'. I was a - mov - in' and a - groov - in',
E♭9
B♭
Repeat and Fade
Optional Ending
I was a - reel - in' with the feel - in'. I was a -

from SESAME STREET
Words and Music by Joe Raposo

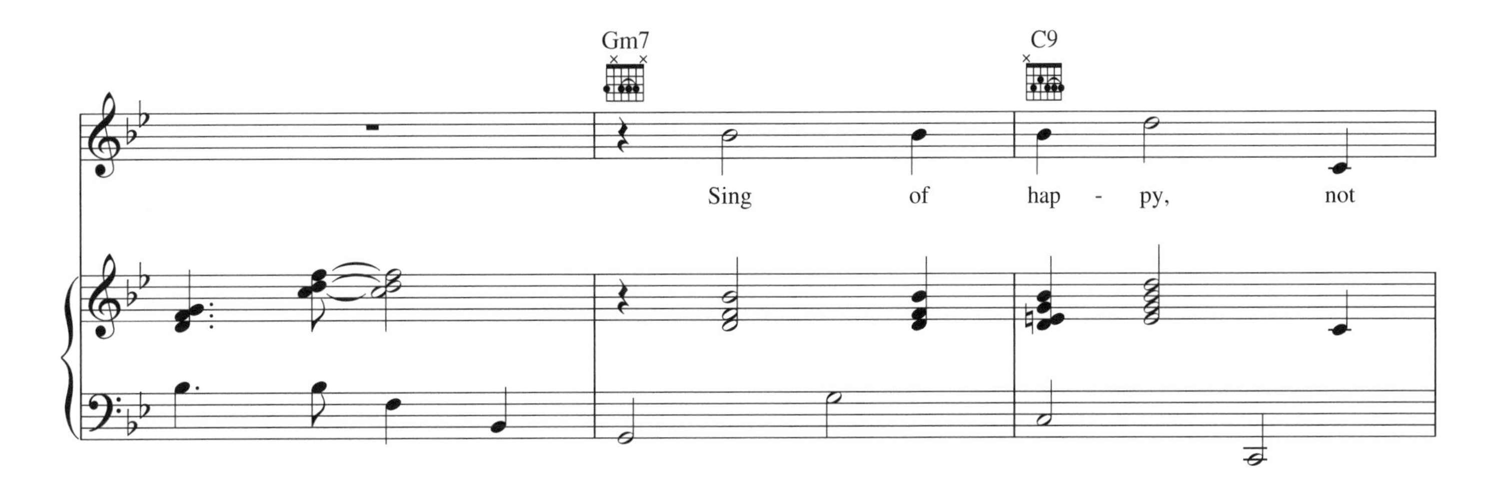
Gm7
C9
Sing of hap - py, not

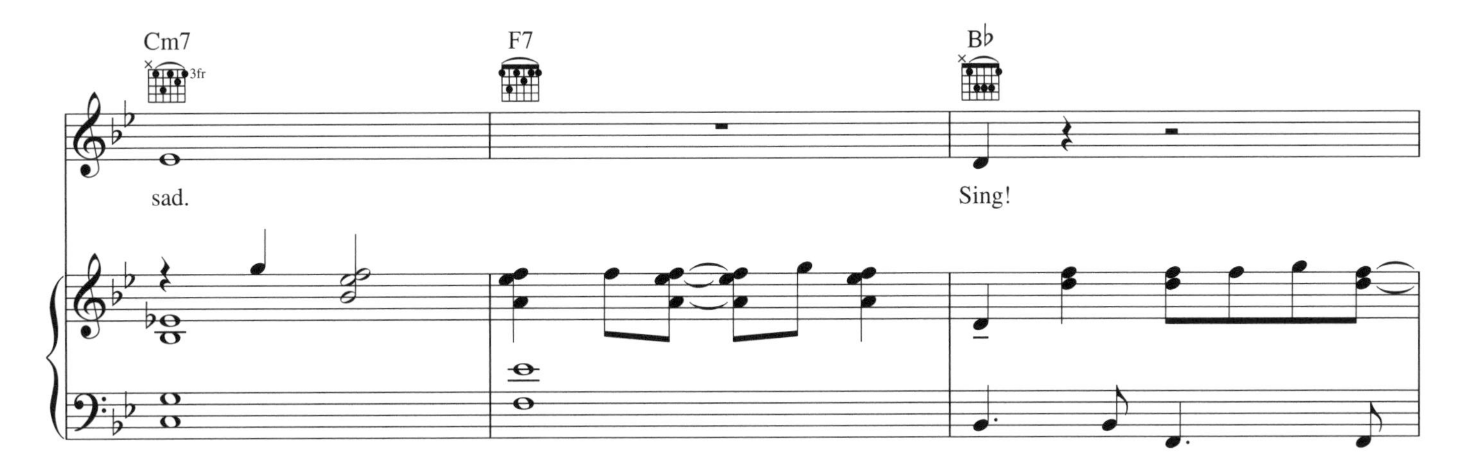
Cm7
3fr
F7
B♭
sad.
Sing!

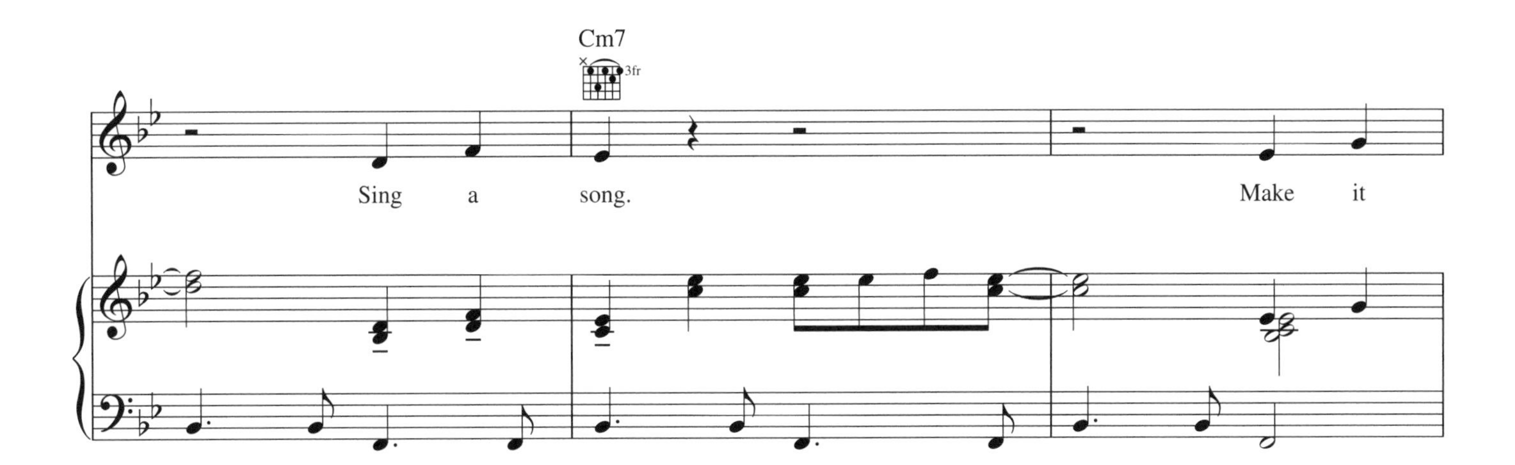
Cm7
3fr
Sing a song.
Make it

B♭
B♭maj7
B♭6
Fm7/B♭
sim - ple to last your whole life long.

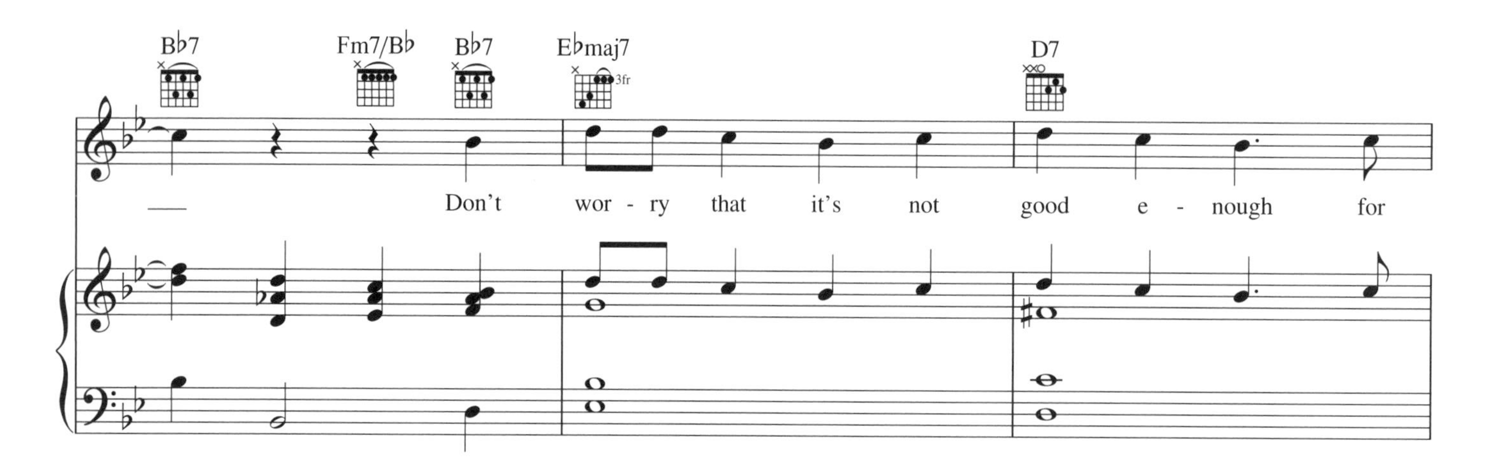
B♭7
Fm7/B♭
B♭7
E♭maj7
3fr
D7
Don't wor - ry that it's not good e - nough for

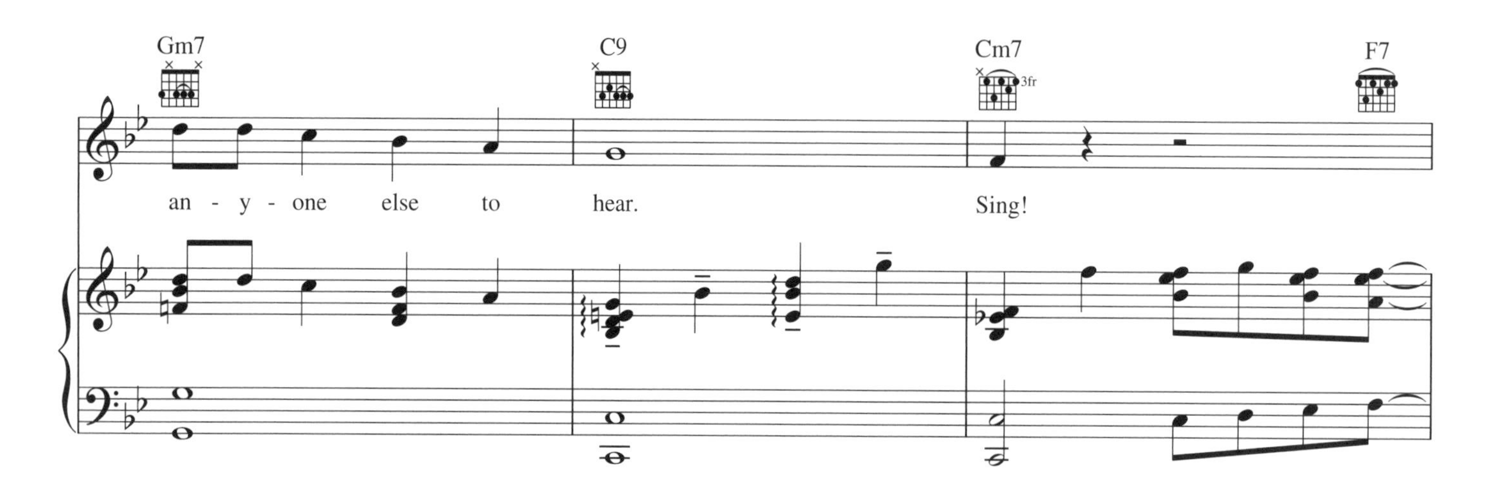
Gm7
C9
Cm7
3fr
F7
an - y - one else to hear. Sing!

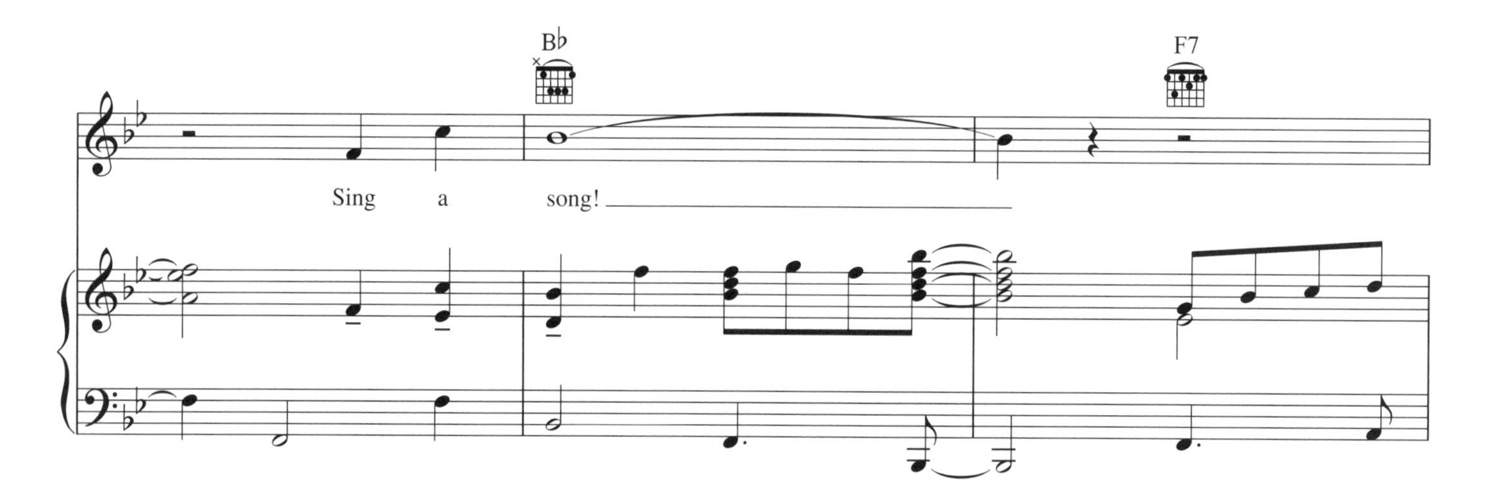
B♭
F7
Sing a song!

B♭
B♭maj7
E♭maj7
3fr
La la do la da, La da la do la da, La da da la do la da.

B♭
B♭maj7
La do la da, La da la la da, Lo

E♭maj7
3fr
1
2
da da la do la da.

B♭
B♭maj7
E♭maj7
3fr
La la do la da, La da la do la da, La da da la do la da.

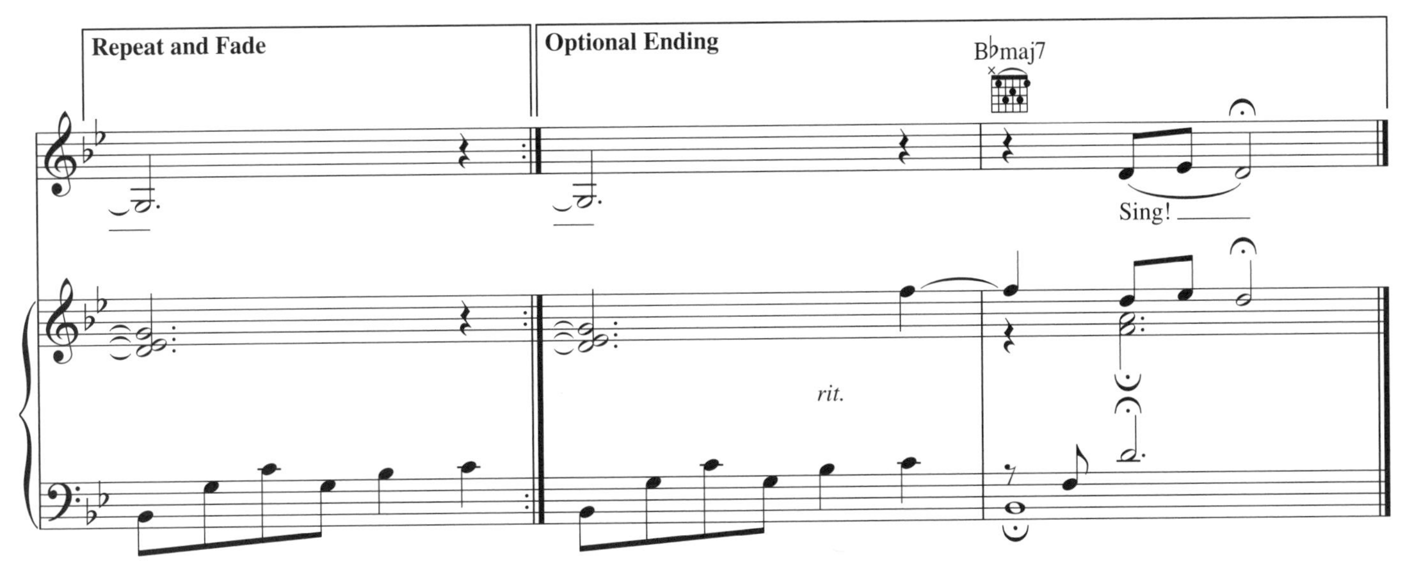
Repeat and Fade
Optional Ending
B♭maj7
Sing!
rit.

SpongeBob SquarePants Theme Song

from SPONGEBOB SQUAREPANTS

Words and Music by Mark Harrison, Blaise Smith, Steve Hillenburg and Derek Drymon

C
Kids: Sponge - Bob Square - Pants! Painty: then drop on the deck and flop like a fish!
3
G
Kids: Sponge - Bob Square - Pants! All: Sponge - Bob Square - Pants!
D
Sponge - Bob Square - Pants! Sponge - Bob Square - Pants! Sponge - Bob Square -
G
N.C.
Pants!
8va

Supercalifragilisticexpialidocious

from Walt Disney's MARY POPPINS

Words and Music by Richard M. Sherman and Robert B. Sherman

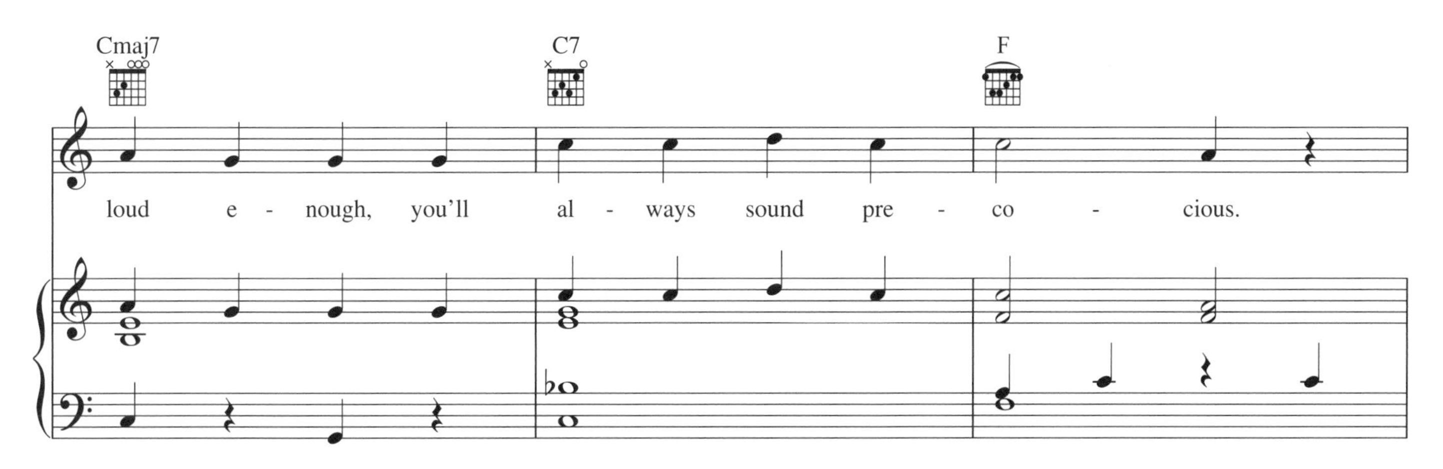
Cmaj7
C7
F
loud e - nough, you'll al - ways sound pre - co - cious.

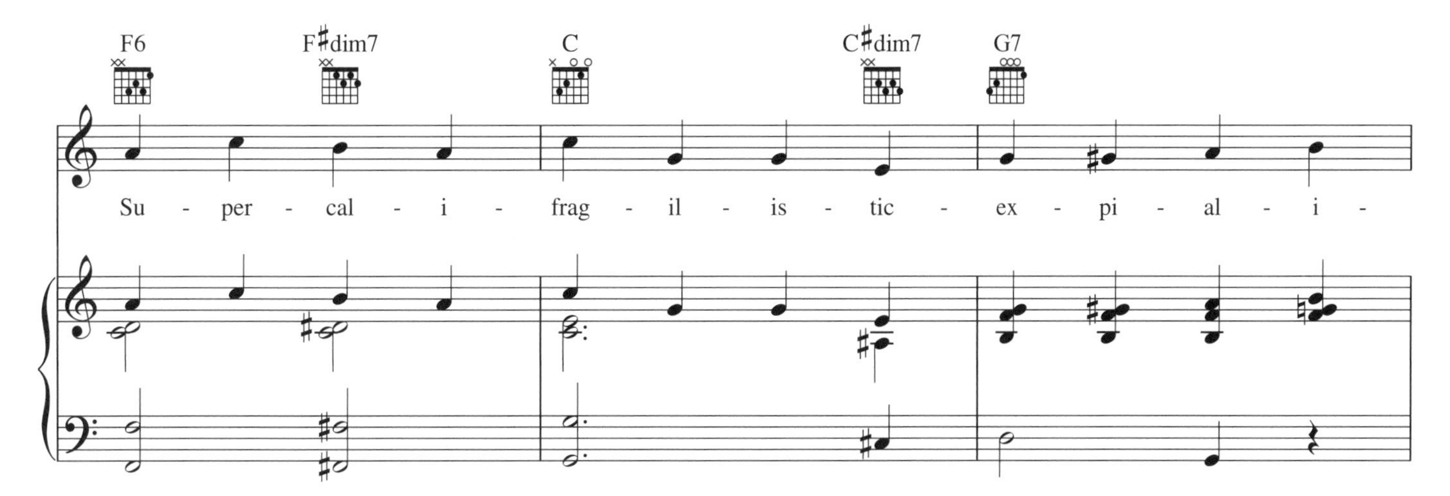
F6
F♯dim7
C
C♯dim7
G7
Su - per - cal - i - frag - il - is - tic - ex - pi - al - i -

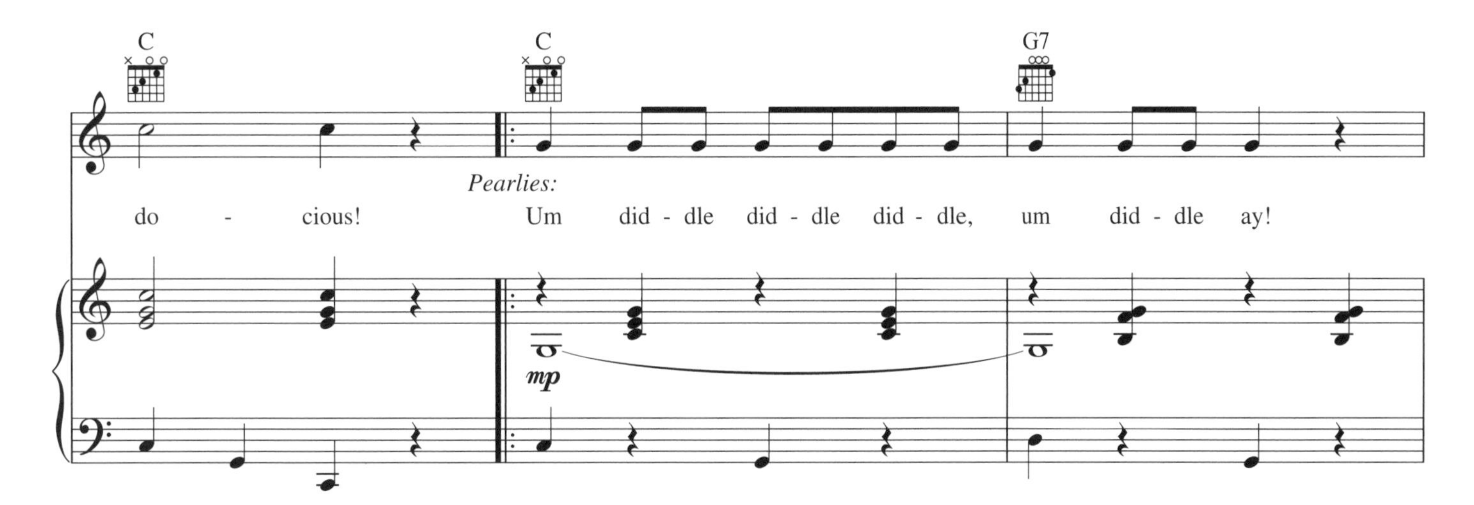
C
C
G7
Pearlies:
do - cious! Um did - dle did - dle did - dle, um did - dle ay!
mp

C
G7
C
Um did - dle did - dle did - dle, um did - dle ay!
Bert: Be - cause I was a -
Mary Poppins: He trav - eled all a -
So when the cat has
mf

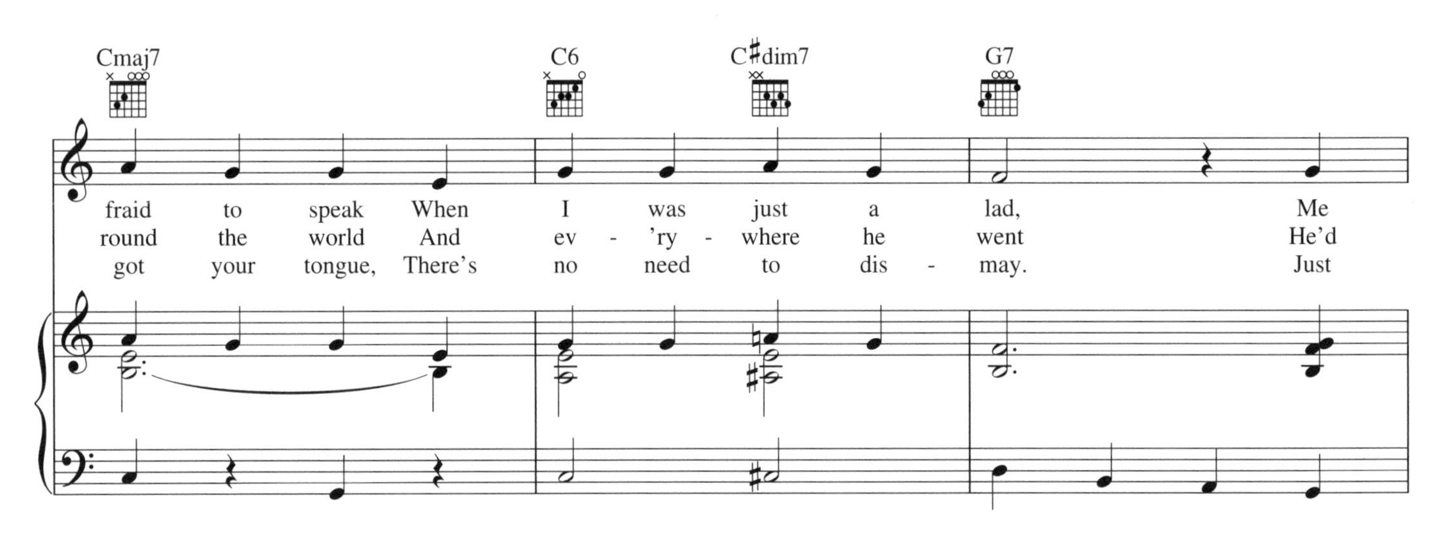
Cmaj7 C6 C♯dim7 G7
fraid to speak When I was just a lad, Me
round the world And ev - 'ry - where he went He'd
got your tongue, There's no need to dis - may. Just

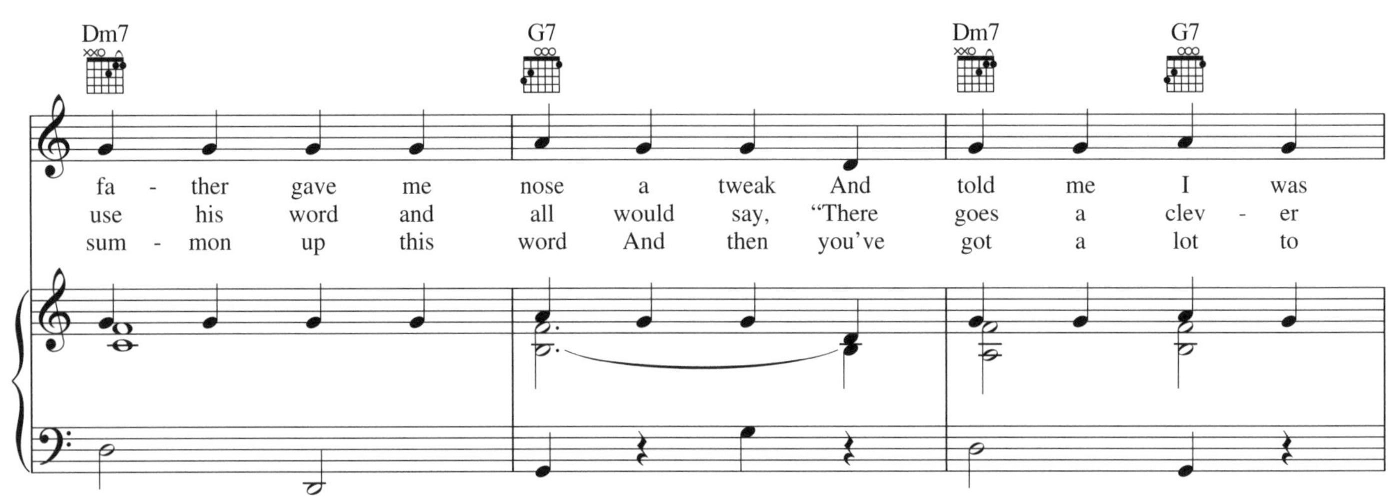
Dm7 G7 Dm7 G7
fa - ther gave me nose a tweak And told me I was
use his word and all would say, "There goes a clev - er
sum - mon up this word And then you've got a lot to

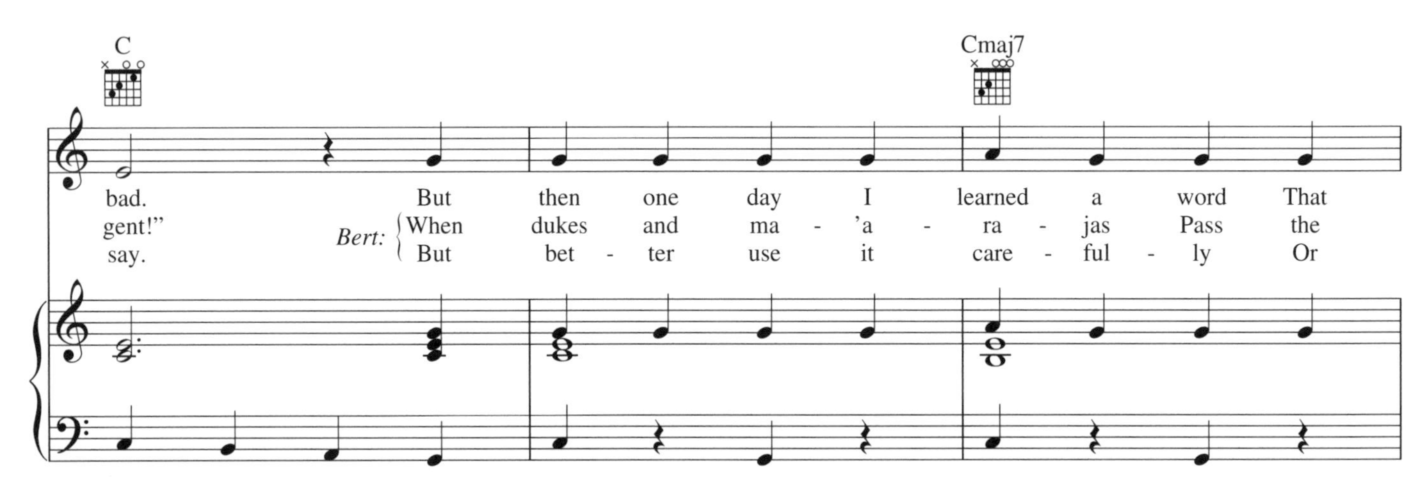
C Cmaj7
bad. But then one day I learned a word That
gent!" Bert: When dukes and ma - 'a - ra - jas Pass the
say. But bet - ter use it care - ful - ly Or

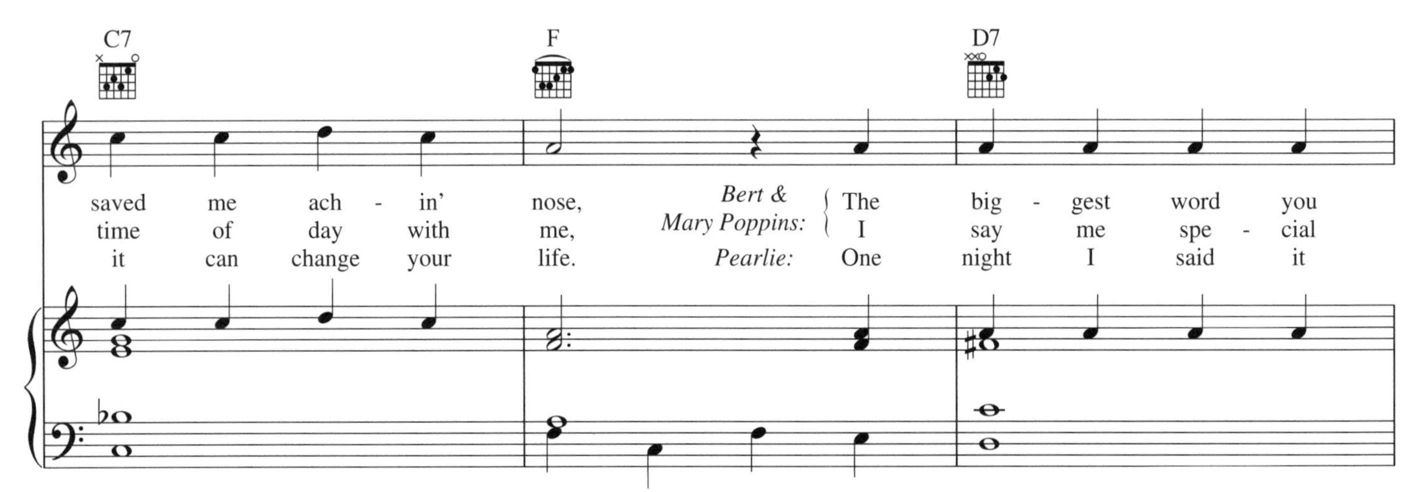
C7 F D7
saved me ach - in' nose, Bert & Mary Poppins: The big - gest word you
time of day with me, I say me spe - cial
it can change your life. Pearlie: One night I said it

G7
ev - er 'eard And this is 'ow it goes: Oh!
word And then they ask me out to tea. All: Oh!
to me girl And now me girl's me wife. All: She's
f

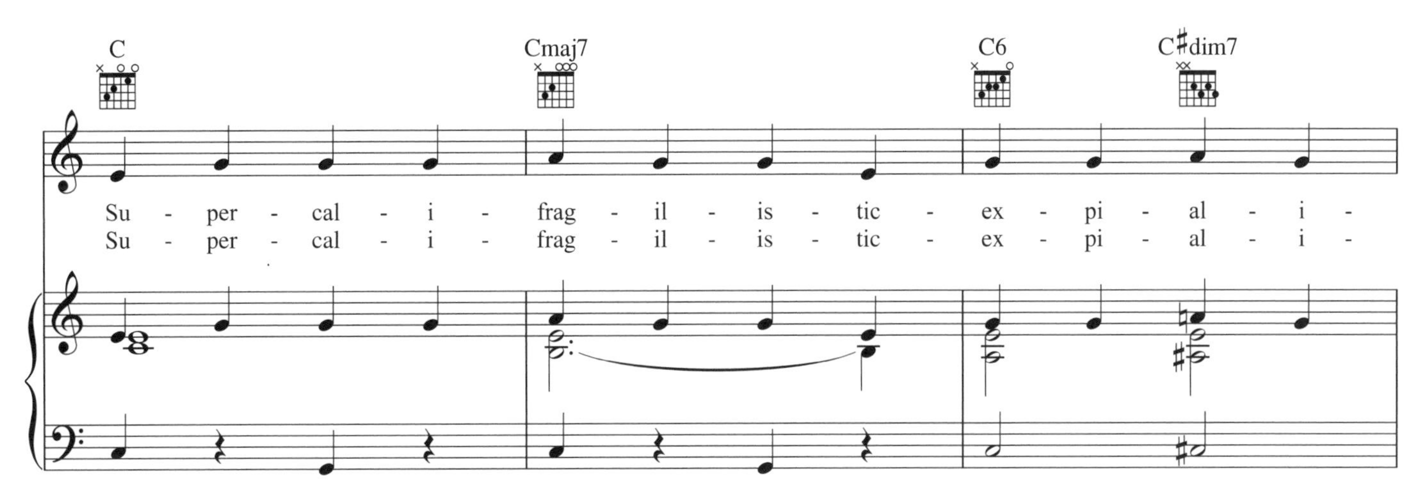
C
Cmaj7
C6
C♯dim7
Su - per - cal - i - frag - il - is - tic - ex - pi - al - i -
Su - per - cal - i - frag - il - is - tic - ex - pi - al - i -

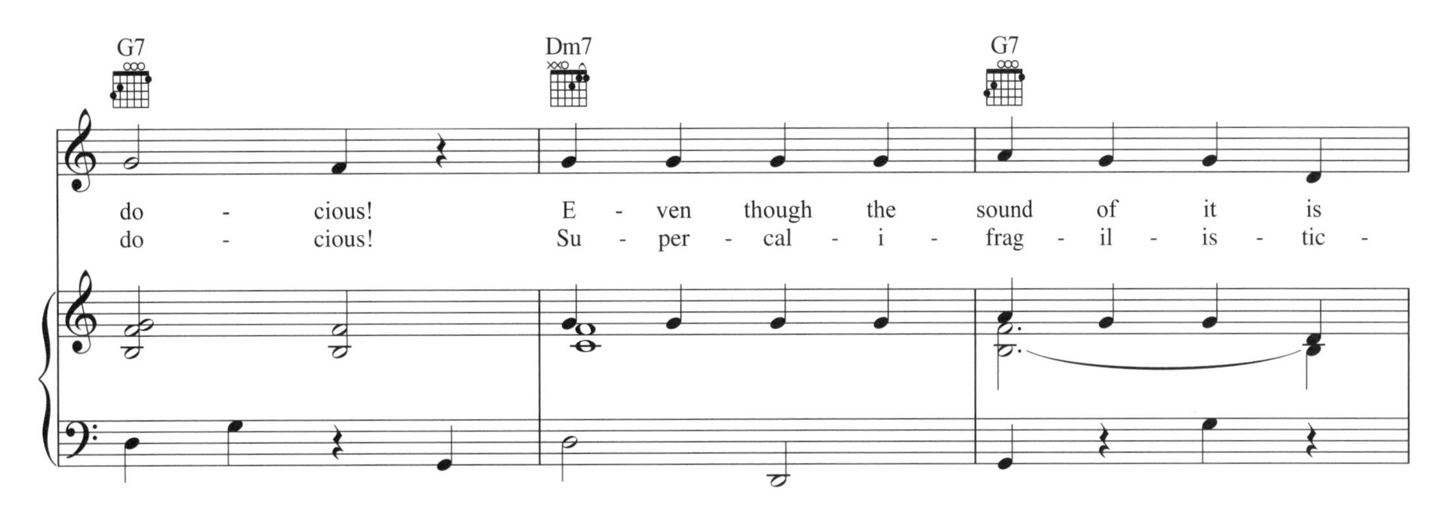
G7
Dm7
G7
do - cious! E - ven though the sound of it is
do - cious! Su - per - cal - i - frag - il - is - tic -

Dm7
G7
C
some - thing quite a - tro - cious, if you say it
ex - pi - al - i - do - cious! Su - per - cal - i -

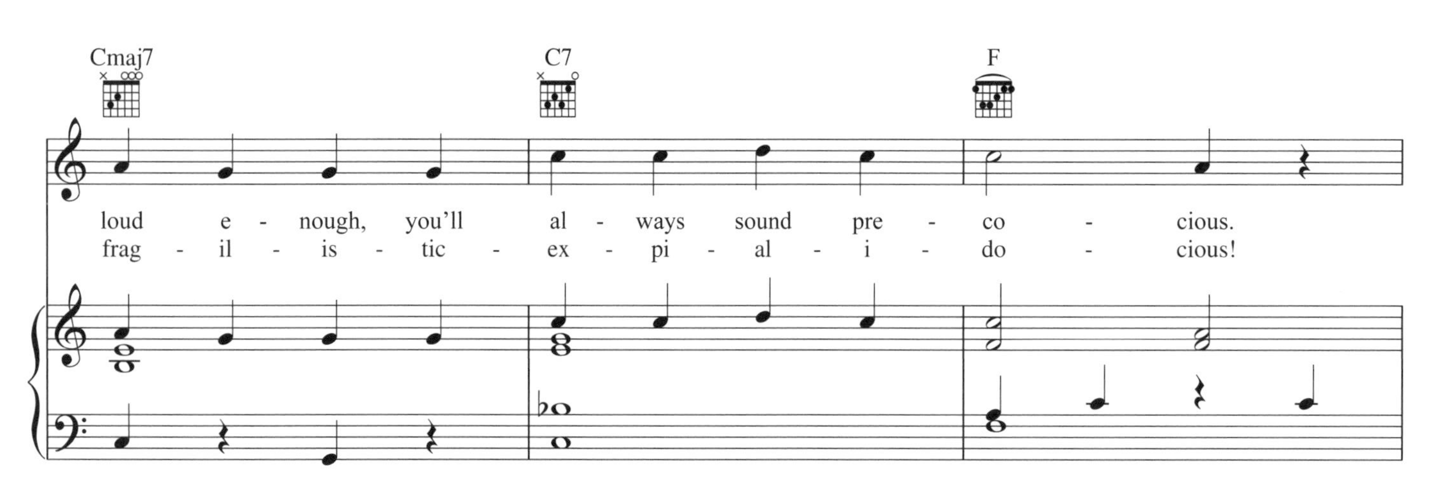
Cmaj7
C7
F
loud e - nough, you'll al - ways sound pre - co - cious.
frag - il - is - tic - ex - pi - al - i - do - cious!

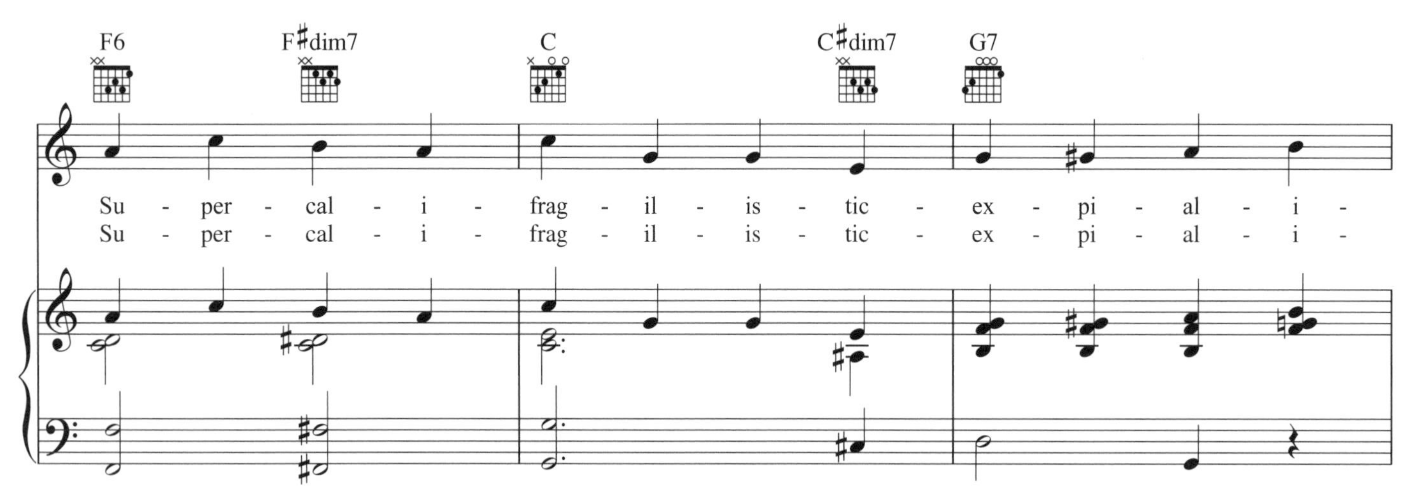
F6
F♯dim7
C
C♯dim7
G7
Su - per - cal - i - frag - il - is - tic - ex - pi - al - i -
Su - per - cal - i - frag - il - is - tic - ex - pi - al - i -

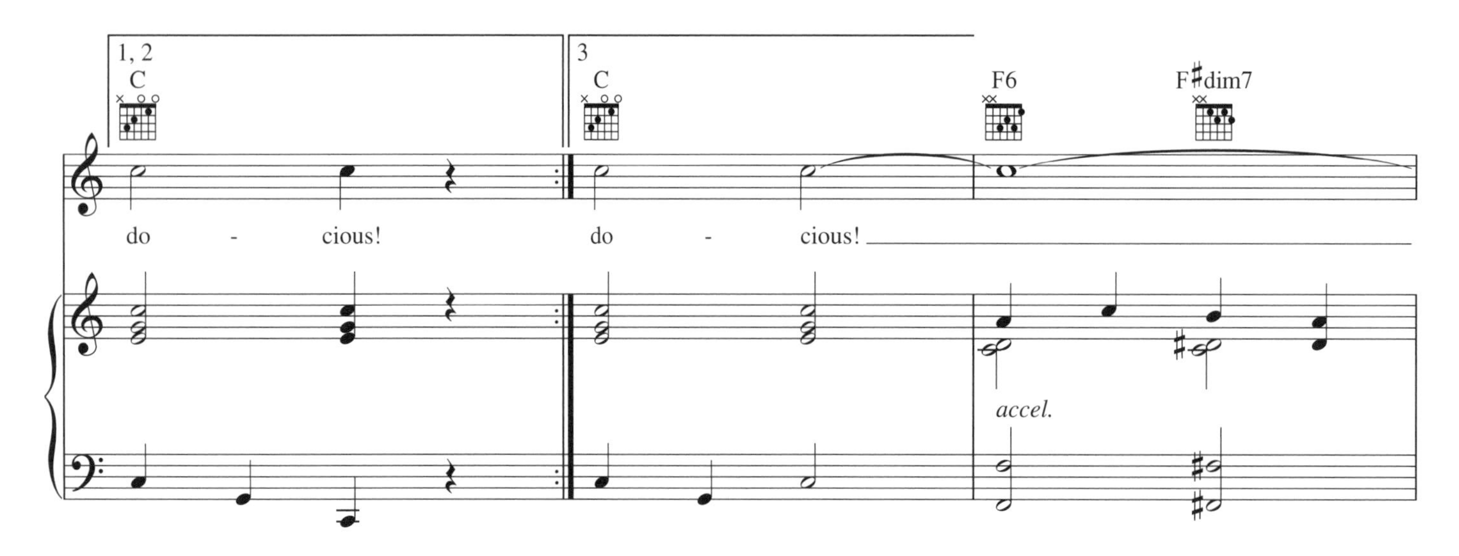
1, 2
3
C
C
F6
F♯dim7
do - cious!
do - cious!
accel.

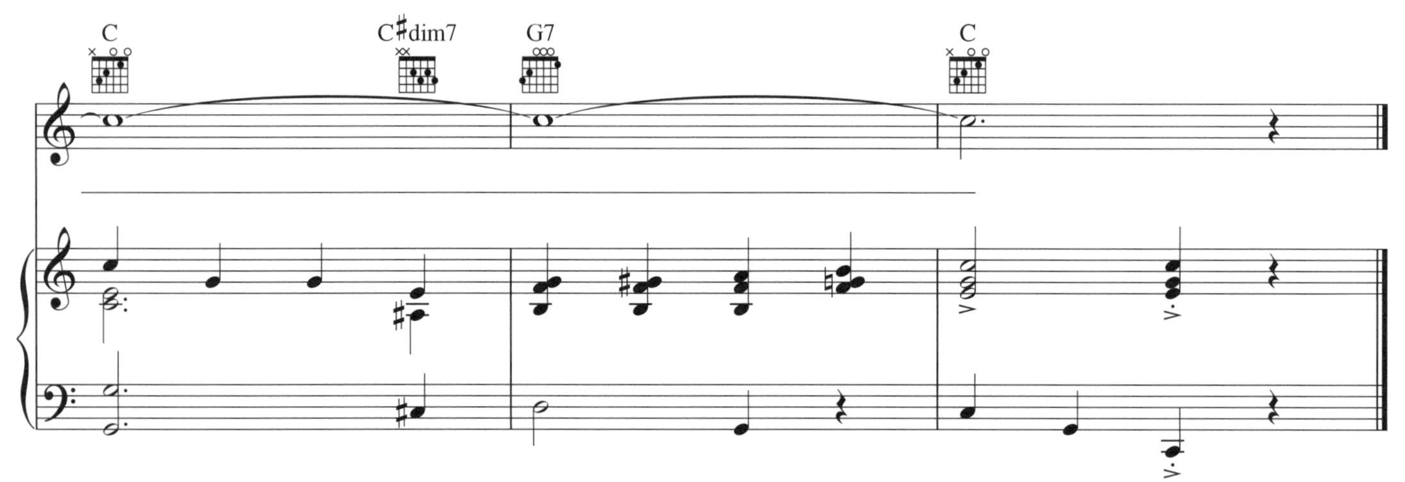
C
C♯dim7
G7
C

Take Me Out to the Ball Game

Words by Jack Norworth
Music by Albert von Tilzer

Spirited, in 1

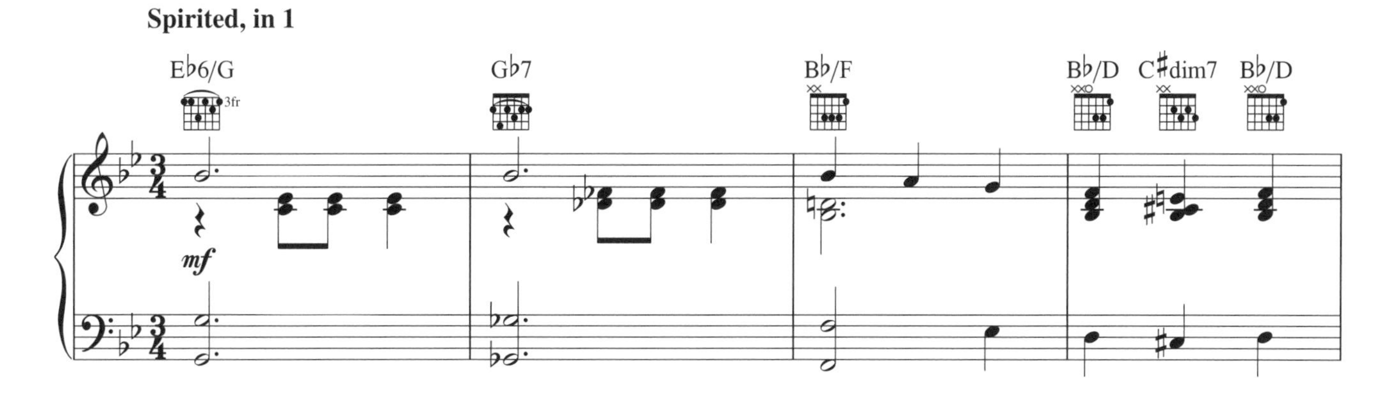

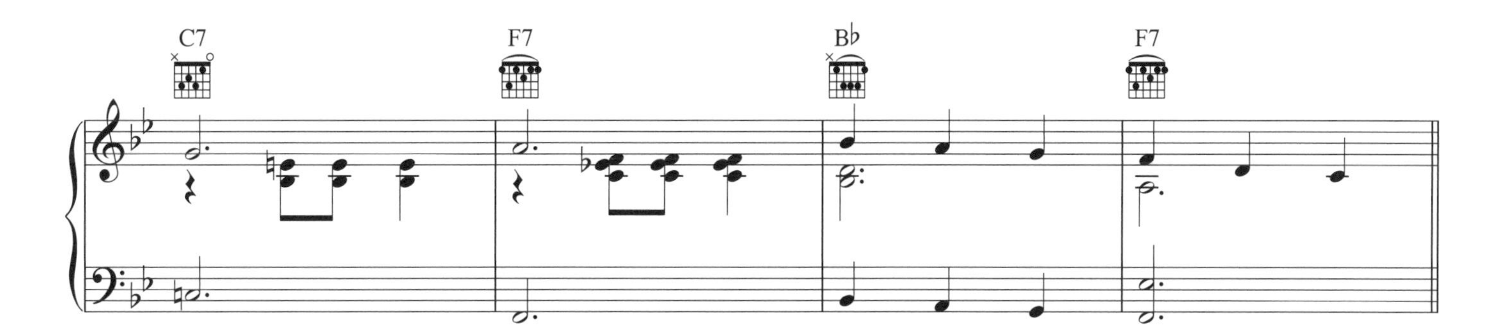

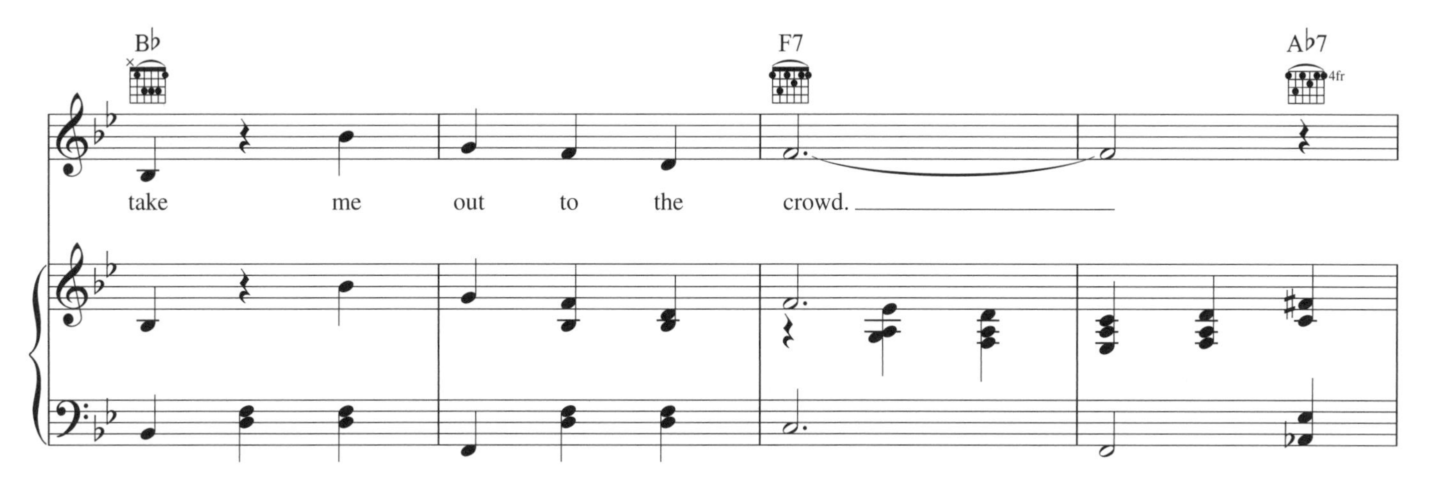

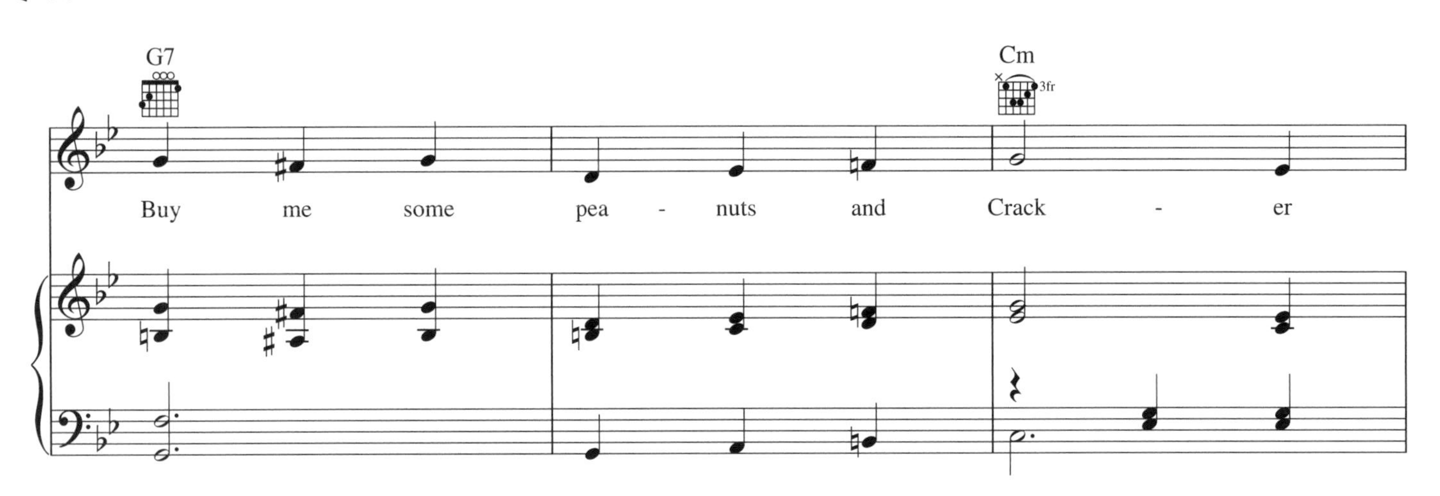
G7
Cm
3fr
Buy me some pea - nuts and Crack - er

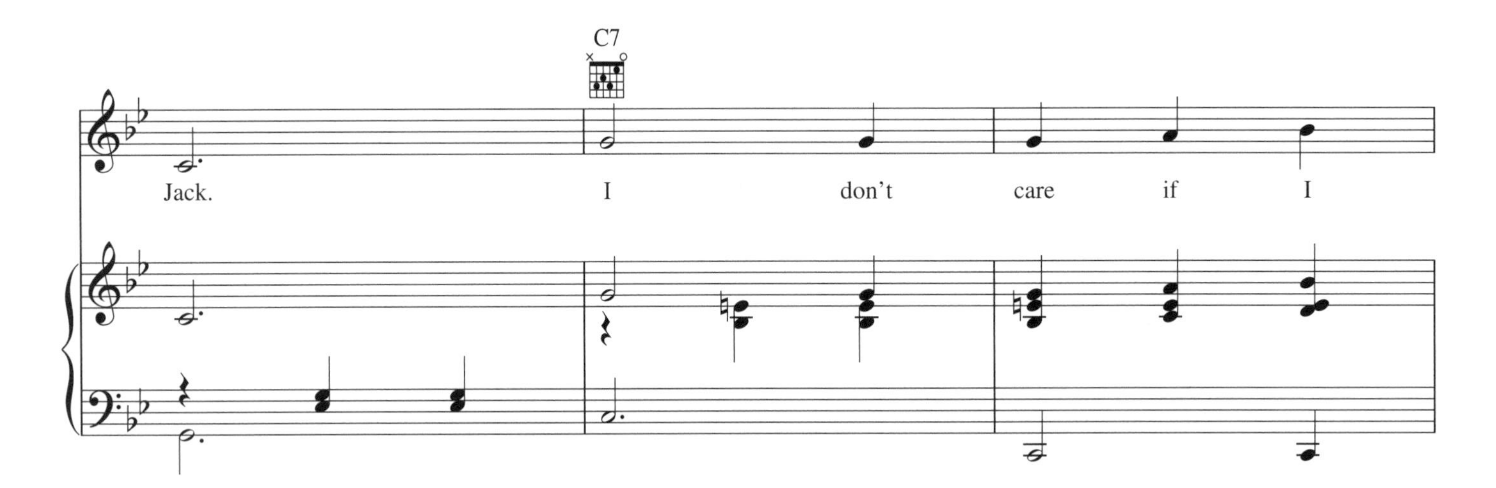
C7
Jack. I don't care if I

F7
B♭
nev - er get back. Let me root, root,

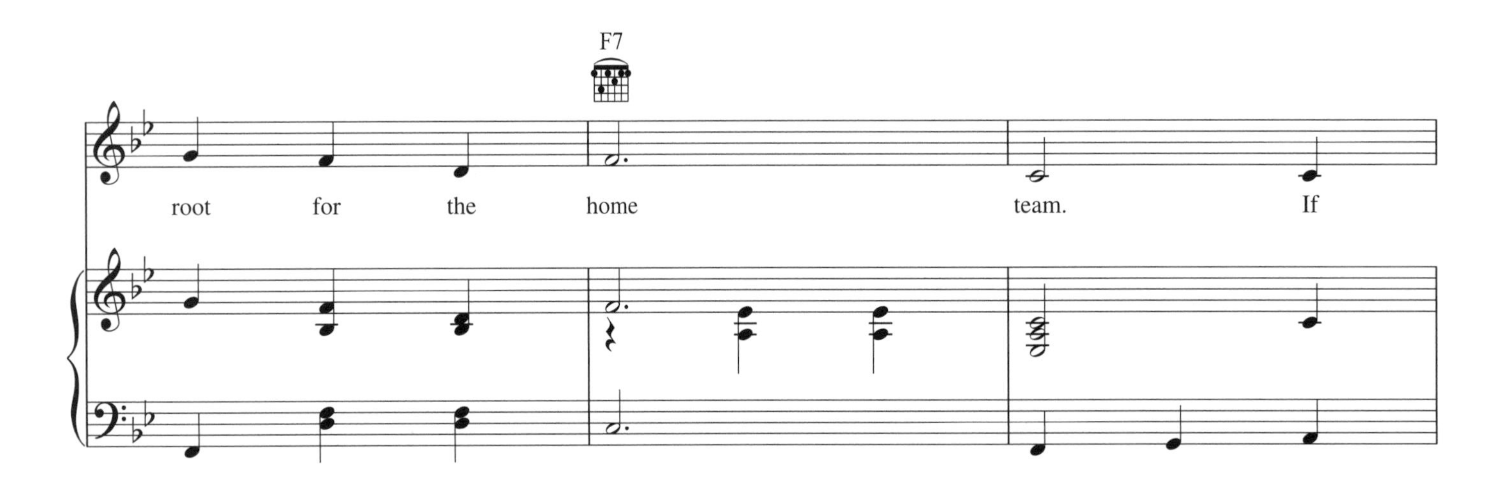
F7
root for the home team. If

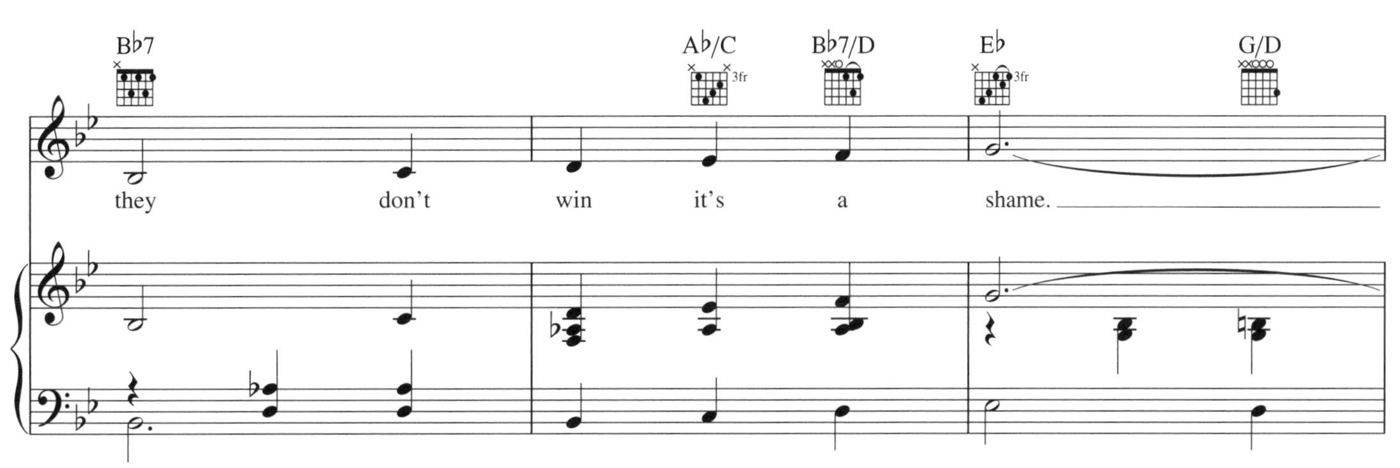
B♭7
A♭/C
B♭7/D
E♭
G/D
they don't win it's a shame.

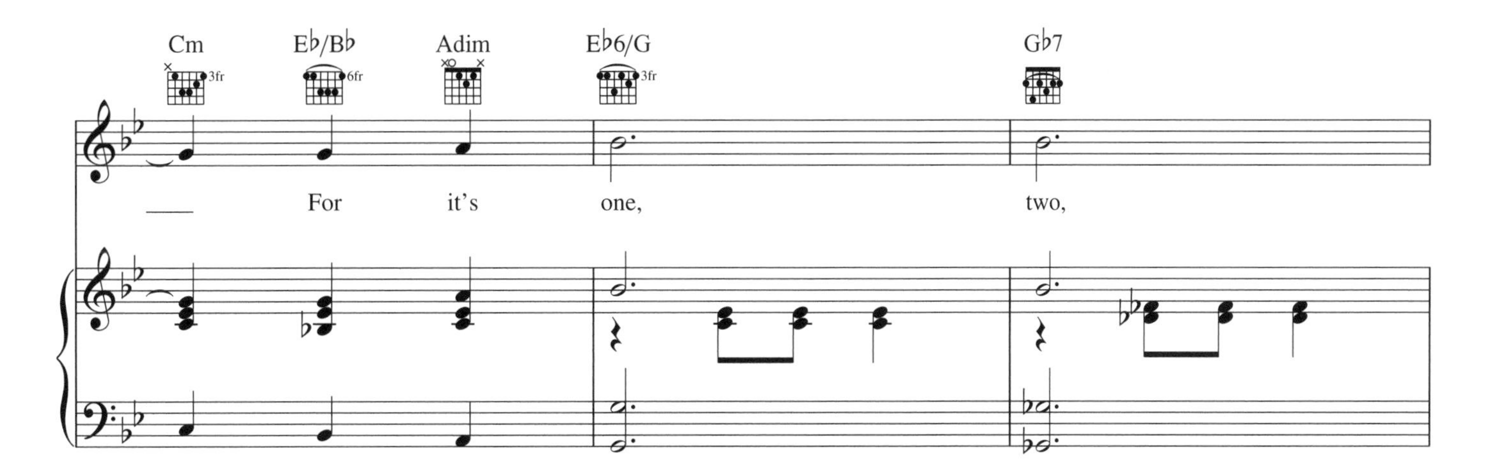
Cm
E♭/B♭
Adim
E♭6/G
G♭7
For it's one, two,

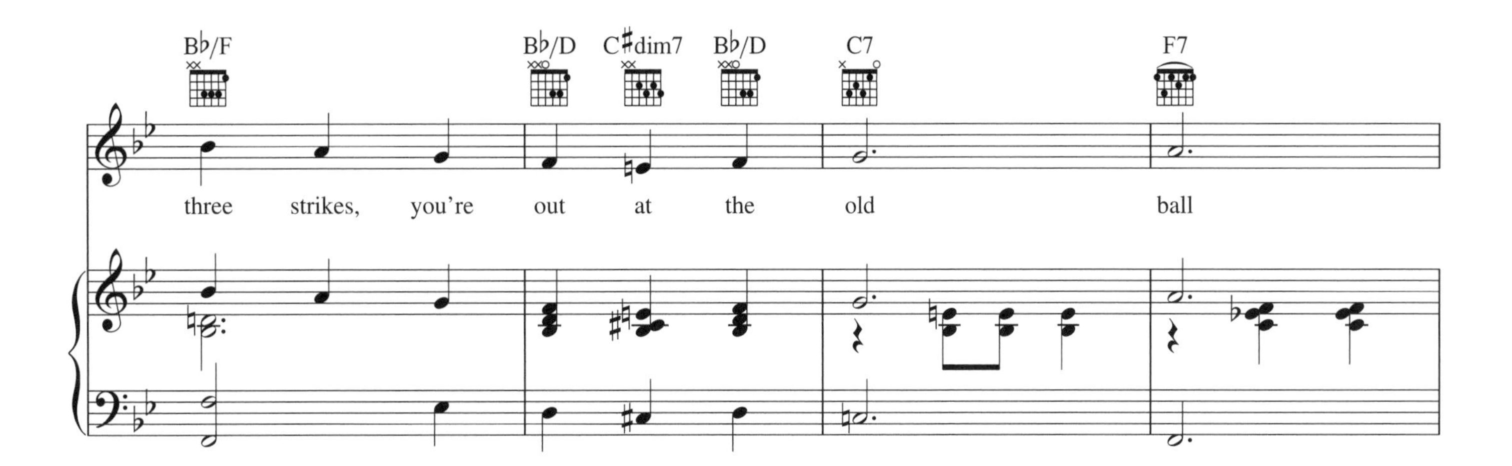
B♭/F
B♭/D
C♯dim7
B♭/D
C7
F7
three strikes, you're out at the old ball

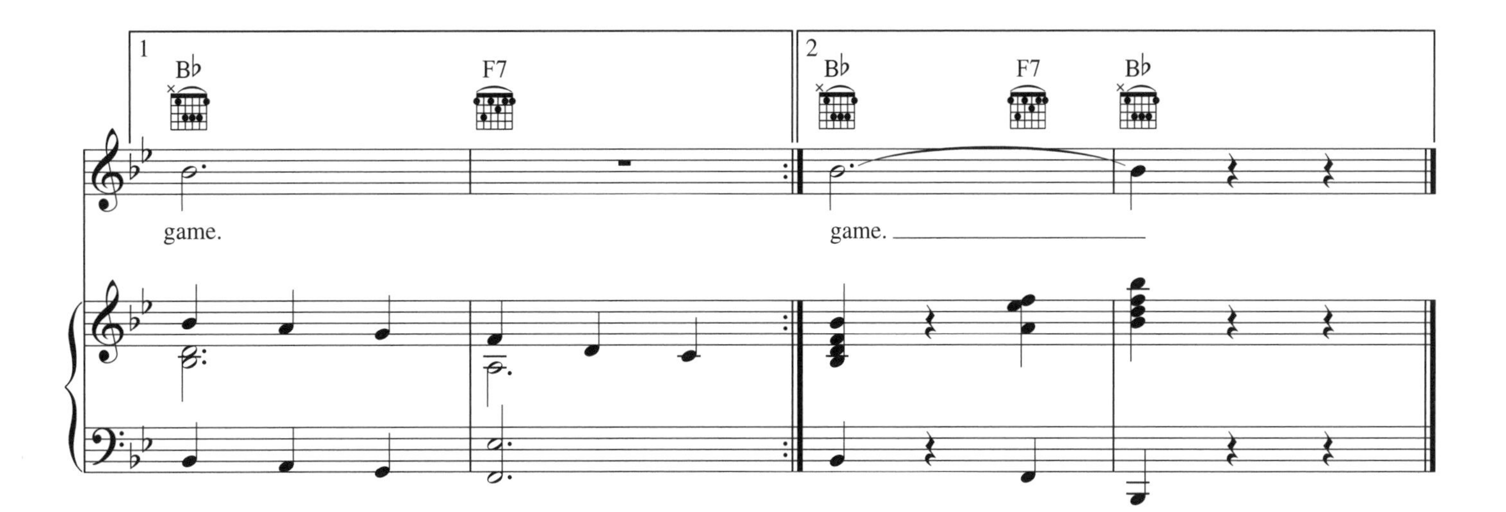
1
B♭
F7
2
B♭
F7
B♭
game.
game.

This Land Is Your Land

Words and Music by Woody Guthrie

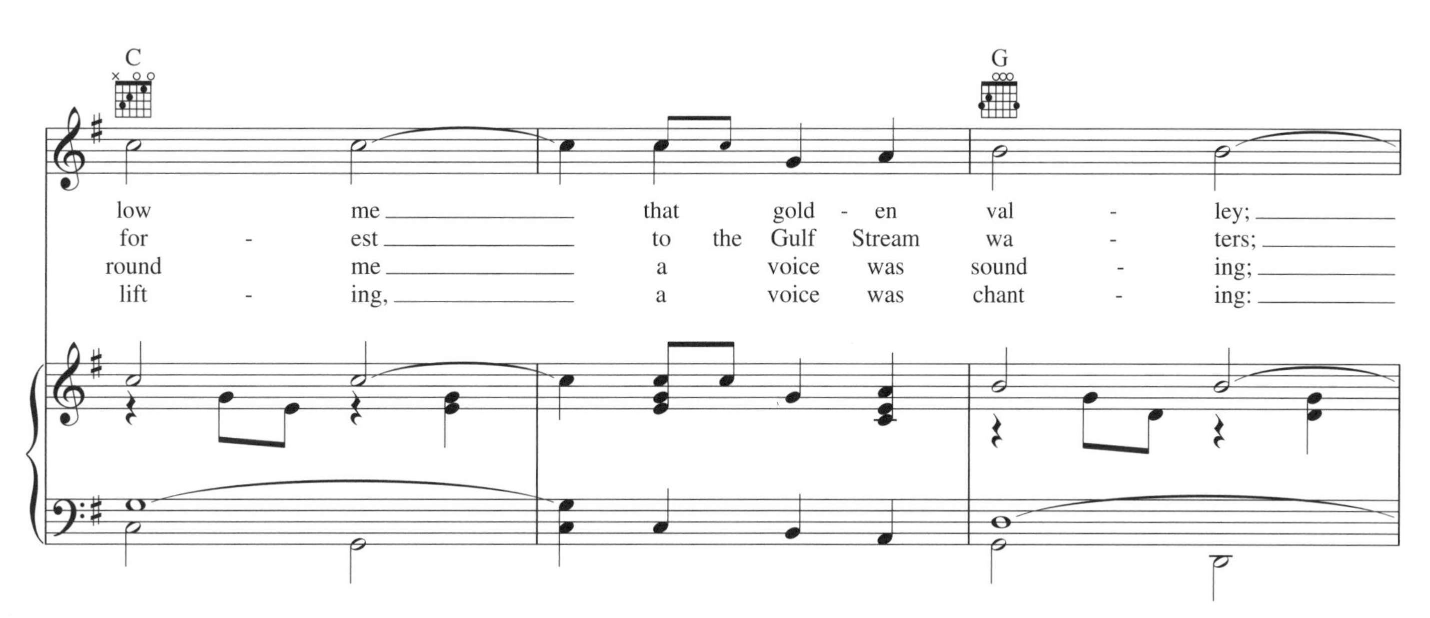
C
G
low me that gold - en val - ley;
for - est to the Gulf Stream wa - ters;
round me a voice was sound - ing;
lift - ing, a voice was chant - ing:

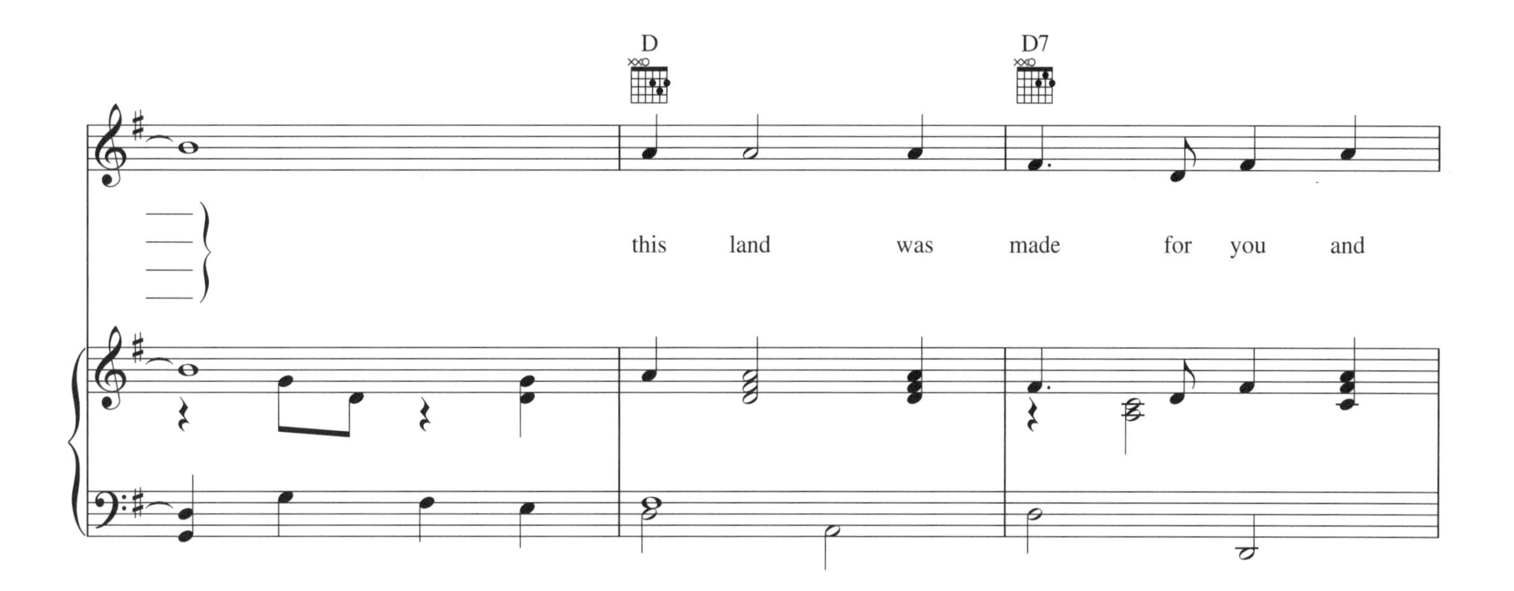
D
D7
this land was made for you and

1–5
G
6
G
me.
2.,4.,6. This land is
3. I've roamed and
5. Well, the sun came
me.
rit.

Words and Music by Saxie Dowell

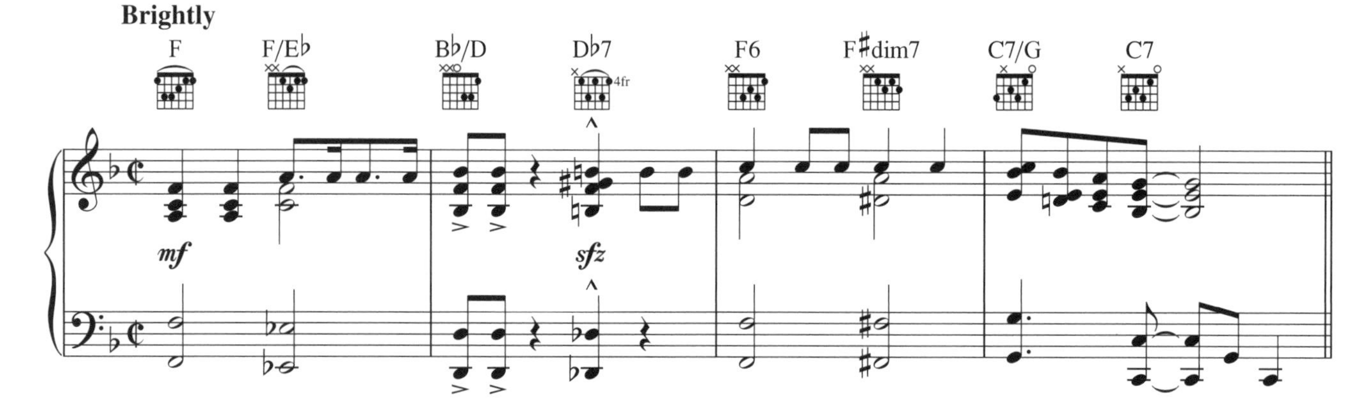

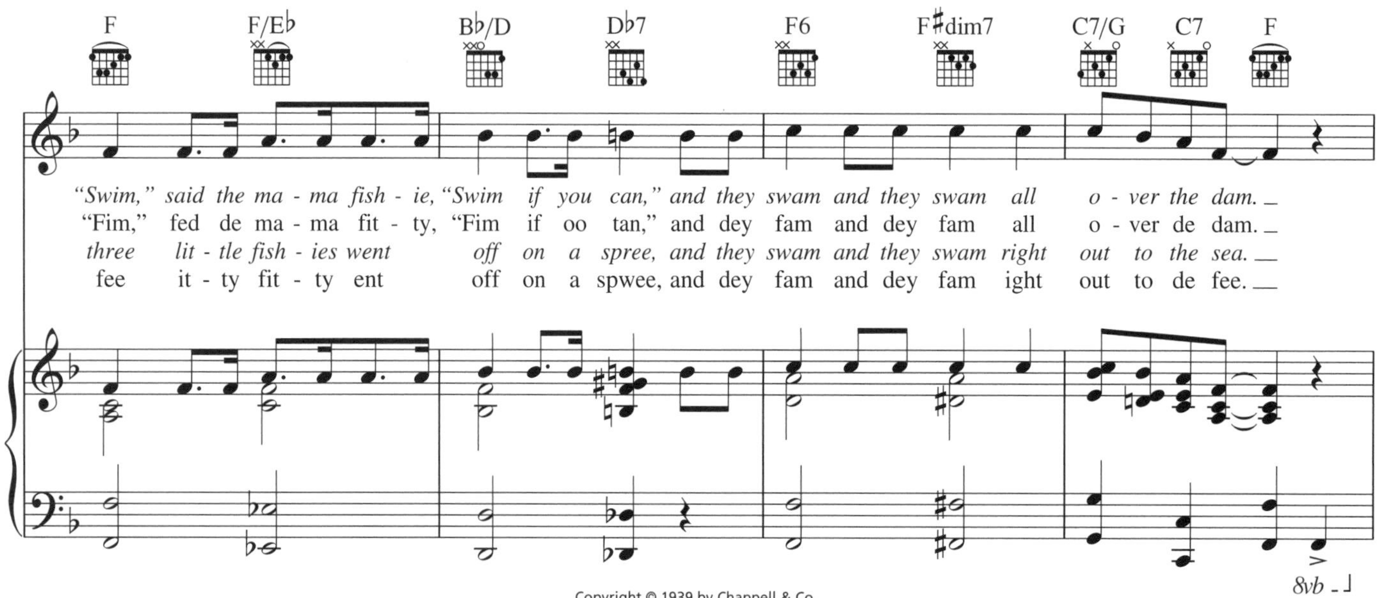

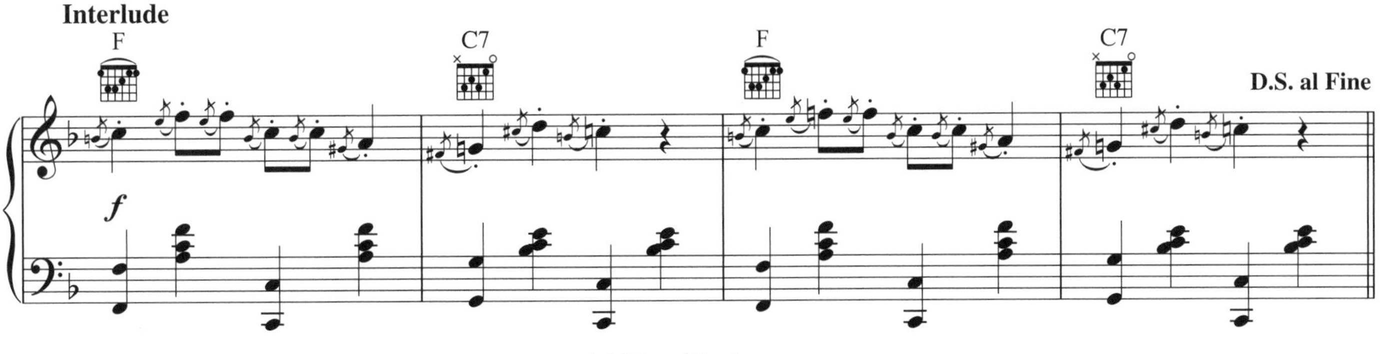

Additional Lyrics

3. *"Whee!" yelled the little fishies, "Here's a lot of fun.*
   We'll swim in the sea till the day is done."
   They swam and they swam and it was a lark,
   Till all of a sudden they saw a shark!

   "Whee!" 'elled de itty fitties, "Ears a wot of fun.
   Ee'll fim in de fee ill de day is un."
   Dey fam and dey fam and it was a wark,
   Till aw of a tudden dey taw a tark!

   Boop boop dittem dattem whattem. Chu!
   Boop boop dittem dattem whattem. Chu!
   Boop boop dittem dattem whattem. Chu!
   Till aw of a tudden dey taw a tark!

4. *"Help!" cried the little fishies, "Gee! Look at all the whales!"*
   And quick as they could they turned on their tails.
   And back to the pool in the meadow they swam,
   And they swam and they swam back over the dam.

   "He'p!" tied de itty fitties, "Dee! Ook at all de fales!"
   And twit as dey tood dey turned on deir tails.
   And bat to de poo in de meddy dey fam,
   And dey fam and dey fam bat over de dam.

   Boop boop dittem dattem whattem. Chu!
   Boop boop dittem dattem whattem. Chu!
   Boop boop dittem dattem whattem. Chu!
   And dey fam and dey fam bat over de dam.

Tomorrow

from the Musical Production ANNIE
Lyric by Martin Charnin
Music by Charles Strouse

B♭maj7
Am7
Dm
Dm/C
clears a - way the cob - webs and the sor - row till there's
B♭maj7
C
Fm
A♭/E♭
none. When I'm stuck with a day that's gray and
D♭
E♭
3fr
A♭
4fr
A♭maj7
lone - ly, I just stick out my chin and grin and
C7sus
C7
say: Oh! the
f
mp

F
Fmaj7
B♭maj7
Am7
sun - 'll come out to - mor - row,
So you / Oh! I
got to hang on till to -
Dm
Dm/C
G♭maj7
C7sus
C7
mor - row come what may! To -
1 (small notes are optional harmony)
F
Fmaj7
F7
B♭
B♭m6
6fr
mor - row, to - mor - row, I love ya to - mor - row, you're
F
C7sus
C7
F
Fmaj7
B♭maj7/F
Gm7(add4)
al - ways / on - ly
a day a - way!
The

2
F
Fmaj7
F7
B♭
B♭m6
6fr
mor - row, to - mor - row, I love ya to - mor - row, you're

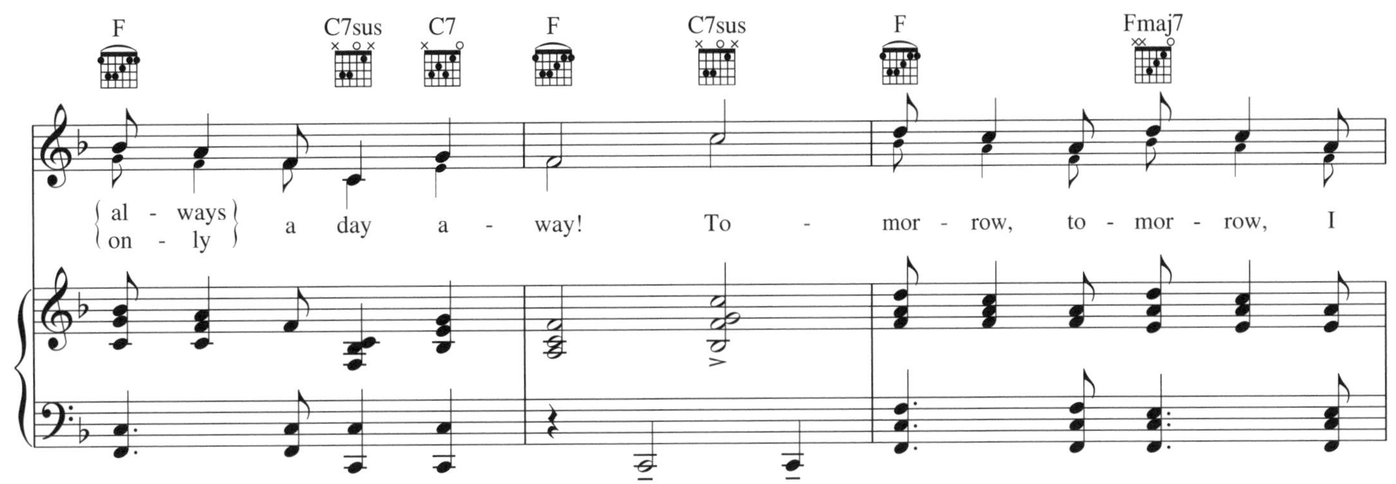
F
C7sus
C7
F
C7sus
F
Fmaj7
al - ways
on - ly
a day a - way! To - mor - row, to - mor - row, I

F7
B♭
B♭m6
6fr
F
C7sus
C7
love ya to - mor - row, you're
al - ways
on - ly
a day a -

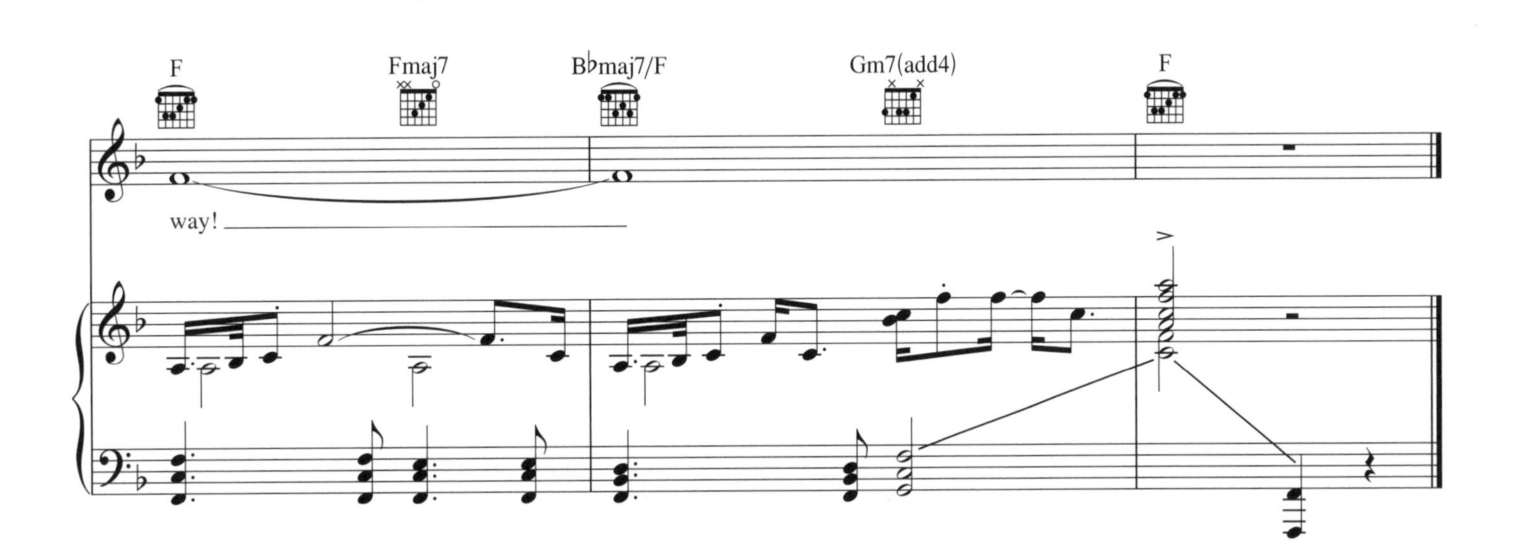
F
Fmaj7
B♭maj7/F
Gm7(add4)
F
way!

When I'm Sixty-Four

from YELLOW SUBMARINE
Words and Music by John Lennon and Paul McCartney

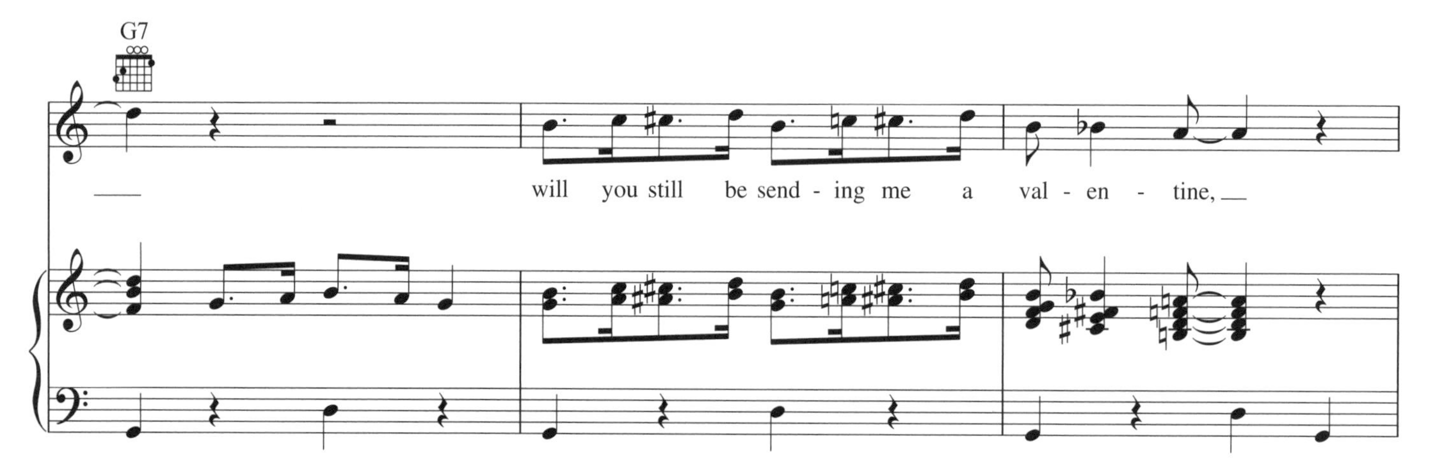

N.C.
C
birth - day greet - ings, bot - tle of wine?
If I'd been out till

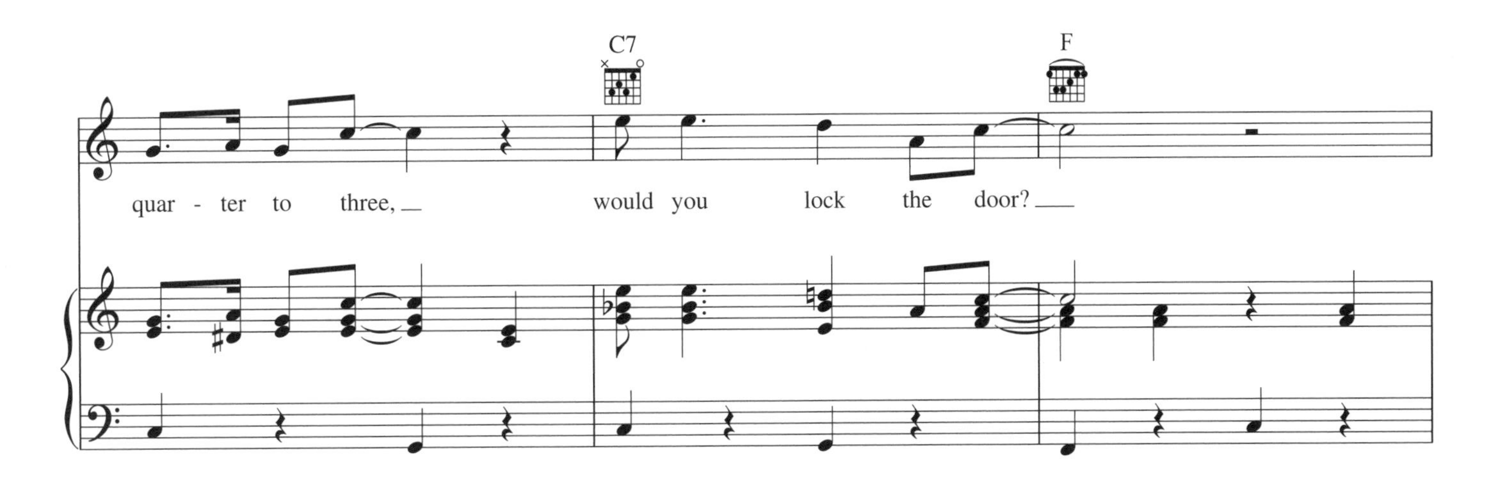
C7
F
quar - ter to three,
would you lock the door?

A♭7♭5/G♭
C/G
A7
D9
4fr
G13
3fr
Will you still need me,
will you still feed me,
when I'm six - ty -

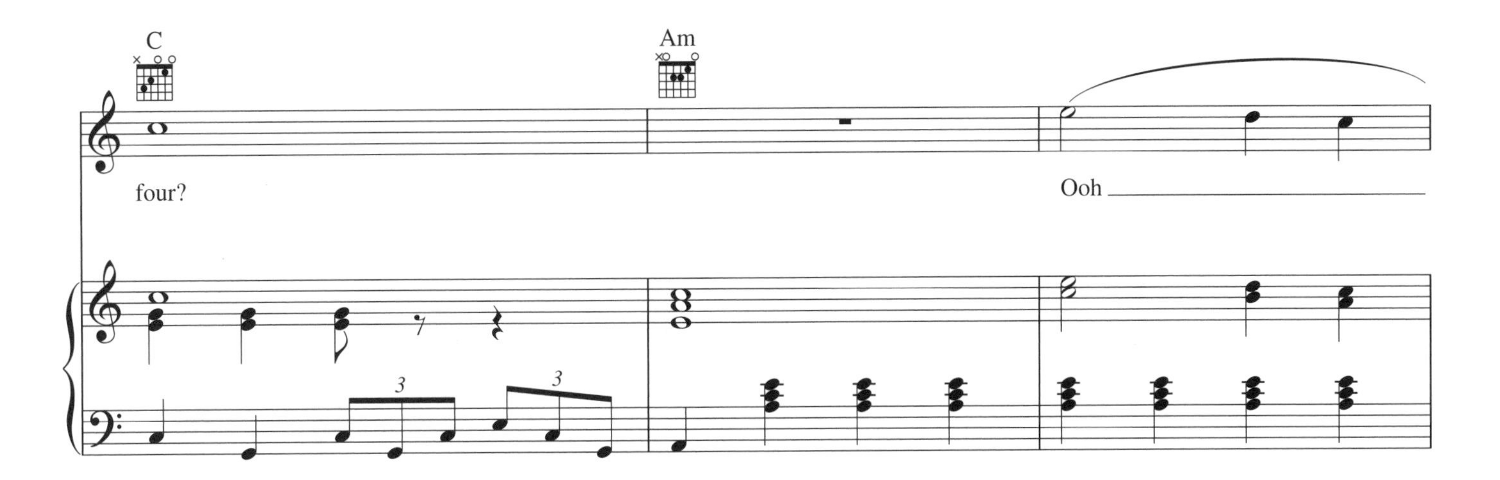
C
Am
four?
Ooh

G
Am
You'll be old - er

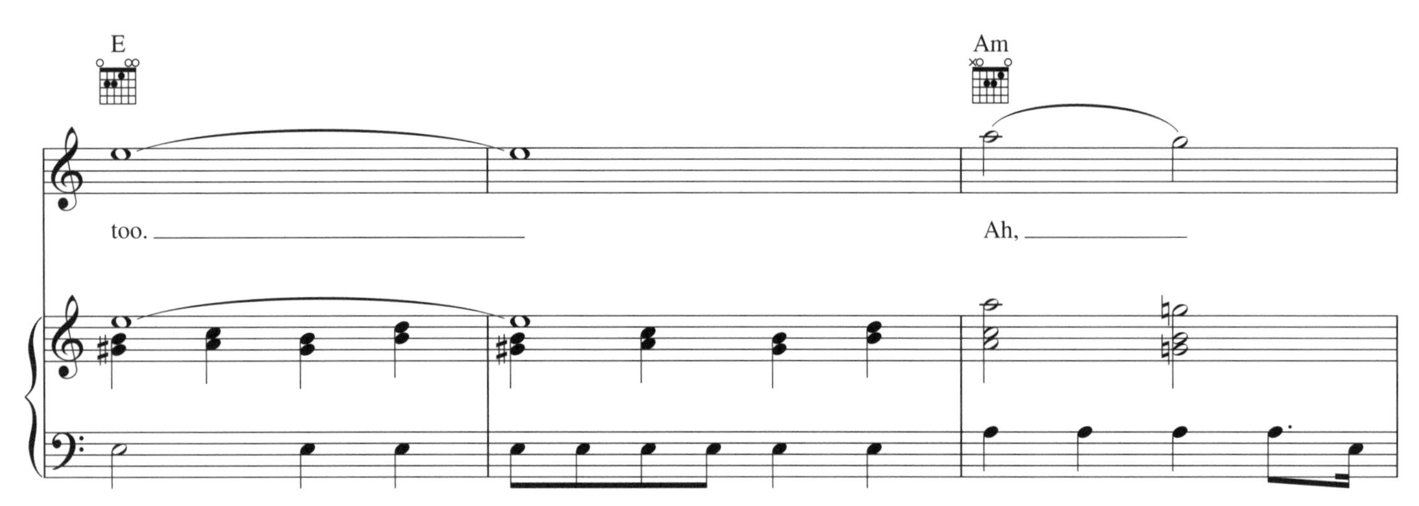
E
Am
too.
Ah,

Dm
and if you say the word,

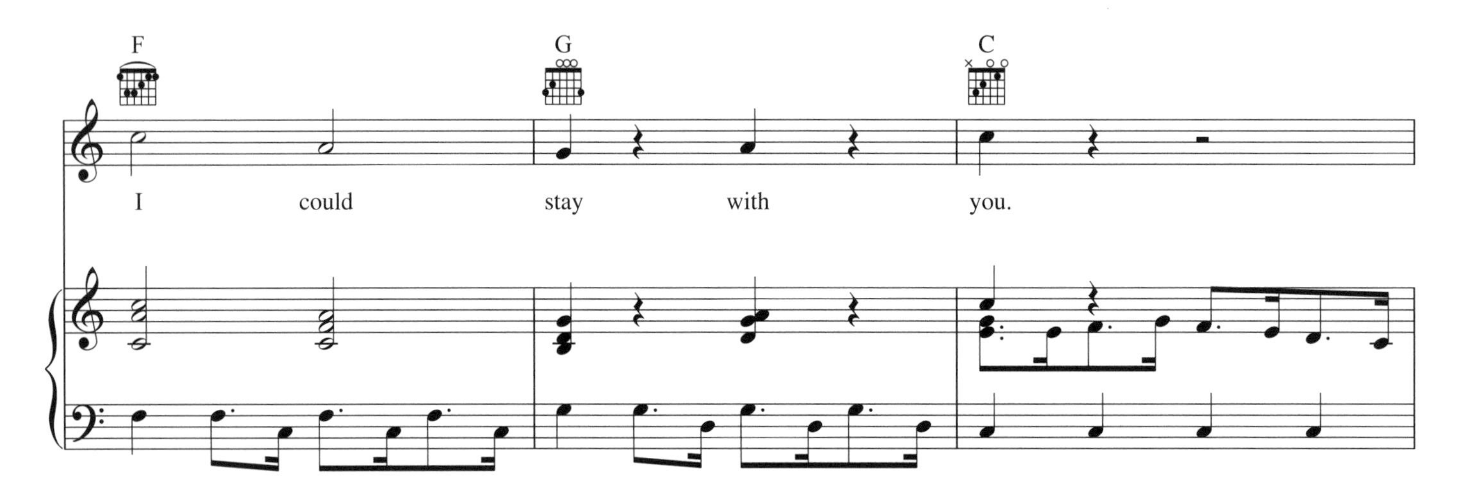
F
G
C
I could stay with you.

G
C
I could be hand - y
Send me a post - card,

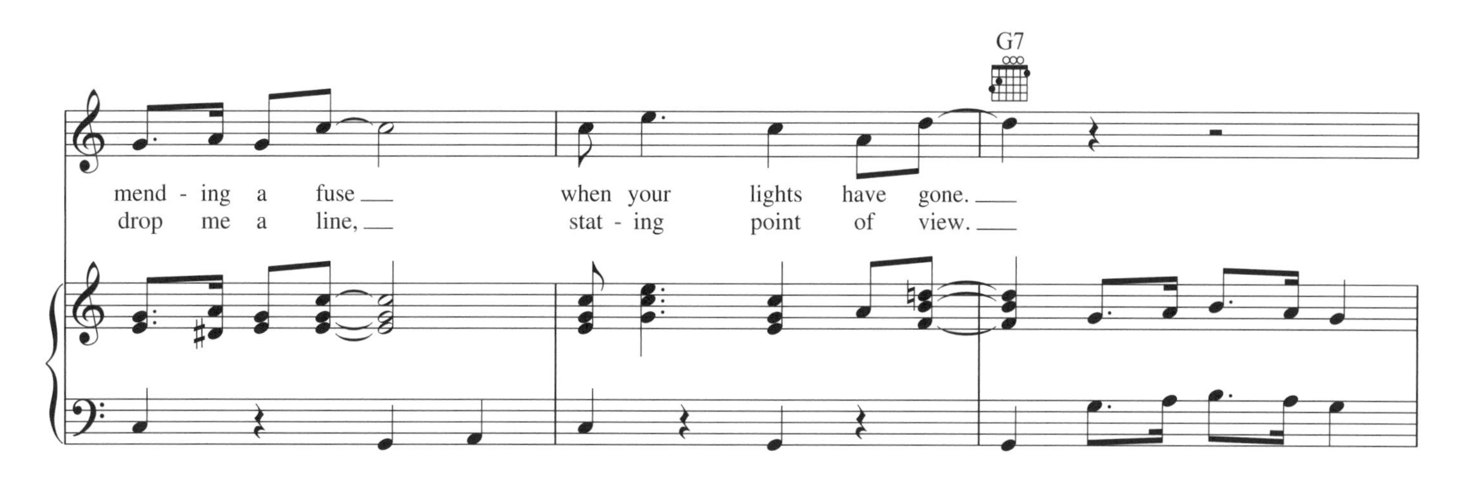
G7
mend - ing a fuse
when your lights have gone.
drop me a line,
stat - ing point of view.

N.C.
You can knit a sweat - er by the fire - side,
Sun - day morn - ings,
In - di - cate pre - cise - ly what you mean to say,
yours sin - cere - ly,

C
go for a ride.
Do - ing the gar - den, dig - ging the weeds,
wast - ing a - way.
Give me your an - swer, fill in a form,

C7
F
A♭7♭5/G♭
who could ask for more?
mine for - ev - er - more.
Will you still need me,
Will you still need me,

C/G
A7
D9
G13
To Coda
C
4fr
3fr
will you still feed me,
will you still feed me,
when I'm six - ty - four?
when I'm six - ty -
3
3

Am
G
Ev - 'ry sum - mer we can rent a cot - tage in the Isle of Wight if it's not too dear.

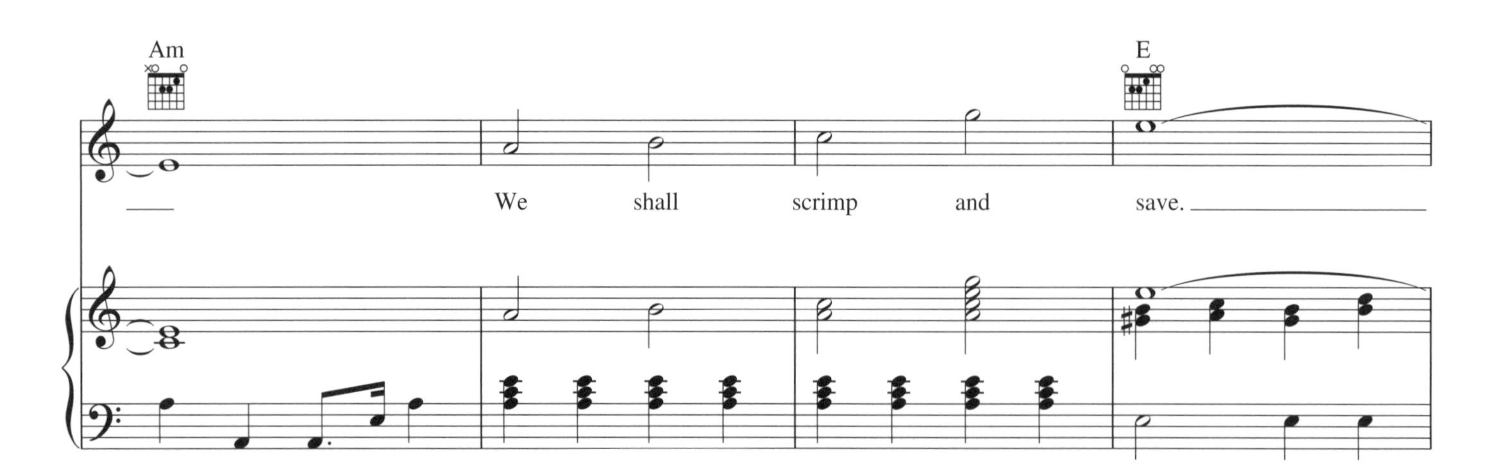
Am
E
We shall scrimp and save.

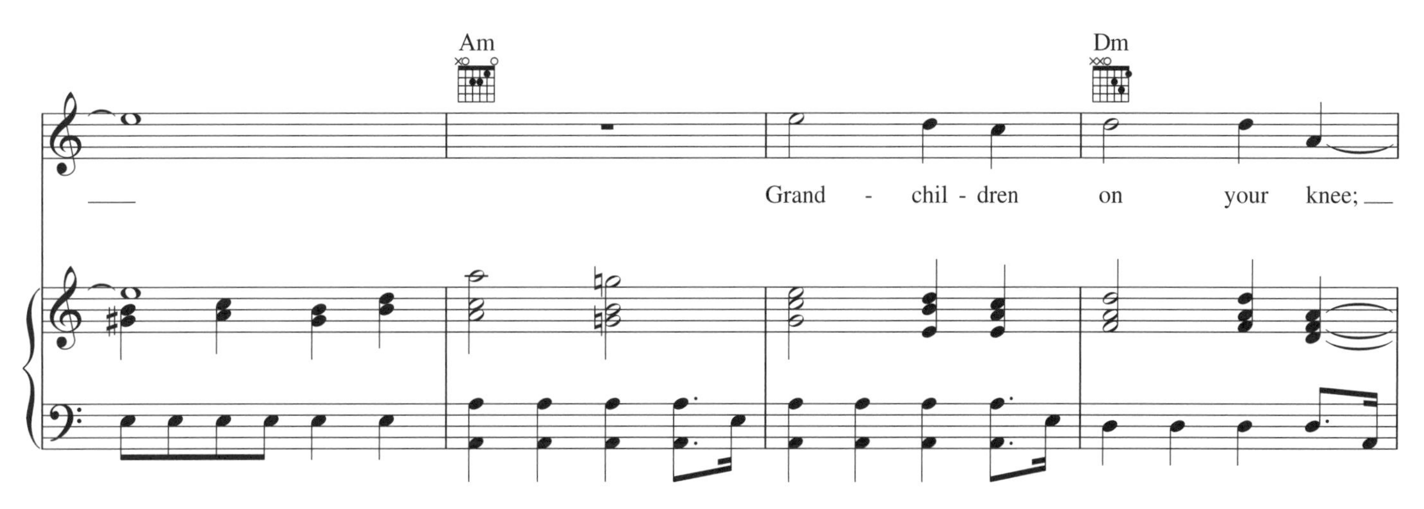
Am
Dm
Grand - chil - dren on your knee;

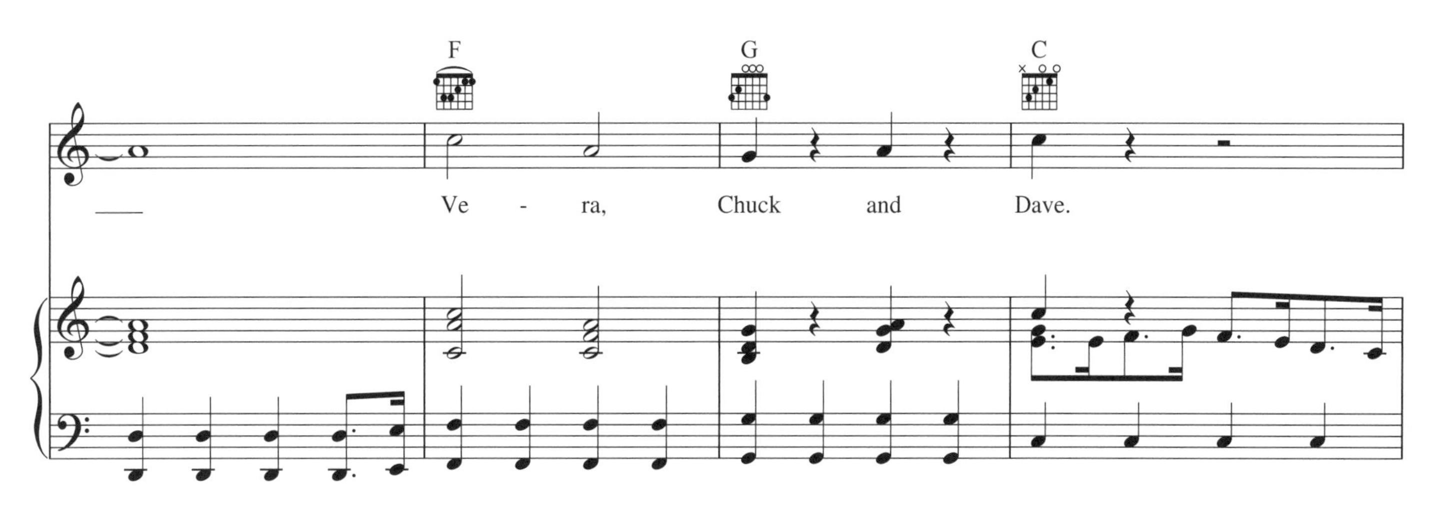
F
G
C
Ve - ra, Chuck and Dave.

G
D.S. al Coda
CODA
C
four? Ho!

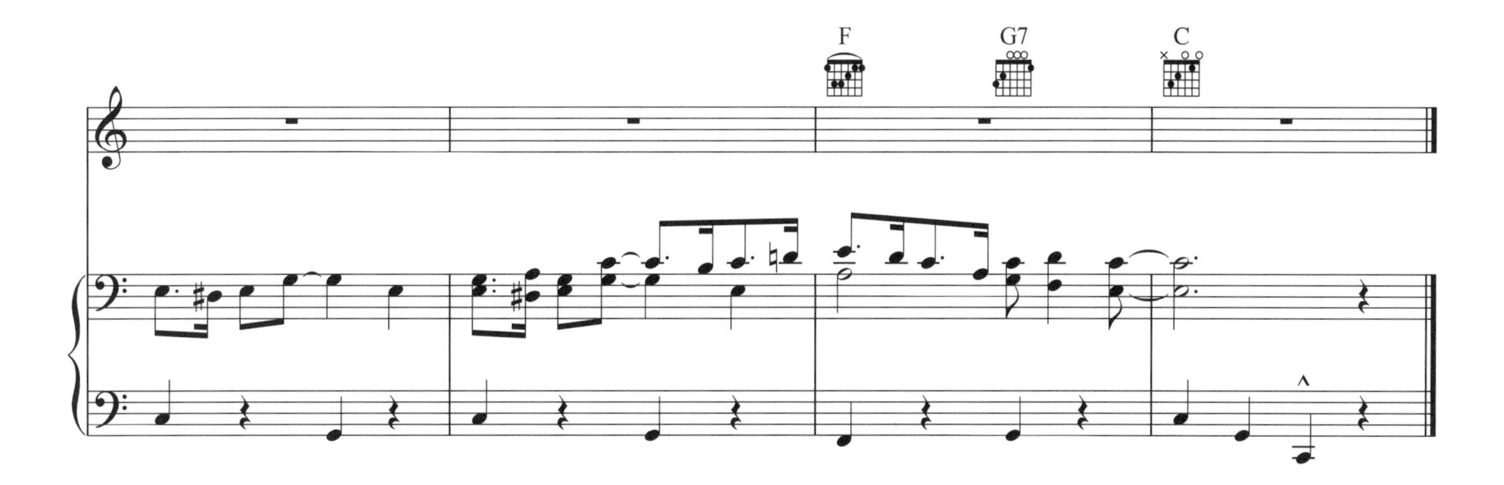
F
G7
C

Won't You Be My Neighbor?
(It's a Beautiful Day in This Neighborhood)

from MISTER ROGERS' NEIGHBORHOOD
Words and Music by Fred Rogers

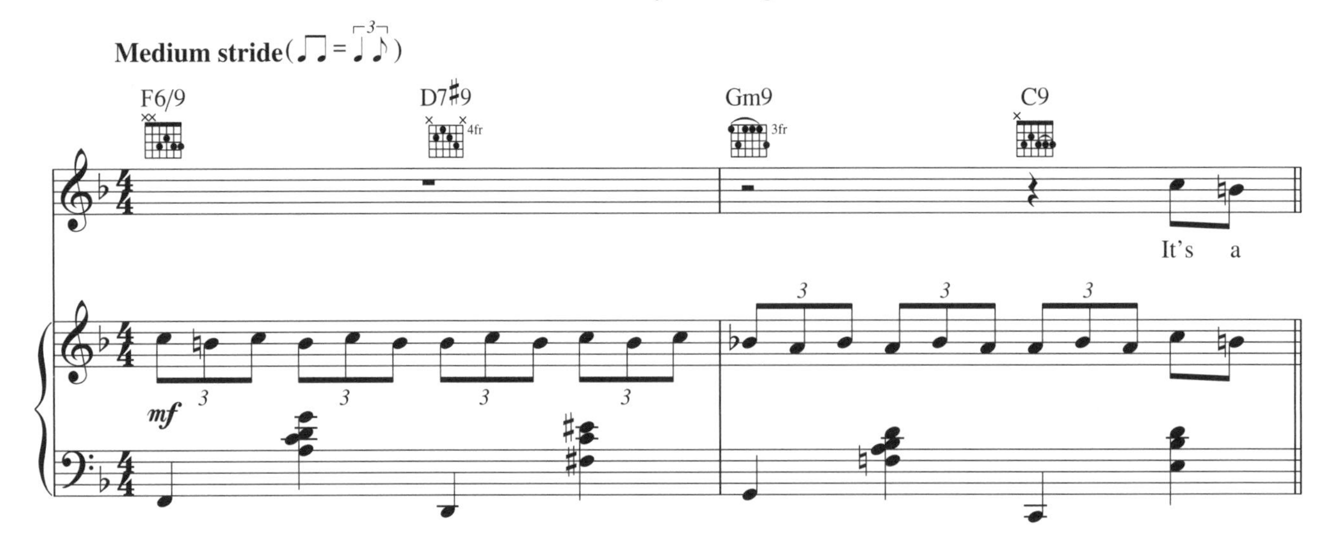

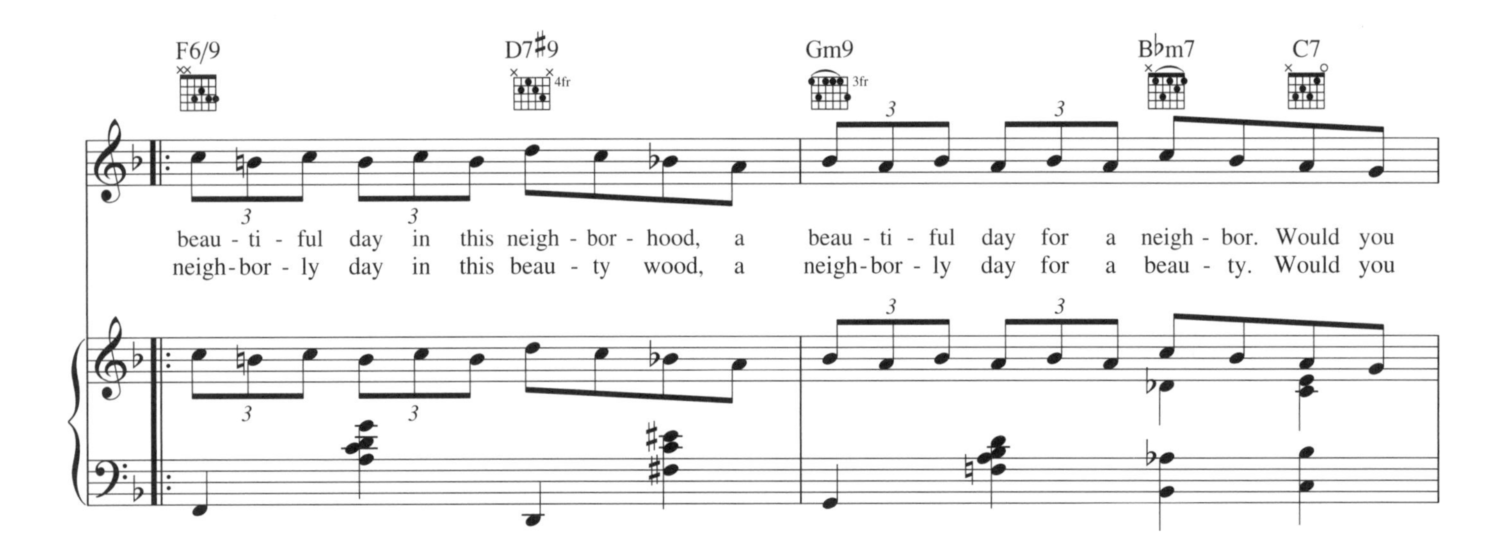

B♭
D7
Gm
D♭
F
Gm7
al - ways want-ed to have a neigh bor just like you! I've al - ways want ed to live in a neigh-bor -
A♭m7
D♭
Gm11
C7
F6/9
Cm7
D7
Gm9
B♭m7
hood with you. So let's make the most of this beau-ti-ful day, since we're to-geth er we might as well say:
To Coda
F
Dm7
Gm7
C7
F
B♭
Am7
Gm
Am7
D7
Would you be mine? Could you be mine? Won't you be my neigh-bor? Won't you please, won't you please?
D.C. al Coda
(with repeat)
Gm7
C7
B♭
F
Please won't you be my neigh-bor?
CODA
Gm7
C7
B♭
F
Please won't you be my neigh-bor?

Yellow Submarine

from YELLOW SUBMARINE
Words and Music by John Lennon and Paul McCartney

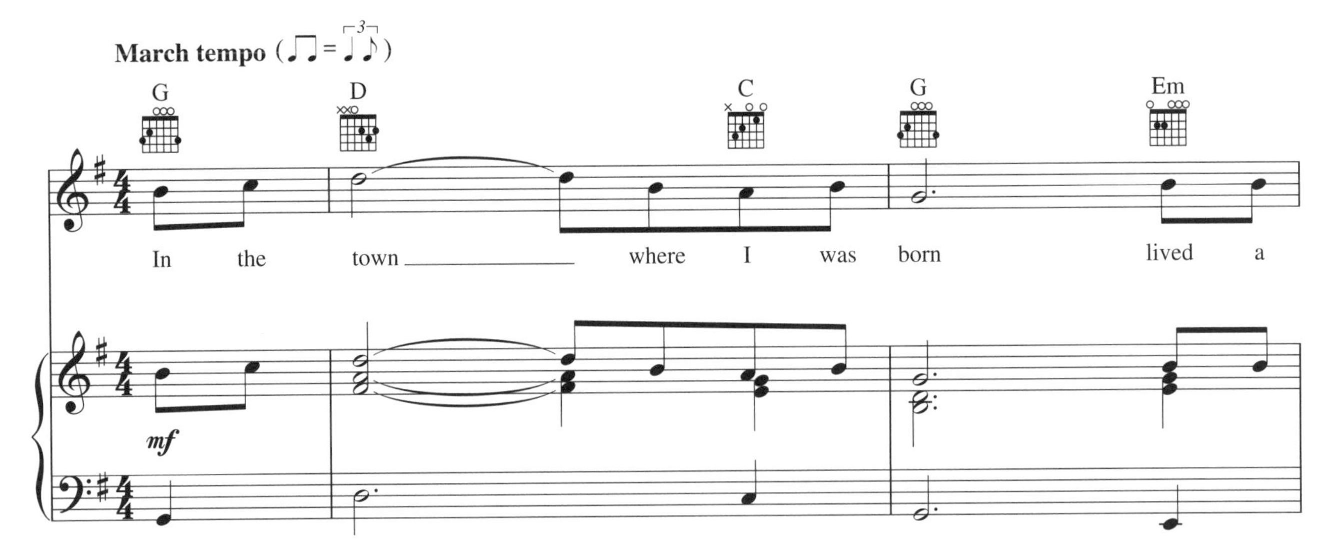

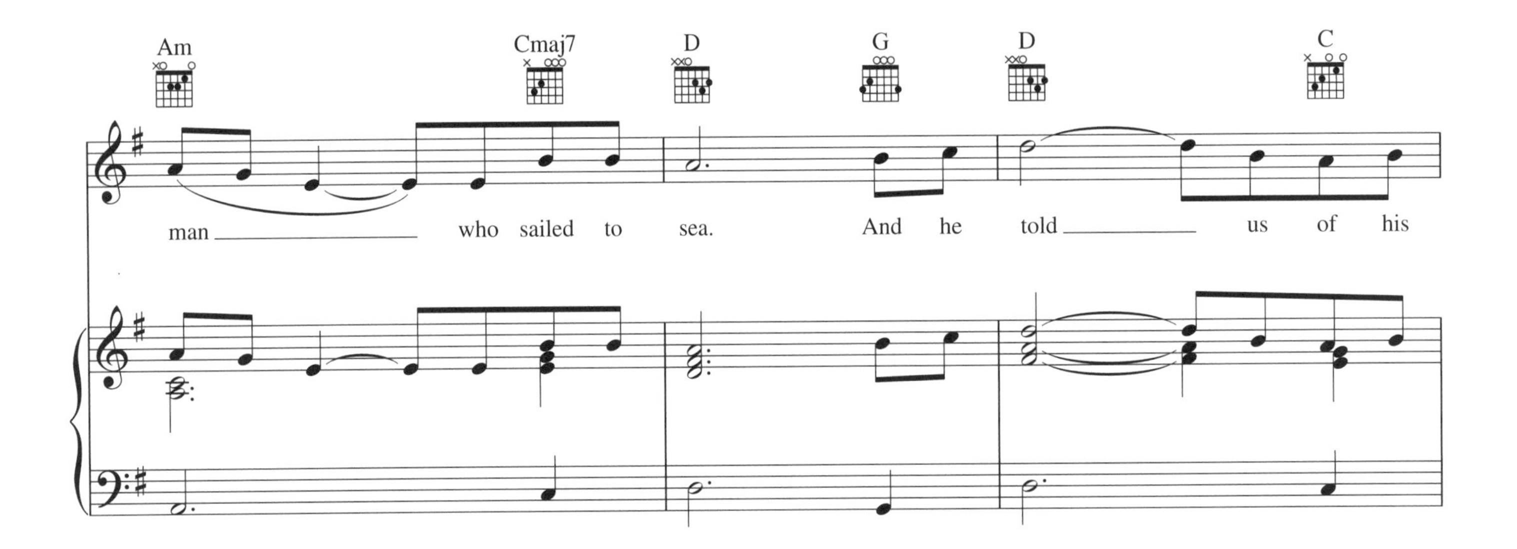

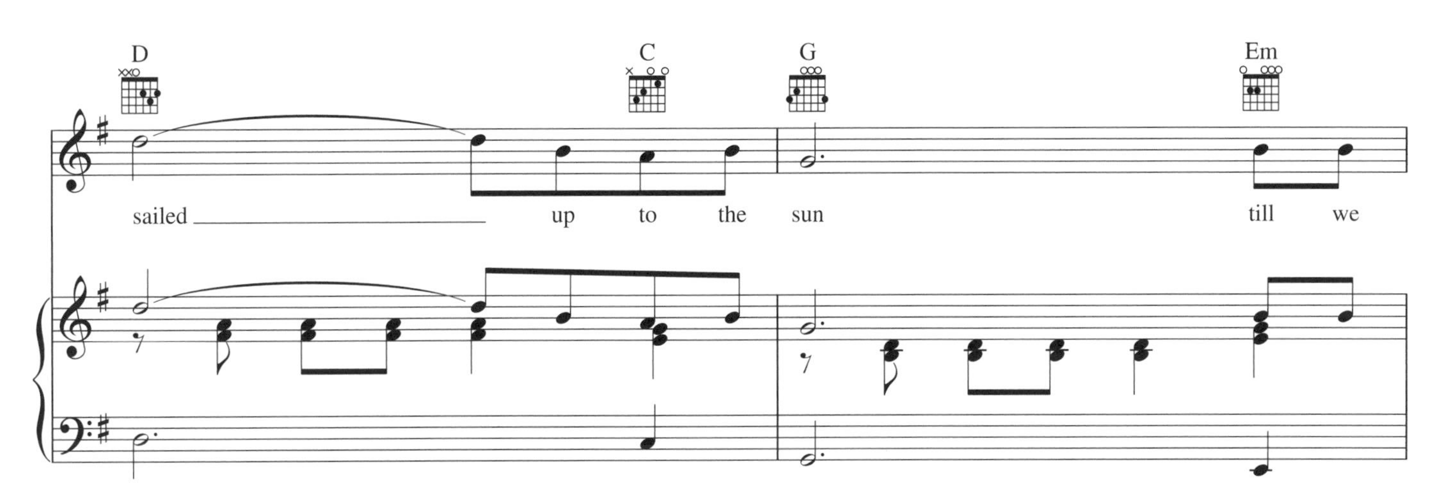
D
C
G
Em
sailed
up to the sun
till we

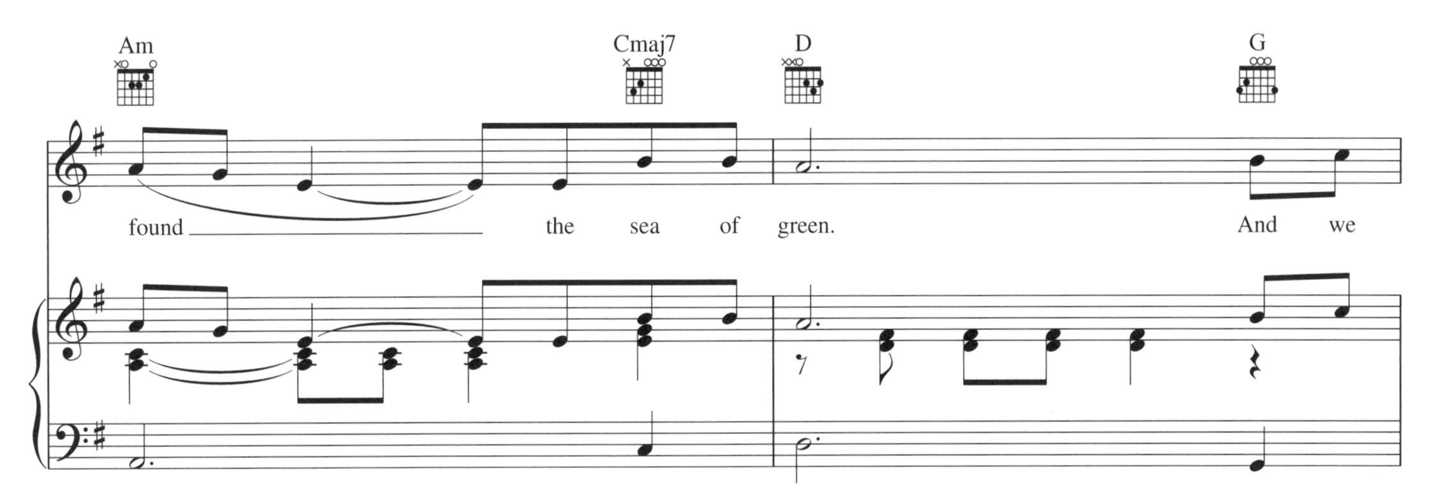
Am
Cmaj7
D
G
found
the sea of green.
And we

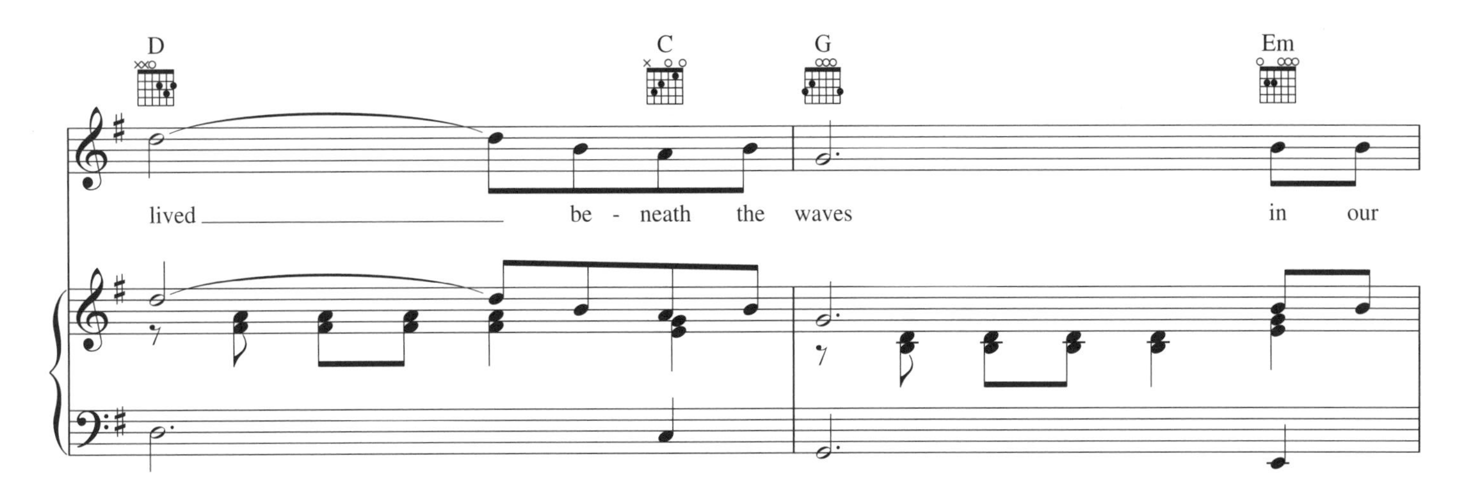
D
C
G
Em
lived
be - neath the waves
in our

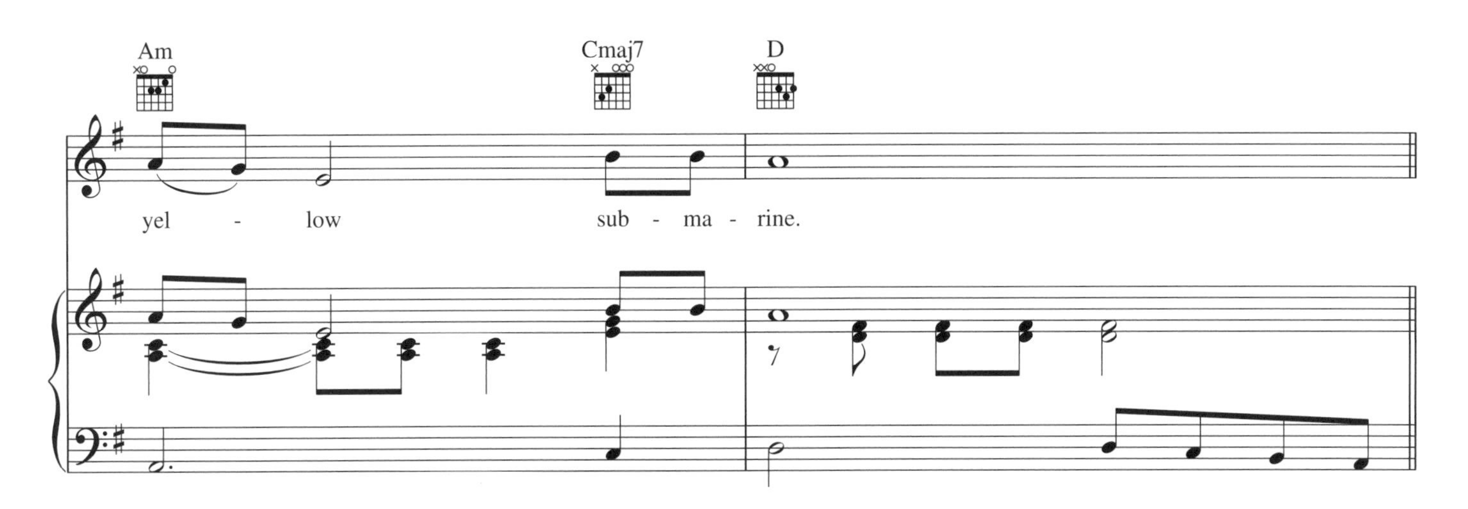
Am
Cmaj7
D
yel - low
sub - ma - rine.

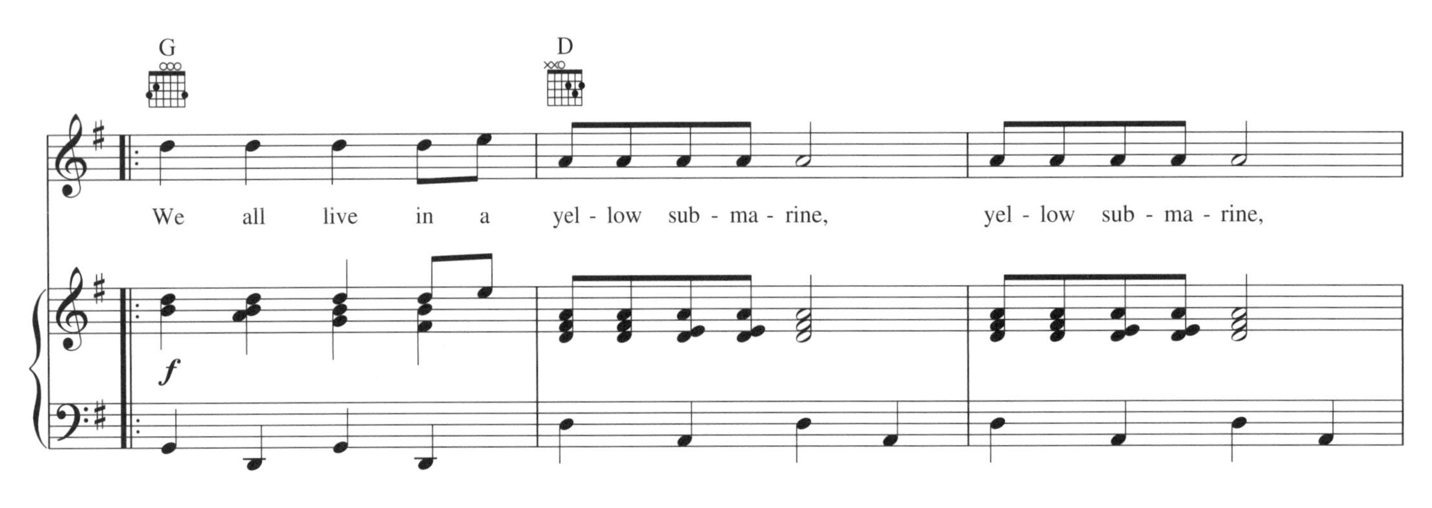
G
D
We all live in a yel - low sub - ma - rine, yel - low sub - ma - rine,

G
D
yel - low sub - ma - rine. We all live in a yel - low sub - ma - rine,

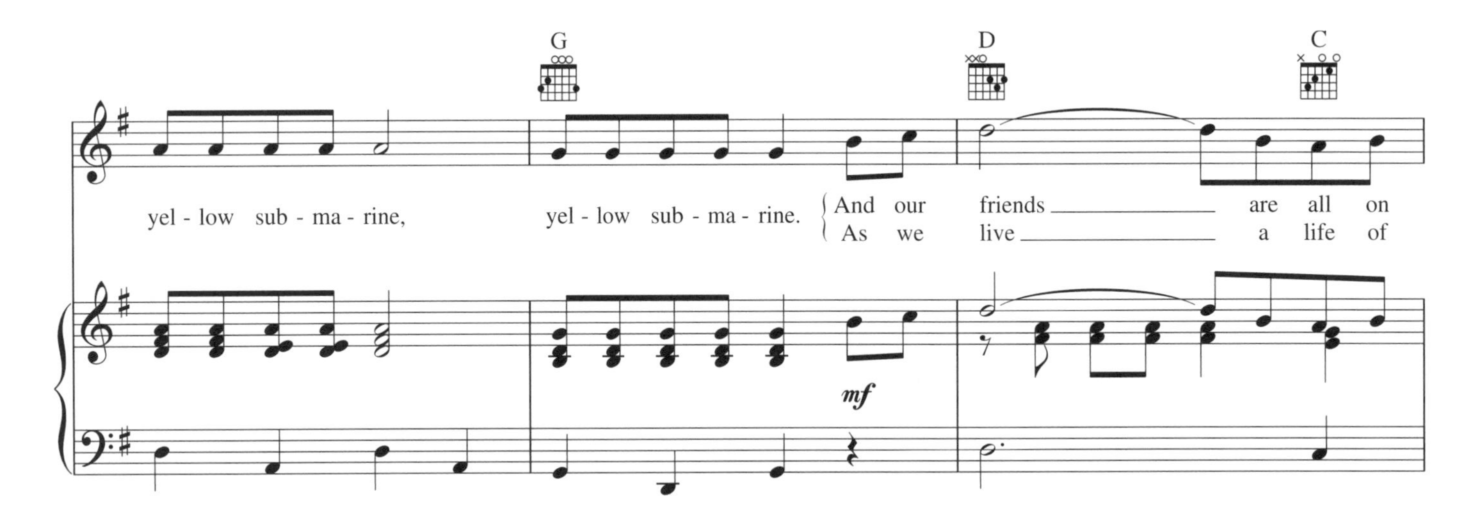
G
D
C
yel - low sub - ma - rine, yel - low sub - ma - rine. And our friends are all on
As we live a life of

G
Em
Am
Cmaj7
D
G
board, man - y more of them live next door. And the
ease, ev - 'ry one of us has all we need. Sky of

D
C
1
G
band be - gins to play.
blue and sea of
3
3
3
3

2
G
Em
Am
Cmaj7
green in our yel - low sub - ma -

D
G
D
rine. We all live in a yel - low sub - ma - rine,
f

Repeat and Fade
G
Optional Ending
G
yel - low sub - ma - rine, yel - low sub - ma - rine. yel - low sub - ma - rine.

Zip-A-Dee-Doo-Dah

from Walt Disney's SONG OF THE SOUTH
Words by Ray Gilbert
Music by Allie Wrubel

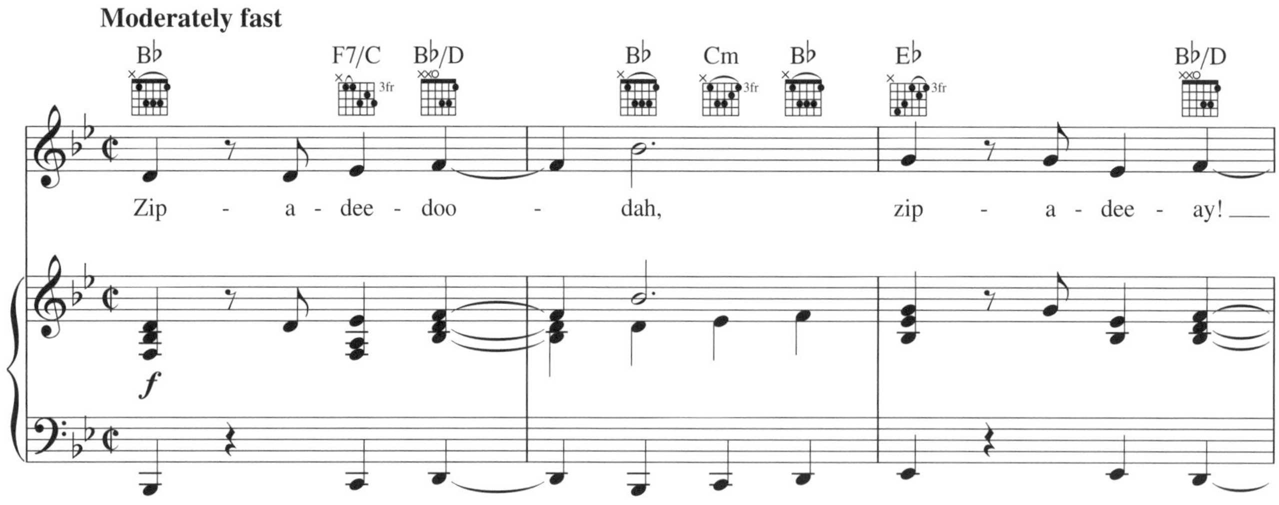

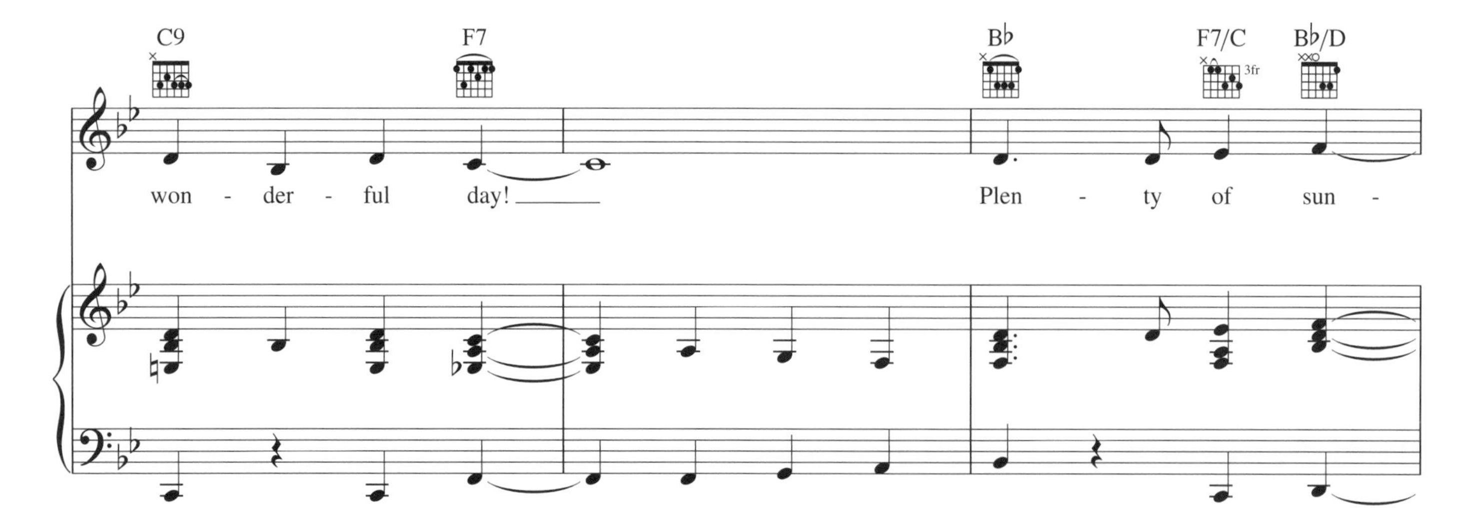

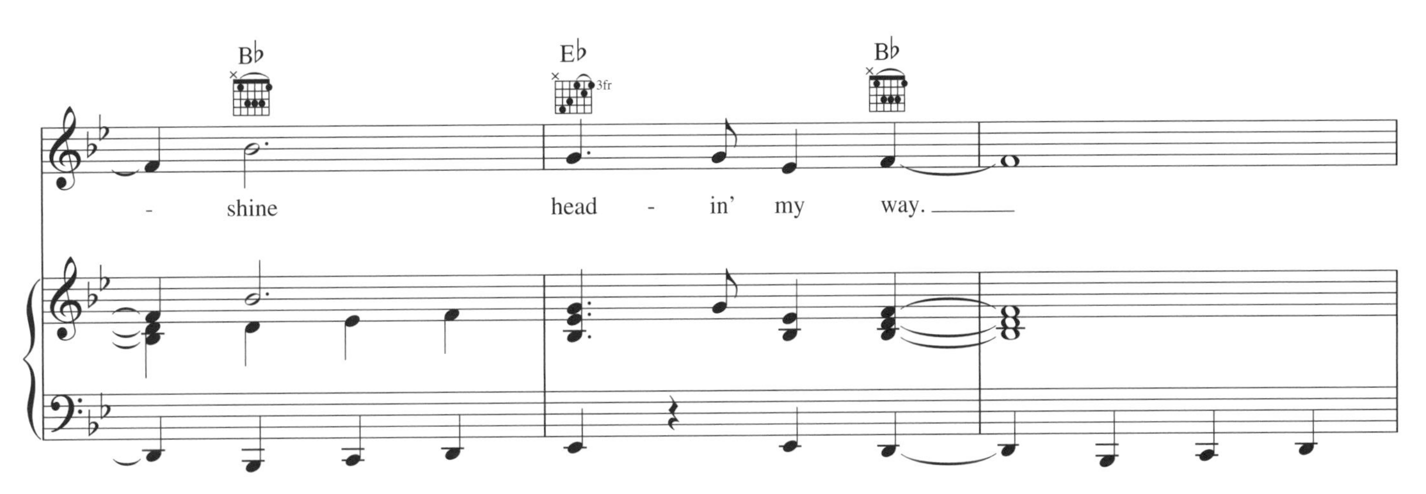
B♭
E♭
3fr
B♭
- shine head - in' my way.

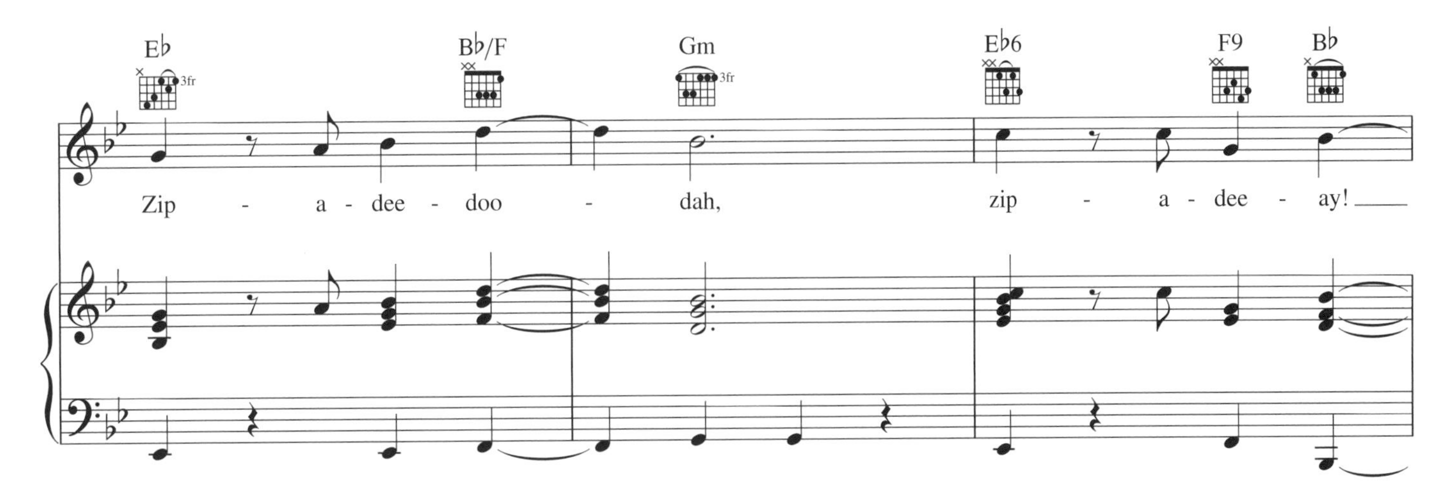
E♭
3fr
B♭/F
Gm
3fr
E♭6
F9
B♭
Zip - a - dee - doo - dah, zip - a - dee - ay!

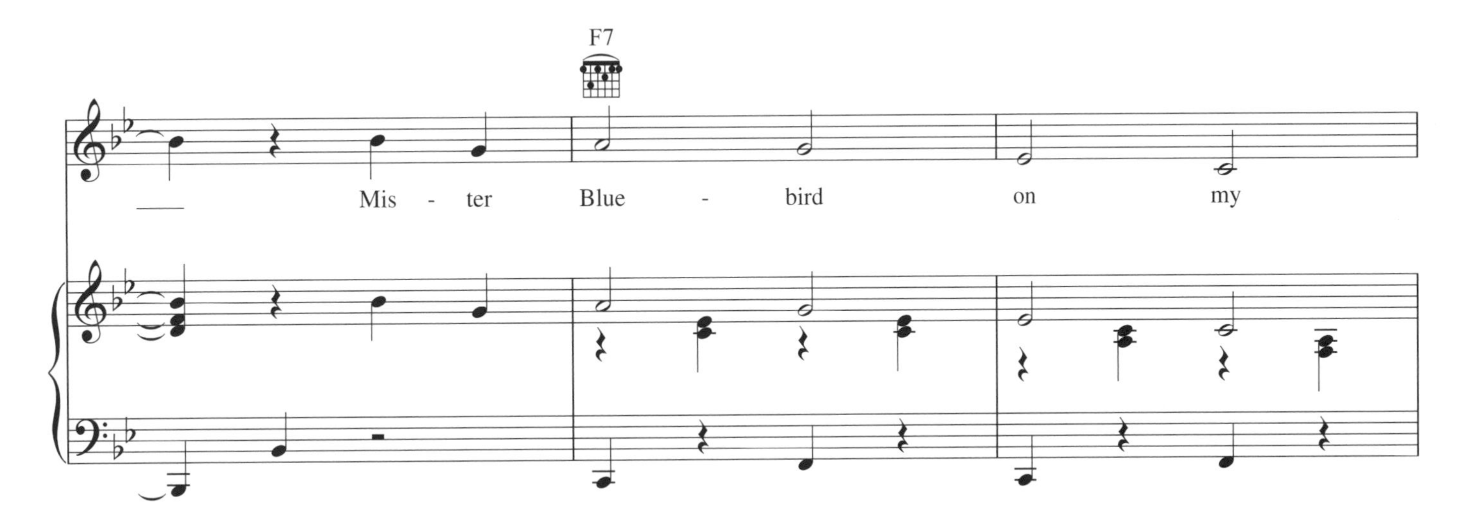
F7
Mis - ter Blue - bird on my

B♭dim7
B♭
Gm7
C7
shoul - der, it's the truth, it's

F
"act - ch'll" ev - 'ry - thing is "sat - is - fact - ch'll."

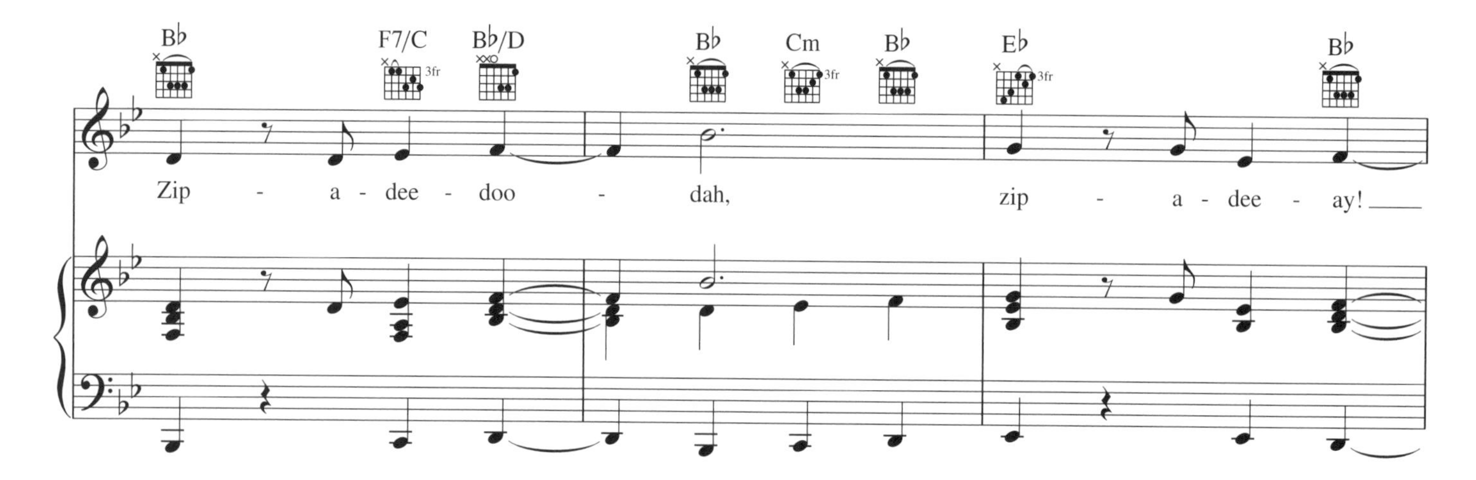
B♭
F7/C
B♭/D
B♭
Cm
B♭
E♭
B♭
Zip - a - dee - doo - dah, zip - a - dee - ay!

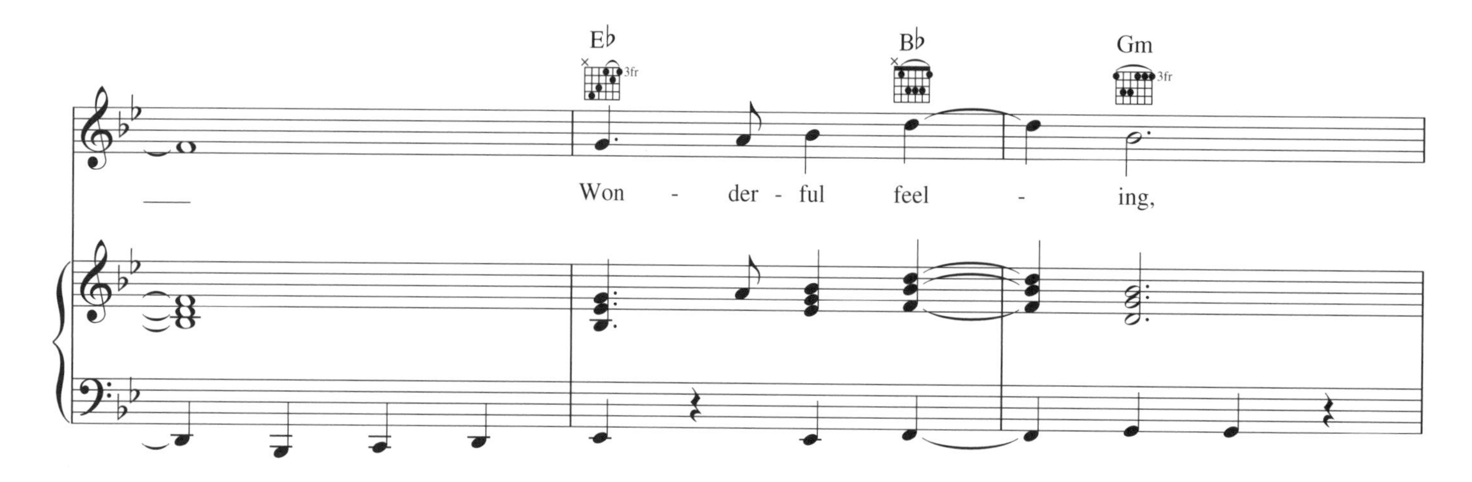
E♭
B♭
Gm
Won - der - ful feel - ing,

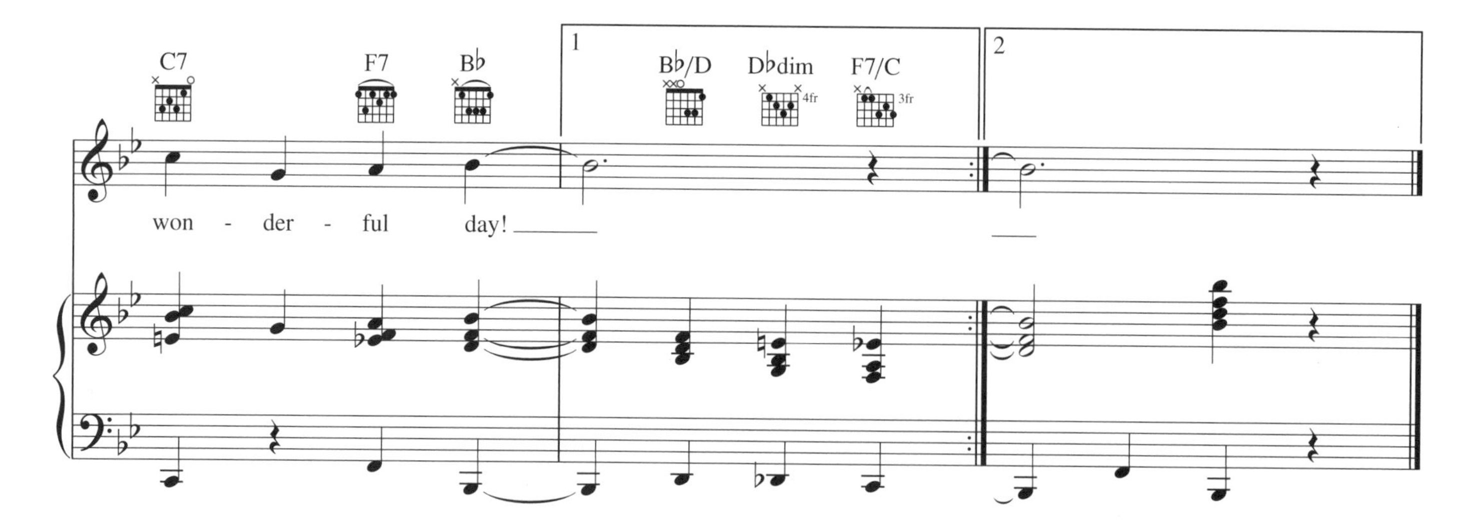
C7
F7
B♭
1
B♭/D
D♭dim
F7/C
2
won - der - ful day!

44. FRANK SINATRA – POPULAR HITS
Come Fly with Me • Cycles • High Hopes • Love and Marriage • My Way • Strangers in the Night • (Love Is) The Tender Trap • Young at Heart.
00311277 P/V/G $14.95

45. FRANK SINATRA – MOST REQUESTED SONGS
From Here to Eternity • I've Got the World on a String • Theme from "New York, New York" • Night and Day • Time After Time • Witchcraft • and more.
00311278 P/V/G $14.95

46. WICKED
Dancing Through Life • Defying Gravity • For Good • I Couldn't Be Happier • I'm Not That Girl • Popular • What Is This Feeling? • The Wizard and I.
00311317 P/V/G $15.99

47. RENT
I'll Cover You • Light My Candle • One Song Glory • Out Tonight • Rent • Seasons of Love • What You Own • Without You.
00311319 P/V/G $14.95

48. CHRISTMAS CAROLS
God Rest Ye Merry, Gentlemen • Hark! the Herald Angels Sing • It Came upon the Midnight Clear • O Holy Night • Silent Night • What Child Is This? • and more.
00311332 P/V/G $14.95

49. HOLIDAY HITS
Frosty the Snow Man • Happy Xmas (War Is Over) • I'll Be Home for Christmas • Jingle-Bell Rock • Rudolph the Red-Nosed Reindeer • Santa Claus Is Comin' to Town • and more.
00311333 P/V/G $15.99

50. DISNEY CLASSICS
Some Day My Prince Will Come • When You Wish upon a Star • Whistle While You Work • Who's Afraid of the Big Bad Wolf? • Zip-A-Dee-Doo-Dah • and more.
00311417 P/V/G $14.95

51. HIGH SCHOOL MUSICAL
9 songs, including: Breaking Free • Get'cha Head in the Game • Start of Something New • We're All in This Together • What I've Been Looking For • and more.
00311421 P/V/G $19.95

52. ANDREW LLOYD WEBBER CLASSICS
Another Suitcase in Another Hall • Close Every Door • Love Changes Everything • Pie Jesu • Wishing You Were Somehow Here Again • more.
00311422 P/V/G $14.95

53. GREASE
Beauty School Dropout • Grease • Greased Lightnin' • Hopelessly Devoted to You • Sandy • Summer Nights • You're the One That I Want • and more.
00311450 P/V/G $14.95

54. BROADWAY FAVORITES
Big Spender • Comedy Tonight • Hello, Young Lovers • I've Grown Accustomed to Her Face • Just in Time • Make Someone Happy • My Ship • People.
00311451 P/V/G $14.95

55. THE 1940S
Come Rain or Come Shine • It Could Happen to You • Moonlight in Vermont • A Nightingale Sang in Berkeley Square • Route 66 • Sentimental Journey • and more.
00311453 P/V/G $14.95

56. THE 1950S
Blueberry Hill • Dream Lover • Fever • The Great Pretender • Kansas City • Memories Are Made of This • My Prayer • Put Your Head on My Shoulder.
00311459 P/V/G $14.95

57. THE 1960S
Beyond the Sea • Blue Velvet • California Dreamin' • Downtown • For Once in My Life • Let's Hang On • (Sittin' On) The Dock of the Bay • The Twist.
00311460 P/V/G $14.99

58. THE 1970S
Dust in the Wind • Everything Is Beautiful • How Can You Mend a Broken Heart • I Feel the Earth Move • If • Joy to the World • My Eyes Adored You • You've Got a Friend.
00311461 P/V/G $14.99

59. THE 1980S
All Night Long (All Night) • Another One Bites the Dust • Every Little Thing She Does Is Magic • Got My Mind Set on You • I Just Called to Say I Love You • Kokomo • Saving All My Love for You • Stand by Me.
00311462 P/V/G $14.99

60. THE 1990S
Don't Speak • (Everything I Do) I Do It for You • Hero • I Believe I Can Fly • I Don't Want to Wait • I'll Be • Save the Best for Last • Walking in Memphis.
00311463 P/V/G $14.99

61. BILLY JOEL FAVORITES
And So It Goes • Baby Grand • It's Still Rock and Roll to Me • Leave a Tender Moment Alone • Piano Man • She's Always a Woman • Uptown Girl • You May Be Right.
00311464 P/V/G $14.95

62. BILLY JOEL HITS
The Entertainer • Honesty • Just the Way You Are • The Longest Time • Lullabye (Goodnight, My Angel) • My Life • New York State of Mind • She's Got a Way.
00311465 P/V/G $14.95

63. HIGH SCHOOL MUSICAL 2
All for One • Everyday • Fabulous • Gotta Go My Own Way • I Don't Dance • What Time Is It • Work This Out • You Are the Music in Me.
00311470 P/V/G $19.95

64. GOD BLESS AMERICA
America • America, the Beautiful • Anchors Aweigh • Battle Hymn of the Republic • God Bless America • This Is My Country • This Land Is Your Land • and more.
00311489 P/V/G $14.95

65. CASTING CROWNS
Does Anybody Hear Her • East to West • Here I Go Again • Praise You in This Storm • Somewhere in the Middle • Voice of Truth • While You Were Sleeping • Who Am I.
00311494 P/V/G $14.95

66. HANNAH MONTANA
I Got Nerve • Just like You • Life's What You Make It • Nobody's Perfect • Old Blue Jeans • Pumpin' up the Party • Rock Star • We Got the Party.
00311772 P/V/G $19.95

67. BROADWAY GEMS
Getting to Know You • I Could Have Danced All Night • If I Were a Rich Man • It's a Lovely Day Today • September Song • The Song Is You • and more.
00311803 P/V/G $14.99

68. LENNON & McCARTNEY FAVORITES
All My Loving • The Fool on the Hill • A Hard Day's Night • Here, There and Everywhere • I Saw Her Standing There • Yellow Submarine • and more.
00311804 P/V/G $14.99

69. PIRATES OF THE CARIBBEAN
All for One • Everyday • Fabulous • Gotta Go My Own Way • I Don't Dance • What Time Is It • Work This Out • You Are the Music in Me.
00311807 P/V/G $14.95

70. "TOMORROW," "PUT ON A HAPPY FACE," AND OTHER CHARLES STROUSE HITS
Born Too Late • A Lot of Livin' to Do • Night Song • Once upon a Time • Put on a Happy Face • Those Were the Days • Tomorrow • You've Got Possibilities.
00311821 P/V/G $14.99

71. ROCK BAND
Black Hole Sun • Don't Fear the Reaper • Learn to Fly • Paranoid • Say It Ain't So • Suffragette City • Wanted Dead or Alive • Won't Get Fooled Again.
00311822 P/V/G $14.99

72. HIGH SCHOOL MUSICAL 3
Can I Have This Dance • High School Musical • I Want It All • A Night to Remember • Now or Never • Right Here Right Now • Scream • Walk Away.
00311826 P/V/G $19.99

73. MAMMA MIA! – THE MOVIE
Dancing Queen • Gimme! Gimme! Gimme! (A Man After Midnight) • Honey, Honey • Lay All Your Love on Me • Mamma Mia • SOS • Take a Chance on Me • The Winner Takes It All.
00311831 P/V/G $14.99

75. TWILIGHT
Bella's Lullaby • Decode • Full Moon • Go All the Way (Into the Twilight) • Spotlight (Twilight Remix) • Supermassive Black Hole • Tremble for My Beloved.
00311860 P/V/G $16.99

76. PRIDE & PREJUDICE
Arrival at Netherfield • Darcy's Letter • Dawn • Georgiana • Leaving Netherfield • The Living Sculptures of Pemberley • Meryton Townhall • The Secret Life of Daydreams.
00311862 P/V/G $14.99

77. ELTON JOHN FAVORITES
Bennie and the Jets • Blue Eyes • Don't Go Breaking My Heart • Don't Let the Sun Go down on Me • Rocket Man (I Think It's Gonna Be a Long Long Time) • Sacrifice • Someone Saved My Life Tonight • Tiny Dancer.
00311884 P/V/G $14.99

78. ERIC CLAPTON
Bell Bottom Blues • I Can't Stand It • I Shot the Sheriff • Lay Down Sally • Layla • Sunshine of Your Love • Tears in Heaven • Wonderful Tonight.
00311885 P/V/G $14.99

79. TANGOS
Adios Muchachos • Amapola • Aquellos Ojos Verdes • El Choclo • Rose Room • Say "Si, Si" • Takes Two to Tango • Tango of Roses.
00311886 P/V/G $14.99

80. FIDDLER ON THE ROOF
Do You Love Me? • Far from the Home I Love • Fiddler on the Roof • If I Were a Rich Man • Matchmaker • Sabbath Prayer • Sunrise, Sunset • Tradition.
00311887 P/V/G $14.99

81. JOSH GROBAN
February Song • Machine • Now or Never • Per Te • Remember When It Rained • So She Dances • Un Dia Llegara • You Raise Me Up.
00311901 P/V/G $14.99

82. LIONEL RICHIE
All Night Long (All Night) • Lady • Penny Lover • Say You, Say Me • Still • Stuck on You • Three Times a Lady • Truly.
00311902 P/V/G $14.99

83. PHANTOM OF THE OPERA
All I Ask of You • Angel of Music • Masquerade • The Music of the Night • The Phantom of the Opera • The Point of No Return • Think of Me • Wishing You Were Somehow Here Again.
00311903 P/V/G $14.99

84. ANTONIO CARLOS JOBIM FAVORITES
Água De Beber • Chega De Saudade • Dindi • The Girl from Ipanema • Meditation • Quiet Nights of Quiet Stars • Triste • Vivo Sonhando.
00311919 P/V/G $14.99

85. LATIN FAVORITES
Bésame Mucho • A Day in the Life of a Fool • The Look of Love • More • Samba De Orfeu • Sway • Watch What Happens • You Belong to My Heart.
00311920 P/V/G $14.99

87. PATSY CLINE
Back in Baby's Arms • Crazy • Have You Ever Been Lonely? (Have You Ever Been Blue?) • Heartaches • I Fall to Pieces • She's Got You • Sweet Dreams • Walkin' After Midnight.
00311936 P/V/G $14.99

88. NEIL DIAMOND
Cracklin' Rosie • Forever in Blue Jeans • Love on the Rocks • September Morn • Solitary Man • Song Sung Blue • Sweet Caroline • You Don't Bring Me Flowers.
00311937 P/V/G $14.99

89. FAVORITE HYMNS
Beautiful Savior • The Church's One Foundation • Crown Him with Many Crowns • Faith of Our Fathers • Holy, Holy, Holy • A Mighty Fortress Is Our God • My Faith Looks up to Thee • Onward, Christian Soldiers • Rock of Ages • We Gather Together.
00311940 P/V/G $14.99

90. IRISH FAVORITES
Cockles and Mussels (Molly Malone) • Danny Boy • I'll Take You Home Again, Kathleen • The Irish Rover • MacNamara's Band • Minstrel Boy • My Wild Irish Rose • Too-Ra-Loo-Ra-Loo-Ral (That's an Irish Lullaby) • The Wearing of the Green • When Irish Eyes Are Smiling.
00311969 P/V/G $14.99

91. BROADWAY JAZZ
Bewitched • Falling in Love with Love • Glad to Be Unhappy • I Can't Get Started with You • I Didn't Know What Time It Was • The Lady Is a Tramp • Little Girl Blue • My Funny Valentine.
00311972 P/V/G $14.99

92. DISNEY FAVORITES
Candle on the Water • Chim Chim Cher-ee • Circle of Life • A Dream Is a Wish Your Heart Makes • If I Never Knew You (Love Theme from *Pocahontas*) • It's a Small World • Supercalifragilisticexpialidocious • Written in the Stars.
00311973 P/V/G $14.99

93. THE TWILIGHT SAGA: NEW MOON – SOUNDTRACK
Done All Wrong • Meet Me on the Equinox • New Moon (The Meadow) • No Sound but the Wind • Possibility • Roslyn • Satellite Heart • Slow Life.
00311974 P/V/G $16.99

94. THE TWILIGHT SAGA: NEW MOON – SCORE
Almost a Kiss • Dreamcatcher • Edward Leaves • I Need You • Memories of Edward • New Moon • Volturi Waltz • You're Alive.
00311975 P/V/G $16.99

95. TAYLOR SWIFT
Fifteen • Forever & Always • Love Story • Our Song • Picture to Burn • Should've Said No • White Horse • You Belong with Me.
00311984 P/V/G $14.99

96. BEST OF LENNON & McCARTNEY
All You Need Is Love • And I Love Her • Can't Buy Me Love • Day Tripper • Let It Be • Penny Lane • She Loves You • Ticket to Ride.
00311996 P/V/G $14.99

FOR MORE INFORMATION, SEE YOUR LOCAL MUSIC DEALER, OR WRITE TO:

HAL•LEONARD®
CORPORATION
7777 W. BLUEMOUND RD. P.O. BOX 13819
MILWAUKEE, WISCONSIN 53213

Visit Hal Leonard Online at
www.halleonard.com

Prices, contents and availability subject to change without notice.

Big Books of Music

Our "Big Books" feature big selections of popular titles under one cover, perfect for performing musicians, music aficionados or the serious hobbyist. All books are arranged for piano, voice, and guitar, and feature stay-open binding, so the books lie flat without breaking the spine.

BIG BOOK OF BALLADS
62 songs.
00310485 .... $19.95

BIG BOOK OF BIG BAND HITS
84 songs.
00310701 .... $19.95

BIG BOOK OF BLUEGRASS SONGS
70 songs.
00311484 .... $19.95

BIG BOOK OF BLUES
80 songs.
00311843 .... $19.99

BIG BOOK OF BROADWAY
70 songs.
00311658 .... $19.95

BIG BOOK OF CHILDREN'S SONGS
55 songs.
00359261 .... $14.95

GREAT BIG BOOK OF CHILDREN'S SONGS
76 songs.
00310002 .... $14.95

FANTASTIC BIG BOOK OF CHILDREN'S SONGS
66 songs.
00311062 .... $17.95

MIGHTY BIG BOOK OF CHILDREN'S SONGS
65 songs.
00310467 .... $14.95

REALLY BIG BOOK OF CHILDREN'S SONGS
63 songs.
00310372 .... $16.95

BIG BOOK OF CHILDREN'S MOVIE SONGS
66 songs.
00310731 .... $19.95

BIG BOOK OF CHRISTMAS SONGS
126 songs.
00311520 .... $19.95

BIG BOOK OF CLASSIC ROCK
77 songs.
00310801 .... $22.95

BIG BOOK OF CLASSICAL MUSIC
100 songs.
00310508 .... $19.95

BIG BOOK OF CONTEMPORARY CHRISTIAN FAVORITES
50 songs.
00310021 .... $19.95

BIG BOOK OF COUNTRY MUSIC
63 songs.
00310188 .... $19.95

BIG BOOK OF COUNTRY ROCK
64 songs.
00311748 .... $19.99

BIG BOOK OF DISCO & FUNK
70 songs.
00310878 .... $19.95

BIG BOOK OF EARLY ROCK N' ROLL
99 songs.
00310398 .... $19.95

BIG BOOK OF '50S & '60S SWINGING SONGS
67songs.
00310982 .... $19.95

BIG BOOK OF FOLK POP ROCK
79 songs.
00311125 .... $24.95

BIG BOOK OF FRENCH SONGS
70 songs.
00311154 .... $19.95

BIG BOOK OF GERMAN SONGS
78 songs.
00311816 .... $19.99

BIG BOOK OF GOSPEL SONGS
100 songs.
00310604 .... $19.95

BIG BOOK OF HYMNS
125 hymns.
00310510 .... $17.95

BIG BOOK OF IRISH SONGS
76 songs.
00310981 .... $19.95

BIG BOOK OF ITALIAN FAVORITES
80 songs.
00311185 .... $19.95

BIG BOOK OF JAZZ
75 songs.
00311557 .... $19.95

BIG BOOK OF LATIN AMERICAN SONGS
89 songs.
00311562 .... $19.95

BIG BOOK OF LOVE SONGS
80 songs.
00310784 .... $19.95

BIG BOOK OF MOTOWN
84 songs.
00311061 .... $19.95

BIG BOOK OF MOVIE MUSIC
72 songs.
00311582 .... $19.95

BIG BOOK OF NOSTALGIA
158 songs.
00310004 .... $19.95

BIG BOOK OF OLDIES
73 songs.
00310756 .... $19.95

BIG BOOK OF RAGTIME PIANO
63 songs.
00311749 .... $19.95

BIG BOOK OF RHYTHM & BLUES
67 songs.
00310169 .... $19.95

BIG BOOK OF ROCK
78 songs.
00311566 .... $22.95

BIG BOOK OF ROCK BALLADS
67 songs.
00311839 .... $22.99

BIG BOOK OF SOUL
71 songs.
00310771 .... $19.95

BIG BOOK OF STANDARDS
86 songs.
00311667 .... $19.95

BIG BOOK OF SWING
84 songs.
00310359 .... $19.95

BIG BOOK OF TORCH SONGS
75 songs.
00310561 .... $19.95

BIG BOOK OF TV THEME SONGS
78 songs.
00310504 .... $19.99

BIG BOOK OF WEDDING MUSIC
77 songs.
00311567 .... $19.95

FOR MORE INFORMATION, SEE YOUR LOCAL MUSIC DEALER, OR WRITE TO:

HAL•LEONARD® CORPORATION
7777 W. BLUEMOUND RD. P.O. BOX 13819 MILWAUKEE, WI 53213

Prices, contents, and availability subject to change without notice.

Visit **www.halleonard.com**
for our entire catalog and to view our complete songlists.